DATE DUE			
~~DUE DEC 1 8 1980~~			
~~DUE JAN 19 1981~~			
~~DUE MAY 1 5 1981~~			
~~DUE JUN 5 1981~~			
~~APR 7 1983~~			
~~FEB 2 4 1984~~			
~~DEC 7 1984~~			
~~APR 2 0 1990~~			

The Railroad Mergers
and the
Coming of Conrail

THE RAILROAD MERGERS AND THE COMING OF CONRAIL

Richard Saunders

CONTRIBUTIONS IN ECONOMICS AND ECONOMIC HISTORY, NUMBER 19

GREENWOOD PRESS

WESTPORT, CONNECTICUT • LONDON, ENGLAND

Library of Congress Cataloging in Publication Data

Saunders, Richard.
   The railroad mergers and the coming of ConRail.
   (Contributions in economics and economic
history ; no. 19 ISSN 0084-9235)
   Bibliography: p.
   Includes index.
   1. Railroads--United States--Consolidation.
2. ConRail. I. Title.
√ HE2757 1978.S28 385'.0973   77-91095
ISBN 0-313-20049-1

Library of Congress Catalog Card Number: 77-91095
ISBN:0-313-20049-1
ISSN: 0084-9235

First published in 1978

Greenwood Press, Inc.
51 Riverside Avenue, Westport, Connecticut 06880

Printed in the United States of America

10 9 8 7 6 5 4 3 2 1

78006

Contents

List of Maps

List of Tables

Foreword

As Professor Saunders makes crystal clear in his fact-packed introduction, this book is essentially an inquiry into why this generation's highly touted railway mergers have—with one notable exception, the Burlington Northern—been such dismal failures. Some, like the cataclysmic Penn Central fiasco, were worse than others, but nearly all fell far short of the hopes and expectations of their sponsors. Was the regulatory system, including the endless delays of the Interstate Commerce Commission, at fault? Or were the petitioning railroads simply unrealistic about the savings and collateral benefits that would accrue from the proposed mergers? Were the 1950s, 1960s, and 1970s just the wrong time to carry out successful consolidations? Were the railways, beset by mounting competition from other carriers and hard put for new capital, just not strong or wise enough to play the parts in the new order that mergers would presumably bring about? Could the roads cope with labor's reaction to fewer jobs together with the howls of communities that might be left without rail service? Or was it varying combinations of reasons that caused so much woe? Could anyone, in short, really predict the effect of these jackstraw undertakings? Was there—is there—any better way to achieve the benefits alleged to come from carefully planned and wisely regulated consolidations?

These are some, but by no means all, of the thought-provoking questions Saunders raises. And as in a masterly crafted whodunit, he saves his final judgments and suggested solutions to the brilliant last chapter. The reader who wants to experience the full impact of these conclusions, however, had best do the homework implicit in the preceding fourteen chapters.

As is well known, rail mergers in this country appeared with the very first roads in the 1830s and 1840s; they proceeded at a brisk pace up to World War I: the Boston & Maine was pieced together from over one hundred small lines, the Burlington from over two hundred, and the Pennsylvania from over six hundred.

Thus the rail industry, the financiers, and the public had some seventy-five years of experience with mergers of various sorts behind them when in

1904 the Supreme Court's dissolution of the Northern Securities Corporation put an end to old-style, privately planned consolidations. It is at this logical watershed that Saunders begins his detailed account. In turn, he depicts the tribulations caused by the vociferous but woefully inept Progressives, the regrettable but inevitable period of government control during World War I, and the brave attempt to fashion, in the Transportation Act of 1920, a positive measure that would, among other things, encourage a system of planned, efficient consolidations. But neither the Ripley Plan of 1921 nor the commission's own scheme of 1929 proved any more acceptable to rail management than had John Barriger's ahead-of-its-day seven-system Prince Plan. A supposedly clarifying act of 1940 contained a noble statement of national transportation objectives that thereupon and thereafter were habitually honored in the breach.

The years 1940 to 1954 were strangely devoid of significant mergers, although such unexpected events as Young's capture of the New York Central kept the rails on the front pages. It is at this point, with mergers definitely on the horizon, that Saunders reminds his readers of Edward Hungerford's keen insight as revealed in his *A Railroad for Tomorrow*, which appeared in 1945. Although rail managers, almost to a man, sniffed at this rail-lover/journalist's plan for a twenty-one-division unified system, Hungerford had a courageous and uncanny way of diagnosing the ingrained weaknesses of the men at the top; ironically his suggestions should find an attentive if belated audience in the 1970s.

The stage was set, and the years 1954 to 1976 are characterized as the high point of the merger movement in every corner of the United States: Northeast Quadrant, South and West. These heady developments Saunders presents both chronologically and by regions. Although heroes—and some villains—emerge here and there, this account achieves a fine balance; the author has praise for jobs well done and lively criticism for opportunities missed. Most of his reportage lies, of course, between these extremes. Despite the facts that crowd these pages, they are eminently clear and in pleasing style. Helpful maps and tables, along with reference notes, support the text; a thorough bibliography of both primary and secondary works is worthy of careful study.

This is a thoughtful book. Only on the basis of hard facts and penetrating analysis does Saunders, in his final chapter, tote up the score as he sees it. Clearly he urgently wants the railways to survive as healthy, essential overland carriers. But the industry's problems, he thinks, need prompt, intelligent attention. This book suggests where a goodly share of that attention should be directed.

Richard C. Overton

Acknowledgments

The Interstate Commerce Commission listened dutifully to the railroad merger cases, taking testimony, receiving exhibits, briefs, and rebuttals, and hearing argument. All of this material, some of it far from complimentary to the commission, is available to the researcher thanks to the helpful staff of the ICC, in the Dockets File Room and in the library, and the staff of the Federal Records Center at Suitland, Maryland. Working with these people was a very pleasant experience.

The idea of exploring the mergers was suggested to me by Robert Sutton of the University of Illinois at Urbana-Champaign. H. Morris Cox, dean of the College of Liberal Arts at Clemson University, made facilities of the college and the university available to me. Alan Schaffer of Clemson read extensively in my early drafts and offered suggestions. Flora Walker of Clemson helped type my drafts. Jim Binger of Clemson's Division of Engineering Services, and Walter Wysocki, also of Clemson, prepared the maps. My parents helped to entertain my Airedale sidekicks while I concentrated on research and writing. Dave Thurston of Clemson contributed photographs from his collection. Clemson friends Cheree Gillespie, Janet Pisaneschi, Tom Taylor, and Doug Carter helped in the final preparation of galleys and index.

The Railroad Mergers and the Coming of Conrail

Introduction

This is a tale of modern regulated enterprise.

Regulated enterprise was the bastard child of private initiative and socialism, denounced by partisans on both sides. Regulated enterprise was the triumph of Western economics that brought the postwar boom, first to the United States and then to the Atlantic community.

This is a tale of the failure of regulated enterprise. Bankruptcy and government bailout, the issues that everyone said they wanted to avoid, were the two most obvious results. The best ideas of management, carefully scrutinized by the regulators, ended in fiasco.

This story is about railroads. Some thought railroads were unique; that their experience would never be duplicated in other industries. But historically, their history foreshadowed things to come for others, for they had always been the first to cross the great watersheds of capitalism. They were the first big business; the first to work out the managerial structures of big business; the first to confront nationally organized labor; the first to face modern regulation. By the mid-twentieth century, they were the first to reach industrial maturity—that point where, though performing functions essential to the economy, capital needs outran profits. This was the situation the mergers were supposed to remedy. This was the situation in which regulated enterprise came to grief.

1

The mergers that will occupy most of our attention—the merger movement, as I will call it—began in 1954, when a number of economic and political factors came together to make consolidation attractive to management. It ended in 1970 with the collapse of the Penn Central. The six years that followed were a kind of epilogue which saw the creation of the government-sponsored Consolidated Rail Corporation, hopefully to clean up the mess the mergers had made. If there are mergers after Conrail, they will be in the hindsight of the Penn Central disaster and will most assuredly be different from the merger movement of the 1960s.

Our story will be told more or less in chronological order, and to do it properly, we must go back to 1904, when helter-skelter consolidation on the railroads' own terms was brought to an end by the federal government. In the years that followed, efforts were made to control the consolidation process for a broader public good through regulation. Several ideas were put forth. The one finally adopted in 1920 was a compromise, as so many things must be in a democracy, but it unfortunately included most of the weaknesses of the original suggestions.

In the second chapter, focusing on the Northeast where intrigue was most intense, we will see how powerful corporations could frustrate the purpose of the law, but not necessarily to their own advantage. In addition, changing conditions worked upon an already weak law, and forced a modification of it in 1940. In the third chapter, focusing specifically on the Pennsylvania Railroad and on financier Robert Young, we will examine the sad aftermath of the interwar years, which helped to shape the tragedy to come. The fourth chapter is an analysis of why certain economic and technological conditions came together in the 1950s to make consolidation suddenly the hottest topic in railroading, the panacea for all its ills.

In the fifth chapter, we move our tripod close to dissect as a case study a single merger, the Erie and the Lackawanna in 1960. We will examine motives and justification, and weigh the heavy hand of history. We will explore the regulatory process and analyze the forces in opposition to merger. Then we will follow Erie Lackawanna through eight years of its merged existence and discover that merger did not accomplish any of the goals for which it was intended. Evidence that the panacea would not work was strewn liberally about, but no one looked back to learn from experience.

The sixth chapter demonstrates how the two richest railroads in the Northeast, the Chesapeake & Ohio and the Norfolk & Western, used consolidation for their own purposes in the early 1960s. Their unilateral actions threatened considerable harm to other parts of the northeastern network, and raised the question of what effect consolidation was going to have, not just on a railroad, but on all railroading. In the seventh chapter, we will examine what was happening simultaneously in the West. There, two merger proposals appeared to be designed primarily to eliminate competition. These would profit railroads, but seemed to threaten harm, without compensating benefits, to others. This included the merger of the "Northern Lines," the empire of James J. Hill, nineteenth-century railroad builder and financier in the Northwest. In the eighth chapter, Congress is made aware that the "panacea" was not turning out well, either in the East or the West, and that the Interstate Commerce Commission, the regulatory agency in charge, probably needed new guidelines. But Congress couldn't come to grips with these tough problems, and the ICC was left to stumble forward with mergers about which the deepest questions had been raised.

In the ninth chapter, "The Rise of the Penn Central," congressional neglect comes home to roost in the merger petition of the Pennsylvania and the New York Central railroads. Though it had a plausible justification, there were plenty of signs of disaster. On M-Day, as it was called, April 27, 1966, the ICC dealt simultaneously with the petition of the New Haven Railroad to discontinue all passenger service, and the Penn Central and Northern Lines' mergers. It was a day that left railroading stunned and the ICC awash in controversy.

In the tenth chapter, we journey south, where the railroad network seemed to fall neatly into four well-balanced but ominously powerful cartels. Merger seemed to work, but at a terrible price. In the next chapter, we revisit the West, where, in contrast to the South, the pieces did not fall into place, and the merger struggle ended in costly deadlock. In the twelfth chapter, back in the East, all the carriers left out of the Penn Central scrambled to protect themselves from what they thought was an onrushing juggernaut. Finally, the courts had to resolve matters where commissioners and congressmen had failed.

The thirteenth chapter, "The Fall of the Penn Central," sifts through the wreckage of a tragic business failure. We will examine the bitter rivalry of executives, the abortive attempt to invest funds outside of railroading, and the accounting techniques which disguised the spreading paralysis from investors, regulators, and even directors. Of greater seriousness, we will proceed step-by-step through the operating breakdown of a railroad. It had been coming on for years, but merger, rather than the panacea, was the catalyst for collapse.

Finally, in the last chapter, government steps in to mop up the mess. The ICC, despite its many mistakes in the merger movement, emerged as the defender of open and methodical plan-making, urging that bridges not be burned in haste. Unfortunately, real plan-making had passed to the Department of Transportation, which seemed determined to repeat all of the ICC's past mistakes, now made even more tragic by what appeared to be its crassly political motives. The story ends with the creation of the Consolidated Rail Corporation on April 1, 1976.

2

If failure were the end result, had there ever been a proper justification?

The merger movement grew out of the special problems of railroads. They had been built to serve the needs of the nineteenth century, in a day when they were the only mode of cheap, overland transportation. Despite the arrival of competition from motor trucks and newly improved waterways, their tonnage grew steadily, except during the Depression. But the composition of that tonnage changed, most noticeably after World War II. They tended to lose the traffic of high-value manufactured items to trucks, especially when they moved over short distances, as in New England, for example, or for that matter, in all of the Northeast. This was traffic that could pay a comparatively high rate per ton. More and more railroad traffic came to be bulk commodities that would move only at minimal rates—grain, ore, coal, cement. Hence, the need for physical capacity increased as the funds available to build that capacity decreased.

At the same time, there were technological developments that kicked the props from under railroading's nineteenth-century structure. Stronger building materials, heavier locomotives, bigger cars, and more sophisticated signals made it possible for a given track to carry many times the traffic of earlier days. This had been an ongoing process, but in the 1950s it accelerated significantly. There was the development of "second-generation" diesel power, capable of hauling more than twice the tonnage of the first diesels; of jumbo freight cars, up to three times the size of steam-era cars; and especially centralized traffic control (CTC), which permitted the operation of all signals and switches along several hundred miles of track from a single console.

The new locomotives were useful only if trains carried 150 cars or more; CTC was expensive, and could not be justified unless traffic volume were heavy. Dividing traffic among half a dozen nineteenth-century lines meant no one could take advantage of the new efficiency. More threatening was the need to rebuild rights-of-way to an engineering parity with the interstate highways. Grades had to be leveled; curves had to be straightened. Railroads had been built with nineteenth-century technology and followed too closely the configuration of the land. This could never be done for a multitude of parallel lines. Add to this the rising demand by railroad workers to share in the good life. Add the government's active sponsorship of highway, air, and water transportation, thus narrowing the efficiency gap between those modes and the railroads. It became more important than ever to take advantage of all that technology had to offer.

These were the "textbook" conditions for consolidation: eliminate duplicate facilities and concentrate traffic on a few good lines. This would save money in operating expenses that could be better used to buy technology; in other words, trade in the obsolete nineteenth-century investment for needed twentieth-century investment.

The public had a stake in this. Everyone who used railroad services, or who produced or consumed products that were carried by rail at some stage of their production, had an interest in seeing that service constantly improved, for everyone's productivity improved as a result. It was especially true if a railroad were getting into financial trouble, if it were moving to what we will call the "point of no return," where it could not afford the capital improvements to remain competitive (thus making it unlikely it would ever be able to afford them again). Consolidation promised to pump life back in, saving the industries and the jobs dependent on those industries along its lines. Since 1920, in fact, this had been why the government had tried to encourage consolidation, for the possible benefits did not flow just to railroads, but to the general public as well.

But there were drawbacks. First, many jobs of railroad employees would be lost, and this was a blow not only to the people involved but to railroad towns—junctions, division points, shop towns—that might be phased out by consolidation. No matter how justified the *coup de grâce,* it was not pleasant to watch, especially if the merger did not produce the good results anticipated.

Second, whether or not all the nineteenth-century railroads were capable of earning a profit, vested interests that were not obsolete or redundant had grown up around every one of them. Phasing out a line in consolidation could ruin industries dependent on it. It could render perfectly useful investment wasted and cause unemployment for more than just railroad workers. Unemployment sent reverberations deep into the bowels of the economy. States and cities felt responsible to see that no extreme violence was done to their economies in this way.

Third, a railroad that was not invited to a merger when its rivals were was denied the advantages they were supposed to be getting. Rivals might become better situated to divert traffic away from it. Thus, it might needlessly be pushed to the point of no return. Industries along the excluded roads, as well as cities and states, had reason to see that all were properly included.

Fourth, consolidation reduced competition. Many commodities were subject to plenty of competition from other modes of transportation, and the issue was of no consequence. But other commodities were bound to the rails, usually by their low value per ton. Here, competition between railroads was a factor of significance. Experience seemed to indicate that where competition between railroads existed, rail service remained good and rates low; that if complacent monopolies let service deteriorate or rates rise, they might lose traffic to other modes they never dreamed of losing.

The mass-consumption economy rested on the concept of division of labor, the extraordinary interdependence of producers and consumers at many levels of production. Transport, including railroads, made that division of labor possible by distributing the specialized products of specialized skills in specialized regions. Neither economically nor politically would the nation tolerate unilateral action by railroads that could disrupt these delicate relationships. There never was the possibility that decisions with such far-reaching repercussions would be left to management alone.

The situation demanded wise and proper regulation. The Interstate Commerce Commission, with three-quarters of a century of experience when the merger movement got under way, was the body called upon to do this work. The real question was whether existing private and public institutions were capable of facing this economic and technological and political challenge.

The issues were never as simple or as clear cut as I have drawn them so far. The overall advance of general welfare was not at the top of any individual's priorities. Managers presumably cared about the good of their own company, but not necessarily for the good of all railroading, and in any event, cared first about their own careers, which a merger might or might not advance. Owners and creditors cared about their securities—hence a consolidation that might make good operating sense to management would be voted down by stockholders. Railroad labor, shippers, local communities, other railroads—all had selfish interests which had to be separated from broader public interests.

The ICC did not make decisions by whim, but according to law, which was sometimes vague, and did not compel anyone to do anything he didn't want to. The commission was more or less insulated from politics, but Congress was not. The decision to change the law under which the commission operated, or not to change it, was political. The railroad mergers, then, become a case study of the intricacies and subtleties of business decisions in a regulated atmosphere.

The story ended in failure, so it seemed that existing procedures were not functioning well. Partisans of more regulation or less may each find solace in this story. It contains few real villains, but not many heroes, either. The deepest questions will be raised about all institutions—management, labor, state and local government, the bureaucracy, the courts, Congress, even capitalism itself. The reader will have to decide for himself what should have been done or what ought to be done in the future. But he should not make up his mind in haste, for all sides had compelling arguments and destructive weaknesses.

3

It has been a number of years since the names of once-famous railroads faded into memory. The flags of the Wabash, the Monon, the Nickel Plate, the Seaboard Air Line, and many more have been furled. With the passage of time, these lines, once vital and familiar, disappear into the attic of our business past.

For those who were not familiar with the configuration of American railroads as they were when the merger movement began in the mid-1950s, it might be useful, before reading on, to take a minute to look at some maps and recall some of the great railroads of days gone by.

At first glance, the structure of American railroads seemed wildly chaotic. There were, in the 1950s, several hundred different companies, of which 134 were called Class I carriers (meaning, in those days, they had annual gross revenues of more than a million dollars). But only about half of those were of national significance, and of that half only a portion are of concern to us here.

Railroadwise, the country was divided into three parts. The Northeast, or trunkline territory, as it was called, extended south to the Potomac and Ohio rivers, and west to a line between Chicago and St. Louis. The South, for our purposes, extended from Richmond, down through the Deep South, and out to the cotton Southwest. The West was everything west of Chicago and the Mississippi River. On the borders between the regions lay the major junction points, or gateways, where traffic funneled on through rates from one region to another. Between East and West was Chicago and St. Louis; between South and West, Memphis and New Orleans; between North and South, Alexandria and Cincinnati.

The Northeast: The Trunks

Astride the East lay four railroads called trunklines that extended all the way from the Atlantic to the western gateways.

The larger two, the greater trunks, were the New York Central and the Pennsylvania. Though they headed out of New York in opposite directions, they turned west, the Central at Albany and the Pennsylvania at Philadelphia, to blanket the entire region that in days gone by had been heartland of all American industry. It was one of the most historic rivalries in American business. Travelers who knew their way around often chose the Central when they could, for the "breakfast run" as it was called, the final sprint of the great express trains from Albany to New York along the Hudson, was one of the world's magnificent spectacles. But the Pennsylvania had an edge on the Central as the bulk mover; of people, along the New York-Washington corridor; of freight in the heavy coal and ore-hauling regions of the midwestern steel districts. Central had its coal lines, going even as far south as Charleston, West Virginia, and Cairo, Illinois. But east of Buffalo, it served an area of light manufacturing where much of the traffic had been diverted to trucks. So as similar as the two railroads appeared, there were differences that were profound.

Of the lesser trunks, the Baltimore & Ohio concentrated on hauling raw materials to the steel districts. The Erie, aside from its seedy financial past as the Scarlet Woman of Wall Street, was best known as a purveyor of perishables and finished goods to the eastern markets.

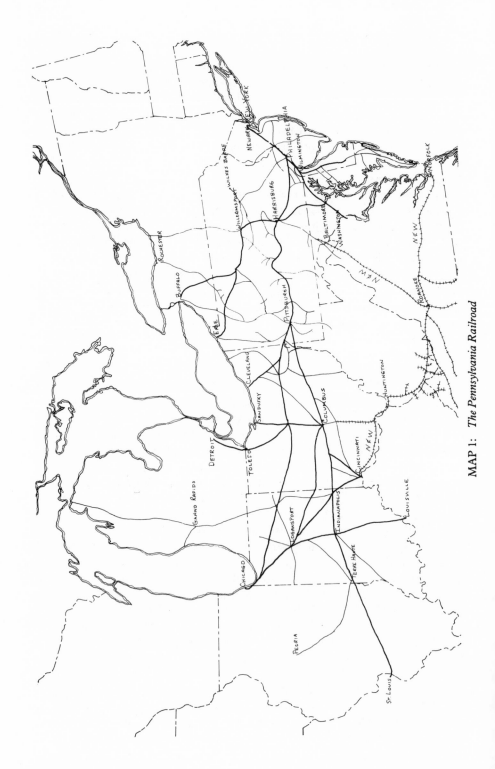

MAP 1: *The Pennsylvania Railroad*

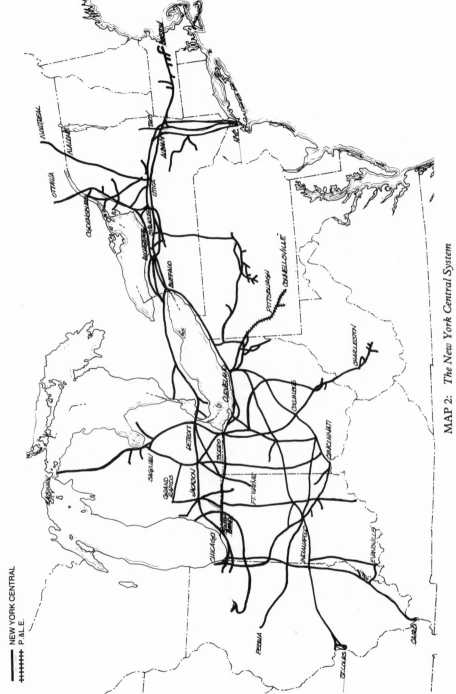

NEW YORK CENTRAL
+++++ P.&L.E.

MAP 2: *The New York Central System*

Though they were grouped together as "the trunks," the discrepancy in their size and relative importance was considerable, as, for example, their 1955 gross revenues indicated:

Pennsylvania	$934,972,870
New York Central	762,666,356
Baltimore & Ohio	432,061,417
Erie	161,447,842

In addition to the trunks, there were some other important groups o railroads in the East: the New England roads, the anthracite roads, the Pocahontas roads, and the midwestern bridge lines.

The New England Roads

New England was like a laboratory of all that was troubled in railroading. First, distances were short. Despite that, two roads of northern New England, the Bangor & Aroostook and Maine Central, carried mostly raw materials to markets farther south, and earned regular, if modest, profits.

In southern New England, in addition to short distances in a region of light manufacturing where traffic was highly susceptible to motor carrier invasions, there were extraordinary terminal expenses. Every carload on every railroad had to be picked up on someone's siding and delivered to someone else's. It required tedious man-hours at slow speeds, usually on heavily taxed trackage, which produced little revenue. Obviously, some railroad had to bear the cost, but the ones that had the least of it, or that had a long line-haul to compensate, were better off. A "bridge line" that received cars from connecting roads and delivered them to connecting roads at the other end was ideally situated. But New England was either the beginning or the end of the line for nearly every shipment that went there, and the New England roads did not have much of a line-haul to compensate.

On top of that, southern New England was a region of heavy passenger traffic. Air, and more significantly, the private automobile, had lured away the most lucrative of this business, and what was left kept the companies that provided it constantly embroiled in politics. Besides, passenger trains were labor-intensive. A full complement of waiters, porters, and bartenders no longer came cheap, and productive machinery could not be substituted the way it could in freight service. Since the roads of southern New England had once depended upon passengers for a major portion of their revenues, they had the farthest to fall.

Only one trunkline, the New York Central, entered New England over its Boston & Albany route.

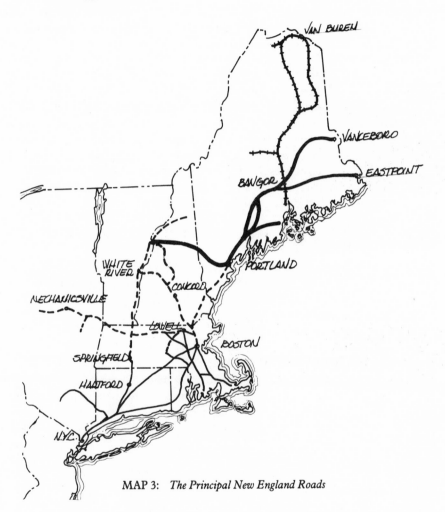

MAINE CENTRAL
BANGOR & AROOSTOCK
BOSTON & MAINE
NEW HAVEN

MAP 3: *The Principal New England Roads*

The Anthracite Roads

It was hard to imagine, in a later day when homes were heated with oil or gas, the significance of anthracite, or hard coal, when it was the principal fuel for space heating. Without coal—at reasonable prices—people froze in the northern winters; therefore, anthracite had once been almost as "political" a commodity as passengers. Five major railroads were specifically built to carry the coal from the anthracite fields in northeastern Pennsylvania. The Jersey Central sent it east to New Jersey and New York City. The Reading carried it south to Philadelphia. The Delaware & Hudson took it north to New England and Canada. The Lehigh Valley and the Delaware, Lackawanna & Western carried it both east to New York and west to Buffalo, where it went on to Canada or the American Midwest. All of these railroads carried general traffic as well—the D&H, wood pulp from Canada, for example; or the Reading, bituminous coal to the industrial complex of the lower Delaware Valley. But when anthracite was replaced with other fuels, the rug was pulled out from under these railroads. Only the D&H, a line which was not also burdened with extensive passenger operations, was able to preserve a semblance of prosperity.

The Pocahontas Roads

On the borderlands between railroading's northern and southern regions lay what was called the Pocahontas District. There, two principal roads, the Norfolk & Western and the Chesapeake & Ohio, together with a smaller one, the Virginian, carried bituminous (soft) coal eastbound to Virginia tidewater and westbound to midwestern industry. Though they had branches extending even into North Carolina, this traffic was so intimately a part of the northern economy that the interests of those roads were generally with the North. In contrast to anthracite, the demand for bituminous was increasing—for fueling steam generators to make electricity and for turning into coke to fuel steel blast furnaces. These roads, therefore, were among the financially strongest in the nation, blue chips to compare with any other industry.

The Midwestern Bridge Lines

There were two roads, the Wabash and the Nickel Plate, between Buffalo and the midwestern gateways, occupying the same region as the western halves of the trunks. If put together with the anthracite roads, like the Lehigh Valley or the Lackawanna, they formed systems similar to the trunks. Their haul was fairly long, across flat terrain. Much of it was of that lucrative "bridge" variety. In days gone by, they had been the country cousins of the rich anthracite roads, but time had turned things around, and in the postwar era they were in a considerably more enviable position.

The South

The major railroads of the South were financially strong, thanks largely to the successful industrialization and urbanization of that region after World War II. The region was subdivided, railroadwise, with comparatively little overlap.

In the coastal plain, the Atlantic Coast Line and the Seaboard Air Line competed mile-for-mile for the lucrative haul of both freight and passengers between Florida, the Carolinas, and the industrial North.

To their west, in the Piedmont and mountain regions, extending as far west as the Mississippi River, were the mighty Southern Railway and Louisville & Nashville systems. The L&N was controlled by the Atlantic Coast Line, although the two were historically operated as separate companies.

Along the Mississippi River, from the Delta cotton lands of Mississippi to Chicago, lay the Illinois Central, like the continent's spine. To its west, into the cotton lands of Texas and the wheat lands of Kansas, were the Missouri Pacific and the St. Louis-San Francisco (better known simply as the Frisco). Earlier in the century, the Southwest had been a railroad wasteland, where poverty-stricken roads served a poverty-stricken region. But the Southwest and its major railroads were booming together after World War II.

The West: The Granger Roads

In the West, there were two distinct types of railroads—the grangers and the transcontinentals. In the nineteenth century, farmers couldn't be more than a day's wagon haul from a railroad. Railroads had been cheap to lay on the flat land. The result was a spaghetti-like network of crisscrossing lines. In a later day, it wasn't necessary to have so much mileage. A farmer, after all, could truck his crop a lot farther to a railhead than he could haul it by wagon. The result was too many railroads in a region where they were too heavily dependent on seasonal grain crops. Many roads operated in the region, but four big ones that served it almost exclusively we will call the greater grangers—the Chicago & North Western, the Milwaukee Road, the Rock Island, and the Burlington. Depending on how successfully these roads had found other traffic to supplement their granger traffic, this tended to be a region of marginally profitably operations.

The Transcontinentals

To the west of granger country lay the great transcontinentals. A long haul, largely bound to the rails because of distance, was the key to their success. From south to north, they were the Southern Pacific, the Santa Fe, the combination of the Denver & Rio Grande Western and Western Pacific, the Union Pacific, the Northern Pacific, and the Great Northern. The

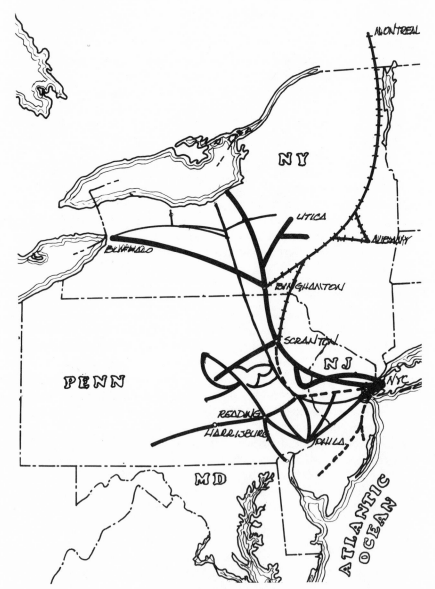

LACKAWANA
LEHIGH VALLEY
++++++ DELAWARE & HUDSON
— — JERSEY CENTRAL
READING

MAP 4: *The Anthracite Roads*

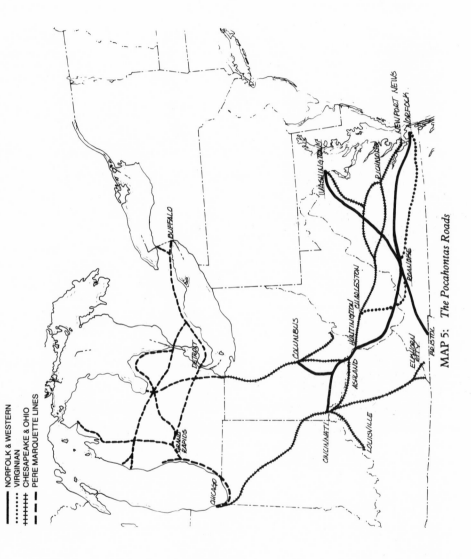

NORFOLK & WESTERN
VIRGINIAN
CHESAPEAKE & OHIO
PERE MARQUETTE LINES

MAP 5: *The Pocahontas Roads*

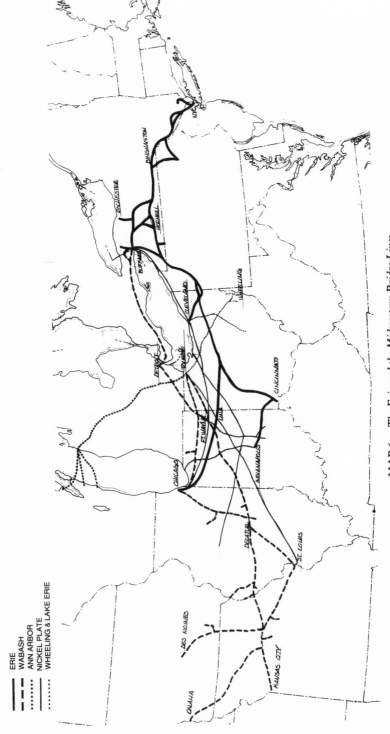

MAP 6: *The Erie and the Midwestern Bridge Lines*

ERIE
WABASH
ANN ARBOR
NICKEL PLATE
WHEELING & LAKE ERIE

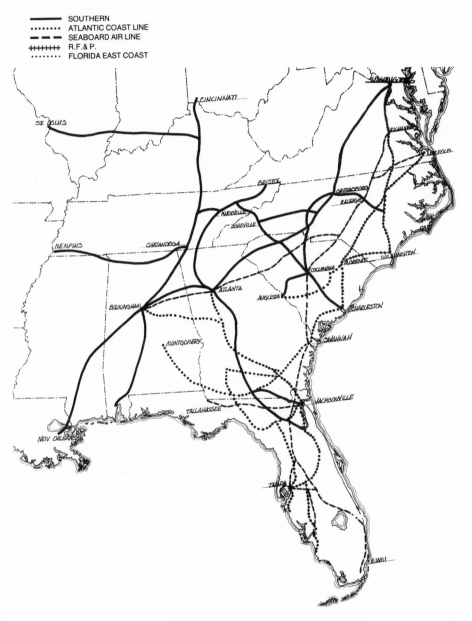

CINCINNATI

ST. LOUIS

BRISTOL

WASHINGTON

RICHMOND

NORFOLK

GREENSBORO

RALEIGH

KNOXVILLE

ASHEVILLE

MEMPHIS

CHATANOOGA

COLUMBIA

FLORENCE

WILMINGTON

ATLANTA

AUGUSTA

CHARLESTON

BIRMINGHAM

MONTGOMERY

SAVANNAH

JACKSONVILLE

TALLAHASSEE

NEW ORLEANS

TAMPA

MIAMI

MAP 7:   *The Deep South Carriers*

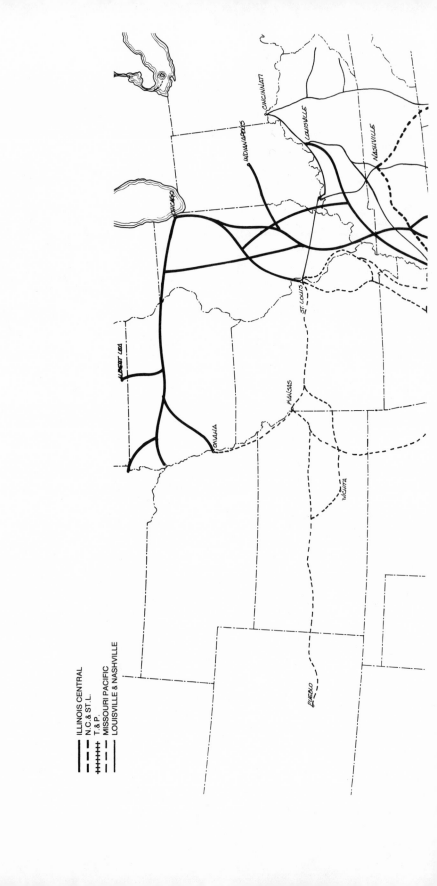

ILLINOIS CENTRAL
N.C. & ST. L.
T. & P.
MISSOURI PACIFIC
LOUISVILLE & NASHVILLE

CHICAGO

INDIANAPOLIS

CINCINNATI

LOUISVILLE

NASHVILLE

ST. LOUIS

ALBERT LEA

OMAHA

KANSAS

WICHITA

PUEBLO

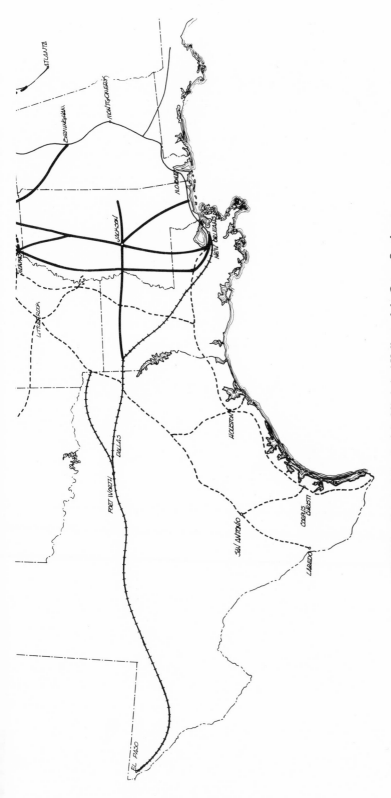

MAP 8: *Principal Roads of the Mississippi Valley and the Cotton Southwest*

CHICAGO & NORTH WESTERN
MILWAUKEE ROAD
ROCK ISLAND
BURLINGTON

SEATTLE

BUTTE

BILLINGS

LANDER

DENVER

TUCUMCARI

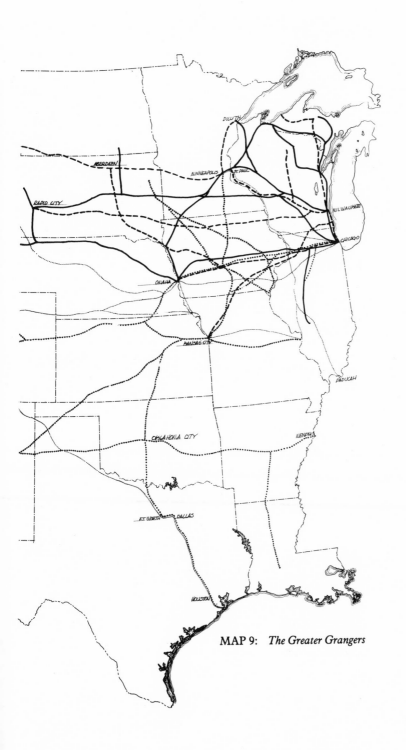

MAP 9:   *The Greater Grangers*

SANTA FE
CONNECTIONS
SOUTHERN PACIFIC
ADDITIONS 1920-40
CONNECTIONS

PORTLAND

OGDEN

RENO

SAN FRANCISCO

LOS ANGELES

SAN DIEGO

PHOENIX

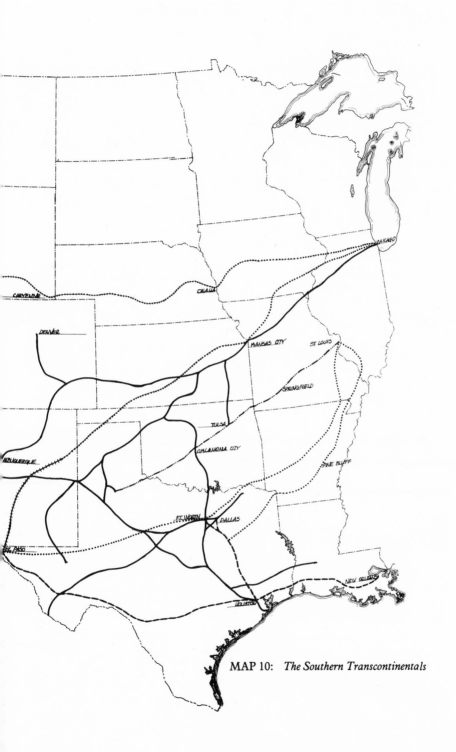

CHEYENNE

DENVER

GALENA

CHICAGO

KANSAS CITY

ST. LOUIS

SPRINGFIELD

TULSA

OKLAHOMA CITY

ALBUQUERQUE

PINE BLUFF

FT. WORTH   DALLAS

EL PASO

NEW ORLEANS

HOUSTON

MAP 10:   *The Southern Transcontinentals*

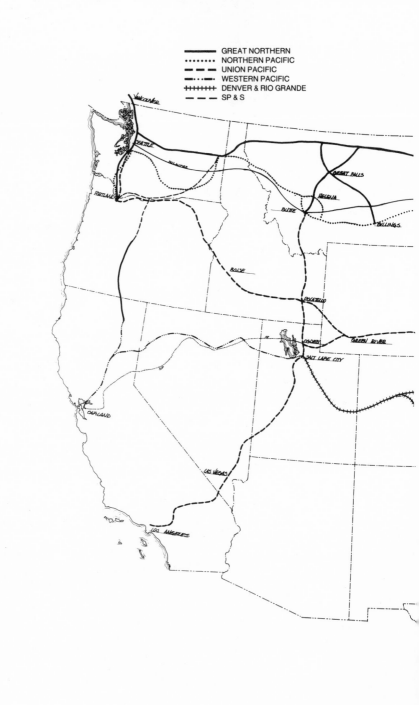

GREAT NORTHERN
.... NORTHERN PACIFIC
— — — UNION PACIFIC
—··—··— WESTERN PACIFIC
+++++++ DENVER & RIO GRANDE
— — SP & S

VANCOUVER

SEATTLE

WALLSNGER

PORTLAND

GREAT FALLS

HELENA

BUTTE

BILLINGS

BOISE

POCATELLO

OGDEN

GREEN RIVER

SALT LAKE CITY

OAKLAND

LAS VEGAS

LOS ANGELES

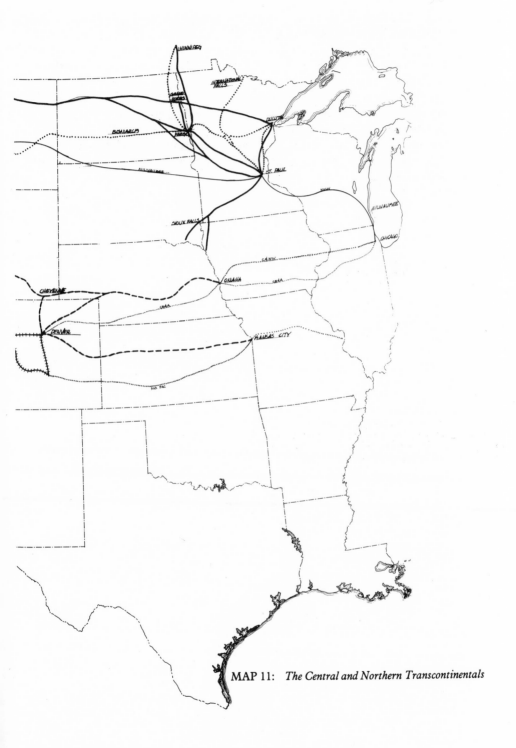

MAP 11: *The Central and Northern Transcontinentals*

Canadian Pacific, in connection with its granger road subsidiary in the American Midwest, the Soo Line, was also a factor in traffic across the country. Only the transcontinental extension of the Milwaukee Road, which I have already described as a granger road, failed to partake of the transcontinental success.

In the course of this story, we will meet some smaller roads—the lesser grangers, for example, and some southern roads that were not quite as well off as their big-time colleagues—which played brief but significant roles in consolidation. In an industry that was in a constant state of flux and which defied very much generalization, this was its basic structure as the merger drama began.

CHAPTER 1

The Problem and the Idea; 1904-1920

It was an anxious crowd that gathered on March 14, 1904, in the old chambers of the United States Supreme Court. The decision expected that day was potential dynamite, one that could set off a panic on Wall Street. Stakes were high on both sides. On the one was James J. Hill's railroad empire known as the Northern Securities Company, backed by J.P. Morgan, accused of seeking to monopolize transportation in the Northwest, a conspiracy in restraint of trade and a violation of the Sherman Act. On the other was the Department of Justice, representing the highest aspirations of the Roosevelt administration and the reform spirit in America, that hoped to limit the size and power of big business, which already seemed to rival elected governments for supreme authority in the land.

Nine years before, the Court had virtually thrown out the law under which the present charges were brought, giving the trusts, as they were known, a green light to restructure business as they pleased. But on that spring day of 1904, a new court and new political pressures pointed to a reversal. Business said a decision against Northern Securities would shatter investor confidence and wreck private enterprise. The Justice Department said a decision in favor of Northern Securities would be tantamount to saying all industry could be run by a few rich men for their own benefit, as much a threat to healthy capitalism as any anarchist scheme imported from Europe.

By the narrowest of margins, the forces of reform won their case. Northern Securities was ordered dissolved and old-fashioned price competition was to be restored, at least in theory. President Roosevelt was pleased, and Republicans generally were quick to take credit, for this decision was popular with their middle-class constituency back home. The trusts were on the run, and there was yet room for small business in America.

As it turned out, Wall Street's dire predictions of panic and ruin were a little overstated. There was no panic; the market actually rose. In the first place, the decision was not as sweeping as it might have been. Morgan was still in control of his empire even if some of the devices to hold it together had been struck down. In the second place, other industry recognized that a decision against the railroads was not necessarily a precedent for them. The railroads were dreadfully unpopular. Sooner or later, the Supreme Court always followed popular sentiment. The railroads could be a useful lightning rod to take the pressure off everyone else.

There was a good deal of irony to the railroads' unpopularity. No other invention had done as much to make industrialization possible. Industrialization rested on the concept of division of labor, which meant essentially that a comparatively few people engaged in mechanized agriculture could raise the food to feed the people of the cities who made the machines that mechanized agriculture. Instead of trying to provide for all its needs, a city or a region specialized in the things it could do best and traded its products for those of other regions. It required massive volumes of cheap transportation, and the railroads had provided it. No matter, as some have argued, that canals could have done the job better. The railroads had done it, and with incredible success. While the roots of industrialization went back to the eighteenth century, most of the transformation had taken place since 1870, well within the living memory of the people who heard the Northern Securities decision that spring day of 1904.

Because the railroad occupied this strategic position in the new order, it had tremendous power. The wheat of Kansas or the shoes of Fall River were worthless until they were shipped to distant markets. Railroad rates and service would frequently determine in what markets these products could be sold and in what quantity. To the producer, however, it often appeared that the railroad was confiscating his profit, except when it was held in check by the competition of another railroad. That was an obvious reason for the railroads' desire to consolidate, or at least for their owners to try to bring them under some kind of common control. It was also the reason why a myriad of interests, commercial and political, wanted to stop the consolidation process.

The love-hate ambiguity ran deeper. If the train, especially the fast one thundering through complicated junctions and into elaborate terminals, symbolized power and progress, it also signaled an end to the self-sufficient man. The yeoman farmer, the pioneer of American lore, took care of his own needs and his success or failure depended on his own efforts. The morals and mores of the entire nation rested on that. The world the railroad created, in contrast, was an interdependent one, and at some deeper level, most Americans must have understood that the idea of every man standing on his own effort was not going to survive intact. There were many who believed their own independence had somehow been handed over to the lords of the railroad. As the railroads grew to blanket whole regions, and as they consolidated and came under the control of bankers, it meant to millions that their destiny was in the hands of remote men in distant places who were unresponsive to their needs and uncaring of their problems. The genie uncorked, in other words, would not go back in the bottle.

If the Northern Securities decision did not, as capital had predicted, ring down the curtain on capitalism, it did send out ripples. The effects were imperceptible to the public at first, but they were going to be profound. For example, the process of railroad consolidation slowed, and then abruptly stopped.

In the nineteenth century, the railroads had combined together, absorbed local lines, built new lines, and shaped themselves into competitive systems through a process that was almost organic in nature. It had taken place in three phases. In the first, before the Civil War, a few companies put together basic through routes under single managements, and lines such as the New York Central, the Pennsylvania, and the Baltimore & Ohio began to emerge as powerful forces. In the second phase, between the end of the war and the panic of 1893, rival companies tried to maintain their competitive positions with each other by absorbing feeder lines. The larger systems in the East and the West, though not yet in the South, began to take the basic shape they would retain until the 1960s. In the third phase, which began at the end of the depression of the 1890s, the giants tried to curb ruinous competition between them by seeking to control each other.[1]

At the time of the Northern Securities decision, the legacy of the second phase was an expensive burden that required high profits to support. The Lackawanna, for example, had absorbed some nineteen separate lines in order to round out its system. It had assumed their debts and guaranteed dividends on their stocks, sometimes for as much as 12 percent. When the future was bright and profits were assured, 12 percent did not seem unreasonable, although even for those days one could sense the speculators and promoters had come out on top. Any threats to profits could turn this mass of semidigested short lines, costing millions of dollars in fixed charges, into a serious liability.[2] Thus the second phase made the third phase almost inevitable.

It was the third phase of consolidation that attracted the attention of the reformers, for its avowed purpose was to eliminate competition. After the depression of the 1890s, there were some spectacular changes in railroad structure. In the South, largely under the guidance of J.P. Morgan, a collection of short lines was forged into three major systems, the Southern, the Seaboard, and the Atlantic Coast Line (which controlled the Louisville & Nashville). In the West, E.H. Harriman put together his giant combination of the Union Pacific, the Southern Pacific, and the Illinois Central. In the Northwest, Hill combined his own Great Northern with the Northern Pacific, and in 1901 added the Burlington, controlling them all through the Northern Securities holding company. Harriman had contested Hill's control of the Burlington. The two had gone at each other's throats and nearly set off a financial panic, concrete evidence of how vulnerable the nation was to the irresponsibility of the giants.[3]

In the East, plans were already under way for the greatest monopoly of them all. Neither a merger nor a holding company, it was a less-structured device known as community-of-interest. It represented the ultimate of the consolidation process when the last surviving giants signed a declaration of peace. The purpose was to end rate competition, the ruinous price war that could drive rates down to where even day-to-day maintenance was sacrificed. It was an elaborate affair, worked out informally between the Pennsylvania and the New York Central and their bankers, to control all the lines in the East, either by stock control or through interlocking directors. The Pennsylvania bought control of the Baltimore & Ohio and the Norfolk & Western, while the New York Central bought a substantial share of the Lackawanna. Together, they bought heavily into the Jersey Central, the Reading, the Chesapeake & Ohio, and the New England roads. Their bankers sat on the boards of each to make sure no one tried to injure anyone else. There was no formal arrangement between the Central and the Pennsylvania, but their very size and power seemed to keep them in check.[4]

At the time of the Hill-Harriman fight over the Burlington, which triggered the panic of 1901, community-of-interest was still in its subtle, formative stages. Northern Securities was not subtle and that made it an easy target for antitrust prosecution. Old-style, privately planned railroad consolidation ended that spring day of 1904 when the Northern Securities decision was handed down. The message was clear to the promoters of community-of-interest: break up now, voluntarily, on your own terms, or have it done for you by the courts.

In case any misunderstanding remained, a few subsequent developments underscored the point. In 1906, the Interstate Commerce Commission launched an investigation of Harriman's empire. The tone of its final report was hostile, and his control of three western carriers was found to be harmful to the public interest. It asked Congress to make *any* combination that might reduce competition illegal.[5] In another investigation, the ICC exposed how the once-prosperous Cincinnati, Hamilton & Dayton line (later acquired by the B&O) was financially broken by the manipulations of the Pere Marquette Railroad. "This sordid tale has been told without adjectives," said the droll commissioners in their final report. "The facts speak for themselves and have been told in all their nakedness."[6]

It was the New Haven affair that finally brought the issue to a head, and brought the wrath of all reformers down upon J.P. Morgan. It involved the abortive attempt of Morgan's New Haven to take over the Boston & Maine. Morgan and his New England lieutenant, Charles Mellen, fully intended to build a total monopoly of New England transportation, and admitted the purpose was to control rates. What was best for the House of Morgan was best for New England, they said, for otherwise the giant trunklines, like the Pennsylvania or the New York Central, would dominate the little New England roads to their own advantage. Morgan's technique, more dubious than his rationale, was to force the hapless New Haven to buy the securities of the little roads, often at inflated prices. Morgan made his money selling securities, not by running fine railroads.

Weighted down with debt, the New Haven did not even have the cash for routine maintenance, a serious thing on a high-speed, high-density passenger line. There followed a series of grisly wrecks which the Hearst papers happily reported in every lurid detail. Louis Brandeis made his debut as a national figure by his relentless pursuit of Mellen in what became a classic progressive-style attack on monopoly. By 1914, Mellen was out, and the New Haven, unable to pay a dividend, had acquired the cadaver-like quality it would retain to the end of its days. New England was left with neither the advantages of healthy competition nor those of a single integrated unit.[7]

In that kind of atmosphere, community-of-interest faded away. The dismantling was done quietly and a few of the new relationships were retained. The New York Central kept the Boston & Albany, for example, and integrated it directly into its system, making it the only trunkline in New England. The Pennsylvania kept its interest in that up-and-comer of the coal fields, the Norfolk & Western. Nevertheless, progressive reform had frozen the railroads into a miscellaneous collection of units that was neither natural nor ideal. Some were big and well entrenched, with good routes and terminals, while others were excluded from lucrative traffic and left to feed on the scraps. Some could earn a respectable return and thus raise more capital for more investment, while others were condemned to a slow death, unable to raise the capital to make the improvements that would keep them competitive.

Despite the Morgans and the Mellens, there was good reason for some consolidation. The concept of efficiency, particularly efficiency through large-scale operation, was new and only vaguely understood at the time of Northern Securities. Had it been fully appreciated, it would surely have been one of the holding company's principal defenses. As it was, it came up only once. The Great Northern Railway had purchased ships to carry the railroad's trans-Pacific export traffic. They were large enough to compete with the ships of the Japan Mail Line, but unless the traffic of the Northern Pacific were also funneled into those ships, they would not be feasible to operate. Splitting the two railroads would deliver the business to a foreign competitor.[8]

In the years that followed, the concept of efficiency came to hold an increasing fascination for American businessmen. In 1909, Herbert Croly's book, *The Promise of American Life*, concluded that big enterprise, properly regulated, was the best means for efficient production. Roosevelt would take up the idea as the major theme of his Bull Moose campaign in 1912—a significant break from his trust-busting past. Perhaps the very concept of antitrust had been ill-conceived from the start.

It was too bad that in order to get soundly consolidated railways, it was necessary to put up with greedy promoters and speculators, but there was going to be a high price for interfering in their little games.

At about the same time as the Northern Securities decision there was another cloud gathering about the railroads, also in the name of progressive reform. The original Act to Regulate Commerce that established the Interstate Commerce Commission as a regulatory and enforcement agency, had halfheartedly tried to curb discrimination in railroad rates. But the Supreme Court, in the closing days of unrestrained laissez-faire conservatism before the advent of progressive reform had poked devastating holes in the commission's rate-regulating powers. The Hepburn Act of 1906 plugged the loopholes of the original act and gave the commission the power to approve maximum rates. The Mann-Elkins Act of 1910 plugged a loophole in the Hepburn Act. The ICC flexed its new muscle over rate-making by denying the railroads' requests for general rate increases in 1911 and again in 1912.

Many little businesses believed they had been nearly ruined by unfair rates. Many people thought the railroad barons lived in luxury because of unfair rates milked from the people's sweat. Many citizens believed the railroad barons had come to possess a power that a democracy of supposed equals never meant to confer on anyone. The clamor for regulation could not be denied.

But it became abundantly clear at those rate hearings of 1911 and 1912 that the railroads had been delivered into the hands of their enemies. Mostly, these were their own customers, big shippers and little ones, from all over the country, who perceived their best interests in low rates right now, regardless of what it did to the railroads in the long run. They had found a way to keep the transportation giants down. Behind government regulation lay not a big-brother brand of creeping socialism, but always a private, vested interest.

The rapid increase in the volume of railroad traffic was the best testimony to the fact that railroad service was not, in general, overpriced. But the increase in volume had brought the railroads face to face with technological crises on more than one occasion. Early on, for example, heavy and long and fast trains would have been impossible without low-cost steel to replace the iron rails and wooden cars and bridges, which the Bessemer and open-hearth processes solved only in the nick of time. By the 1890s, especially as the depression began to dissipate, volume required double tracks, electric signals, heavy locomotives and cars, and elaborate line relocations to level grades and straighten curves. It all took money—lots of it.

The money had to be borrowed. Borrowing took confidence—that profits would be sufficient to repay the money in fifty or seventy-five years. The railroads had greeted the new century with unbounded optimism. The decade that began with the waning of the depression and ended about 1907, a year of financial panic on Wall Street and the first year of life under the Hepburn Act, was probably their most expansive period ever, with investment in improvements that exceeded the great construction boom of the 1880s.

After 1910, investment began to fall off, even in the face of rising volume, which indicated that confidence was also falling off. The adverse rate decisions and the ICC's hostility to consolidation were too coincidental to be irrelevant. Railroads could neither set their prices like other businesses nor arrange their routes and facilities as they thought best. In other words, the apparent victory of the people might be brief and hollow if the long-run effect was to discourage the investment that made improvement possible.

So the railroads arrived at World War I shorn of their confidence, though not always their arrogance, and expressed it by decreased investment. When the war came, they had neither the equipment nor the capacity to handle the load. That was before there was any serious competition from other kinds of transportation. The reformers thought they would simply curb the industry; they wound up crippling it. Commonly known as progressives, one writer has called them "archaic progressives" for their remarkable shortsightedness.[9]

1

Winter came early in 1917 and it came with a vengeance. The nation was at war, and the cold snap was going to be a burden on railroads already buckling under the heavy load of war traffic. Switches froze and trains stalled. Hopper cars filled with coal could not be unloaded until fires were built to them out. Most of the traffic was moving east to the Atlantic ports, which were already clogged with trains waiting to be unloaded. Cars were in short supply when the war began, and now were scarcer than ever. This bad break in the weather was going to plunge all deliveries into chaos.

The first alarm was over fuel supplies in the cities, for with the railroads breaking down the cities were going to run out of coal. At Toledo and Columbus, for example, trains on the Chesapeake & Ohio were stalled for lack of terminal space. Back at the mines, production had stopped for lack of hopper cars, while at the Drop Forge Company at Alliance, Ohio, and at war industries all across the state, production stopped for lack of fuel.[10] The public demanded action.

Knowing they were up for judgment, the railroads tried to cooperate to keep the trains moving. In a few cases, even the bitterest of rivals were able to work out emergency agreements. When the Baltimore & Ohio ran short of locomotives to double-head its long freights over the heavy grades from Pittsburgh to New Castle, a bottleneck that threatened to shut down the entire railroad, rival Pittsburgh & Lake Erie permitted B&O trains to use its low-grade line. The railroads set up no less than five voluntary committees to coordinate operations between November of 1916, when munitions shipments first began to clog eastern terminals, and December of 1917, when everything finally broke down.

Only the last, the so-called Railroad War Board, was given any real authority by its constituent companies. For example, in order to redistribute equipment, it ordered the Lackawanna to dispatch 1,100 empty hopper cars westward in a single day for delivery to connecting lines. The B&O was ordered to send nine solid trains of empty boxcars from Baltimore to St. Louis, regardless of owner or routing, to ease car shortages in the west. The board received hourly reports on the location of trains and the availability of cars, with the power to re-route if necessary to avoid congestion. After the fact, the board was accused of mismanagement, though its failings were not always its fault. For example, it ordered trains away from badly congested Cleveland, but Governor Cox defied the directive, comandeered the trains, and ordered them to Cleveland anyway.[11]

If the railroads had been more extensively consolidated when the war began, coordination might have succeeded. As it was, voluntary efforts did not work, for these were competing railroads, and there were limits on their ability to cooperate, even under duress. Trains of war materials rolled into congested eastern ports while southern ports remained idle, yet what railroad, congested or not, would turn its traffic over to another route? Coal roads had solicited their own special customers, which meant that coal was frequently cross-hauled—Pennsylvania coal going to customers in the west, Kentucky coal moving east, for example—but what railroad would let a rival serve its customers? And beyond practical matters, there was always a gut rivalry that imbued management at all levels. A casual remark by a New York Central executive on the Railroad War Board said it all. "I've always wanted to issue orders to the Pennsylvania Railroad, and now I have my chance."[12]

On December 29, 1917, President Wilson took over the railroads. Ownership would remain in private hands, but operations would be conducted by the United States Railroad Administration. Some thought this smacked dangerously of socialism, but the men selected to run the new system were hardly socialists. There was Hale Holden of the Burlington and Henry Walters of the Atlantic Coast Line; Walker Hines of the Santa Fe and A.H. Smith of the New York Central; John Williams was serving as comptroller of the currency but was formerly of the Seaboard. As chief administrator, Wilson chose William Gibbs McAdoo, his son-in-law, frequently cited as the most able man in the cabinet. Congress held hearings in January and readily approved the president's action, for the good of the country and for victory.

Under the new administration, the railroads retained their separate identities and their own operating officers, but any routes or operations might be integrated, regardless of whether previously competing carriers were involved. Efficiency was the only criterion that mattered; maintaining competition did not. The very thing "archaic progressivism" had tried to preserve was out the window. That was of little matter, for by 1917 the only real support for old-fashioned railroad-busting came from a hard core of railroad-baiting southerners and westerners. The more sophisticated element of the reform movement had long since gone over to new ideas of efficiency and scientific management.[13] That meant large, integrated units, and if the USRRA was not exactly what they had in mind, it was on the right track.

As an experiment in the new "efficiency progressivism," the USRRA was a mixed disappointment. It kept the war trains rolling and never broke supply lines on the homefront. Both McAdoo and his successor, Walker Hines, thought that was significant. Wartime was not a good time to experiment with untried procedures and operations. Even so, car and locomotive design was standardized. The highly individualized locomotives of the various roads could never wander far from their supplies of parts, and so could not roam around the country like ordinary boxcars. Standardization was a prerequisite to truly unified operation. But few services were actually coordinated. Baltimore & Ohio passenger trains on the *Royal Blue* line were brought into Penn Station in New York instead of ending their runs in Jersey City, and since that was the only coordination project readily visible to the public, the USRRA made the most of publicizing it.[14]

Less visible was the fact that 1.9 percent more ton miles were performed by 2.1 percent fewer train miles, which meant that more trains were operating as solid units through to their destinations. A number of circuitous routes, all of them in the West, were eliminated, and the bottleneck at Cincinnati was eased by coordinating traffic over the Ohio River bridges. The accuracy and completeness of statistics was improved by adopting the procedures of scientific management, and that was essential for good managerial decisions.[15] Nevertheless, this was hardly the sweeping coordination that had been anticipated, and besides, the operation had incurred a serious financial loss (mostly the result of substantial wage increases).

At the end of the war, there was some support for continued government operation, but not among the Republican majority in Congress. Debate focused on the conditions by which the lines would be returned to private control. John J. Esch, chairman of the House Committee on Interstate Commerce, a conservative from Wisconsin, wanted to re-create the prewar status quo. His counterpart in the Senate, Albert Cummins of Iowa, sensed this was a golden opportunity for some experimentation in "efficiency progressivism."

2

Albert Cummins had been an "archaic progressive." As a freshman in the Iowa legislature in the 1890s, he had heard the antirailroad diatribes of the populists, even though he wasn't one of them. Later, he was twice defeated for the Senate by the railroads' political machine. When he was elected governor in 1902 as an insurgent Republican, it was on a militantly antirailroad platform. In three terms as governor, he guided a series of measures through the legislature that gave Iowa comprehensive railroad regulation. There was an increased assessment on railroad land and a maximum passenger fare of two cents a mile. A two-way demurrage law made railroads subject to penalty for failing to furnish shippers with cars and there was a law against free passes (even though Cummins himself regularly accepted passes until 1905). A complicated rate law forced substantial reductions, and antilobbying and primary election laws were meant to destroy the railroads' political machine.[16] These were immensely popular measures for they reined in giant out-of-state corporations to the benefit of small local businessmen, a class to whom men like Cummins, a young lawyer from a moderately well-to-do background, were usually responsive. Railroad men thought it was a vendetta that smacked of pathological hatred.

When Cummins was elected to the Senate in 1908, his reputation as an "expert" in railroad matters was well established and he quickly assumed a leading role on the Commerce Committee, where he sat for hearings on the Mann-Elkins Act. Albro Martin, in his book *Enterprise Denied,* singled him out as the arch-villain of the progressive clique that destroyed the railroads. Until 1917, he never veered from the notion that bigness was badness. He voted enthusiastically for the Clayton Act in 1914, which tightened the strictures of the Sherman Act and became the controlling law in railroad antitrust cases. But in 1917, he accepted the USRRA without qualms, even though the railroads were going to be operated by railroad men as a monopoly. He never asked himself if the policies he had previously sponsored created the impasse of 1917. Regardless, his switch to "efficiency progressivism" was complete. In the long debate on what to do with the railroads after the war, Albert Cummins became the principal spokesman for large, consolidated railways. For better or worse, he was the architect of modern consolidation policy.

The heart of the railroad problem, he said, was that some roads were financially weak. (In other words, he denied that railroad problems were general, the result of "archaic progressivism   He would reel off an example or two from back home in Iowa, where the Chicago Great Western earned a meager 1.7 percent return, while its competitor, the Chicago & North Western, earned a handsome 6.13 percent. A level of rates adequate for the North Western would starve the Great Western, while one to support the Great Western would give the North Western excess profits, something that he, for one, would never tolerate.

To reconcile the dilemma, he worked out a complicated plan, much of which was eventually embodied in the Transportation Act of 1920. Rates were to be set at a level that would produce a fair return, which he determined was 6 percent. This rule of rate making was a significant departure from past regulatory philosophy for it recognized the paramount need to attract capital. A 6 percent return was meant for railroads in general, not for any one road in particular, and it was to be based on a fair valuation of the property, not merely the face value of securities that happened to be outstanding. Any earnings in excess of 6 percent were to go into a special fund, and the moneys thus "recaptured" would be distributed to roads that failed to earn 6 percent.[17]

Recapture, however, could never give the weak roads more than a little short-term help. The ultimate solution lay in consolidation. Cummins wanted a new agency, a Transportation Board, free of the past record of the ICC, to draw up a plan for general consolidation. There were to be not less than twenty nor more than thirty-five operating companies. Competition was to be preserved, along with "existing routes and channels of trade." Weak roads were to be absorbed by strong roads so that the surviving companies would be of roughly equal earning power. Once the plan was drawn up, railroads would have seven years to consolidate on their own terms according to the plan; after that, consolidation would be compulsory. Did the government have the constitutional power to compel? Was that not confiscation of private property? Cummins said no; the state's power of eminent domain provided all the authority that was necessary.[18] Thus the Cummins plan gave the government a major role in economic engineering, a creative role that was a new departure from the nay-saying regulation of the past.[19]

3

Meanwhile, in union halls across the country another idea was making headway which seemed wildly radical to men like John Esch, or even Albert Cummins. It was the brainchild of one man, a lawyer by the name of Glenn Plumb.

Plumb never regarded himself as a radical, but only as a pragmatist who saw problems and tried to find solutions that were fair to all. To him, "all" included labor, and in the context of 1919 that made him a radical. As a young lawyer, Chicago's Mayor Dunne had chosen him to fight the city's battle against the street railways whose ironclad franchises made them bastions of privilege. It was one of urban progressivism's most classic fights, one which Plumb carried all the way to the Supreme Court. In 1916, the railway brotherhoods asked him to be their general counsel. It was in that capacity that he addressed a militant labor rally at Atlantic City in June 1919. Brotherhood leadership was dubious of it but the crowd cheered and applauded, and the fight for the Plumb Plan became a fight of the rank-and-file.[20]

Capital, labor, and the public all had vested interests in the management of railways, said Plumb, yet only capital was represented on the boards of directors. Excluded from all decision-making, labor had turned to unions and the public to government regulation. That created a system in which management, the unions, and the regulatory agencies worked at cross-purposes, with every incentive to be irresponsible. No one was happy: management said it could not earn a fair return, labor said wages were too low, and the public said rates were too high. With each trying to press its case to the limit, the railroads were going to be destroyed.

Plumb saw no reason why capital had the right to be the sole manager of railroad property. Much wiser, he thought, that capital, labor, and the public share in the responsibility. It could be done in the following way:

1. The government should acquire all railroad property, paying prices based on a fair valuation. To pay for it, the government should issue its own securities at the lowest obtainable rate. Once paid off, capital would have no further claim on railroad profits, except as holders of government securities.
2. The government should lease its newly acquired railroads to a federally chartered corporation.
3. The corporation should have a nominal stock issue (its primary capital being operating skill). The stock should be trusteed for the benefit of its employees. Workers would be divided into two categories: class A would be managerial employees and class B, wage earners.
4. One-third of the board of directors would represent the public, appointed by the president with advice and consent of the Senate. One-third would represent class A employees and one-third class B.
5. The corporation would:
   a. pay all operating expenses and arrange for capital improvements;
   b. provide a sinking fund to extinguish government bonds, and
   c. divide any net equally between the government and its own stockholders (up to a total return of 5 percent, after which the ICC would order a reduction in rates).
6. Half the dividends would go to the small number of class A employees and half to the large number of class B employees.

The stock would give employees a vested interest in efficient operation. The possibility that employees might use their dominant position on the board to vote themselves higher wages was precluded by their conflicting dividend desires, as class A employees would benefit more from higher dividends than higher wages. The 5 percent limit on profits would guarantee the lowest possible rates to the public.[21]

This was 1919, the year of the great steel strike and general strikes in Seattle and Winnipeg. The IWW still sounded its fire and fury and red flags still waved at socialist rallies. Bolshevism was in power in Russia and on the verge of it in Germany and Hungary. By that fall, the United States was gripped in an anti-Bolshevist hysteria that would send to oblivion any idea supported by the underprivileged. So the campaign against the Plumb Plan was shrill. Hoke Smith of Georgia called it "simon-pure Bolshevism" and John Esch called it "sovietism." To the Guaranty Trust Company, it was "class rule and class profiteering," something that banks naturally loathed and despised, especially in others.[22]

More devastating was the opposition of Samuel Gompers, for that doomed a united front by labor. The plan violated his theory of industrial relations which held that labor and management must always be separate, each free to bargain to its best advantage. As for Glenn Plumb, he was engulfed by the movement he spawned. In August, he presented it to the Esch Committee, which listened politely, then denounced him publicly. Plumb spent the next two years in an arduous speaking campaign. The Plumb Plan League and its publicity organ, the newspaper *Labor,* kept the flame alive until Plumb, exhausted, died in 1922.

None of the other Western democracies found ideas like the Plumb Plan too radical. Faced with problems that were similar, though not identical, to those of the United States, they all turned to solutions that would bring labor and the public in on managerial decisions.

1. The British Railways Act of 1921 provided that all railroads be amalgamated into four regional systems. If railroads could not agree on terms voluntarily, they would be determined by an Amalgamation Tribunal. A Minister of Transport would supervise the standardization of operations and services, a Railroad Rates Tribunal would set rates, and a Central Wages Board would determine wage scales.

2. In France, the six regional systems (five of them privately owned; one, the *Ouest,* state-owned) would continue as separate corporations, but they would be managed as a single unit by the *Comité de Direction,* composed of representatives of the managements of the six companies. Above them, serving as an advisory board to the government, was the *Conseil Supérior des Chemins de Fer,* a body of seventy-one members, including twenty-one delegates from the railroad companies, fourteen from the labor unions, thirteen from the government, and twenty-three from agricultural and industrial associations. It was to supervise the

standardization of rates, operations, equipment, and wages.

3. In Germany, railways previously owned by the individual states were taken over by the federal government. All operations were supervised by the Railway Administration, composed partly of technical experts and partly of delegates from the employees' work councils that were similar to the Russian soviets.

4. In Canada, the Canadian National Railways was created in 1917 to assume operation of all government-owned lines. A crown corporation owned by the government, it was free to run its own affairs (and compete with the privately owned Canadian Pacific). It was a monumental consolidation project that eventually created a single operating unit of 23,000 miles spanning five time zones.[23]

What was good for other countries was not necessarily good for the United States. Every railroad executive before the Cummins Committee was asked if regional consolidation was desirable, and they all said no. Their reasons were partly personal, no doubt—too many executives would lose their jobs—but they all said it was impractical. The American network was too complex and too busy to be managed in monopolistic units. Even the USRRA had maintained the identity of the separate lines.[24] While the Cummins Plan made consolidation essential to a long-range solution of the railroad problem, it did so within a framework of competing private systems.

As for the Plumb Plan, flawed as it may have been, it died a victim of hysteria and class intolerance. It was a bold proposal for a new order of industrial relations that was ill-suited to an era that craved "normalcy." It had tried to come to grips with the fact that regulation was not working and that the three-way antagonism between capital, labor, and the people was destructive. The railroad plans of the other democracies underscored, even at this early date, how isolated the United States was in its rigid defense of the inviolability of private capital.

4

The Cummins Plan avoided philosophical issues and stuck to the nuts-and-bolts of railroad reorganization. Had it been enacted *in toto,* it might have had a chance for success. But the conservatives in the House tore the heart out of the plan and guaranteed its failure. Instead of Cummins's rate-making principle that was meant to produce a fair return, it reiterated the old progressive nostrum of "fair and reasonable" rates, to be determined by a strengthened ICC. Consolidation, while held to be desirable, was not to be compulsory. Planning was allowed to proceed, but the ICC would do it, and the railroads would be free to accept or reject its suggestions as they chose.[25]

Cummins knew this gutted his whole scheme. He knew railroad men liked everything about the consolidation idea except the compulsory part. He had listened to them all—Carl Gray of the Union Pacific, Julius Kruttschnitt of the Southern Pacific, Samuel Rea of the Pennsylvania, Howard Elliott of the Northern Pacific. They had all offered nearly identical testimony on why they should be freed of the Clayton Act without further obligation. They wanted to be free to take what they wanted and strengthen their own strong companies. They had no interest in solving the weak-road problem.[26]

Cummins never thought the watered-down version would amount to much. The final bill was only a gesture in the direction of "efficiency progressivism," the more dangerous because it looked like the real thing. Perhaps the ICC could draw up a plan so suitable, so wonderful, everyone would rush to consolidate and the problem would be solved. It was unlikely.

By 1920 the issues were drawn. The railroads would solve their crisis of capital investment only if given the right to monopolize, which was unacceptable to the public. Congress showed that it did not have the nerve to buck private desires nor the imagination to go through with any meaningful idea. Only labor, and that an unofficial spokesman for the movement, had tried to rise above the battle with a plan that permitted large-scale efficiency without banker control. But within a few years, seeing no initiative from public or private quarters, labor also retreated to a pursuit of its own selfish interests.

The real problem was an absence of leadership and of goodwill, an absence that would never be filled in the long history of railroad consolidation.

CHAPTER 2

The Legacy of the Transportation
Act of 1920 in the East;
1920-1940

The Interstate Commerce Commission seemed to move with gusto into its new role as a planning agency. It engaged Professor William Ripley of Harvard to draw up a tentative plan that would be the basis of discussion in future hearings. He was the author of treatises on rates, regulation, and finance, and seemed as well qualified for the job as anyone could be. But the law specified that all railroads must be combined into twenty-five or thirty systems of *equal size and earning power which preserved competition and existing routes and channels of trade*. It was not long before Ripley discovered that what seemed so reasonable in the abstract was devilishly elusive when it came to specifics.

The only plan he could devise which met the rigid strictures of the law rested on two controversial expedients. First, he wanted to dismember certain existing systems where necessary for the sake of balance. That was essential in the West, he thought, where there were just not enough trans-continental lines to match up with the many granger roads of the Great Plains. Second, he wanted to create monopolies in geographic subregions, namely, Michigan and New England, where there were not enough independent lines to give one to each major system. Whether or not this was good railroading, it was terrible politics. A lot of people who were now very important had joined in the shrill attack on Morgan for trying to do what the expert now said was the right thing to do.

At first, the difficulties seemed minor. The Ripley Plan was a *tour de force* that reduced all the railroads in the United States to twenty-four systems. The ICC held brief hearings on it in the summer of 1921, made a few modifications, and labeled this its "tentative plan." The New England monopoly was too hot to handle and was thrown out (although the one for Michigan was retained). The idea of forced dismemberments was also thrown out, except for the Wabash, one of only two major railroads to straddle that invisible line between Chicago, St. Louis, Memphis, and New Orleans, which railroads crossed only to deliver cars.

Hearings for the tentative plan went on for twenty-one months in cities coast to coast. Out of them was supposed to come a final plan, as directed by Congress. But even at this stage, something seemed to have gone wrong. Peripheral issues took up most of the hearing, which was really not surprising, since the commission relied entirely on private parties to put into the record only what they saw fit. In the East, for example, most of the time was spent on an inconclusive debate between the Baltimore & Ohio and the New York Central over who should get the Jersey Central and the Reading. When the hearing was over, it was assumed the final plan would soon be forthcoming. Instead, there was silence from the commission, which had evidently split over what to do. Three years later, it notified Congress that it was unable to devise a plan, and asked to be relieved of the duty altogether.[1]

Congress considered the matter in 1926. Albert Cummins was discouraged and repeated that without compulsion, consolidation would come to naught. He introduced a bill that would excuse the commission for five years from making a final plan, during which time the railroads might consolidate voluntarily. After that, the commission was to go ahead with a compulsory final plan, and from that point forward permit no deviations from it.[2] But the bill failed, and Cummins's death later that year frustrated efforts to revive it. Two years later, Senator Fess of Ohio introduced similar legislation, more friendly to the railroads, but it failed as well.[3] Looking back, the concept of planning was dead the moment the commission announced it could not come up with a plan. After that, all meaningful initiative came from the railroads.

1

The northeastern United States was crisscrossed with railroads, as befit the nation's prosperous and populous manufactory. These were not granger branches, as in the Midwest, but for the most part, mainlines, usually double- or quadruple-tracked. But under the veneer of a double track lay some very weak railroads. Despite the long coal trains that came curving up out of Scranton, for example, or the procession of passenger trains that clattered back and forth to the Catskills on a summer weekend, no one was fooled that the New York, Ontario & Western was the equal of, say, the Lehigh Valley. The East needed consolidation, and the major roads were eager to have it. So the region was a good laboratory for the functioning or malfunctioning of the Transportation Act of 1920.

In the rough-and-tumble days before planned consolidation, the powerful could expect to get always more powerful. With planning, the powerful were to be held in check while the others were brought up to a rough equality. The nation's most powerful railroad, the Pennsylvania, deeply resented any plan in which it did not remain the most powerful. The Pennsylvania, therefore, was going to present the concept of planning with a severe test. Both the Ripley Report and the tentative plan tried to impose five major systems on the region, when in fact, there were only four railroad powers to begin with—the Pennsylvania, the New York Central, the Baltimore & Ohio, and the Van Sweringen empire. From the start, the Pennsylvania suspected the fifth system was going to be created, like Eve, from its own ribs, and it was not pleased. The central theme of the experience of the 1920s was how the most powerful railroad used the process for its own purposes. All efforts to plan consolidation in the East would fall upon the machinations of the Pennsylvania Railroad.

Planned consolidation offered the B&O an expedient way to do what it could not do on its own—develop its extremities. Its middle portions were healthy enough, but its lines to the eastern seaboard and to the Midwest reached out like dangling strings, devoid of branches and friendly feeders. Since the New York Central or the Pennsylvania could outbid it for any acquisition that might remedy this, the B&O needed strong government. By adding the Reading and the Jersey Central, it would get lucrative anthracite and passenger traffic, an entrance to one of the nation's most intensely industrialized areas, and highly developed port facilities at New York and along the Delaware River. The addition of the Western Maryland would bring it a rich bituminous coal traffic plus an eastbound gradient over the Alleghenies more favorable than its own mainline. The addition of the Alton would help it corner some of the midwestern grain traffic, while the Alton line to Kansas City would give it the longest haul of any eastern trunkline. A strong B&O was crucial to balance in the East, and Ripley and the ICC treated it well. No road stood to gain as much and lose as little from planned consolidation as the B&O.

New York Central, the Vanderbilt road, was more powerful than the B&O, less powerful than the Pennsylvania, but fully capable of protecting its own interests. The tentative plan offered it little, so it was hardly enthusiastic. But on the surface, it seemed strangely compliant, its strategy a subtle one to stymie the whole scheme. All it had to do was stalemate the ambitious designs of others, and planning would be discredited. So it demanded the Virginian Railway as an entrance to the West Virginia coal fields, which neither Ripley nor the ICC had offered to give it. It knew that would be unacceptable to the Pennsylvania, which coveted the Virginian, and a blow to the Van Sweringens' C&O, which was then the Central's favored connection to the coal fields. Then it mounted a frontal assault on the B&O by demanding the Jersey Central and the Reading. It claimed its mainline was congested and wanted an alternate route between Cleveland and New York through the Clearfield district of Pennsylvania. It seemed unlikely that the Central would actually divert freights from its water-level mainline and send them over a single-track route that crossed some of the most difficult terrain in the East.[4] But what a beautiful way to frustrate the plan.

Neither Professor Ripley nor the ICC had calculated that the Van Sweringen brothers, real-estate developers from Cleveland, would emerge as a

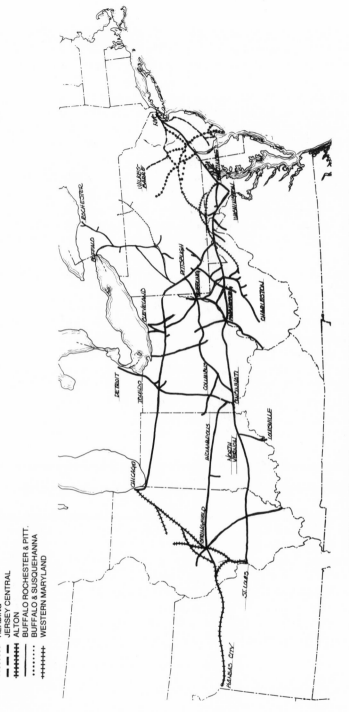

B & O ▬▬▬▬
READING ⋯⋯⋯
JERSEY CENTRAL ┼┼┼┼┼┼
ALTON
BUFFALO ROCHESTER & PITT. ▬▬▬
BUFFALO & SUSQUEHANNA ⁺⁺⁺⁺⁺⁺
WESTERN MARYLAND ┼┼┼┼┼┼

MAP 12:   *The Baltimore & Ohio, with Additions Recommended in the Tentative Plan*

dynamic force in eastern railroading. Before World War I, they developed land known as Shaker Heights, Ohio, and to get the right-of-way for a rapid transit line to downtown Cleveland, bought the Nickel Plate Road from the New York Central. Nickel Plate paralleled the Central's Lake Shore route for five hundred miles between Buffalo and Chicago. Central had controlled it ever since its completion by speculators in the 1880s, who figured correctly the Vanderbilts would pay dearly to crush this unnecessary competition. Presumably the threat of an antitrust suit induced the Central to sell, and since the Vans cared about only seven of the Nickel Plate's five hundred miles, it was doubtful they would ever do much to hurt the Central. Furthermore, J.P. Morgan was the banker for both the Central and the Vans, which gave rise to rumors (never proven) that they were merely the Central's stalking horses. The Vans took advantage of the Nickel Plate's one great asset, its high-level crossing of the Cuyahoga Valley in Cleveland, much superior to the Central's heavily graded line to the valley floor, and built the Cleveland Union Terminal beside it, on four acres of land they had purchased on Public Square. It was an early urban-renewal project, and became the focus of rail and rapid transit lines in the city. The Central had cooperated enthusiastically, but it was hideously expensive; bonds would still be outstanding on the terminal even after the last Central passenger train departed in 1971.[5]

A taste of big-time railroading whetted the Vans' appetite for more. By their astute use of the holding company, they were able to collect and control a number of railroads with a minimum investment and without the need for ICC approval. Even as the hearings on the tentative plan were in progress, they acquired the Lake Erie & Western and the Toledo, St. Louis & Western (the Clover Leaf Route) and in 1923 merged them into the Nickel Plate, providing it with valuable feeder lines and entrances into the important midwestern gateways of Peoria and St. Louis. This was consistent with the Ripley Report and the ICC's tentative plan, and so there should have been no substantive objection. Instead of requesting approval under the consolidation provisions of the 1920 act (paragraph 6 of section 5), however, they applied under paragraph 18 of section 1 for permission to operate constituent railroads, and under section 20a to issue stock in exchange for the stock of constituent roads. Thus, if the ICC approved this transaction, which it already acknowledged was in the public interest, it would set a bad precedent on method. It could pave the way for future consolidation that did not conform to a plan and undermine the commission's authority to plan at all. The commission subjected the Nickel Plate unification to intense scrutiny, but finally gave its approval. Ironically, it turned out to be the only significant consolidation of the 1920s.[6]

It was their later acquisitions that gave the Vans their clout in eastern railroading. The Erie, Pere Marquette, Hocking Valley, Wheeling & Lake Erie, and the big, coal-rich Chesapeake & Ohio all came under their control through holding companies. On two occasions, they tried to merge all these properties into a unified system. The first attempt failed due to the opposition of certain C&O stockholders, who did not want their equity in a strong road diluted by these weaker ones. The second failed because the ICC, while professing not to care if this would ruin its five-system plan, said the holding company was too shaky a structure on which to base a major trunkline. A lot was at stake here. As long as the Erie and the Nickel Plate remained under the same control, a five-system East was impossible.[7] Therefore, unless the commission was willing to break up the holding companies, which it clearly was not, there could be no consolidation at all, and the commission would be blamed for the failure.

Finally, there was the Pennsylvania, large, powerful, profitable, and content to remain, as it fancied itself, "the standard railroad of the world." It was not about to have a meddling government hold it in check while lesser lines were strengthened. It viewed the situation with the social-Darwinist perspective that was always characteristic of the powerful—if there was to be a feast, the largest should get the most. The Pennsylvania demanded trackage along the south shore of Lake Erie (which the New York Central would never tolerate) and an anthracite road—either the Lackawanna or the Lehigh Valley would do. It wanted a route between Chicago and St. Louis—either the Wabash, the Alton, or the Chicago & Eastern Illinois. And it made it very clear that it would not gracefully give up its interest in the Norfolk & Western.[8]

Furthermore, the Pennsylvania had something in its favor that none of the others could match—an articulate spokesman for its cause. Albert J. County was officially the vice-president of accounting; unofficially, however, he was the secretary of state to deal with other railroad "powers." Dublin-born, beginning his career on the Irish Railways, he was graduated from the Wharton School and went directly to the secretary's office of the Pennsylvania. He was present at all the public and private consolidation conferences of the 1920s, and his obstinacy was the rock upon which the ambitions of the others foundered.

What County did was to raise fundamental questions about consolidation that had evaded Cummins, Ripley, and planning's most articulate defender on the ICC, Joseph Eastman. First, he said, no one, certainly not the congressmen who wrote the law, *knew* if consolidation would solve the weak-road-strong-road problem or provide cheaper transportation; they only guessed it. Studies were needed, and he was not at all certain they would show what the proponents of consolidation wanted them to show. Second, he said, no one had really asked if the weak lines were essential at all. He thought the motor truck was about to open a new era of intermodal transport; instead of maintaining a number of weak, under-utilized railroads, trucks would feed the traffic to the strong roads. Finally, he said, repeating forcefully what railroad men had been saying all along, the need was for capital, not for pie-in-the-sky plans, and if government really wanted to be helpful, it ought to supply the capital at low rates. There was no reason why it should not do this, for railroads served communities, employed people, and paid taxes. This point, he hastened to add, was just a helpful observation about the weak-road problem. The Pennsylvania was capable of raising all the capital it needed.[9]

2

As long as there was no official plan, each of the big four hoped to influence the final outcome in its favor. If they could agree on a plan to divide the spoils among them, they could present a united front to the commission. Failing this, they could each hasten to grab what they wanted and present each other with *faits accomplis*. In a series of more or less secret great-power conferences, it became apparent that the Pennsylvania and the other three were polarized into implacable camps.

Determined to have its power unchallenged, the Pennsylvania became the promoter, always in the shadowy background, of fifth-system schemes that would keep the pie divided in small pieces. One of these rested on the dynamic personality of Leonor Loree, once a rising young executive of the Pennsylvania, who had gone on to become president of the independent Delaware & Hudson. He hoped to combine the D&H with some other medium-sized lines, among them the Lehigh Valley and the Wabash, into a circuitous trunkline that would have little chance of success against the established routes. The Pennsylvania nurtured the idea for its nuisance value, and Loree attended the great-power conferences as a full-fledged spokesman for the "fifth system." When the Loree plan failed, the Pennsylvania fell heir to his sizable blocks of Lehigh and Wabash stocks.[10]

A second scheme, to which the Pennsylvania was attracted in its later stages, was the ambitious plan of the Taplin brothers to create a new lakes-to-the-sea system. The two men owned coal mines along the Pittsburgh & West Virginia Railway, a sixty-mile line from southeastern Ohio to the Pittsburgh industrial area. It was the remnant of the old Wabash-Pittsburgh Terminal Railway which George Gould intended as the final link in his ill-starred transcontinental system, one of the last swashbuckling ventures of the robber-baron age. The line was built to elaborate specifications, some of it double- and quadruple-tracked, with gradients superior to the competing St. Louis line of the Pennsylvania. The Taplins hoped to win control of the Wheeling & Lake Erie, itself a coal-hauler of vast potential, which would extend their rails to lake ports at Cleveland and Toledo. Then they wanted to build forty miles of new line, the forty miles that ultimately de-

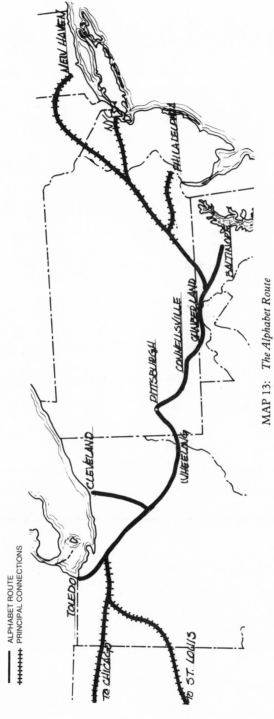

MAP 13: *The Alphabet Route*

feated Gould, from Pittsburgh to a connection with the Western Maryland Railway at Connellsville, Pennsylvania. If then they could get control of the WM, they would own a potentially formidable east-west service route.

Since the B&O already owned enough stock to control the WM, the project was in trouble from the start. Nevertheless, three of the big powers, the B&O, the Central, and the Vans, were sufficiently frightened to snap up joint control of the Wheeling. At first, the Pennsylvania thought the Taplins were stalking horses for the other three, and threatened to cut off all interchange with the P&WV if the Connellsville Extension went through. But it did go through (in 1928) and the Pennsylvania, unable to stop it, decided to use it for its own purposes. When the Taplins found their empire beyond their grasp, and tired of the whole thing, the Pennsylvania paid them handsomely for the P&WV. Although a unified Wheeling-P&WV-WM system never materialized, and despite the fact that various segments belonged to rival camps, it did become an important freight-service route, nicknamed the Alphabet Route, that would be a factor in developments to come.[11]

When the buffer schemes collapsed, some less subtle tactics were in order. The Pennsylvania tried to lease the Norfolk & Western, but was rebuffed by the commission.[12] Then N&W tried to merge with the Virginian, but that was also refused.[13] Next, the Virginian extended its line across the Kanawha River at Deepwater, West Virginia, to a strategic connection with the New York Central, a liaison with profound significance for the future.[14] The Pennsylvania hung securely onto the Wabash and Lehigh Valley, but Central also began to buy Lehigh stock, then sold it and bought Lackawanna instead. It began to resemble the robber-baron age so much that Daniel Willard of the B&O was moved to call it "a return to Harrimanism."

Congress had refused to relieve the ICC of the duty to make a plan. By 1928, as fifth-system plans collapsed, with vital segments of the eastern network falling into the hands of the Pennsylvania, it was soon going to be impossible for any consolidation except under the railroads' own terms. To undo some of the damage, the ICC instigated a number of Clayton Act proceedings to break these newly acquired holds and at the same time intimated it was going ahead with a final plan.[15] Within a year, Central, B&O, and the Vans had to give up the Wheeling, and B&O had to quit the Western Maryland.[16] The Pennsylvania was ordered to sell the Wabash and Lehigh, but it appealed and kept the case in litigation through the crucial years that followed. In 1934, the Supreme Court, in a four-four decision (which sustained a lower court ruling), found for the railroad.[17] So the result of these proceedings was to further strengthen the Pennsylvania while weakening the others.

In the short run, they unleashed a new acquisitive binge by the great powers known as the "scramble" of 1929. Each tried to grab and hang on to anything it could. It was the year of the great bull market, and some of the roads were speculating like everyone else. Most of the purchases were on money borrowed at 6 percent or more, and when the crash came, constituted a fearful overextension of credit. New York Central bought heavily into Lackawanna, while B&O increased its hold on the Reading.[18] The Vans formed a new holding company, the Alleghany Corporation, to control all of their railroad enterprises, and then bought massive blocks of Missouri Pacific, Kansas City Southern, and Chicago Great Western.

None used the holding company device more skillfully than the Pennsylvania. It feared the final plan more than the others and had the most to lose if it did not checkmate the ICC with strategic stock purchases of its own. The venerable (1870) Pennsylvania Company, wholly owned by the railroad, and with identical officers, owned the Wabash and Lehigh stocks that were under litigation. But its principal vehicle of expansion was the new Pennroad Company, formed in 1928 and owned by the railroad's stockholders, not the railroad itself. By selling stock to stockholders, the railroad had been able to tap new sources of capital, and since all that stock was trusteed for ten years, there would be no loss of control. The Pennsylvania's record for astute stock purchases had been so good that Pennroad was quickly oversubscribed. Many of its acquisitions were strictly for investment, but they strengthened the Pennsylvania's hold on the Wabash and Lehigh, and made it the dominant force on the Detroit, Toledo & Ironton, which it purchased from Henry Ford. Most significantly, in the summer of 1929, it bought large blocks of New Haven and Boston & Maine (whereupon the Pennsylvania named a vice-president for New England affairs).[19]

Since the commission's announcement of a final plan had triggered the scramble, publication of such a plan might end it, but all through 1929 no plan was forthcoming. It was known that the commission was divided between those who wanted a four-system East (which would ratify what the great powers had already done) and those who favored a five-system East (that would require major divestitures). No attempt was made to bring the 1923 hearings up to date, even though the situation was quite radically changed. Then, in December, it released a final plan that shocked everyone. It called for a five-system East, with none of the five having an entrance to New England. The Pennsylvania was to be stripped of everything but the Long Island Railroad; the New York Central was to get the Virginian; the B&O was to have everything it wanted; the Vans' empire was to remain intact.

The fifth system was the surprise. Based on the financial strength of the Lehigh Valley and the Norfolk & Western, it included the Wabash, the Alphabet Route, and the Seaboard Air Line, of all things, making it a railroad from Omaha to Miami via Buffalo that was utterly devoid of geographic cohesion. Henry Sturgis of the First National Bank of New York recalled how he used to kid friends on the Lehigh Valley that they would probably wind up with the doubtful honor of caring for the weak Wabash. "I intended it as a joke," he said, "and I'm afraid the joke has gone a little far."[20]

The final plan was so bizarre, in fact, that it terrorized the Great Powers into settling their differences. The secret conferences were reopened and the fifth system was eagerly parceled out among the four, with the Pennsylvania keeping a firm grip on the N&W. In the entire settlement the eastern railroads presented to the commission, there was not a single word about economy or coordinated service or the time or method by which all this consolidation was going to be carried out. It had nothing to do with public interest. It was a paper plan that served the railroads' private interest, just in case consolidation should ever become compulsory.[21]

3

By 1930, Herbert Hoover was almost desperate to stimulate capital investment and thought consolidation would provide a good stimulus for railroads. Railroad security owners were tired of managements' evasions and wanted action as well. They had come to see consolidation as a means for operating economy, including the elimination of duplicate executives. Once again Professor Ripley was summoned, this time to shuttle between the railroads and the White House in search of commitments. Recognizing the signals from the White House, the commission quickly modified its "final" plan to suit the whims of the Great Powers, thereby exposing its lack of will or ability to enforce anything the railroads opposed. This was the revised final plan and was seldom heard of again.

The president was so hopeful that this really would pave the way for consolidation that he announced the new plan himself on December 30, 1930. He said the purpose of the consolidation legislation of 1920 was to provide more adequate service, a simplified rate structure, and lower operating costs, which was, of course, not quite right. Congress had not talked about any of those things in 1920.[22] They were the reasons consolidation was needed in 1930, and it looked as if Walker Hines and the scientific management people of the USRRA were about to be vindicated.

Labor took careful note of this new enthusiasm for economy and correctly surmised that it was going to be the principal victim. The spirit of the Plumb Plan was dead. Senator James Couzzens of Michigan introduced legislation to have the consolidation provisions of the 1920 Act repealed and subject the railroads to the same antitrust legislation as everyone else. Hearings on the Railroad Unification Act of 1931 showed that it had become a political issue, with owners in favor of general consolidation, and labor and management united in opposition (which was natural enough; both were the owners' hired men). The debate went straight to fundamentals; should prosperity be revived by helping business—in this case by encouraging consolidation—or by preserving jobs by preventing it? The problem was passed to the new administration.

Franklin Roosevelt's campaign speech on transportation, delivered at Salt Lake City in September 1932, repeated the Hoover policy of encouraging consolidation to stimulate investment. Between them and the inauguration, a Boston banker, Fredrick H. Prince, past president of the Pere Marquette Railroad, speaking as the president of the Association of Railroad Security Owners, published a plan for consolidation more sweeping than anything since the Plumb Plan.

The Prince Plan's greatest attribute was that it concentrated maximum traffic on minimum trackage and still preserved competition. Radical consolidation was essential, said John Barriger, the young engineer who did most of the work on it, because the downward trend of commodity prices was going to make many commodities unshippable. Railroads would have to economize so they could reduce rates. The entire network was divided into seven systems, two in the East, two in the South, and three in the West. Each would be a new corporation that would acquire railroads by leasing them and paying rent to their owners. The Reconstruction Finance Corporation would buy the new companies' 4.5 percent debenture bonds at par, the funds to be used as needed, even for buying the stock of leased lines when offered at a discount. For two years, all wage earners displaced by the plan would receive a protection allowance of one-half to two-thirds their previous salary.[23] The plan attracted considerable attention and President Roosevelt was intrigued by it. Raymond Moley explained that it was novel and Roosevelt liked anything that was novel.[24]

It was with the Prince Plan in mind that emergency transportation legislation was passed by Congress in 1933. It established the office of the Federal Coordinator of Transportation to encourage the carriers to reduce duplication and reorganize their finances. Consolidation was one way, though not the only way, to reach that goal. But the law was vague and the coordinator's power to coerce was doubtful. Joseph Eastman seemed like a good choice for the job, but he was too confident of his ability to persuade and unwilling to risk a showdown in the courts. Labor was never confident of the scheme. Earl Latham, author of a comprehensive study of it, said labor thought it was the "typical right-wing remedy for the ills of industry—deflation without regard to the social cost."[25] Management responded by creating its own coordinating agency, the Association of American Railroads, similar to the cartel-like structures being created in other industries as part of the Blue Eagle recovery program. The AAR coordinated the railroads' lobbying activities in Washington.[26] So, as in 1920, a faulty piece of legislation aroused strong opposition and failed to produce the results anticipated. It was temporary and was not renewed when it expired in 1936.

Since there was no coordination under the act, it was easy to forget how much Coordinator Eastman had tried to get it, and how much of his agency's time was devoted to it. His tenure began with promise. He appointed William B. Poland, a railroad engineer of long experience, to test the findings of the Prince Plan. In the East, Barriger had planned two systems—the northern, including the New York Central, the Van Sweringen lines, and all of northern New England, and the southern, to include the Pennsylvania, the B&O, the N&W, and the New Haven. Poland found no quarrel with these groupings but questioned the extent to which they would produce the savings Barriger said they would. For example, Barriger had calculated that between Pittsburgh and Chicago, the Pennsylvania could carry all the traffic and the B&O could be eliminated as a mainline. Poland felt the traffic not only warranted two lines but that the B&O was the superior route anyway. Between Washington and New York, Barriger put all traffic on the Pennsylvania and anticipated the elimination of the *Royal Blue* line. Again, Poland questioned the ability of the Pennsylvania to handle all the traffic. Poland reduced Barriger's anticipated savings from $743 million a year to $218 million, which was still a substantial amount.

The first annual report of the coordinator contained not only the Poland Report, but an opinion by Duke University law professor Leslie Craven that the government did have the constitutional power to require consolidation. It could use its power under the commerce clause to create federal corporations and have them acquire railroad property. Existing companies that did not acquiesce could then be forbidden to engage in interstate commerce.[27] Despite this ammunition, Eastman could find no support in any quarter. By his fourth and last report, he was disillusioned and put the blame on railroad executives:

Their habit of mind is intensely individualistic and suspicious of collective action. When such action is proposed—notwithstanding that it may be for the good of the industry as a whole—the normal executive will at once seek to determine how it may affect his railroad in comparison with others. . . . He is particularly wary of any collective proposal which has a nationwide aspect, for he sees in it what he regards as a tendency toward "nationalization" of the railroads, and at all events, a decrease in the importance of local managements.[28]

As if to underscore his point, the Association of American Railroads released its own studies on locomotive and car supplies, which concluded that no coordination efforts were needed or desirable.[29]

Roosevelt first appointed a Committee of Three to make recommendation and on it put the ICC's most progressive commissioners, Mahaffie, Eastman, and Splawn. They suggested all railroads be consolidated into a single unit under private management and ownership. The idea was breath-taking, and the President said he liked it. On May 8, 1938, he hinted publicly that sweeping, compulsory consolidation might be in the offing. Labor was so terrified that he meant it that it negotiated the so-called Washington Agreement to provide temporary compensation for the men who might be displaced. Management signed—nearly all the roads did outside the South, and they came to terms later on—because it did not want disruptive strikes in case consolidation should come about.

But Roosevelt knew labor and management feared consolidation about equally, so he appointed another committee, the Committee of Six, three from labor and three from management, to make their recommendation. They suggested nothing stronger than voluntary consolidation on company initiative, and with heavy restrictions on that. Security owners denounced this handiwork of the hired men before the Senate committee headed by Burton K. Wheeler of Montana, then conducting hearings on new omnibus legislation for transportation.[30]

The law that came out of those hearings, later known as the Transporta-tion Act of 1940, would be the governing law for the mergers of the 1960s and largely embodied the recommendations of the Committee of Six. Con-solidation was to be encouraged and supervised by the ICC, but without compulsion. Most labor leaders were content with the Washington Agree-ment and wanted no statutory provisions, although Congressman Vincent Harrington of Iowa, at the request of the Brotherhood of Railroad Train-men, got an amendment that guaranteed four years at full previous salary for all displaced employees.[31] Some thought that would so substantially re-duce any benefit to management or owners that consolidation would be a dead letter.

Recounting the failure of Albert Cummins's inspiration for planned con-solidation, economist William Leonard blamed three parties. First, there was management, because strong roads wanted to get stronger, medium roads wanted to build up their equity, and weak roads wanted to be free to bargain to their best advantage. Second, the ICC fumbled, perhaps de-liberately, since many of its members were Harding appointees sympathetic to management. Finally, the law was faulty. Instead of emphasizing ef-ficiency and economy, as the technocrats said it should, it was offered as a panacea for the weak road problem, which it could not solve. Leonard himself was convinced that planned, compulsory consolidation was possible and desirable. But the railroads had found a new incantation—that con-solidation could not be planned by so-called experts. The experience of the 1920 act proved, they said, that it would not work. In fact, no such thing had been proven at all. What had been shown was that a poorly devised plan based on ill-conceived legislation, administered by an indecisive com-mission upon a troubled but nonetheless powerful industry, would not work

CHAPTER 3

Dead Ends under the Transportation Act of 1940; 1940-1954

During the hearings on the Transportation Act of 1940, the railroads said, in essence, "free us of straight-jackets, free us of plans, and we will consolidate." This was after twenty years of evasion, and came on top of soft rumblings by the Association of American Railroads that consolidation was not really necessary at all. That should have been a clue. But the act gave the railroads exactly what they asked for—voluntary consolidation. The result was that virtually no consolidation took place at all in the next fifteen years.

In the East, however, the scene of all the abortive jousting of the 1920s, there were some subtle shifts in the structure of railroading in the 1940s and early 1950s. To some extent, these were out of the public eye, but they would have profound effects on events to come.

1

No railroad had used the planning experience of the 1920s to its advantage better than the Pennsylvania Railroad. It had wrapped its tentacles around a number of important eastern lines—among them the Norfolk & Western, the Lehigh Valley, the Wabash, the New Haven—so that very little consolidation could take place in the East without the Pennsylvania's approval. In the 1940s, it would tighten its grip on this empire—on all of it except the New Haven—until it could virtually dictate the pattern of eastern railroading, unless, that is, the government were willing to move forcefully against it. However, all did not start out so well for the giant of Philadelphia.

Back in the heady days of the 1929 bull market, everything the Pennsylvania touched seemed to turn to gold. Investors eagerly bought shares in the Pennroad holding company, for example, just to get in on a good thing. The railroad took this money to make its strategic purchases of the New Haven, Boston & Maine, Detroit, Toledo & Ironton, and Pittsburgh & West Virginia lines. The purchaser of a Pennroad share received only a trust certificate, without voting rights, to be exchanged for the actual share only after ten years. It didn't seem to matter; the stock was immediately oversubscribed.[1]

By May Day of 1939, the day those Pennroad shares could be exchanged, a lot had changed for the Pennsylvania and for the railroad securities market in general. The certificates had been actively traded and many of them were now in hands not necessarily friendly to the railroad. Most of Pennroad's holdings had been purchased on the bull market at speculative prices, and after it collapsed, Pennroad never paid a dividend. So many of those who gathered at the Pennroad stockholders' meeting that May Day bore a certain grudge—a grudge that turned to rage when old A.J. County got up to announce that Pennroad was going to write off $84 million as dead loss. When the pandemonium quieted, and dissident stockholders had their motion for an investigation beaten back by management, four lawsuits were initiated, charging the officers of Pennroad and the Pennsylvania Railroad with mismanagement and moral turpitude. The charges were serious enough that Pennroad officers resigned and were replaced by nominees of the dissident stockholders. From that point on, the railroad lost control of Pennroad.[2]

The railroad insisted that everyone who put their money in Pennroad knew these investments were for strategic, not beneficial purposes. It had not paid exorbitant prices, it said; its only fault was not to have foreseen the depression. Its main defense, however, was the statute of limitations, hardly a demonstration of clear conscience. Judge Walsh exonerated the officers but held the company liable for $25 million in damages. On appeal, the judgment was reversed solely because of the statute of limitations. Pennroad threatened further appeal, and the railroad finally settled out of court for $15 million, still proclaiming its innocence.[3]

The Pennroad affair left deep scars on the Pennsylvania; stockholders had lost $15 million, management had barely avoided conviction for moral turpitude, and plans for expansion were set back so severely, they were dormant for nearly a decade. Furthermore, it must have strained relations between the railroad and its principal banker, Kuhn, Loeb and Company, for back in 1928, it had paid Kuhn, Loeb $4.75 million just for the advice to establish Pennroad.[4] Most significantly, it was the *coup de grâce* for the holding company as a vehicle for railroad consolidation. It was costly, dangerous, and actually hindered constructive restructuring.

The Pennsylvania's sphere was crumbling in other places as well. It had paid $77 a share for 119,000 shares of Wabash in 1927, then saw the price of that stock drop to one-tenth of that four years later. The old granger road, never a strong earner, was the second major railroad insolvency of the depression. For a moment in 1937, reorganization seemed around the corner, but earnings fell again and action was postponed until 1941. Even then, it was unlikely the old common stock would have any value at all, and Pennsylvania stood to lose its influence as well as its investment.[5]

That was exactly what happened to the New Haven. It entered receivership in 1937, and when it was reorganized in 1941, its old common stock was written off as worthless. Pennsylvania dearly wanted to keep its leverage in New England and its lawyers did their best to convince the federal district court in Connecticut that the stock did have value. Most New Englanders wanted the Pennsylvania out. With a committee of New England governors and the Boston Port Authority as their spokesmen, they argued the Pennsylvania had controlled New England traffic to the region's disadvantage. It had forced traffic over the Hell Gate Bridge route to the New Haven's Bay Ridge Yard on Long Island, where it had to be transferred by lighter to the Pennsylvania on the New Jersey shore. It was a slow, circuitous, and expensive route that did not compare to the service of all-rail routes. The Pennsylvania was furious that it should be harried from New England when the New York Central was allowed to remain (with its Boston & Albany line), but the court's decision was final and the New England adventure came to an abrupt end.[6]

The Wabash might be saved if the Pennsylvania could persuade the other creditors to accept the idea that the old common stock still had value. It presented a reorganization plan based on the premise that former bondholders would not be interested in any new common stock. They would have first claim on it, of course, but would have only 90 days to withdraw it from escrow. After that, former stockholders could purchase it at $12.75 a share in amounts proportional to the number of old shares they owned. If, after all this, the Pennsylvania was still not the largest stockholder, it offered to buy stock from others at $12.75. For $7 million, it thought it could retain its dominant position.[7] It also asked the ICC for permission to control.

In its attempt to show that control was in the public interest, the Pennsylvania instead made a glaring demonstration that absolutely no real economic benefit could come from a transaction like this. Its entire case rested on the following:

1. It cited the *Detroit Arrow* service, a joint passenger operation between Detroit and Chicago via Fort Wayne, and implied, without being specific, that other joint services would come. Yet the *Detroit Arrow* service was already operating, which implied that control was not necessary, and it was such a marginal service anyway that it was one of the first name-train runs to be discontinued (in 1949).
2. It suggested that yards would be combined at Buffalo, Detroit, Toledo, Fort Wayne, Chicago, Decatur, and St. Louis. It did not mention that at Buffalo, for example, there was a five-mile gap between Pennsylvania and Wabash trackage filled only by railroads hostile to control in the first place. In fact, none of these yard consolidations was ever carried out.

3. It noted that interchange traffic destined for points on the Wabash west of St. Louis was exchanged at Logansport, Indiana, even though the Pennsylvania deliberately short-hauled itself by doing that. This was supposed to show how strong roads benevolently helped the weak. It did not mention that on eastbound traffic, the Wabash was similarly getting short-hauled. Logansport was never a major interchange for either carrier, and after control, the Wabash's share of total interchange received at that point increased only from 3 percent to 4 percent. [8]

In short, there was no reason from the standpoint of better transportation for the Pennsylvania to have the Wabash. That was why neither Professor Ripley nor the ICC had combined the two in the plans of the 1920s.

It was rare for the two great trunklines to confront each other directly before the ICC, but the New York Central could not abide Pennsylvania domination of the Wabash. In the first place, it was an invasion of the Central's Detroit enclave, from which it dispatched a million cars a year and would defend the traffic against all comers. Second, it was not about to see the Pennsylvania create a Wabash-Lehigh Valley trunkline serving all the same points as its mainline. It had fought this fight before, and told the ICC it was ready to subpoena all the Pennsylvania's private papers into the public record, if need be, to stop it. It was time for the superpowers to make a deal; if Pennsylvania would put its Lehigh stock in trust, Central would withdraw. [9] That was the Agreement of 1941, which would play a role in the confrontations of the 1960s.

Walter G. Peterkin was convinced the Pennsylvania was not playing by the rules. He was a small investor in Wabash bonds who had taken a loss and was ready to fight. He insisted the Pennsylvania had controlled the Wabash illegally ever since it first bought that stock back in 1927. It had forced the Wabash to pay dividends in 1931 even as revenues were declining. Funded debt was increased at an alarming rate even as the company hurtled toward receivership. The outward sign of this control was the presence of former Pennsylvania men in Wabash executive positions, like Walter Franklin, who would later return to the Pennsylvania as president. He believed, though he could not prove, that there was an intricate web of conflicting interests between Equitable Life, the Chase National Bank, and the two railroads. [10]

Even if these were interesting allegations, Peterkin was fighting alone, and had neither the skill nor the resources to pursue it to the end. All he wanted was more than $12.75 a share, the ceiling he said the railroad had put on it. If it were so valuable, said the railroad, he should go and sell it to somebody else. The point this all raised was one of ICC procedure. Serious charges had been raised about the railroad's ethics, with supporting evidence that demanded investigation. The ICC would have known nothing about this had this disgruntled bondholder not happened along. When Peterkin quit and the Central withdrew, things like the *Detroit Arrow* carried the day, for the commission was absolutely dependent on adversaries to counter any proposal. Peterkin made it clear there were gaping holes in this record.

In July 1941, the Wabash, which *Business Week* called "one of the biggest chips in the great consolidation poker game" of the 1920s, came under the control of the Pennsylvania. No attempt was made to integrate operations. In fact, the Wabash traffic department continued to solicit as it had in the past, in active competition with the Pennsylvania. There were no savings and no efficiencies. Control merely denied the Wabash to anyone else who might wish to consolidate it legitimately—anyone, that is, who did not have the approval of the Pennsylvania.

That was the Pennsylvania's attitude to the rest of its empire as well. It had clung on by the narrowest of margins but could now shape general consolidation in the East to its own desires, a negative factor of tremendous importance.

2

Like Pennroad, the Van Sweringen empire had fallen on evil days. The Vans' last super-holding company, the Alleghany Corporation, had to be propped up by massive loans from the Reconstruction Finance Corporation, and when even that was not enough, creditors, notably J.P. Morgan and Company, demanded the whole thing be auctioned off. The auction was a strange affair, conducted in a loft over 30 Vesey Street in New York. One of the brothers, Mantis James, was mortally ill, and the other, Otis Paxton, wept, and said, "I would rather have paid my bills." Within a year, they were both dead. Robert Young, a Wall Street upstart from Texas, bid at the Vesey Street auction, but it went to George Ball, the glass jar manufacturer from Muncie, Indiana, a friend of the brothers and a big Nickel Plate shipper. After the brothers were gone and Ball had made his money by manipulating Alleghany through his tax-free foundation, he sold it to Young, whom he remembered from the auction. That was how the man who would be the most aggressive figure in consolidation in the 1940s came to railroading.

Young was a speculator. He had quit the University of Virginia in his sophomore year, worked from statistician to assistant treasurer of General Motors in the 1920s, had hobnobbed with the DuPonts at GM, and had met Jacob Raskob, GM's chief financial officer and manager of Governor Smith's 1928 presidential campaign. In 1929, he became Raskob's personal financial advisor, but left in 1931 to join his GM friend, Frank Kolbe, in speculating ventures. They invited some other GM friends to help them swing the Alleghany deal, but the group tried to dump Young and buy control without him. The plot might not have been discovered had it not been for Senator Wheeler, then conducting hearings on transportation legislation. He was interested that men connected with GM were about to buy railroads on which GM was a major shipper, and warned them off. Young had gone to another friend, the silent Allan P. Kirby, conservative heir to the Woolworth fortune, and together they gave Ball a promissory note for a controlling interest in Alleghany. It got both Young and Kirby seats on the board of Alleghany's most important subsidiary, the Chesapeake & Ohio.[11]

Young's early days at Alleghany were difficult, and he could not quite keep the empire intact. As a result of reorganization, Alleghany's holdings in Erie and Chicago & Eastern Illinois were so drastically reduced that both stocks were sold. His greatest obstacle was the bankers. Before the Wheeler Committee, he had faced the intellectual heirs of "archaic progressivism" who were implacably hostile to speculators. Knowing how to please an audience, he had treated them to a stump speech on the need for competitive bidding in railroad security issues. It was not customary practice, but it was necessary if the power of the big investment banking houses was ever to be broken. The committee liked that, and it seemed to ease his difficulties with them. The bankers did not like it, and plotted to get rid of him altogether.

Back when the Van Sweringens were trying to make their faltering securities more salable, they had written a clause into the C&O's indentures which said that if any C&O security ever fell below 150 percent of par, voting power would go to a trustee. Morgan, Stanley and Company and Guaranty Trust were the trustees and C&O securities were selling below 150 percent of par. However, when Morgan and Guaranty tried to use this to get Young off the board, he sued, and got an injunction on the grounds that the bankers had engineered this unreasonable contract in the first place. Then he began a campaign against bankers and absentee control to win the support of C&O management and thousands of small C&O shareholders. He conducted it with messianic enthusiasm. By accident, he, an absentee controller (from his home in Newport, Rhode Island), had become the champion of the plain people against the banker-insider clique that had manipulated railroads since the days of the robber barons.

Before that business was settled, the promissory note to George Ball came due and could not be paid. Young picked up a tip that the SEC was about to investigate Ball for the manipulation of Alleghany stock, and so he got another injunction, eventually settled with Ball out of court, and by the narrowest of margins, held on to Alleghany.

All of this aroused the curiosity of the ICC, which launched one of its rare independent investigations. The report by Examiner C.E. Boles in 1945 concluded that while the Alleghany roads were well managed, permission to control them had never been sought, and forced divestiture was recommended. Desperate, and furious that the commission held him to a standard to which it did not hold the bankers, Young worked out a compromise. All railroad stocks other than the C&O would go into a voting trust administered by Guaranty.[12]

In 1938, while recovering from something resembling a nervous breakdown, Young had penned a few lines:

> Until today, it seemed my path led ever upward.
> But now, I find myself upon a constant downward slope
> Which gains in pitch until I see
> Dim, distantly a void,
> From which departed friends have turned their tired faces,
> The quest of fortune ended.
> While none but liars house the halls of state.[13]

But he had held on. By 1945 all his railroads were sound and making money, and it looked as if he had been a mighty poor prophet.

3

Of the four railroads that remained under Alleghany domination, two were financially strong and two had to be made strong. The C&O and the Wheeling & Lake Erie, the two coal-haulers, were historically sound. C&O was the core of the empire and had been a prime money-earner ever since World War I when West Virginia coal first became competitive in eastern markets. Dependence on a single commodity was not healthy for any railroad, but profits were dependable even in the depression. The C&O was a rock upon which a mighty system could be built. The Wheeling was much smaller but it had a lively coal traffic and was a vital link in the Alphabet Route. Over 3,000 cars a month were using the Alphabet now, five times as many as in 1929. The public knew little of the Wheeling, but it was a freight line whose star was rising.

Nickel Plate and Pere Marquette were the weaker components, but both were on the threshold of greatness. Nickel Plate had failed to cover its fixed charges in the depression and had been forced three times to postpone payment of a $10 million bond issue originally due in 1932. Its only liquid asset was the Wheeling trust certificates it held on its own account. In 1941, when it could not meet that $10 million obligation and receivership seemed inevitable, C&O bought the certificates to keep Wheeling in Alleghany hands and Nickel Plate out of the courts.[14] Despite its financial problems, the road had excellent management, and in the late 1930s began a capital improvement program to upgrade its engineering standards.

On the eve of World War II, it found its niche in eastern railroading. Behind new Berkshire-type steam locomotives, it dispatched frequent fast freights, and rolled them at a steady 60 mph over the flatlands. Shippers responded with enthusiasm. Most traffic was overhead (received from connections and delivered to connections), which meant the railroad got the full mileage rate with virtually none of the terminal expenses. Unlike its arch rival, the New York Central, it had none of the costly multiple tracks or the passenger congestion. In short, it was ideally suited to do what railroads could do best in the latter half of the twentieth century, and it was destined to become rich and important. It was never financially embarrassed again after 1941.[15]

The Pere Marquette had been built to carry lumber and tourists. When the timber was gone and the vacationers had found other ways to get to the lakes, the future of PM was grim. It was saved by the development of the automobile industry in Michigan, particularly General Motors.[16] But its profits were dissipated in improvident dividends paid to the Vans' holding companies. In 1929, it did not have a single creosoted tie or a piece of rail heavier than 90 pounds to the yard. That year, it floated bond issues to finance improvements, then could not meet the fixed charges, and had to be kept afloat by short-term loans from the RFC. By 1938, it had to borrow just to meet mid-year taxes. The banks lost confidence and only a loan from the C&O helped save it. In 1942, Young ended an old Van Sweringen practice of common officers on C&O and PM, and PM vice president Robert Bowman was put in full command, with orders to bring his railroad up to C&O standards. He abandoned many of the unused branches in the cut-over timber districts and began systematic reduction of debt and a program of physical rehabilitation. The PM was being groomed for inclusion in the C&O.[17]

In 1943, a terse statement from Alleghany said that a committee had been formed "to consider ways and means to bring about full or partial unification." Nothing more was heard for the next two years. Then, shortly after V-J Day, Young called a meeting of the four railroads' presidents. Young himself did not attend, but they were told the time was ripe for merger and it would proceed immediately. After a long recess, the C&O men, accompanied by an "expert" from Standard and Poor (whom no one but the C&O people seemed to know), presented a stock exchange ratio and pretty much demanded its acceptance. This ratio, the amount of C&O stock that would be exchanged for the stock of the other companies, meant a lot of money to a lot of people. Calculations were based on the closing market prices of the previous day, which did not necessarily reflect a fair price, if indeed there was such a thing as a fair price.[18]

In the last week of September 1945, representatives from each of the roads conferred with Young. Pere Marquette was granted certain modifications, but no agreement could be reached on the demands of certain Nickel Plate preferred stockholders.[19] Sometime between then and the Nickel Plate's October 30 board meeting, they formed a protective committee and promised to fight the terms offered before the ICC and before the courts.

Under Ohio law, where Nickel Plate was chartered, these minority stock-holders had the power to block merger. Nickel Plate President Davin in-formed Young that the situation was hopeless. Nickel Plate could not join, and without it, there was no point in bringing in the Wheeling, as that road did not connect with the C&O.[20]

It was a stunning development. A merger that had been expected since the early 1920s just collapsed, for reasons that most people did not under-stand at all. Some thought it was Young's fault. Had he tried to force the merger too soon? Apparently he feared that while the four roads stood at about equal financial strength in August 1945, the situation might not last long, for a postwar depression was generally anticipated. For years after-ward he would tell the story of how the C&O had saved the Nickel Plate and its preferred stockholders from certain receivership. They were ungrate-ful and unwise, he said, and the C&O would "never again bend its knee to the Nickel Plate Road."[21]

4

There were some important developments from the wreckage. The first was a merger of the C&O and the Pere Marquette. Two months after the Alleghany merger collapsed, C&O offered to take in the PM on the same terms as before. There were complications with Michigan law, and the legis-ature showed signs of resistance. Many in the state wondered if C&O were as interested in serving the branches of the forested interior as it was in the auto plants of Flint and Saginaw. But the governor wanted the merger, and enabling legislation was secured. Before the ICC, C&O claimed its own good credit would allow PM to refund its debt and reduce its fixed charges. The commission wondered if PM's auto traffic might go the way of lumber and tourists, as the auto industry was already beginning to decentralize out of Michigan. It also questioned the stability of Young's management on the C&O, particularly the rapid turnover of presidents.[22]

Preferred stockholders could be an obstreperous lot, especially when their guaranteed dividends were in arrears and their rights supposedly pro-tected by a mass of state laws that varied wildly from state to state. Michi-gan law, for example, provided that when a company was going to "wind up its affairs," preferred stockholders were to be paid the full value of their shares before the common stockholders got anything. Since the owners of PM common were going to get C&O stock, the preferred holders said they were entitled to $100 a share par value plus $72.50 in accrued arrearages.[23] The commission said complaints of this nature would have to seek redress in a Michigan court and went ahead and approved the merger. So the pre-ferred stockholders went, not to a Michigan court but to federal court to have the whole merger set aside. The suit made its way to the Supreme Court, which handed down a sweeping decision. The commission erred, it said, in its implication that Michigan law superseded the Interstate Commerce Act. It did not. Federal law superseded all state laws in the matter of railroad consolidation.[24] For the C&O and for all railroads, the *Schwabacher* decision swept away all hindrances from state laws, including charter restrictions. Few Supreme Court decisions were as important to the future structure of railroading as this.

On May 20, 1947, the Pere Marquette became the Pere Marquette District of the Chesapeake & Ohio. Unlike its Pocahontas twin, the N&W, C&O was now more than just a coal road. It had direct access to one of the nation's most industrialized areas.

The second development from the Alleghany wreckage was the combination of the Wheeling and the Nickel Plate. On the same day that C&O sent its offer to the Pere Marquette, it announced it would dispose of its Wheeling common stock. The C&O had kept it in a kind of trust for Nickel Plate, but no favors were owed now, and C&O wanted a lot more money than it had paid for the stock initially. Nickel Plate had embarked on another capital improvement program, but it had no choice but to come up with the $5.5 million that was asked. Only the troublesome preferred stockholders were opposed; if the railroad had $5.5 million for an old coal road, why could it not pay their dividends in arrears?[25] If Nickel Plate did not get the Wheeling, the Pennsylvania probably would, for C&O had already asked the Pennsylvania for a bid.[26] If the Alphabet Route should fall to the Pennsylvania, it would be a disaster for Nickel Plate. So the preferred holders were strong-armed, the money was paid, and Nickel Plate was granted first permission to control the Wheeling, and then permission to lease it. (A merger would have required the seating of Mrs. Taplin and someone from Pennroad on the Nickel Plate board, which was further than the preferred holders would go.)

In the fall of 1947, the C&O distributed its Nickel Plate stock as a very handsome dividend to its own shareholders. Nickel Plate was being expelled from Alleghany altogether. It was not unexpected. More than once, C&O had hinted that since merger was off, it had no intention of being an investment trust for 4 percent securities. Cast from the protective umbrella of the C&O, it looked as if Nickel Plate ownership had been scattered to the wind, into thousands of independent portfolios, making it an independent railroad for the first time in its history. Then, for the next two months, the price of Nickel Plate common inched up steadily, a sign that someone was buying systematically and for a purpose. Who? The Pennsylvania? Perhaps. Nickel Plate President Davin just said he would "stick to his knitting" and serve the stockholders to the best of his ability, whoever they turned out to be.[27]

5

The mystery was revealed shortly before Christmas in a letter to Davin from William White of the Lackawanna. Lackawanna had nearly 10 percent of Nickel Plate's common and planned to seek control with intent to merge. It was the most natural merger in the East. The two roads were each other's best connections, interchanging whole trains daily at Buffalo. Their traffic departments solicited together and their operating departments maintained joint schedules. It was an old relationship that seemed to grow stronger with the years. Robert Young had always said that if the Alleghany consolidation had gone through, Lackawanna would have been the most natural addition, and Professor Ripley had paired the two back in 1921.

Back then, Lackawanna was paying 7 percent dividends, among the highest in the nation. With an aristocratic haughtiness that was very typical, it said it would be impossible to bring the Nickel Plate up to Lackawanna standards.[28] Now things were the other way around. Anthracite was no longer "black gold" for the railroad because people weren't heating with it anymore. Lackawanna crossed the mountains with double tracks, hauled lots of passangers and commuters, and served congested terminals that required expensive lighterage operations in New York harbor. Everything about the Lackawanna was a liability, and unless it could pull off this Nickel Plate deal quickly, time would work against it. It had wasted its years of wealth and greatness when it could have expanded anywhere it wished. Nickel Plate, in contrast, was just coming into its greatness. No matter how right, how logical this combination might be, there would surely be those same preferred stockholders at Nickel Plate who would not want their securities jeopardized by this stuffy has-been.

William White invited Nickel Plate's officers and directors to a joint meeting with the Lackawanna board in January 1948. The Nickel Plate men were ushered into the Lackawanna's sumptious board room, seated, and bluntly asked to resign. As one Nickel Plate director put it, "It took me some time to recover from my surprise."[29] The meeting ended in a stalemate. By the next May, a group of Nickel Plate directors representing certain minority stock interests made it clear they were opposed to any kind of affiliation with Lackawanna. White, disastrously unheeding of these people, told them they could not dictate what the Lackawanna would do. They were human, he said, and would die, but the Lackawanna was a corporation that would survive them all, and it could wait for a propitious time.[30]

But the Lackawanna was in bigger trouble than was discernible from its well-manicured mainline. White retreated from his demand for common officers and said he would be content if two Lackawanna directors were seated on the Nickel Plate board. They would be forceful railroad men and would give Lackawanna effective control. No agreement could be reached on that either, and a running litigation began that lasted for seven years. By 1957, Lackawanna could ill afford a forced divestiture of that dividend-paying stock, its last big liquid asset, in case the litigation should go against it, and it agreed to put the stock in trust.[31] It had lost its last chance for independent greatness.

6

Young did not conceal his disappointment over the collapse of the Alleghany consolidation. One day shortly afterward, Robert Bowman, his lieutenant at the Pere Marquette, came into his office and said it was a good thing the Nickel Plate had turned them down, for there was a much bigger prize waiting to be won—the New York Central. Indeed! It was a giant of American business, an aristocrat of corporations, with showy passenger trains favored by celebrities. Young loved celebrities. From that day on, he said, he could think of nothing but the New York Central.[32]

Perhaps as early as October 1, 1946, he asked Merrill, Lynch, Pierce, Fenner and Beane to buy Central common for Alleghany as quietly as possible. Few on Alleghany's board and no one at the C&O was told, although rumors began to circulate on Wall Street, one report naming the backers as Young's old friends, the Duke and Duchess of Windsor.[33] Central common was low—$16 in the fall of 1946, down from $30 in 1945. Even at the height of Alleghany's buying in the fall of 1946, it rose only to $18. Young and Bowman asked for seats on the Central's board, a body composed mostly of the same bankers Young had defeated in his fight for Alleghany back in 1938, who loathed Robert Young and everything he stood for. But they offered the seats as long as the ICC would allow it. They had read the Boles Report and knew the ICC was hostile to Young. And when Young went to the ICC to ask for permission, none other than C.E. Boles was appointed to conduct the hearings.[34]

Robert Young's ambitions, and his tactics for realizing them, were becoming more bizarre with the passing months. He had tried to buy the Pullman sleeping-car service and had been frustrated by a consortium of railroads. He carried that campaign to the public in the same fashion he used to win the support of small C&O stockholders. He sponsored an advertisement on how hogs could cross the country in the same railroad car but people could not.[35] That made him a celebrity. Some even thought he should run for president (of the United States). Then he went off to Georgia to confer with Governor Arnall on that state's litigation against the eastern railroads over rate-fixing. He said he was trying to negotiate a settlement for all; other railroads said it was to make a special deal for the C&O.[36]

They pushed their rate-fixing bill, the Reed-Bulwinkle Act, through Congress, and Young denounced them for it and yanked the C&O and Nickel Plate out of the Association of American Railroads. At the time of the New York Central affair, C&O was still outside the AAR, heading up its own Federation for Railway Progress and hoping others would join.

Meanwhile, Young had become preoccupied with stainless steel passenger trains. For C&O and Nickel Plate, he bought the finest cars that could be procured, even though both were only minor passenger carriers. He established a central reservations bureau, a no-tipping policy and credit cards (each with appropriate fanfare). Then he ordered a new train, the *Chessie*, to be an eye-popping dream train for the Washington-Cincinnati run, with movie theaters, dancing lounges, scenic domes, childrens' play rooms, and aquariums.

After the "hog" ad, he was a folk hero, and fancied himself a David against the Goliath of the "damnbankers" he liked to taunt in public. "How can slave railroads serve the public?" he asked in one of his more controversial advertisments, which portrayed dull-eyed steam locomotives on a leash held by a pompous, bloated banker.[37] Yet within his own Alleghany, there was something less than perfect harmony. There were frequent rumors of monumental confrontations between Young and other C&O directors, over *Chessie*, over the mediocre performance of the road's securities, over the cheap publicity about "goddamn bankers," over foul-mouthed temper tantrums by Kirby. Company lawyers were beside themselves over those advertisements which insulted everyone over the emblem of the Chesapeake & Ohio.[38] Such was the world of Robert Young when he arrived in Washington in September 1947 to testify before the ICC on why he should sit on the board of the New York Central.

His opposition should not have been all that serious. Chrysler Corporation and the Packard Motor Car Company did not want the Central under the domination of a railroad (Pere Marquette) that was known as a "General Motors" road. The PM had recently sponsored a rate schedule on new automobiles highly favorable to GM. Young said he was not familiar with little details like freight rates on automobiles.[39] The Virginian Railway feared it would lose its valuable role as the Central's connection to the coal fields. Young said the Virginian was merely a tool of Morgan and other "damnbankers." The Central was not present, although some thought the Virginian, in its ruthless cross-examination, was its stalking-horse.[40]

Young only wanted a seat on the Central board, yet his plans for molding Central in his own image were very ambitious. How could he do all this if he were only a director? Historically, his opponents pointed out, interlocking directorates only reduced competition and never led to innovative programs. Robert Bowman tried to explain: forceful directors, experienced in railroad affairs, would have a great deal of influence, especially alongside the Central's present directors, who were mostly bankers.

To support this, renowned professors of transportation, Julius Grodinsky and William Leonard, both authors of important books on consolidation, were brought in to testify on the theoretical desirability of interlocking directorates as a first step to merger. Grodinsky had his testimony shredded by a withering cross-examination. After pontificating on how we must "strive to achieve a golden mean between competition and cost control," he was exposed as having only the most superficial knowledge of commodity rates and movements in the Northeast, and no concept whatever of the effect an interlocking directorate might have on them. He barely avoided trick questions meant to trap him, but his credibility as an expert witness was demolished anyway.[41] Professor Leonard did somewhat better, but it was an embarrassing reminder that academicians' oversimplifications did not go far in the real world.

The star witness was Robert Young himself. It was not testimony; it was a performance. About bankers, he said:

And what did they do about [the depression]? Come down here and oppose everything Mr. Roosevelt tried to do to take care of their employees, and ended up paying ten times more through the tax route than if they had spent it in a constructive way rehabilitating the rundown railroad system. I say it would have been a lot more constructive if the unemployed had been reducing curves and building sleeping cars rather than chasing starlings around the sidewalks of Washington. The railroads couldn't spend because the bankers had loaded them down with debt, so they could sell and resell their bonds and make their five points, and its going to happen again if people like Chrysler come down here and oppose the railroads' making a 2% return on their investment.

About Chrysler and Packard:

As a matter of fact, it appears that a lot of steel can go to Chrysler and Packard so they can make a 30% or 40% return . . . and the railroad car builders who need steel for cars and stuff, to relieve the suffering abroad, they cannot get steel, but it's going to Mr. Chrysler and Mr. Packard. . . . It reminds me of Doris Duke intervening in a wage proceeding to see that her footman doesn't get a raise.

About railway progress:

Yes New York Central uses diesels and the C&O uses steam on passenger trains, but we are not reactionary as some people say, because we are experimenting with steam turbines. . . . and I say further that railroads are using up oil at a rapid rate and should not use diesels, and some government agency ought to investigate and see that they go back to coal.

On the New York Central:

The first thing is to improve the passenger service. Coal you just haul one way, but people, if you treat them well, you can haul them back and forth two or three times a month. I look at the Central with envy, and just dream of what I could do if I had their kind of opportunities.

Lets talk about sleeping cars. . . . I came down here and laid $75 million on a silver platter and said I will put it in this dead duck and I will replace every damn one of them, and we will get some people seeing this great country of ours instead of locking them up and treating them so miserably on trains they hope the planes and the highways do take their business away from them. But the railroads turned me down. They said I was a sucker and they wouldn't take my sucker money.

On why he should go on the Central board:

If one man can never serve on the boards of directors of two railroads, you will never get any railroad consolidation. It is something that goes to the key of the national defense. It goes to the key of the national economy, and it's at the root of the present spiral of inflation and living costs.

Q [by the examiner]: Your going on the board of the Central is the key to all these problems?

A: I think the railroad industry is the key to the national defense, and if it goes along at this 2% starvation diet that Mr. Chrysler and others want it to operate on, I say that at the first sign of a depression in this country, tens of thousands, hundreds of thousands of men are going to be laid off by the railroads of sheer necessity.

Q: And the cure for all that is Robert Young on the board of the New York Central?

A: It will go a damn long way in the direction of curing it—for a little fellow.[42]

At the very end of the hearing, the Virginian Railway put on its star witnesses, the officers of the Central. Under subpoena, they nevertheless talked freely of their opposition to Young and the C&O, knowing, they said, that such talk would probably cost them their jobs if Young should win. The Central did have problems and they were doing something about them. Flashy streamliners were not the answer. Their testimony was a stiletto thrust that was devastating to Young's cause.[43]

Examiner Boles was quick to recommend against seating Young. The official reason was the effect on competition; the real reason was a lack of confidence in Young. "The applicants have given only the most general consideration to the problems with which they would be confronted." And that was it.[44]

Young thought the deck was stacked and was furious. "It's difficult for us to take the Commission's two-faced justice," he said. "Henry Hagerty of the Metropolitan Life Insurance Company was quietly granted the right, without a hearing, to sit on the boards of the New Haven and the Erie, at the very time we were required to appear before the Commission."[45] Then he launched a series of peculiar advertisments headlined "Memo to the New York Central." There were five of them altogether, and they challenged Central to imitate the C&O's progressive passenger train innovations.[46] *Trains*, in an imitation of the ads, urged Young to "get off the branch-line and onto the mainline" and worry about the Central's real problems like low rate of return and intermodal freight competition.[47]

On May 10, 1948, the full commission gave Young's scheme its *coup de grâce*. After that, all was quiet. There were rumors that Young was trying to work out a three-way deal to include the Virginian, but little came of it. Then there was a rumor that Alleghany purchases of Seaboard and Rock Island anticipated a Young-controlled transcontinental, but nothing came of that. Alleghany continued to buy Central common, until by 1950 it had doubled its holdings since the end of the hearing. In 1951 there was a wild rumor that Young was about to resign from the C&O and seek control of the Central independently. It was denied, and all was silent, except that at the Central they were preparing for the onslaught.[48]

7

The announcement came on January 19, 1954. Young wanted the Central so badly he was ready to give up the C&O for it and run the risk of a proxy fight against the Central's entrenched management. He used all the persuasive power at his command in his appeal to thousands of small stockholders and the public. He promised to end banker domination and put an employee (retired engineer William E. Landers) and a woman (*Reader's Digest* publisher Lila Belle Acheson Wallace) on the board of directors. There was national publicity—lots of it—including a debate between Young and Central President William White on "Meet the Press." White was a worthy adversary. He liked streamliners, too—he had pushed his board at the Lackawanna to buy the *Phoebe Snow*. But he had little respect for Young's preoccupation with the flashy side of railroading. "If we should get licked in this fight," he said, "I want to see Mr. Young up there on the 32nd floor [of the New York Central Building] meeting our day-to-day problems. I'd just like to see him sit down, by God, and stick it out for five years."[49]

The crux of the case was the 800,000 Central shares owned by the C&O in trust at the Chase National Bank. The Chase would almost surely vote them against Young, so he got his friends, Texas oilmen Sid Richardson and Clint Murchison, to buy them for him. There were legal maneuvers by Central to block this, and countermaneuvers by Young. On May 26, 1954, both Young and White rode the *Stockholders' Special* to Albany to the annual meeting. They rode in different cars and did not speak to each other, but were busy soliciting proxies all the way. It took two breathless weeks to count the votes; Young had it by 1,026,000 shares.[50]

The change at Central was complete. No Vanderbilt would serve on the Young slate, so all connection with the founding family was severed. Young chose Alfred Perlman of the Denver & Rio Grande Western Railroad to be his president and chief operating officer. Perlman had taken a second-rate mountain railroad and turned it into a first-class competitor of the Union Pacific. Hopefully, the same magic would work at the Central. He and Mrs. Perlman arrived in New York the night the final proxy count was announced, and before a battery of excited reporters at Grand Central he pledged to serve Young and the Central.[51] The next day, Young, Perlman, Mrs. Wallace, and others made a triumphal march from Alleghany headquarters to the New York Central Building on Park Avenue. So began the Young era on the Road of the Vanderbilts.

Young's biographer, Joseph Borkin, put it this way: White and his directors were in possession of a terrifying fact—Central was bankrupt. Perlman toured the line and was heartsick. The road was even more passenger-oriented than he had imagined. The property was littered with elephantine stations that resembled pagan temples. The four-track mainline was a millstone, with the passenger tracks signaled for 80 mph, useless for freight, and the two freight tracks signaled for 30 mph, useless for a service that could compete. On the flat straightaway south of Buffalo, along the Lake Erie shore where the Central and the Nickel Plate ran a dead parallel heat, the short, fast NKP freights darted past the Perlman inspection train in a dazzling display of technological superiority, and Nickel Plate was doing it with steam locomotives.

Young and Perlman were lucky for a while; 1955 and 1956 were good years. Net income was up and Young found enough cash to experiment with his low-slung dream trains, christened the *Ohio Xplorer* and the *Great Lakes Aerotrain*. But they were immediate and dismal failures. The "travel-tailored" timetable in the fall of 1956, the penultimate effort for a super passenger service, resulted in a $12 million out-of-pocket loss. The spirit of progress was ebbing rapidly, along with morale. Stock that had soared to $49 a share in the heady days after the Young victory, sank to $13. With the onset of recession in the fall of 1957, everything went sour, and that apparently sparked the first merger talks with the Pennsylvania. The first quarter dividend was omitted in 1958.

After breakfast on the morning of January 26, 1958, at his home in Palm Beach, Robert Young shot himself to death. His body was taken by train to Newport, where he was buried beside his daughter. He had sold all of his

Central holdings in the weeks before, but his friends, who had bought stock to help in the proxy fight, had taken terrible losses. Facing them must have been unbearable, although Kirby remained steadfastly loyal. There were stories of a letter from a disillusioned "Aunt Jane" who had lost everything, that lay before him on the table where his body was found, but Borkin and others discount this as a cause of his death. It is not certain he even read it, and it was quite obviously in the same hand as other crank mail he had received. Central and Alleghany denied that the state of their fortunes had anything to do with his death and the only man who could verify that was silent. Everyone recalled those disturbing lines of poetry he had penned just as his career was beginning and speculated that beneath the optimistic exterior, there lay a will for self-destruction.

At Elkhart, Indiana, a new electronic classification yard was named in his honor, one of the few reminders on the latter-day Central of his colorful association with it. Perlman, in full command, immediately began the transformation of the New York Central from a four-tracked passenger line into a double-tracked, high-capacity, fast freight line. That was far removed from Robert Young's dreams of merger, streamliners, celebrities, fame, and the New York Central he once coveted with the eagerness of a little boy who dreamed of a Lionel train at Christmas time.

CHAPTER 4

Consolidation Is the Panacea;
1954-1960

Edward Hungerford loved trains, and it showed in his histories of the Baltimore & Ohio, the New York Central, and the Erie. But he was not always so fond of railroad men. He loved the hoggers and the brass-pounders and the gandy dancers, for they were real men who dedicated their lives to the trains. And when the executives put trains above profits, he loved them, too. He wrote a book on such a man, Daniel Willard of the B&O. It distressed him that most of the industry's leaders were not men like Willard, but bureaucrats and financiers ruled by pride, greed, tradition, and inertia, who would let the trains die before giving an inch to the prerogatives of private property.

Like many of those who loved trains, he shared a sense of foreboding about their future. The Depression hit railroads harder than other industries, and he sensed that lack of leadership was their special problem. Then came World War II, which proved what a magnificent machine the railroad was, and that an industry recently reduced to self-pity could come alive when duty called. More than ever, he knew the trains must not be allowed to die.

In 1944, he put his feelings in a book, a science-fiction novel called *A Railroad for Tomorrow,* which described what things would be like in far-off 1960.[1] When the war was over, the story went, and the depression had settled in again, the railroads were helpless because the war had sapped the last of their strength. William Wiggins was a shortline railroader from Maine, now a United States senator, who put before Congress a plan to save them. He would charter a new corporation, the United Railways, which would assume the debts of all the roads that wished to join. Once so united, the efficiency of consolidation would make them strong.

At first, only the weak roads joined, like the Erie and the Seaboard, and the big roads snickered that the United would never amount to much. But they underestimated William Wiggins. He forged them into a real system, and soon all the other railroads were trying to coordinate their operations in self-defense. Still, they could not overcome their age-old jealousies. By then, the United was a confirmed success. Great streamliners were streaking coast-to-coast over its rails, and the public was aghast at what consolidation had wrought.

It was then that Wiggins brought forth the United States Railroad. A successor to the United, it coordinated the operations of all the nation's railroads. It was governed by a board of directors that conducted business in public, like a legislative body in a democratic society. It included representatives of the twenty-one operating divisions, the labor brotherhoods, shipper associations, and the public, as appointed by the president.

Such a step was completely without precedent. . . . At no time in the history of our railroads had the head of a brotherhood even been invited to sit in on a board meeting, to say nothing of becoming a member. . . . Some of the ultra-progressive old-time railroad presidents—farsighted men such as Daniel Willard of the B&O and Sir Henry Thornton of the Canadian National (both these many years gone) would have liked to take the step. They never took their own boards too seriously. Even with all their power, neither of them was quite powerful enough to accomplish such a sweeping change under the ever-watchful eye of the God of Tradition.

There was not to be a single banker.

On this point, Wiggins was adamant. He knew far too well the evils of absentee management on American railroads. Of the so-called banker control, he was especially abhorrent.

"We won't have any of those moneybags on our board, not if I can prevent it," he said bluntly. "I've seen for myself the damage those fellows did in the old days."[2]

The new company was launched on September 1, 1952. Needless to say, since this is fiction, it was a great success. It had no trouble raising capital, for the entire nation was entranced with its railways. Containerization became so efficient trucks did not even try to compete for long-distance traffic. No one flew in airplanes anymore, not with those wonderful scenic-domed streamliners sweeping all over the country. William Wiggins, in spite of being a stuffed shirt, became a national hero. Public galleries were packed for board meetings of the USRR, and the crowds gasped in awe as the great man brilliantly led the proceedings. Alas, he was overworked and had a coronary and died. Too bad it was such an ordinary way to go. No one had been groomed for the succession and Wiggins was going to be a hard act to follow.

That was how Edward Hungerford thought national socialism would come to American railroads. Naive? Perhaps. But like Glenn Plumb before him, he had seen a few things with sparkling clarity:

1. The salvation of railroads lay in coordinated action, but operating units should not be too large as they would be unmanageable; hence, twenty-one operating divisions. Ruinous competition was bad, but healthy rivalry was good.

2. Labor had better be brought in on the arrangement; otherwise, it had the power to wreck it.
3. The rights of capital had better be limited for it also had the power to wreck.
4. Business ought to conduct its affairs under the scrutiny of public and press for the haughty secrecy of old would never wash in the postwar world.
5. Finally, there was no substitute for an able leader.

As the real story unfolds in the pages that follow, the reader would be well advised to keep some of this in mind.

1

There had been a merger—somewhat more modest than the United States Railroad—and it had been so successful, in its modest way, that in 1947 the ICC permitted the same railroad to merge again.

The Gulf, Mobile & Northern and the Mobile & Ohio served the clay and pine hills region of eastern Mississippi. The farms were poor and the forests cut over. According to the roads' historian, James Lemly, their chief claim to fame was that more broken-down old cows per mile were run over by their trains than anybody else's—cows left to roam by dirt farmers who needed the little bit of indemnity they knew the local judge would award them. Success rested largely on the personality of Issac B. (Ike) Tigrett of the GM&N, who molded that road into a viable entity in the 1920s and then put out cautious feelers to the bankrupt M&O in the 1930s. What Tigrett shaped into the new Gulf, Mobile & Ohio, said Lemly, was a railroad that had to expand or expire. The new company never set railroading on fire, but it remained solvent and was able to generate capital for basic improvements.

Under Tigrett's firm hand, the GM&O merged once more in 1947, again successfully, with the Alton Route, a road that had wallowed through the interwar years as an orphan of the B&O. A few years later, GM&O became the first major railroad to be 100 percent dieselized. Perhaps it can be called the Lemly Thesis that honest mergers by honest men for honest reasons could produce solid results.[3] It was a heart-warming experience.

2

Yet despite the happy success of the GM&O, or the inspired trumpeting of Edward Hungerford, merger was a dead topic in railroading in the late 1940s. Why so little interest? Two explanations seem at first contradictory —one, that the railroads were too prosperous, and two, that they were too poor.

Edward Hungerford guessed wrong when he predicted postwar depression; instead, there was prosperity. With industry booming and capital

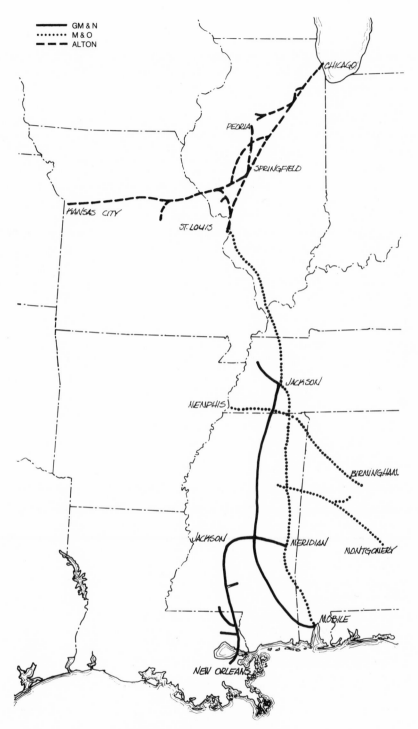

MAP 14:   *The Gulf, Mobile & Ohio*

investment high, demand for transportation was great, and the railroads helped share in this. All but one of the roads forced into receivership during the depression were able to reorganize; the exception, the Missouri Pacific, was not for lack of profits.

In these good times, there was enough capital for the railroads to make a dramatic investment, the switch from steam to diesel power. It was accomplished in the same eight-year period that interest in consolidation was at its lowest, 1946-1954. While steam buffs argue the point, the savings from diesels were substantial, immediate, and dramatic, especially when new locomotives replaced depression- and war-ravaged units that were obsolete even in steam technology.[4] It is a moot point whether dieselization utterly preoccupied management or whether it simply enabled it to show enough profit to keep the stockholders quiet and not demand more drastic action such as consolidation.

For railroads, doing modestly well in a booming economy was no big accomplishment. On front after front they seemed to be in trouble. The truck, once limited to short hauls of light-weight commodities, was cutting into longer hauls and heavier commodities with each advance in its technology. Government highway construction, paid for in part by the taxes on railroads, was demoralizing. A good history of this competitive struggle is yet to be written, but even now it is clear that railroaders were behaving as if they were spooked. That explained their efforts, which ultimately backfired, to set up dummy "public interest" lobbies in the state capitals to get severe restrictions put on the truckers. They even went so far as to infiltrate state PTA organizations to make sure the railroad message reached those of an impressionable age.[5]

In their efforts to compete, railroads frequently ran against a wall of restrictive legislation which they came to believe existed solely to harass them. (Truckers, in contrast, always insisted the ICC was railroad-dominated.) The situation produced the "crying-towel syndrome" in which most of the railroads' paltry efforts at public relations were given over to wails of woe on how unfairly the world was treating them. No one admires a loser, especially a sore one. Labor never accepted the idea—if railroads were so poor, how come they could pay dividends? By the late 1950s, even sympathetic sources (including *Trains*) suspected the campaign had backfired and poisoned labor-management relations.

On top of this came the demise of the passenger train. It was a victim of rising costs and public preference for other kinds of transportation. By the 1960s, it would be almost a measure of a railroad man's virility to be hard-nosed about passenger service, which meant get rid of it as fast as possible. But deep in their hearts, railroad men loved those trains. They showed the company's flag. The quality of the trains reflected on the people who ran them. Domed streamliners serving five-course meals, rolling beds swathed in acres of starchy sheets, trips to remote corners of the land—this was show business, not utility. Yet hardly a railroad executive protested the purchase of these trains for millions of dollars. Appropriations were not cut back until well into the 1950s, because these were things of the heart. In the 1950s, as the crowds thinned and the upholstery got ragged and the paint began to peel, railroad morale went to pieces.

This spirit of gloom that hung over the railroads affected consolidation in a particular way. Simply put, the new problems fell more heavily on some railroads than on others, and the old status quo of strong roads and weak ones was changing remarkably. The roads that were suffering the most were, by and large, yesterday's blue chips, particularly in the East. They had the heaviest passenger traffic. They served the old industrialized areas which were not sharing in the postwar expansion as dramatically as the West and South. They covered an area where distances were short and were more susceptible to truck competition. Many served the Ohio River Valley or the Great Lakes area where water competition was intense. Most were built when trains were short and frequent, hence, multiple tracks, now redundant in an age of electronic signals. The availability of oil and natural gas pulled the rug out from under the railroads built specifically to carry anthracite. The result was that yesterday's desirable merger partners were today's dogs. Until the new economic factors sorted themselves out and a new status quo emerged, consolidation was in the deep freeze. The Lackawanna-Nickel Plate affair in the previous chapter was a case in point.

Thus the railroads were too rich to be forced into consolidation and too unsettled for it to take place naturally. Besides, railroad executives said the ICC would not let them consolidate anyway, because it was so morbidly concerned with preserving competition. That fit the crying-towel mentality and was a fine excuse for not even trying. Men who had insisted that consolidation was a good thing, who had fought for and received a law that put the burden of initiative on them, and then did nothing about it, had to have some rationalization.

Since the Transportation Act of 1940 encouraged consolidation and the Clayton Act prevented it, it appeared the politicians had contradicted themselves, which many businessmen thought was typical. But that was not the case. The wording and legislative history of the Transportation Act of 1940 showed that Congress wanted to encourage consolidation as long as it was in the public interest. Knowing that businessmen were capable of planning many kinds of affiliation that were not in the public interest, it chose not to alter the Clayton Act. The issue had been resolved by the Supreme Court in the *McLean* case of 1944.[6] The McLean Trucking Company charged the commission had paid insufficient attention to the antitrust statutes when it allowed a number of small truckers to merge into the Associated Transport. The Court held that when the advantages of consolidation outweigh the disadvantages of reduced competition, Congress intended the merger should go through. Subsequently, the ICC approved the C&O-Pere Marquette merger, the Nickel Plate's lease of the Wheeling, and the merger of the Alton and the GM&O. It was an impressive record in favor of consolidation.

The ICC was not rubber-stamping these proposals, as Robert Young found out. But the railroad establishment showed little remorse for Young's defeat. It was a second denial that brought a whirlwind of abuse down about the commissioners' heads.

When the GM&O acquired the Alton in 1947, it thought seriously of selling its Kansas City line. Ike Tigrett wanted to concentrate on developing the north-south traffic and not spread his resources thin on the east-west routes. The Burlington and the Santa Fe, both eager for a direct line across Missouri, leaped at the opportunity. It would allow improvements in certain Burlington and Santa Fe services, but shippers were already getting those services from other southwestern carriers, all of whom would be hurt if this went through. Advantage would flow only to two powerful corporations; the public could actually be hurt if it diminished the southwesterns' ability to compete. Denouncing the proposal as a power grab, the commission turned the application down, and the GM&O eventually kept the line.[7] Economist William Leonard lambasted the commissioners for ignoring what he thought were obvious economies, and much of established railroading joined in the clamor.[8] It seemed to suit them to pout over the decision. For some it was an excuse for not proposing consolidation of their own; for others it was a way to badger the commission into accepting their own power grabs more gracefully.

3

In fact, the ground was already being prepared for the wild chain reaction of mergers to come.

1. The *McLean* decision set aside antitrust laws.
2. The *Schwabacher* decision set aside restrictions by the states, including charter restrictions.
3. The *New York Central Securities* decision provided a simple test for that elusive term "public interest." A railroad needed only show that its proposal had a "direct relation to the adequacy of transportation services and to its essential condition of economy and efficiency."[9]
4. The so-called *DT&I conditions*, stemming from the Pennsylvania's request to control the Detroit, Toledo & Ironton, specified that merging railroads must maintain "all routes and channels of trade via existing junctions and gateways" and "all present traffic and operating relationships." This silenced objections from the most formidable opponents to railroad consolidation—other railroads.[10] Furthermore, since no adequate provision was made to enforce it, merging railroads would still be free to rearrange traffic patterns as they wished.

The contest for the control of the Toledo, Peoria & Western seemed to set a precedent of particularly ominous importance, namely, that when a railroad was being sought by more than one other railroad as a consolidation partner, the larger and stronger of the contestants was to be preferred because it offered more financial security. The TP&W's history was not a happy one. Although it was not a passenger carrier, one of the worst wrecks in American history took place on its line—eighty-two Niagara Falls-bound weekenders died at Chatsworth, Illinois, in 1887. In the 1940s, it wrote a turbulent chapter of industrial relations which culminated in the assassination of its president, George P. McNear, Jr., in 1947. Nevertheless, it had become a modestly profitable bridge line, speeding long freights between the Pennsylvania and the Santa Fe on a line that bypassed the congestion at Chicago.

The Minneapolis & St. Louis line, under the aggressive leadership of Ben Heineman, a young Chicago lawyer, bid $69.50 a share; like GM&O, this minor granger road had to expand or expire. But Santa Fe and Pennsylvania wanted it, too, and put in a higher bid which Heineman had a hard time matching. The ICC decided the big carriers could better maintain the TP&W's physical plant.[11] One conclusion could be drawn: consolidation was not going to be a way for little lines to pull themselves up.

The most significant precedent came with the abortive bid of the Atlantic Coast Line to acquire the Florida East Coast. What *Trains* called "Mr. Flagler's pretty railroad by the sea," carried citrus and tourists and was a logical extension of the ACL's Richmond-Jacksonville mainline. It had been in receivership since 1931, but one Edward Ball had snapped up a majority of its bonds at bargain prices. Together with his brother-in-law, Alfred I. DuPont, he put together an empire consisting of some of the state's major banks, the so-called Florida National group, the big St. Joe Paper Company, and the railroad. The conglomerate was important in Florida commerce, with roots sinking deep into Florida politics. Ball loved Florida, wanted the FEC to remain small, independent, and Florida-oriented and, some thought, a giant Lionel for him to play with. The ICC thought a merger with the ACL made good operating sense and made it a condition of FEC's reorganization. Did that smack of forced consolidation? Ball thought so and got the Supreme Court to agree. Any kind of forced consolidation was out.[12] If anything frightened big railroads about consolidation, it was the threat of being forced. Now, they were free and clear.

4

One by one, all the impediments to mergers on managements' terms had fallen. To labor, consolidation was a code word for retrenchment and job reduction. Capital, it was convinced, would arrange the mergers to suit itself, and the workingman who could least afford it would pay most of the cost. But management had long experience dealing with the unions. It believed that if it were protected with sufficient agreements and precedents, even if they were costly, it was assured of a docile work force that would accept whatever mergers management decided on, and never disrupt service. The process of neutralizing labor began in the 1930s, and by the late 1950s was established fact.

Back in 1936, when time expired on the emergency legislation of 1933, both labor and management had wanted an agreement on consolidation. Under the Washington Agreement, men who were forced to take less desirable jobs received a monetary allowance to make up the difference. Men who lost jobs received a stipend of 60 percent of their previous salary. All protection lasted five years and began the day the person was actually affected, so long as that was within three years of the official date of consolidation. Since men were subject to recall (and would lose all benefits if they did not return), a provision was made for a lump-sum settlement. The company paid moving expenses of men transferred, including losses on canceled leases or hastily sold property.[13]

There had been no statutory requirement for labor protection, although the ICC had imposed such conditions and been upheld by the Supreme Court.[14] Most labor leadership had not wanted the Washington Agreement written into the Transportation Act of 1940, preferring collective bargaining to rigid codification. But during floor debate in the House, Congressman Vincent Harrington of Iowa asked that all consolidation or coordination be prohibited if it resulted in "the impairment of existing employment rights of . . . employees." "If you want to pave the way for ghost railroads and ghost towns," he thundered, "if you want the blue envelope and the pink slip going out to 200,000 railroad employees, then do not vote for my amendment."[15]

Members of the Interstate Commerce Committee were furious. They had taken days of testimony from brotherhood leaders and written a bill that included everything they had asked for. Only one, A.F. Whitney of the Brotherhood of Railroad Trainmen, wanted this ironclad prohibition, and Harrington was his mouthpiece. The House passed the amendment, the Senate refused, and an interunion fight now threatened to wreck the whole bill. Finally, there was a compromise. The law would require four years of 100 percent protection for every railroad wage earner affected by consolidation.[16] Thus, he had two kinds of protection: four years of full coverage beginning the day the ICC gave approval, as a matter of law; and five years of 60 percent protection beginning the day he was actually affected, by private agreement.

It took the ICC a few tries before it found a way to meet the new requirements and not prevent all consolidation. But with the so-called *Oklahoma* conditions of 1944, railroads were allowed to rearrange their work forces to suit themselves so long as a person's compensation remained the same for four years.[17] The *Oklahoma* conditions became routine, usually imposed for the benefit of nonagreement employees, for in the Pere Marquette and Wheeling cases, for example, labor and management preferred the Washington Agreement, which they were free to substitute under the terms of the law.

When the railroads of New Orleans petitioned to build a new consolidated passenger terminal in 1948, a situation arose with which the *Oklahoma* conditions could not cope. The new station would not be completed until four years after the ICC gave its approval, during which time every job would remain unchanged. Then, just when statutory protection ran out, there would be massive dismissals. The following solution emerged: men received the full protection of the *Oklahoma* conditions for four years. After that, any protection that might still accrue under the Washington Agreement was imposed as a matter of law. The so-called *New Orleans* conditions were the basic statutory protection for labor as the merger movement got under way.[18]

5

It would be wrong to imply that all these agreements and precedents had been arranged conspiratorily so that management would have a clear track for any kind of arrangement it wanted. But the fact was, there they were. All systems were go. In 1957, the process came to fruition in the merger of the Nashville, Chattanooga & St. Louis into the Louisville & Nashville. There are some who think this case set in motion the mania for railroad mergers.

The NC&StL had been controlled by the L&N since 1880. The L&N was controlled in turn by the Atlantic Coast Line, which at first made the plan seem merely a corporate streamlining within the Coast Line family. Yet both the motive for merger and the obstacles that stood in its way anticipated things to come. Merger would save $3.75 million in operating expenses which could be spent on new capital investment. A study showed how these savings were going to come, mostly from the elimination of duplicate facilities and staff. This was the first merger whose principal objective was retrenchment.

The pattern of opposition would become familiar. Other railroads protested, in this case the Illinois Central and the Central of Georgia, for they would lose interchange traffic. The city of Nashville protested, for competition at that point would be virtually eliminated. Stockholders of both roads protested, for each group believed the other was getting a better deal. Labor protested, for a total of 550 jobs would be lost, mostly in Nashville and surrounding Davidson County.

The ICC faced the issues head on. The L&N was ordered to retain all joint routes as per the *DT&I* conditions, but IC and CofG were told they would have to pay a price for the strengthening of railroads as a whole. Nashville was told benefits outweighed the damage of lost competition, as per the *McLean* decision. Stockholders were denied reconsideration, with the implication they had tried to turn the merger to their own advantage. Labor was told existing agreements gave it all the protection it was going to get.[19]

Furthermore, the ICC concluded the proceedings with dispatch. The two roads agreed to merge on November 28, 1954, but did not submit their proposal until January 28, 1955. Hearings were held in August, giving all parties time to prepare their cases. Then briefs were filed. The hearing examiner prepared his report, and exceptions to it were filed. The commission listened to oral argument, after which briefs were filed again, a report prepared, and further exceptions filed. The decision was handed down on March 1, 1957. Merging railroads always insisted the process was too slow. Delay was an enemy of consolidation, for if the fortunes of one of the merger partners should undergo a significant change while the case was in progress, the stock exchange ratio might have to be renegotiated or the whole deal called off. But those who believed their ox was being gored, including fellow railroads, expected due process and that took time. The noise about the ICC's snail's pace lay somewhere between a genuine desire by management to get something, once decided on, over with, and yet another effort to badger the commission into accepting management's desires more dutifully.

Deep in the mass of technical exhibits presented by the L&N lay a curious item. By itself, it meant little, but it said something about the mentality of the men who made the mergers. It seemed the NC&StL's locomotive repair shops at Nashville were to be phased out and all work transferred to the L&N shops at South Louisville. But the cost of repairs per unit, as revealed in such available sources as *Moody's Transportation Manual*, were less at the NC&StL shops. It showed that some of the assumptions about the efficiency of large, consolidated facilities needed rather close scrutiny. It seemed to indicate the desire to merge had come first, the justification after, and when statistics indicated some facets would be counterproductive, they were ignored.

6

While the ICC struggled with the mundane issues, there was excitement outside. Two weeks before the L&N and NC&StL made their first announcement in 1954, the Milwaukee Road and the Chicago & North Western announced they were going to study coordination. Said David

Morgan in *Trains*, "The slim statement handed out to the press was hazy in exact meaning but immense in its implication." Early the next year, Patrick McGinnis, a gadfly in the mold of Robert Young who won control of the New Haven in a similar kind of proxy fight, said he would seek control of the Boston & Maine to create the New England monopoly that eluded J.P. Morgan. William White, who had gone to the Delaware & Hudson after Young ousted him from the New York Central, proposed the B&M join his D&H, and together with the Lackawanna and the Nickel Plate, form a new trunkline in the Northeast. Lackawanna, in the meantime, announced it would boldly abandon seventy miles of its mainline and use the parallel tracks of the Erie. While no mention was made of merger, the names of the two roads were frequently linked from that day on. Consolidation had suddenly undergone a bit of a revival.

Why? Coincidence, perhaps, for none of the proposals were related. But the time was propitious for merger. Traffic levels and profits were good during the Korean War. Even the New Haven was paying dividends and ordering new equipment. Strong road-weak road incompatibilities were not so pronounced. Then came the recession of 1954, short, but severe enough to scare railroad men. In an industry with high fixed costs, even a mild recession brought a big reduction in earnings.

To make it worse, the spectacular impact of the diesel was over. In the early days of dieselization, the new locomotives replaced obsolete steamers and were put on runs where they were utilized to their fullest. As the change-over neared completion, new locomotives replaced steam power built since 1940 which was not obsolete and had to be assigned to those marginal tasks which did not permit full utilization.[20] What had once spelled dramatic savings was now a lot less dramatic, and it was time to look beyond the diesel. Merger was one answer, and as soon as the recession was over, it was time to pursue it. Mergers take place naturally when futures are bright and profits assured, a balm for all disagreements. The Interstate Highway System, the St. Lawrence Seaway, and commercial jet aircraft were already on the drawing boards. It was the time to strike. The moment might never come again.

The initial spate of mergers washed out; a new management on the North Western in 1955 discontinued talks with the Milwaukee; Pat McGinnis was ousted from the New Haven; Nickel Plate spurned the Lackawanna. But general talk about consolidation continued in the trade press, and in 1956, there was a whole new series of proposals. In the West, Great Northern, Northern Pacific, and Burlington announced they would re-create the Northern Securities empire. In the South, Frisco said it would take the Central of Georgia. In the East Perry Shoemaker of the Lackawanna prodded William White to substitute Erie for Nickel Plate and propose an Erie-Lackawanna-D&H merger.

David Morgan in *Trains* was the first to sense the significance of it all. Commenting on the Milwaukee-North Western proposal, he noted that 1954 was not a good year for either road, and that when the directors began their studies, "they would see parallel lines in thinly-trafficked territory, two yards handling the tonnage of one. All railroaders," he said, "have much at stake. . . . A great many of them will be looking over the shoulders of this committee of directors as they sit down to study coordination." As for the Northerns, he recalled the *Northern Securities* decision of 1904 and asked who was right after all, Teddy Roosevelt the trustbuster or James Hill the empire builder? Hill was accused of immoral and illegal action, but what he tried to do back then seemed like the right thing now. It was time to recall the words of Frank Spearman, the banker, back when "Northern Securities" was a tainted phrase:

That which will be incredible to men 50 years from now is that [Hill] should have been assailed as a wrong-doer. It should console Mr. Hill that in the cannonization of really great men, the first appropriation is for faggots, the quarrying of the marble being left to the third and fourth generations.[21]

7

In 1957, there began a recession that decisively altered the course of consolidation. Had there been a few good years after the 1954 recession for some of the early proposals to work themselves out, the final combinations of roads would almost surely have been different. The decline that began in the midsummer of 1957 was more serious and persistent than the one of 1954. For railroads, it continued without interruption until 1961. As usual, high fixed costs meant that a marginal drop in revenue (4 percent in 1957) produced a major drop in net earnings (17 percent). Nineteen fifty-eight was worse. New York Central and Pennsylvania reported declines in gross earnings of $100 million each and return on investment fell to 0.6 percent. The Jersey Central, the Lehigh Valley, the Erie, the Lackawanna, the New Haven, and the Boston & Maine all suffered net losses on operations. The New York, Ontario & Western applied for abandonment and the Lehigh & New England prepared to do the same.

In January 1958, George Smathers and his Senate Subcommittee on Surface Transportation began hearings on an administration bill to ease the latest railroad crisis. Company presidents who came to testify were all pessimistic—posturing, perhaps—but it seemed as if doubts, doubts about the principle of the railroad itself and its ability to survive, doubts that recent prosperity had barely glossed over, came welling up from the depth of frustration. The proposed bill dealt with problems of credit and passenger service and few thought it was going to help very much. Perry Shoemaker of the Lackawanna, in his outgoing speech as president of the New York Chamber of Commerce, said it was "distressingly full of compromise, concessions and inertia." Earl Moore of the Jersey Central said it would help the roads ride out the storm but little more. Walter Tuohy of the C&O excoriated the ICC for being so negative about consolidation, and ICC Commissioner Howard Freas, himself in favor of consolidation, shot back that the initiative was on the railroads, and for all their talk, they had come through with precious few concrete proposals. Benjamin Fairless of United States Steel thought that if Congress did not hurry up and do what business wanted, the communists were probably going to take over.

The most important thing to come out of the sessions was the appointment of Maj. Gen. John P. Doyle, United States Air Force, to head a study group on transportation problems. The Smathers bill was vague about consolidation, but he wrote an article in *This Week* in which he called for four regional railroad monopolies, one in each quadrant of the nation, an idea *Trains* dismissed as "old as the hills."

8

On November 1, 1957, the Pennsylvania and the New York Central announced their "mutual intent" to make "further studies" into the possibility of merger. It was a thunderclap that shook all railroading, one of the "best kept secrets in financial circles," said the *New York Times*. These were the industry's superpowers, two of the most historic and intense competitors in American business. They dominated the East. Together, they would overshadow any other combination that could possibly be put together. The press quickly settled down to a recitation of superlatives: assets of $5 billion (tenth largest of U.S. corporations), revenues of $1.5 billion, 80 million passengers a year, 378 million tons of freight, 184,000 employees. No small road thought it could survive against such a combination. Yet for all their size, Central and Pennsylvania earned less than 1 percent on invested capital. They were marginal operators, said Robert Bedingfield in the *New York Times*, not sleek and powerful lions ready to pounce, but dinosaurs, big, obsolete, and dying.

Robert Young and James Symes made the announcement separately, from New York and Philadelphia. Merger, they said, was going to save $100 million a year, and a committee was appointed to find out if this were so. The *New York Times* said "many railroaders" doubted it would ever come to pass, and thought Central and Pennsy were equally unsure themselves. George Alpert of the New Haven thought it was a gimmick to dramatize the plight of the eastern railroads. John S. Tompkins in the *Nation* thought it was all Young's doing, a way to blame his troubles on his "whipping boys of Wall Street" and "fight in the battlefield of the front pages for his legion of 'Aunt Jane' minority stockholders.''[22] After Young's death, there was some question whether his successor cared about merger at all. Alfred Perlman and Robert Young differed on just about every other way to run a railroad, although for the present, Perlman still wore a little button in his lapel that said "merge."

The Penn Central proposal threw all other merger talk in the East into a state of panic, distorting it, compromising it, and making rational planning impossible. Whenever executives of the smaller roads met, at directors' meetings of the AAR or the Eastern Railroad Presidents' Conference, they would huddle over lunch or dinner to plan strategy. They came from an incompatible lot of roads. There was the wealthy C&O, and the attractive, rather swaggering Nickel Plate, which contrasted sharply with, say, the Jersey Central, whose burden of commuters, short hauls, and New Jersey taxes made it what F. Scott Fitzgerald would have called a "sad bird." Nobody quite knew what to do with the Pennsylvania's satellite roads, the Norfolk & Western, Lehigh Valley, and Wabash, including those roads' own officers. Were they going to be part of Penn Central or not?

The outcasts had to assume the worst, that Penn Central studies would soon be completed and would go to the commission. Should they oppose it separately, or together, and if so, on what grounds? Should they acquiesce and hope for the best, or should they submit counterproposals of their own? In the second week of November 1958, they met together in Cleveland in a kind of summit conference of the "outer seven"—the Erie, Lackawanna, D&H, B&O, C&O, Nickel Plate, and Reading. William White was thought to be the instigator.[23] No commitments were made, but channels of communication were open.

The same month, the New England roads held their own summit in Portland, on the initiative of Maine Central's E. Spencer Miller. Those roads were not compatible either. Bangor & Aroostook and Maine Central were wiry enough to stand alone or merge with a trunkline, but the New Haven was skidding toward bankruptcy and the Rutland toward total abandonment. It was said that George Alpert, violin-playing president of the New Haven, and Pat McGinnis, who had gone to the Boston & Maine after Alpert helped oust him from the New Haven, couldn't tolerate each other. One *New York Times* "Wall Street observer" wondered, "How are these railroads going to sit down and work out a merger when they can't even work out the freight charges between them on a bushel of potatoes?"[24] Nevertheless, the Portland gathering put Spencer Miller in charge of a committee to study consolidation and hire consultants if need be.

Even by the time of the "outer seven" and New England conferences, the rumor was rife that New York Central was no longer interested in merger. Perlman was still wearing his "merge" button, but otherwise seemed strangely silent. Then, on January 8, 1959, he said simply that he thought merger would be unwise at that time, although coordination short of merger might be worth looking into. "Before we marry the girl," he said a few days later, "we want to make sure there is no other heiress around that might fall into our lap." The "outer seven" and New England talks abruptly ended. Perlman proposed that all eastern railroads get together and plan a series of rational mergers. *Trains* thought the idea was statesman-like. "Railroad merger talk to date has been remarkable for its disregard for industry-wide implications."

Some thought Perlman was just weaseling out of a merger in which he and his company would play second fiddle. If that seemed selfish, Central thought the Pennsy was downright grasping. After the deal was off, Pennsylvania said it was not interested in coordination short of merger no matter what the savings might be, which implied it was never as interested in savings as in getting the Central. Perlman said the merger was the Pennsylvania's idea in the first place, James Symes had been its only real protagonist, and the Pennsylvania people had badgered him about it ever since.

9

What bothered Perlman was the way he thought the Pennsylvania had tried to force his hand. Norfolk & Western was the Pennsylvania's satelite in the coal fields. Many railroaders, including Perlman, thought the Pennsylvania controlled the N&W, although the Pennsylvania denied it. Central did not have a satellite in the coal fields, but it had a friendly connection, the Virginian. Just after the New Year holiday, Perlman got word that N&W and Virginian were going to merge. He was furious and was sure the Pennsylvania was behind it.[25]

The N&W-Virginian merger has usually been treated as textbook-perfect. Both roads went from the coal fields of West Virginia to tidewater at Hampton Roads. Both crossed three mountain ranges. The Virginian had better grades over the Allegheny and the Blue Ridge, while the N&W had better grades over Elkhorn Mountain. If connections were built at Roanoke and Kelleysville, West Virginia, trains could take advantage of the best grade over all three ranges and helper service on the N&W could be eliminated. If all coal were routed through a single set of piers at Norfolk—in this case, the N&W's Lamberts Point Terminal—the quantity of tonnage would justify the finest of automatic unloading equipment. After combining yards, shops, and executive staffs, merger could save $14 million a year.[26]

The United Mine Workers and every community along the two lines gave hearty endorsement. West Virginia bituminous was used for coking (steel-making) and for steam-generated electric power. There was still a growing demand for it, but it was threatened with oil, gas, waterpower, and perhaps by fuels yet unknown.[27] It was important for these communities and the miners to get the coal to market as cheaply as possible to fore-stall the development of substitutes. Stuart Saunders, the ambitious presi-dent of the N&W, prepared a little pep talk on merger which he delivered before citizens' meetings in school gymnasiums up and down the line. It convinced everyone. It even dispelled lingering doubts by the Virginian's owners, Eastern Gas and Fuel Associates, a subsidiary of Koppers. Vir-ginian had no traffic but coal; linking up with N&W, which did have a general merchandise traffic, would insulate it against a collapse of the bituminous market.

Railroad labor was not so enthusiastic. When Saunders delivered his pep talk to the lawyers for the Railway Labor Executives' Association, he added as a finishing flourish the promise that no railroad man would lose his job as a result of merger. The lawyers asked if he would put that in writing. He said he would have to talk to his lawyers, and scurried out of the room. When he returned, he said yes. The result was the first "attrition agreement." Men whose jobs were rendered obsolete by merger could be transferred to other parts of the system, at company expense, and at no loss of salary. When they retired or died, they would not be replaced. But no man then employed by either road would lose a job.[28] Probably not even Stuart Saunders realized what a major victory labor had won without even going before the ICC or the courts.

The merger was approved October 8, 1959, and work began immediately on the new connections at Roanoke and Kelleysville. A parallel merger was a reality, and Stuart Saunders was a man to watch.

10

On the surface, the Virginian merger seemed to be a smashing success. The ICC was able to demonstrate that it looked favorably on merger. Management, labor, local communities, and even other railroads all seemed to emerge in harmony. Only a few knew the high price that had been paid for that harmony or how it had affected Alfred Perlman. Merger, now more than ever, seemed like the salvation of private railroading.

Yet way down the track, yellow caution lights flickered their warning. Capital sent up one of these messages. In 1960, the Canadian Pacific merged its three subsidiaries in the midwestern United States, the Soo Line, the Wisconsin Central, and the Duluth, South Shore & Atlantic, all under the Soo Line banner. Opposition was minimal, except over the loss of jobs at DSS&A installations on the Northern Peninsula of Michigan. But the price of Soo Line bonds fell abruptly after merger, hardly a vote of con-fidence by investors. Soo Line President Leonard Murray insisted it was because of poor grain harvests brought on by bad weather. If so, the euphoria that was supposed to accompany a merger certainly didn't last long.[29]

Labor sent up its warning. After Ben Heineman left the Minneapolis & St. Louis and won control of the Chicago & North Western, he arranged to buy the railroad properties of the M&StL. (The old M&StL corporation, now an empty shell, restructured itself into a holding company conglomerate, called itself MSL Industries, went primarily into hardware and finished steel products, and was finally bought out by Alleghany Corporation.) Despite the agreements between labor and management, carrying them out required specific "implementing" agreements, which meant that each lodge (local) of each brotherhood (union) had to consent to, among other things, the merging of seniority rosters. The engineers refused to sign and threatened a strike. An eleventh-hour settlement did not disguise the fact that labor might not docilely accept managements' merger decisions.[30]

Shippers sent up a warning. The small M&StL had a legion of loyal shippers on the Albert Lea route, where it connected with the Illinois Central for through service from the Twin Cities to Chicago. Despite the *DT&I* conditions, the North Western effectively closed the Albert Lea route by making sure trains were scheduled to miss the IC connection. Shippers didn't like it and told the Minnesota Railroad and Warehouse Commission.[31] The *DT&I* conditions were ineffectual, and merger had resulted in a deterioration of service contrary to what the railroads said it would do but consistent with what had happened in the past whenever competition was reduced.

The commission sent up a warning. In 1954, the Frisco began to buy stock in the Central of Georgia, intending to seek control. The Alabama and Georgia Public Service Commissions fell in line immediately behind the plan in what would become a familiar pattern for southern political agencies. Only the Illinois Central seemed to object, fearing the disruption of its friendly Central connection at Birmingham. (The IC had controlled the Central before the Central's receivership in the Depression.) With regard to routine economies, the proposal seemed to have merit, especially in light of the Central's demonstrated inability to generate income for capital improvements; therefore, the commission gave its approval in July 1957.

Then there surfaced some unseemly charges that Frisco actually had control before permission was given. It had kept secret the full extent of its purchases. Even as the hearings were in progress, it had borrowed money without revealing the purpose of the loans, and bought Central stock until it had more than 66 percent. Fearing this would be discovered sooner or later, it had put the stock in a trust which the ICC later implied was phony. "The public interest is concerned not only with improvements in transportation service," said the ICC, "but with . . . respect for and observance of the law."[32] The permission for control was revoked.

No matter how some executives may have felt privately about the matter, the commission got little flak over this. It was quite apparent the moment for consolidation had arrived, and it was no time for preemption and piracy among the railroads like there had been in the 1920s, especially not from relative small-fry like the Frisco. When the stakes were high, railroads, like everyone else, wanted the regulators to keep order.

11

"I hear a lot more serious talk these days about merger than I can remember," said *Railway Age* editor Jim Lyne in December 1959. "People doing the talking were not serious advocates of it in the past. The head of a medium-sized road told me he had no enthusiasm for mergers until recently, but changed his mind because the growth of competing transportation was forcing railroads to concentrate traffic on low-cost routes."

John Barriger, veteran of the Prince Plan studies of the 1930s, now a New York Central lieutenant as president of its Pittsburgh & Lake Erie subsidiary, suggested transcontinental systems, like the Canadian National and Canadian Pacific. All the American railroad builders of the nineteenth century thought in transcontinental terms, he said, and were frustrated by accidents, not economics. Consolidation, he said, began in the 1950s as a plan for orderly retreat, but would become an advance in force if pursued according to his plan. He suggested the carriers hold their own "Congress of Vienna" to get the process going.[33]

"What's holding up railway mergers?" asked *Railway Age*. In the *New York Times,* Robert Bedingfield concluded that "when something everyone loudly asserts should be done is not done, there are two possible answers. Either it can't be done, or some of the vocal advocates have their fingers crossed." After a year of talk since the "fuse was lit on Penn-Central, it was as firmly anchored to its launching pad as when it started." The usual process in mergers, he said, was "dramatic announcement, long 'study' and nothing."[34]

If anyone expected the Doyle Report to cut through the fog, they were in for a disappointment. It called for national planning but said no carrier should be forced to do anything it did not want to do.[35] For anyone who had been around since the Transportation Act of 1920 that seemed to have a familiar ring. Edward Hungerford's fiction had been more perceptive than that.

As the new decade began, consolidation was long on talk and short on action. Erie and Lackawanna had a proposal in the regulatory works. The others were still huddling late over lunches and dinners. Ten years later, the structure of American railroading would be unrecognizable.

CHAPTER 5

Erie Lackawanna, The Ideal Merger That Didn't Work; 1960

There were smiles up and down the Erie and Lackawanna railroads in the early autumn of 1960. The ICC had approved the long-awaited merger. Presidents Von Willer and Shoemaker smiled as they shook hands for cameras in front of a giant wall map of the newly created empire. Erie fireman Truman G. Knight smiled as he received 20 shares of Erie Lackawanna stock, his prize for designing the company's new diamond-shaped emblem. Painter Harold Johnson smiled as he applied the new emblem to the nose of an Erie diesel. Passenger agents smiled as they gathered to design the new timetable. Freight agents smiled at the unveiling of the new gray-and-maroon boxcars. It was front-page news in the *New York Times* and in papers throughout the system. In that fleeting moment the future seemed bright. Two companies with long but different histories, well-run despite growing adversity, honestly hoped that by joining together they could overcome their weakness and be strong again. This was private enterprise at its best, run not by profiteers but by technocrats who believed in the railroad, who sensed a public as well as a private duty, and mobilized the meager resources at their command to save their companies and help all railroading.

Two weeks later, labor got a temporary restraining order to stop any substantive changes in operations pending a settlement of grievances. The company could go ahead and call itself Erie Lackawanna and display the new emblem, but otherwise had to remain un-merged for the time being. It was then the smiles began to fade—it was the beginning of the long travail of Erie Lackawanna.

At no time did EL have a silver spoon in its mouth. *Trains*, in giving the merger its blessing, added ominously that "it was like a man in a leaky boat lending a hand to a man in shark-infested waters."[1] Ultimately, the promised economies of merger were not real, and merging a weak railroad into another weak one, even though they were parallel, did not produce a strong one. The story of Erie and Lackawanna showed exactly why consolidation was not going to work, why it was no panacea.

1

The Erie was familiar with poverty. It was completed across southern New York State in the 1850s, financed on a shoestring that plunged it into bankruptcy in 1857. The infamous Erie Ring of Drew, Fisk, and Gould milked its profits and watered its stock in the seamiest business scandal of the robber-baron age and plunged it into a second bankruptcy in 1875. Depressions in the 1890s and again in the 1930s forced it to insolvency twice more, until it was called the Scarlet Woman of Wall Street. It used to be said that when Erie common paid a dividend, hell would freeze over.

It went from New York to Chicago missing every major city in between, except over branches. The smaller cities it served shared the same relationship to Buffalo and Pittsburgh, say, as the Erie did to the New York Central and the Pennsylvania. Therefore, between the Erie and the people of its region there developed a certain warmth in adversity. Perhaps that was why, despite its financial problems, Erie was a well-maintained property, a railroad man's railroad, with an army of loyal followers of which few private enterprises could boast. The volumes of unsolicited letters by individuals to the ICC about the merger, offering advice and help (many of them remarkably anti-Lackawanna) attested to this.[2] "Erie was a funny old road," said Edward Hungerford in his *Men of Erie*, "but once folks got to know it, they rather liked it."

The Delaware, Lackawanna & Western, once upon a time, was rich. That was the salient fact of its history. It had so much money that when a curve was too sharp or a gradient too steep, miles of track would be ripped out to make it perfect.[3] The fortune came from anthracite (and until the commodities clause forced a divestiture in 1911, much of it was produced in the railroad's own mines). In its heyday before World War I, Lackawanna regularly paid dividends of 20 percent, and in 1909, dividends plus Christmas bonuses resulted in an incredible 50 percent. Its technological excellence made it a strong competitor for general merchandise and passengers against the entrenched likes of the New York Central. In 1903, it dressed a beautiful young lady in Gibson-girl finery, all of it sparkling white, and put her on the train to Buffalo. The point was that she could ride all day and not get her pretty outfit full of soot because only Lackawanna locomotives burned expensive anthracite.

> Said Phoebe Snow about to go
> Upon a trip to Buffalo:
> "My gown stays white from morn to night
> Upon the Road of Anthracite."

Forever after, she symbolized the aristocratic elegance that was the soul of Lackawanna.

"I won my fame and wide acclaim
For Lackawanna's splendid name."

Lackawanna trains departed from an enormous ferry and rail terminal on the Hoboken waterfront, then barreled through multiple-track tunnels under the Palisades and headed for the Hackensack River, Newark, and the West beyond. Not far from the Palisades Tunnel, they crossed the main line of the Erie, at that point just a mile from its terminal in Jersey City. From there to Binghamton the two roads took different ways around the mountains, the Lackawanna heading squarely for the anthracite fields, the Erie sticking pretty much to New York State along the Delaware and Susquehanna Rivers. After Binghamton, for seventy miles to Corning, the roads were parallel, sometimes adjacent, until the Lackawanna turned north to Buffalo and the Erie continued its meandering course to Chicago.

In the Depression, Erie and Lackawanna came to have more in common than similar routes. They both shared excessive debt which depression earnings could not support, and both had to be reorganized. For Erie, there was no choice; a sudden downturn in revenue in 1937 plus a maturing bond issue put it in the courts. The reorganization, which lasted until 1941, cleaned up a hodgepodge of debt issues that dated back to the nineteenth century and replaced them with three main series of bonds, the first not due until far-off 1964. To compensate the old bondholders, they were given 80 percent of the new common stock, which wiped out the Chesapeake & Ohio's control that dated to Van Sweringen days. The C&O fought to hold the Erie and even hired a young consultant by the name of William Wyer to do a study of consolidating the two roads. The study showed consolidation would be worthwhile, but the creditors wanted compensation now, not vague promises of a merger later.[4] Banker Henry Sturgis helped spurn the C&O, and when it was all over, was so proud of what he had done that he wrote a booklet praising the 29 percent reduction in Erie funded debt. But Erie still had one of the highest debt-per-mile figures in the country, a fault that four reorganizations had been unable to correct.[5] The sins of past management would be visited unto their heirs and help wreck railroad consolidation in the Northeast.

Lackawanna was never forced to receivership, but its new president in 1941, William White, recognized that unless fixed charges were reduced, every bit of net income would go for debt service with nothing left for modernization. It was not easy to convince the owners of Morris & Essex stock, for example, whose dividends were guaranteed at 7 percent in the bygone days of wealth, to take in its place DL&W bonds at a lower rate of interest. White was able to jawbone and twist arms, but Lackawanna retained the highest debt-per-mile of any major road.[6] For a prospective merger partner, it was not an attractive dowry.

However incomplete, the reorganizations enabled both roads to begin the postwar era with a relatively clean slate. Erie was able to dieselize quickly after the war; a steamer in mainline service was rare after 1949. With its roadbed in superlative condition, it was able to attract high-rate traffic, notably merchandise and perishables, most of it long-haul, Chicago to New York. It claimed to deliver more western perishables to New York markets than any other railroad. It pruned its passenger service (Rochester Division service ended during the war; Buffalo Division service in 1951) but what it kept was lovely, a service that remained popular with people on New York's southern tier long after the Thruway had decimated the New York Central's *Great Steel Fleet*. Erie was paying dividends now, and its bonds were selling close to par. To celebrate its centennial in 1951, it sent a special train all over the system, which included the original train that made the inaugural run in 1851 (including the flatcar on which Daniel Webster had perched in a rocking chair to better view the engineering wonder). Erie was happy to have the public inspect it that year, for it was a company with a great sense of tradition that was doing an honest job of being a good railroad. One could stand beside the polished rails of its double-tracked mainline that gently curved through the river valleys of southern New York, and watch train after train of refrigerator and boxcars, each led by a sparkling black-and-yellow four-unit diesel. It was riding at the peak of its fortunes and seemed to have adjusted well to the postwar age.

At about ten o'clock each morning during the 1950s, a crowd used to gather at the Lackawanna Terminal in Buffalo to wait for the departure of the day train to New York, the streamliner *Phoebe Snow*.[7] *Phoebe* was still new, and a very beautiful train at that, favored by many travelers over its principal rival, the *Empire State Express* on the New York Central, because of its earlier departure. A ticket to New York on the *Phoebe* cost $14.99, less than half the cost on American Airlines. The crowd, at least on summer holidays, might number upwards of 250 or 300. From the windows of that train a passenger saw a railroad that looked to be doing well in the fat years of the mid-fifties; if he was observant, however, he could see the terrible, insoluble problems that lurked beneath the surface.

The terminal building was a monument to the extravagances of an earlier day, its cavernous immensity a bit embarassing when contrasted to its diminishing usefulness. The sweeping marble staircases that led to the second-story concourse, the seventy-five foot ceilings, magnificent in their decadence, symbolized the drafty discomforts of a bygone day. Fourteen trains on three railroads still used it. Over on track 5, the B&O local to Pittsburgh prepared to head down the mainline of the old BR&P, its steam locomotive wheezing quietly in the murky shed. On tracks 1 and 2, a collection of Nickel Plate head-end cars and coaches were being serviced, but the next blue-and-silver Nickel Plate train was not due until noon, as no connection was scheduled for the eastbound *Phoebe*.

But on this summer morning, there were waving hands, farewells, and then the familiar "all aboard." *Phoebe Snow* began its daily passage—past the Michigan Avenue tower that controlled the throat of the terminal, past the flour mills of Pillsbury and General Mills, and low on the horizon, the smokestacks of Republic and Bethlehem Steel. Past rank after rank of Buffalo row houses, the German, Polish, and Italian neighborhoods of the east side, then through the East Buffalo Yard, here and there a piggy-back trailer car, but still lots of hopper cars emblazoned "Lackawanna—Road of Anthracite." Rolling eastward across the dreary fields of Erie County, four railroad mainlines, the Central, the Lehigh, the Lackawanna, and the Erie, were parallel, underused, and all headed for the same destination. The Erie would shortly drop out of sight to the south, but the Lacka-wanna would still be close to the other two until it turned south at East Bethany.

Now the *Phoebe* was on the heavily ballasted speedway, built to the old Lackawanna's exacting standards, hitting a steady 70 mph. The citizens of Leicester, New York, said every building in town shook as the *Phoebe* passed, but on board there was only a low rumble of steel wheels on highly polished rails and nary a vibration to disturb the reader of *Collier's* or *Look*. On the westbound track, a long train of salt cars passed, headed from the Retsof Mines to the electrochemical plants at Niagara Falls. The train slowed on the steep grades out of Dansville as it crested from the Genessee to the Cohocton valley, but by Wayland, it was back at 70 mph. Here, in 1943, a crowded wartime *Lackawanna Limited* going the same speed behind a mighty Pocono-class 4-8-2 struck a switch engine and thirty-three had perished in the scalding wreckage.

The dining car opened at Bath. There was normally a long line, so it was wise to heed an early call. Welsh rarebit was a luncheon specialty. At Corning, the train swung over the Erie on a curving overpass, then passed the immense glass works. From here to Binghamton, the two lines were parallel, sometimes adjacent, sometimes on opposite banks of the Chemung River. Frequently along here the *Phoebe Snow* would race the *Erie Limited*, its gray-and-maroon diesels pacing the green-and-yellow units of the Erie mile-for-mile along the convolutions of the river bank.

Every hour or so the smooth glide of the *Phoebe* was interrupted by the rush of a train in the opposite direction. South of Mount Morris, the *Owl* passed, a long mail train with a coach and a sleeper, bound for a noon arrival at Buffalo. The HB-5 passed somewhere near Corning, with ba-nanas, merchandise, and piggyback out of Hoboken. Next came HB-7, what railroad men called a junk train, with many empties and a lot of cement. Closer to Binghamton, three long merchandisers passed in rapid succession, bound mostly for Nickel Plate and Wabash connections at Buffalo. The BB-3 was from New England, off the Delaware & Hudson at Binghamton. Most of SB-3 was from the Jersey Central at Taylor Yard near Scranton. The HB-9 was about half from the Hoboken docks and half from New England via the Lehigh & Hudson River Railway at Port Morris, New Jersey. Lackawanna was running sixteen scheduled redball freights, plus numerous extras, and eight passenger trains each way on the mainline, with heavier freight and passenger traffic east of Scranton. Piggyback was just coming in, and after the favorable ICC rulings in 1954 the increased volume of this business was noticeable at trackside.

In the autumn, the valley below Corning was flushed with color, and through the winter blizzards, crowded *Phoebes* brought Christmas home-comers to Waverly and Owego, but there was not a great deal of industry until the Endicott-Johnson City-Binghamton corridor. Cars were added here, two from the local that came down from Syracuse and one or two for the crowds expected at Scranton and Stroudsburg. At Great Bend, east of Binghamton, the train turned south into the mountains, going slower now for the grades were steep. Freights needed helpers through here, but the scenery was lush. In the tavern-observation car at the rear of the train, beneath a portrait of the original *Phoebe Snow* as she looked in 1903, Phelan Goree might serve up a highball to pass the pleasant afternoon hours, just as he would on that gloomy Sunday after Thanksgiving 1966, when the *Phoebe Snow* made its final passage into the mountains.

There was always a breathless interruption in the afternoon's conversation as the train crossed the Nicholson Viaduct, perhaps the most beautiful multiple-arch concrete bridge in the world. Villagers at Nicholson, Pennsylvania, in the valley below said the bridge pervaded their whole life, its rumbling trains beckoning their children away from the coal country forever. This was the anthracite region, and it was not doing well. Scranton looked poor, even from the first glimpse of the city as the train swung around Nay Aug mountain. Anthracite was dying, and even a small manufacturing revival, like the new Capitol Records factory, had not seemed to change things. East of Scranton was the Pocono resort country—Mount Pocono, Pocono Summit, and Stroudsburg. In the springtime New Yorkers liked to ride this train to view the dogwood blossoms and the snow-fed creeks. Then came the scenic climax of the trip, the Water Gap, where the Delaware River broke through the mountains and the train crossed into New Jersey.

As afternoon shadows lengthened, the train rumbled down the old Morris & Essex. After Dover, there was electric catenary over the tracks and the first of many commuter trains passed. Electrification of the suburban district was bravely pushed to completion in 1931, just as the Depression closed in, the final engineering feat of the old Lackawanna. Farther on, the stations were more frequent, the posters of the current Broadway hits, *South Pacific* and *Kiss Me Kate*, a blur in the gathering dusk. Many passengers detrained at Summit in the heart of the suburbs, while most others were restless after a long day. No freights here; they were on the Boonton line several miles to the north. Residential suburbs faded into industrial parks; sidings branched off into manufacturing plants, many of them new, the result of the railroad's effort to recruit new industry. Then, the last leg of the journey through the dingy expanses of Newark, the Hackensack River, and the Jersey Meadows, a hellish swamp and dump ringed by the belching smokestacks of one of the nation's most intensely industrialized areas. Finally, the Palisades Tunnel and Hoboken.

Most of *Phoebe's* passengers hurried to the far side of the station for the ferry to take them across the Hudson. It was a pleasant time to travel eastbound; the crowds of commuters were on the westbound boats. It was always quiet on the water, a breeze whipping up from the harbor, the sun in the west casting a reddish glow on the city skyline, which in the distance seemed devoid of humanity. Freight car floats plowed in and out of the Lackawanna slips carrying a final cut of cars for HB-3, the fast overnight manifest, due out for Buffalo at 8 P.M. At the trans-Atlantic piers on the Manhattan shore, the usual complement of liners was in dock. If this were a lucky day, perhaps some of the new ones would be there—the *Flandre* of the French Line, the *Andrea Doria* of the Italian Line, or the *United States*. In little more than a decade, these ships, the Hoboken ferries, and the *Phoebe Snow* would all be gone. For the moment, it was the most memorable way one could choose to arrive at the nation's greatest city.

During the second week of August 1955, tropical Hurricane Connie swept much farther north than usual, battered the Jersey shore, and saturated the ground. A second storm, Diane, had followed Connie northward, sliced briefly into the Carolina coast, and returned to sea. On Wednesday, August 19, the sun shone brightly across most of New Jersey, although by noon, a heavy cumulus bank appeared over the Delaware Valley. It began to rain at Trenton shortly after noon, and hard rain was soon falling in a wide arc around New York City from Asbury Park to Newport, Rhode Island. The torrent continued unabated into the night. Even by late afternoon, water was sweeping down the Pocono hillsides, the saturated ground unable to hold it. Mountain streams left their banks, and the Delaware began to rise ominously. In the middle of the night, the people of northeastern Pennsylvania bundled up themselves and their families to flee their homes and seek higher ground.

East of Tobyhanna at about 7:00 P.M. a trackside signal flashed red for Lackawanna train 44, the afternoon local from Binghamton to Hoboken. Unknown to the engineer and the eighty-nine passengers, the track was already washed out both ahead of and behind the train. At Cresco, Pennsylvania, the engineer of the *Twilight*, westbound out of Hoboken, noticed the sporadic operations of the signals, and at 8:00 P.M., with visibility zero and sections of the track under water, stopped his train to await orders while his 235 passengers bedded down as best they could as the rain pounded the silent cars. Early the next morning, the railroad announced that all service on the mainline east of Binghamton was suspended indefinitely. President Shoemaker and Chief Engineer Bush flew by helicopter over the disaster area and discovered the worst. Seventy-five miles of the mainline were obliterated. An order for 3,000 tons of rail went to Bethlehem Steel, which gave it the emergency designation "rights above everything."[8]

On August 22, the *Phoebe Snow* picked its way into Scranton over temporary trackage, but it was a month before normal operation was resumed. Lackawanna lost $5 million in revenue and paid $8.5 million for rehabilitation. No money was borrowed; it was paid entirely out of cash on hand. Like a disease-ravaged patient, it left the road vulnerable to the slightest economic infection. Still, it was nothing that time could not heal—say, five solidly prosperous years. The year 1956 was a good one. Revenue was up 8 percent, ton miles climbed above the Great Lakes region average, anthracite revenue was up 7 percent, bituminous up 9 percent, merchandise up 8 percent, passengers up 7 percent. Net income was $5.5 million.

After that, however, everything began to go wrong. In 1957, a long cement strike cut bulk loadings and a longshoremen's strike closed the Port of New York for most of February. Refunding the Morris & Essex bond issue strained credit; another $5.5 million had to be found to replace the Hackensack River Bridge where the Army Corps of Engineers found a faulty foundation. The St. Lawrence Seaway opened in 1958, threatening all traffic through the New York port, and anthracite tonnage declined precipitously as the conversion to oil and gas was nearly complete. Most seriously, there was recession. Ton miles were only 68 percent of their post-war high, and there was a $4 million deficit at the end of the year. In 1959, a prolonged steel strike helped send the deficit to $4.5 million. Like a caged animal, Lackawanna struck out at its tormentors. After wage increases in 1958, it pared employment to a subminimum, creating bad morale. It angrily intervened in a Mohawk Airlines application for increased mail pay.[9] Syracuse passenger service was discontinued and two Buffalo trains were combined. On December 8, it advised New Jersey authorities that it "would move as quickly as a statistical case could be prepared to eliminate commuter service on the electric line."[10]

Over on the Erie, the decade was ending almost as badly. Hurricane Diane had inflicted only moderate damage, while anthracite had never been important and its loss not felt so dearly. But recession cut into the high-rated merchandise traffic on which Erie depended. The steel strikes in 1956 and 1959 were disastrous, as were rising production costs in the rubber industry which were causing it to decentralize out of Akron. Erie reported its first deficit since the depression in 1957. The next year its executives took a pay cut of 10 percent.[11] (Lackawanna, with younger, more mobile management, felt such a move would hasten the departure of its most talented men, and hesitated for over a year to make a similar cut.)

Despite hard times, all amenities were not dropped. Erie, for example, still brought long strings of commuter coaches up to Buffalo or Rochester on autumn weekends for the ever-popular rambling excursions through the colorful countryside, the long conga lines of happy revelers snaking past the gin-spiked watercoolers as the trains rumbled and swayed over the Buffalo Division.[12] Management remained innovative. Lackawanna experimented boldly with guaranteed rates (on crushed stone moving from Janesville to Vestal, New York, for the manufacture of asphalt) and on Plan V piggyback, which established joint rates with truckers and allowed delivery beyond the railroad terminal.

2

The boldest innovation was coordination. Back during the short recession of 1954, Erie and Lackawanna had agreed on two projects—joint use of a single passenger terminal on the Hudson River and joint use of seventy miles of mainline trackage in southern New York State. In the good years that followed, the details of these projects, both fraught with possible misunderstanding, were worked out with remarkable smoothness. When bad times returned at the end of the decade, coordination was living proof that partial salvation lay in plant reduction.

Lackawanna's Hoboken Terminal was an elaborate affair, with eighteen tracks, ferries to Barclay and Cortlandt streets in Manhattan, buses to the Port Authority Bus Terminal near Times Square, and tube trains to Hudson Terminal in the financial district and near Penn Station. There were restaurants, a newsstand, and a delicatessen. A half-mile away, in Jersey City, the Erie operated a similar but less pretentious facility, a wooden building with only a bar and a newsstand, with ferries to Manhattan but fewer buses and no tube trains.

A study determined the Hoboken Terminal could handle all of the Lackawanna's 292 daily trains plus the Erie's 154, with an average of 85,000 passengers a day. Similarly, the Lackawanna ferries could absorb the Erie traffic, for unlike the Erie boats, they could unload two decks at a time, greatly reducing turnaround time. The necessary changes in track connections would cost $2,211,956, but the estimated *annual* savings were $2,297,594.[13]

Over on the Manhattan side, the ferry terminals of the two railroads were only about 1,000 feet apart, so no one was really going to be inconvenienced. The ICC noted that joint terminals were frequently a source of friction, not often used without the buffering device of a terminal or union station company. But the need for savings was controlling. The first

Erie Limited from Chicago entered Lackawanna Terminal on October 13, 1956.[14]

There were greater pitfalls to coordinating mainlines. Of the many miles of parallel trackage in the United States, only a small amount was shared. Trackage right, the arrangement whereby one railroad permitted another to use a segment of its track, was fairly common for short distances, but even there, the room for misunderstanding was great. The Wabash, whose line from Detroit to Buffalo was on trackage rights over the Canadian National, and which carried 30 percent of Wabash's traffic, was the exception. The chance an owning road might choose to harass a tenant was great, which led railroaders to talk more about coordination than to actually do something about it. Back in the 1920s, for example, the C&O had used rights over the N&W between the Ohio River and Columbus, but N&W had seen fit to delay trains or reschedule them arbitrarily until C&O was finally forced to pull out and build its own parallel line.

In spite of this, the decision to coordinate was irresistible. The only major expense was the installation of a common signaling system, which amounted to a one-time cost of $816,000 for each road. The annual savings were expected to be $488,000 for a first-year return of 66 percent. In addition, tearing up one of the lines would yield salvage of $2.3 million. Admittedly, the multi-page contract gave a glimpse of the dangers that were inherent, filled with minute detail on the sharing of expenses and liability, and even then it was suggested a great deal was left to good faith.

An immediate problem was the selection of a route. In many ways, the Lackawanna was the superior line. It was newer, and because of that usually skirted the perimeter of towns while the Erie went right through their center. The Erie was two miles longer, and was built, for the most part, parallel to U.S. Highway 17 along a geologically unstable bank of the Chemung River. However, most local industry was on the Erie, and that settled it. Opposition in the city of Elmira was intense, mostly out of fear that doubling traffic on a line close to commercial and residential areas would destroy property values and endanger school children. Pathetic letters came from small businesses close by the Erie mainline, the Foothills Motel, the Del Motel, the State Line Cabins, and the Paramount Diner and Night Club. They fully expected that trains rumbling all night would wipe out their little investments. The railroad said that sixty trains a day would use the line, fourteen of them fast passenger trains—less than either line had handled during the war. That raised another question—what if there were another war? The railroad said that would be no problem—trains could run on a five-minute headway, which only served to further aggravate those near the tracks.

Regardless, the ICC gave its approval.[15] It was 1958 now, and the Lackawanna was having a hard time coming up with the cash to make the change.

But on August 31, 1959, the last train over the old Lackawanna, #15 (the westbound *Owl*), arrived at Corning at 9:42 A.M., and two years of planning culminated in a major coordination project. Once those tracks were gone, there was no going back, whether someday those companies merged, or whether they remained forever in rival camps. Within a year, some hardy weeds had taken root in the DL&W roadbed. Where once the *Erie Limited* and *Phoebe Snow* had raced, all was quiet.

Two points had been made, however. First, the *most* important coordination projects could be done short of merger, despite later protestations of railroad officers. Second, even the most obviously duplicating facilities did affect innocent parties outside of railroading, and it was not going to be easy to determine which vested interest ought to have its way.

3

After 1956, talk of merger eased the path of coordination. The taste of early savings whetted the appetite for more. Joining with the Delaware & Hudson, the three railroads retained Wyer, Dick and Company of Upper Montclair, New Jersey, to determine what savings were possible from a three-way consolidation. Wyer was a veteran of the Prince Plan studies back in the 1930s and had turned to independent consulting in 1938. Known as a troubleshooter for sick railroads, he served briefly in top executive posts on the Jersey Central and the Long Island. As one of the few firms capable of merger studies, Wyer did not come cheap—$250 a day, double for court appearances. It took two years to study physical plants and traffic patterns, but when the report was finished early in 1959, it looked so good that managements could hardly wait to conclude the deal. Then the recession hit Erie and Lackawanna hard, leaving D&H relatively unscathed. William White sensed the trouble ahead and brought in financial consultants, the First Boston Company, to see if a three-way exchange were possible.

When it was all over, Harry Von Willer said, "We knew First Boston was having a hard time coming up with an answer, but no one expected a wholly negative report."[16] But negative it was. There was Erie with twice the gross revenue of Lackawanna, nearly three times the D&H, yet less than one-twelfth of D&H's net income. By 1959, Erie and Lakawanna common had skidded to half their 1956 highs, while D&H was unaffected. The only formula First Boston could suggest gave D&H stockholders 67 percent of the merged company, Erie 27 percent, and Lackawanna 13 percent. It was certain that neither Erie nor Lackawanna stockholders would approve, and in the second week of April 1959, the three-way merger just fell apart. The statement given to the press was terse—unspecified "adverse conditions." Harry Von Willer said more publicity might hurt future possibilities for merger. "The mere fact that three railroads tried to merge and found it wasn't feasible from a financial standpoint didn't need to be advertised,'' he said.[17]

Anticipating what was coming, Erie and Lackawanna asked Wyer to extract figures from his report to see what advantages there would be to a two-way merger, excluding the D&H. He was instructed to keep the cost of consummating merger to a minimum, and so plans for a new general office building in New Jersey, an electronic hump yard at Binghamton (impractical without the D&H), and an insurance subsidiary to handle all company insurance were omitted. This was called the "Quickie" report, and the decision to merge was made on that.[18]

This was only a week after the unpleasant meeting in the offices of First Boston. On the night of April 21, 1959, business cars were attached to the rear of train #17, the *Westerner,* and the Lackawanna merger committee began its journey to Cleveland to meet its counterpart on the Erie. All evening, as the train climbed into the Poconos, they planned strategy for the next day. Perry Shoemaker explained that after living side by side with the Erie for so many years, knowing the Erie was twice as large, with twice the revenue and twice the employees, you pretty well expected Erie stockholders to hold twice the stock of the Lackawanna's. The final ratio agreed upon was 65 percent Erie, 35 percent Lackawanna. The meeting in Cleveland lasted all day. No minutes were kept; a few penciled notes by Perry Shoemaker were later destroyed. Erie director John Thompson described it this way:

. . . We didn't develop any formula of 65-35 by taking these various factors and adding them together or anything like that. We had a number of things before us in our discussions. . . . About half a dozen of us were on one side of the table and half a dozen on the other, and we talked about expenses and earnings and where-do-we-go-from-here, and stock prices and all sorts of things. . . . And with a composite of all that discussing and thinking . . . we agreed to the 65-35 relationship.

There was discussion of whether future development would be more in the territory west of Buffalo than east of it. There was discussion of the anthracite coal situation. There was discussion of the possibility of additional traffic because of electric power developments east of Buffalo. Everybody on both sides had the right to bring up whatever he wanted and it was discussed.[19]

Shortly after 6:00 P.M., April 22, 1959, the roads announced to the press they had agreed on terms. On July 1 the formal petition went to the ICC, and by August 6 a full report by Wyer was submitted as the principal exhibit. Stockholders' meetings were held on September 22, and they gave overwhelming approval. The ten largest stockholders of each company, including the New York Central, which held 114,000 shares of Lackawanna, voted unanimously for merger.[20]

Everyone with an interest *pro* or *con*—at least everyone who could afford a lawyer certified to practice before the ICC—gathered at the Hotel Buffalo

on September 29, 1959, as the merger hearings got under way before ICC
examiner Hyman Blond.

4

The first item of business was the presentation of the Wyer Report.[21] It
determined that through merger, Erie and Lackawanna could save $13 mil-
lion *that could not be saved in any other way*. From that point forward, the
$13 million became a magical figure, an *idée fixe*, self-justifying or self-
condemning, depending on one's point of view. The report itself, compiled
from a condensation of working papers and data sheets, was remarkable for
its thoroughness. There were details right down to the savings that would
accrue from supplying less steam heat to waiting Pullman cars when
passenger services were combined—which showed that $13 million was not
going to drop like manna from heaven. Savings were going to come from
many small categories and were going to take an extremely skilled management to realize.

Wyer himself suggested two shortcomings to the study. First, the data on
which it was based was collected in 1956. By the time it was presented, three
years had passed in which there had been radical changes in the nature of
railroad traffic. Second, Wyer's liaisons with the two railroads, the men
appointed to work with the Wyer engineers and supply them with information, were the wise old men, Stanley McGranahan for the Erie and Philip
Jonas for the Lackawanna. When it came time for implementation, they
had retired; there was no one who could interpret the decisions that had
been made.[22]

In another sense, the Wyer Report was unsatisfying. It cited cost figures,
for example, of $1 a mile per 1,000 gross tons for trains on the Erie line
between Hornell and Buffalo, but gave no hint of how that figure was calculated. At major terminals, x crews were to be eliminated and x dollars
saved, but there was no indication of why those crews, or how it was calculated. There were assurances under oath that all this had been carefully worked out. Certainly, the public did not need these details, nor even
the ICC. They were internal matters. But it would have been nice to have it,
to feel it, to know it was there, to know that management knew what it was
doing when it came time to implement the merger. The Wyer Report for
Erie Lackawanna was the prototype on which later merger studies were
modeled. It set a precedent for a showy summary that could either be
honest or easily faked. At this early date, the ICC failed in not demanding
more explicit evidence to justify merger.

The Wyer studies promised their most significant advantages in yard and
terminal consolidation. On the New Jersey waterfront, the Erie's Croxton
Yard would become the principal marshaling point, while a new coal dock
for anthracite could be built on the site of the old Jersey City passenger

station, concentrating all marine operations close by the Hoboken ferry. In Buffalo, the combined traffic of the two railroads would permit the construction of an electronic yard that would get incoming cars onto the proper outgoing tracks at twice the speed, with half the labor, as ordinary yards. This was the kind of yard their competitor, the New York Central, had already installed at Buffalo.

But for all the miles of parallel track that were supposed to be out there waiting for mergers to eliminate them, there wasn't much that could actually be abandoned. West of Binghamton, it was determined that the Erie route to Buffalo (via Hornell) was the low-cost line, but the Lackawanna route through Dansville could only be downgraded (reduced to branchline status) because it served too many on-line industries. Only an Erie branch parallel to the Lackawanna mainline up the Cohocton Valley, a branch the Erie had nearly been allowed to abandon without a merger in 1944, could be dropped.[23] East of Binghamton, there could be no meaningful abandonments or downgradings. The Erie mainline was thought to be the superior for through freight and provided the vital connection to the New Haven Railroad at Maybrook, New York, while the Lackawanna had virtually all the on-line industry, served what was left of the anthracite traffic, and was the superior passenger route. So one of the great justifications of general consolidation came tumbling down.

Another sweet premise of consolidation theory fell through in the Erie case as well. Combining trains to take advantage of the pulling power of the diesel was a great idea, except on these two railroads. Since each scheduled around-the-clock redball freights between New York and Buffalo, less than two round trips per day could be eliminated because most trains were already operating to capacity.

Any notion that one administrative staff could do the work of two, for those naive enough to believe it, was dashed as well. Wyer calculated that no more than 18 percent of the combined staff could be cut. The department to take the most severe cuts was sales, which seemed like a particularly unfortunate one to demoralize.

5

There were three principal adversaries to the Erie Lackawanna merger—labor, other railroads, and a small group of dissenting Lackawanna stockholders, each exhibiting the kinds of obstacles every merger would have to overcome. Aside from what the merging railroads chose to tell the ICC, all that it learned about the merger and those it would help or hurt came from these parties.

We are trying to find employment for people, not unemployment. By this merger, more than 100 men will be out of work regardless of what they promise.

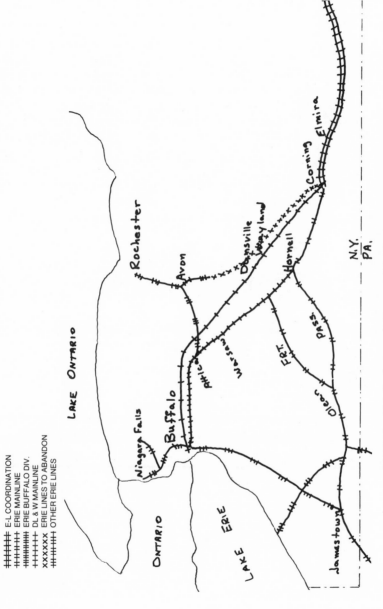

######## E-L COORDINATION
++++++++ ERIE MAINLINE
######## ERIE BUFFALO DIV.
++++++++ DL & W MAINLINE
xxxxxxx ERIE LINES TO ABANDON
######## OTHER ERIE LINES

LAKE ONTARIO

Rochester

Niagara Falls

Buffalo

Avon

Attica

Wyoming

Wassaic

Dansville

Wayland

Hornell

Corning

Elmira

FRT.

Olean

PASS

Jamestown

ONTARIO

LAKE ERIE

N.Y.
PA.

MAP 15: *Erie Lackawanna's Proposed Line Changes in Western New York*

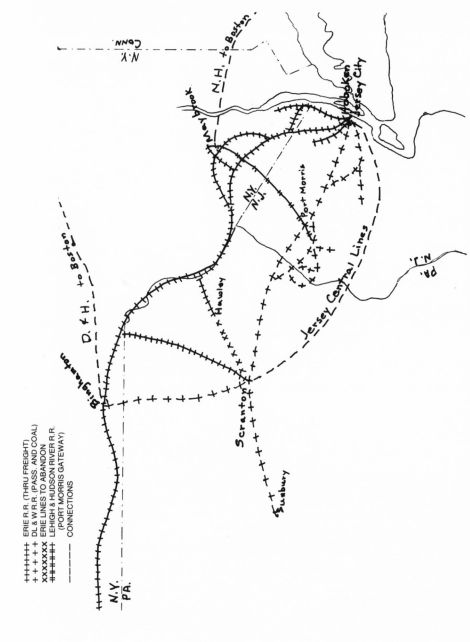

MAP 16:   *Erie Lackawanna's Proposed Line Changes East of Binghamton*

Our country was built around railroads. What should happen . . . if we should have another war . . . with all the railroads that have been taken up. Stations have closed. People stand out in the cold and stormy weather. No way to tell whether trains are late or even running.

Why not let these high salary people take a cut rather than sit in offices and figure out how to take trains off and raise rates. What man is worth $19,000 a year plus a private car and an expense account? I am for the railroads with some good service and reasonable rates. I am not a stormy day passenger. I use the railroads for all my traveling.

Sincerely,
A friend of railroads, but not
of unemployment caused by merger.[24]

That was a voice from the public, to be dismissed at one's peril. The editors of small-town papers took the railroads' word that merger was a good thing and that only shortsighted labor stood in the way, but a good part of the public never believed it. "A friend of railroads" would have been shocked to know that the president of the Erie was getting $103,000, but he knew that merger was retrenchment, and the price of retrenchment was going to be paid by folks like him.

Better than half the projected savings were going to come from labor. No responsible person was insisting that useless jobs should be preserved, but there was legitimate disagreement over what was useless. Honest people had taken honest jobs in good faith, jobs that had never been called redundant until now. There was a moral problem in using little people as pawns to save big business. Every lost job reduced spending power in a community, and that sent reverberations deep into the bowels of the economy. Railroad employment had become notoriously unstable, falling from 28,103 on the Erie and Lackawanna in 1956, for example, to 23,002 in 1958, with the junior levels filled essentially by nothing more than floating pickup help. It was little wonder that working people were touchy, and someone who had worked hard for eight hours didn't like to be called useless.

The day was over when these people could simply be cast to the wolves. Assuming a final settlement would be based on the *New Orleans* conditions, Wyer attempted to calculate the cost that would have to be deducted from savings, at least in the first several years after merger. He was not stymied, but the equation had so many variables, the final result could only be regarded as a good guess. Was it really possible to separate job reductions that resulted from merger from those that came from other causes? He could figure with precision the number of crews that were going to be abolished, but he could not guess how many of the men were going to be taken care of by attrition, how many would choose lesser jobs on the railroad, or how many would take lump-sum settlements. In metropolitan areas, where there was a variety of job opportunities, a higher proportion would probably take lump-sum settlements. In railroad towns like Hornell, it would probably be reversed, but he couldn't be sure. Eventually, he came up with a figure of $3 million as the cost of a settlement, less 52 percent for savings in federal income taxes, which left it under $1.5 million.[25]

By the time the hearing began, labor had already won an attrition agreement in the Virginian merger and would have liked to get one here. The two railroads refused, however, for theirs was a different kind of merger. Savings for the Pocahontas roads, already profitable and in top physical condition, would be translated immediately into higher dividends for stockholders. For Erie and Lackawanna, job reductions would permit the capital expenditures to keep the roads competitive, save the jobs that remained, and be the only way to create sound jobs in the future.

However, if labor was supposed to be such a terrible obstacle to consolidation, its opposition in this case was less formidable than dissenting stockholders and much less formidable than other railroads. In the hearing, labor said virtually nothing.

After the hearing, labor's lawyers thought they had found a novel approach to section 5 (2) (f) of the Transportation Act of 1940, the so-called Harrington Amendment governing merger settlements. It said no employees shall be put "in a worse position with respect to their employment." Since 1940, that had been interpreted to mean that compensation would substitute for a job.[26] But on the premise that a job must be provided, labor went to court. Within seven months, the Supreme Court had thrown the premise out, and the *New Orleans* conditions, as traditionally interpreted, governed in the merger. The dissent of Justice William O. Douglas was eloquent and disturbing. This was a minor episode, he thought, in an important chapter of modern history—the effect of technological change upon workers. It was not the first instance, he thought, "of a controversy settled in Congress by the adoption of ambiguous language and then transferred to the courts." But he would resolve the matter in favor of the people:

Many men, at least, are not drones. Their continued activity is life itself. The toll which economic and technological changes will make on employees is so great that they, rather than the capital which they have created, should be the beneficiaries of any doubts that overhang these legislative controversies when they are shifted to the courts.[27]

By Wyer's estimate, only 7.5 percent of the total savings were to come from the diversion of traffic from other railroads. Yet the other railroads were prepared to fight tenaciously for this. Their opposition was formidable because they were always present at the hearings with a battery of lawyers and elaborate exhibits. Though it wasn't advertised that way, money could buy a lot of succor before the commission.

Wyer had analyzed each car separately to determine whether it might be diverted from an old Lackawanna connection at Buffalo to an all-Erie route west, or whether it might be diverted from Erie Lackawanna altogether in retaliation by one of those connections.[28] He concluded that Erie Lackawanna stood to gain a net of $1.3 million in additional revenues, while some other railroads would suffer net losses—a whopping $3.6 million for the Nickel Plate, for example.

The study had been done with a computer, which was rather new then, and everyone was very proud of how up-to-date it was. But it turned out that each car, that is, each computer card, represented a guess, perhaps knowledgeable, perhaps not (no one could check), as to whether a car would be diverted or not. Sometimes a decision rested on nothing more than whose traffic agent was most friendly with a plant's traffic manager. And a guess was a guess, whether it was computerized or not. As computer people say, "garbage in, garbage out." When the other railroads demanded that the cards be rerun through the computer, the tabulations came out differently and there was a blushing explanation that something must have gotten stuck, either the first time around or the second.[29]

Assuming it could not stop the merger, Nickel Plate wanted ironclad guarantees that service would be as good into Buffalo after the merger as it had been before. It had worked hard to develop traffic jointly with the Lackawanna, and to hone that interchange in Buffalo to twenty-eight minutes of split-second railroading, almost as fast as the New York Central could put a train through the city. If traffic were diverted from Buffalo, fewer trains would make the Nickel Plate connection and fewer shippers would choose the Nickel Plate route the next time. Erie and Lackawanna were not going to own up to this and insisted the proposed electronic Bison Yard was proof of their commitment to Buffalo. Everyone knew, however, that the purpose of merger was to rearrange traffic patterns as the controlling railroads saw fit. As the ICC told the Nickel Plate, it was "part of the everyday risk of railroading in highly competitive territory." One question nobody asked: might this trigger retaliatory mergers?

The Wabash and the Lehigh Valley wanted more than a guarantee of service. They wanted to use the proceeding to get trackage rights over Erie Lackawanna in the city of Buffalo so as to improve their connections with each other. Since this was something they couldn't get on their own, it was an example of how a company could use regulation to its benefit. Perry Shoemaker of the Lackawanna and Harry Von Willer of the Erie were summoned to a meeting with Herman Pevler of the Wabash. There they were given an ultimatum: give the trackage rights that would make the Wabash-Lehigh route competitive with Erie Lackawanna or face prolonged

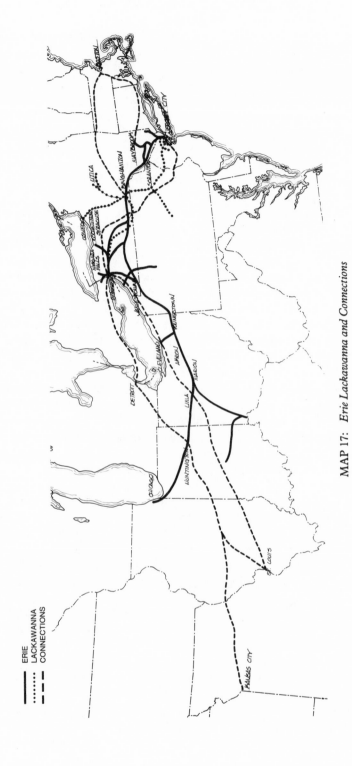

ERIE
LACKAWANNA
CONNECTIONS

MAP 17:   *Erie Lackawanna and Connections*

harassment.[30] When the hearing was over, Shoemaker could barely disguise his rage:

The opposition of the Wabash and Lehigh Valley . . . reflected no credit upon the industry. . . . I know of no precedent for the price of merger being the supplying of property investment to improve a competitor's product, even if it is a product badly in need of improvement. It was a phony issue having no part in the merger proceedings.[31]

Erie and Lackawanna then proceeded to make a deal. On April 26, 1960, in a letter to Shoemaker and Von Willer, Pevler of the Wabash confirmed that the desired trackage had been made available "on terms mutually satisfactory," whereupon the two railroads withdrew from the case. "Both of you know," he added, "that we on the Wabash basically feel your merger is for the good of our whole industry."[32]

In the midst of the hearings, James Symes, president of the Pennsylvania, dropped by to say—officially—how important mergers were for railroading. *Trains* recognized that Symes never did anything without a purpose. It was quite proper, it thought, for a man of his stature to offer theoretical support and give credence to railroad orthodoxy, while his lieutenants who were "close to the cash register" should oppose it.[33] Pevler was one of those lieutenants, for Wabash and Lehigh were both Pennsylvania satellites. The Pennsylvania sphere always seemed to get what it wanted, and this was just the beginning of a mysterious relationship between it and the hapless Erie Lackawanna.

One last obstacle lay in the path of merger—a shadowy group of ten speculators who never appeared at the hearing, whose purpose was never to block the merger but simply to get a better price for their stock. They owned 14,950 shares of Lackawanna common. It was never clear whether they bought stock thinking all the hoopla about merger would make it go up and then discovered they had guessed wrong, or whether they intended from the beginning to use the threat of litigation to blackmail the company into paying off. Commission files were full of pathetic letters from people who had bought DL&W stock back in the glory days of anthracite, when it was a "widow and orphan" issue, who had now lost practically everything. But the ten speculators were not old-line stockholders. "They are new," said Perry Shoemaker after they disrupted the 1960 stockholders' meeting, "and they have as their purpose the harassment of the company."[34] Both the ICC and the courts, where they appealed after the merger was approved, dismissed their case.[35] The following letter in ICC files is self-explanatory:

LACKAWANNA
140 Cedar Street, New York, N.Y.

AUGUST 12, 1959

Mr. *XXXXXX*

You suggested at our meeting that a "deal" could be made, by which you and your associates would withdraw your opposition to the merger of the Erie and the Lackawanna. That "deal," according to you, would involve the purchase by the Lackawanna, or some concealed entity on behalf of the Lackawanna, all of the Lackawanna stock owned by you and your associates at a price based on the average 1956–1957 value, "take a point or leave a point." You stated that for this purpose, your group had about 20,000 shares in Lackawanna stock, and that the purchase could be covered up in some way.

Despite your threats of a suit through retention of an attorney on a contingent fee basis of over $20 per share if the Lackawanna refuses to accede to the foregoing arrangement, I can only repeat what Mr. Shoemaker stated at our meeting: the Lackawanna will not be a party to such a transaction at that or any other price. We do not believe it to be either ethical or legal. With respect to any such suit, I am sure your attorney is aware of *Schwabacher* v. *United States* (334 US 182). Under this case, the appraisal statutes of New York and Pennsylvania are rendered inapplicable to the proposed merger, and if the merger is approved by the necessary vote of the stockholders and by the Interstate Commerce Commission, the terms are binding on all stockholders.

I do not believe that further discussions will serve any useful purpose.

signed: *Rowland L. Davis, Jr.*
VICE PRESIDENT AND
GENERAL COUNSEL.[36]

Since the company would not deal, the speculators engaged a lawyer and sent him off to do battle at the hearing. Day after day, he put company witnesses through grueling cross-examination trying to prove that Lackawanna was worth more than it was getting, and that its management had conspired to sell it off cheaply to the Erie. Nothing seemed to stick. For example, had it not sold off a great deal of real estate—perhaps a plot to cannibalize the railroad? No, it had sold land to General Foods and the Post Office Department and others who built facilities that produced traffic for the railroad.

Questioning that went nowhere got tedious, and the rest of the lawyers, for Erie, Lackawanna, the opposing railroads, and even labor, felt they had more important things to do. Most of them were friends, members of the same country clubs and alumni clubs, who met each other frequently at professional meetings and before the ICC, sometimes working together, sometimes in opposition. They shared a common acknowledgment that what the other was doing was important and were hostile to this intruder who wasted their time. It was not a waste of time, because the speculators' lawyer was getting potentially relevant information on the record that the ICC would never have known about, in case there had been hanky-panky along the way—another reminder that reliance on the adversary system was inadequate and dangerous. It was also an insight into how the regulatory process worked. There were insiders and there were outsiders, and stockholders, among the outsiders, were best neither seen nor heard.

The cross-examination reached its climax over the sudden sale by Lackawanna of its Nickel Plate stock, without warning to its merger partners, on March 2, 1959. At the time, Nickel Plate stock was paying dividends of $1.2 million, and there was speculation that the D&H pulled out of the merger because of the sale. Erie people denied having a hand in the matter, particularly insinuations that it was Erie which, at that moment, needed an immediate infusion of cash. The questioning kept coming back to the point that after the terms of merger were announced, the price of Erie stock pulled ahead of Lackawanna and stayed there, implying the terms favored Erie. Frustrated by the unsubstantiated insinuations and at the end of his patience, Perry Shoemaker finally interrupted the questioning and delivered a moving obituary of eastern railroading in the 1950s:

The purpose of that sale was to make one last desperate effort to put the Lackawanna's financial situation on an even keel before we found ourselves in bankruptcy. I think it is important that you understand the seriousness of our situation. We did not come to the decision to sell the Nickel Plate stock lightly. It was a hard decision to make. It was the last big liquid asset the Lackawanna had.

What was our situation? We had more than $3 million of unpaid bills, some of them several months old. We had suppliers indicating doubt they would continue to to give us material on a credit basis. We had just taken down, on February 1, the last million of our [Hackensack River] bridge loan and were under obligation to have the first million paid back by August 1 of this year, and the income to accomplish it just was not in sight.

We had the normal tax load to meet for this year. We were behind in our tax accounts. Seriously behind. We were not taking advantage of any discounts in the buying of supplies because we couldn't do it. We couldn't pay for them quickly enough to do that.

We were in a very unhappy and serious situation, with no traffic upturn in the immediate prospect to change it quickly. All of these things, together with the realization that we were building up deferred maintenance, the realization that we had already put our supervisory people on a psychologically bad basis, certainly with the pay cuts that went into effect January 1 of this year—all of these things were considered by the board, and we came to the conclusion that we had one opportunity to put our house in order, and that was to dispose of the asset, to clean up our bridge loan, to pay our back bills and to restore our cash position and net working capital.[37]

That was the climax of the hearing and the record on which the commission gave its approval.

6

The merger was a disappointment. When things did not work out the way they were supposed to, the official word was that it would have been much worse if there had been no merger.[38] According to the head of purchasing, Carl F. Bayer, "there were a hell of a lot of things we didn't know until we got into this merger." "We're having our problems," said another executive, "but they may not seem too bad when compared with future mergers."[39]

The recession continued and so did the decline in traffic. Then the blizzards set in; the trains were late and the plowing costly. Little things kept cropping up that no one had thought of. Erie locomotives, for example, used electric devices to spray sand under the wheels, while Lackawanna units used pneumatic devices, which meant that motive power could not be mixed. And so the two fleets began to mingle, but individual units had to be kept separate; it was a headache and it was expensive. Said the *Wall Street Journal,* "almost to a man, Erie Lackawanna department heads concede pre-merger planning was inadequate."

Labor gave management a convenient excuse to shroud its shortcomings with the litigation that delayed consummation of the merger. But seniority rosters had to be merged and rates of pay equalized. What about men transferred from one division to another—how much seniority could they take with them? All of this had to be worked out with the local lodges. It was not until February that agreements were signed with most of the unions, and until those agreements were made, no real changes could have been made anyway. By holding up the merger, labor may have saved the company a terrible debacle by making sure it did not plunge into physical changes without laying the necessary groundwork. As it was, a number of employees had to resort to the ICC with grievances, as both company and union were too preoccupied. The nakedly bureaucratic replies they received must have been disheartening.[40]

The true dimension of the problem was revealed by the fiasco in the accounting department. All revenue accounting was to be handled by the former Erie offices in Cleveland, all disbursements by former Lackawanna offices in Scranton. But in Scranton, the Lackawanna's revenue and disbursement clerks were all on the same seniority roster. For those revenue clerks to move to Cleveland would mean a substantial loss of seniority, so they bumped junior disbursement clerks and stayed in Scranton. Shortly after merger, 70 percent of all disbursements were being handled by inexperienced people, and the bungling was incredible. Bills went unpaid. One New Jersey trucker had to call Perry Shoemaker personally to get the $110,000 the company owed him. "Nothing but time will cure our accounting problems," said Eugene Root, the comptroller. The same thing happened in locomotive repair. All shopwork was to be concentrated at the former Erie shops in Hornell, and 75 skilled mechanics were to be transferred from former Lackawanna shops in Scranton. But only a fraction of them decided to move and while there was a shortage of qualified men at Hornell, others were getting unemployment benefits in Scranton. Under the circumstances, morale did not hold up well.

Morale was poor in the executive suite, too. Few arrangements had been made in advance as to which man would fill each post. Without security, many of the best men left as soon as they had a good offer elsewhere. Lackawanna traffic manager William G. White, for example, left in advance of merger for a post at Consolidated Freightways. Rowland Davis, its general counsel who had brilliantly guided the merger through the regulatory process, left immediately after merger. All executives took a 10 percent pay cut in January 1961, their second in two years. There was never enough rivalry between former Erie people and former Lackawanna people to attract public attention, as would later happen with the Penn Central. But Perry Shoemaker, the logical successor to Harry Von Willer, was passed over in favor of another Erie man, Milton McInnes. Erie men were in charge of most departments. When things began to go sour, however, Shoemaker did move up to the chairmanship and Lackawanna men took over key departments. Then Shoemaker resigned to become president of the Jersey Central, taking a 30 percent pay cut, which implied his departure was not under the happiest of circumstances.[41] Thus, when skilled, experienced management was most needed, there was nothing but instability.

Even some of the key recommendations of the Wyer Report did not work out. It turned out, for example, that the Erie route from Binghamton to Jersey City was not the best route for through freight (although part of its attractiveness was lost when the Maybrook interchange with the New Haven collapsed, an event the planners could not have foreseen). By that time, however, the Lackawanna's Secaucus Yard had been abandoned in favor of the Erie's Croxton Yard, and trains coming down the old Lackawanna line could enter Croxton only by a long back-up operation through a tight wye that caused a number of derailments and bottled up the throat of the terminal for long periods. Later, a balloon track was built to turn the trains 180 degrees as they came out of the yard, but derailments were still common.

Traffic diversion turned out to be a wash. Erie was able to garner more traffic for its long haul, but there were complaints from shippers who liked the old service, usually in connection with the Nickel Plate, and resented that EL was making the old routes deliberately unattractive. Norwich Pharmaceuticals at Norwich, New York, for example, had liked the old Lackawanna-Nickel Plate piggyback service, traffic the two railroads had solicited jointly, and became so annoyed at the new EL sales people that they gave the long haul to the New York Central.[42]

The only way the railroad could raise the cash to make the physical altera- tions called for in the Wyer Report was to borrow. A consortium of credi- tors, notably the Mellon National Bank and John Hancock Life, were will- ing to loan $15 million in 5.25 percent collateral trust notes if the ICC would guarantee under the terms of the Transportation Act of 1958. Approval was given and work went ahead on the yard changes at Jersey City and Hornell, the new piggyback ramps at Chicago and Croxton, and the electronic Bison Yard at Buffalo.[43] But operations in 1961 produced a $26 million loss.

The next year, business showed confidence by locating 153 new traffic- producing plants on line, but the operating loss, even as recession abated, came to $17 million. The EL was beginning to show signs of desperation. Maintenance of the freight car fleet was drastically curtailed (14.5 percent of all cars out of service) and rental of off-line cars became a hemorrhage of cash.[44] Shippers, unable to get the proper cars at the proper time, deserted in droves, mostly to Alfred Perlman's lean and traffic-hungry New York Central. Sizable chunks of real estate were being sold and mortgage trustees became so alarmed that they demanded the proceeds be used only for capi- tal improvement. The passenger service was cut to shreds. The Buffalo Ter- minal closed in 1962 and neither sleepers nor diners were operating through from New York to Chicago. All passenger cars were in such a shabby state of repair they were barely operable. The nadir was in 1962 on a pre- Christmas *Erie Lackawanna Limited*—standing room only because there were not enough cars, no food left in the diner, water from leaking toilets flooding the floors, heat failing utterly on this zero-degree Indiana night, some people forced to leave the freezing train to seek the shelter of a hotel, eight hours late into Hornell because of repeated mechanical breakdowns— hardly an edifying performance.

Of the dark forces that were gathering about Erie Lackawanna none was more ominous than the growing encirclement by the Pennsylvania sphere. In March 1960, the first rumors began to circulate that Norfolk & Western, star of the Pennsylvania's empire, was going to take over Wabash and Nickel Plate. A year later, Pennsylvania said it was taking control of the Lehigh Valley. To a frantic Erie Lackawanna, its worst fears were to be realized—the creation of a firm link between the Lehigh and the Lacka- wanna's former Buffalo connections. Interchange between Nickel Plate and

Erie Lackawanna declined precipitously from 150,000 cars in 1960 to 99,000 in 1964, by which time Nickel Plate and Lehigh were operating run-through freight service. For Erie Lackawanna, there was no choice but to seek inclusion for itself within the Pennsylvania sphere. Not only had its own merger been a disappointment, but other mergers were now going to engulf it.

To be included in another merger, it was going to have to make itself attractive, and new leadership at the top seemed to be the first prerequisite. William White, former president of the Lackawanna and former president of the New York Central (until Young ousted him in the proxy fight), was then serving as chairman and chief executive officer of the Delaware & Hudson. The EL people knew him and trusted him and believed he was the man they needed. He was not willing to give up his D&H post. Would the ICC let him assume the chairmanship of EL simultaneously? "I did not seek the position," said White later, "but on Erie Lackawanna's board are old friends and associates who thought I could help them. One doesn't easily refuse a request from those with whom he has always had pleasant relations."[45]

In May 1963, the railroad wanted to take down another loan because there was not enough money in the till to pay daily bills. Somehow, a creditor was found, the New York Teachers' Retirement System, willing to loan the money at 4.75 percent if the ICC would guarantee. White arrived in the meantime and had barely gotten a grip on his office when the ICC announced it would not grant the guarantee because, it said, it saw no way the company could repay. It was a body blow. There were already $2.5 million in unpaid bills. The next month (December 1963) $4.5 million in New Jersey taxes were due and $1.5 million in interest charges. On the next October 1, $11.5 million of Erie Railroad consolidated mortgage bonds were due and default was at more than even odds. If that were not enough, the entire locomotive fleet was rapidly approaching the end of its service life. Diesel units last about 15 years before maintenance becomes uneconomic. Erie and Lackawanna had dieselized early, mostly before 1949, and so a crisis of major proportions was rapidly approaching.[46]

"How would you like to be in the shoes of William White?" asked David Morgan in *Trains.* "Luckless Erie Lackawanna, the problem child of the East . . . is the road for which merger has yet to underwrite a miracle."[47]

Some thought White chose an odd place to start. He ordered the *Phoebe Snow's* old tavern-observation cars out of storage and back into service. The ersatz *Erie Lackawanna Limited* was rechristened the *Phoebe Snow,* the cars were fixed up, and it was made lovely again. It was a master stroke. The train flew the company's flag proudly and the morale of employees, customers, and creditors rallied.

The taxes were paid, though this momentarily drew working capital down to the danger level. Holders of the mortgage bonds (Metropolitan Life and

First National City Bank were the big ones) expressed a willingness to negotiate an extended deadline. Equipment trusts were secured for new cars and
locomotives. The next year, White found a competent lieutenant, Gregory
Maxwell, who took over the presidency under White's chairmanship.

Next, White turned to the most terrible cash drain on the railroad, the
commuter service. Nothing could make it profitable, Perry Shoemaker had
told the ICC, even if every seat on every train were filled.[48] The day was
rapidly approaching when all of it, both the ancient Stillwell coaches on the
Erie lines and the electric installation of the Lackawanna, would have to be
replaced. Raising the capital was beyond the remotest capability of the company. So it began a persuasive campaign to make the State of New Jersey
assume the responsibility it had avoided so long, to either take over this
public service or pay for it.[49] The politicians bellowed, but finally came
through, and this greatly enhanced EL's chances for inclusion in the N&W.
With sufficient funds well spent, honest men were capable of a fine job. In
the blizzard that crippled New York City on Monday, February 11, 1969,
the only commuter line to report a normal schedule in the metropolitan area
was Erie Lackawanna. On Saturday night, when it was apparent the storm
was really settling in, the crews came out voluntarily, on their own time, to
run the trains back and forth over the tracks to keep them clear.[50]

William White turned Erie Lackawanna around. For 1965, it was finally
able to report a net income of $3.8 million; not much, but the first black ink
since 1956. "In mid-1963, when we set for ourselves the goal of getting in
the black in 1965, we knew it would be difficult to accomplish . . . and there
were times in late 1963 and early 1964 when we feared bankruptcy could not
be avoided because the cash available was $1 million less than the bills the
treasury was holding unpaid. We weathered those bad times, and favored by
good business conditions and running a tight ship, the company in 1965
turned a profit. It is a big boost to the morale of our entire staff."[51]

There was a somewhat smaller profit in 1966, too, but tiny profits in the
booming 1960s were an accomplishment only in context. When William
White died suddenly on April 6, 1967, Erie Lackawanna's fortunes never
rode so high again. Shortly afterward, it came peripherally in the sphere of
the N&W, and that will be the subject of a later chapter.

The point was that merger had not really accomplished very much. Certainly it had been no panacea. If there were savings, and there were some,
there were unforeseen expenses and problems which only the rarest of men,
the master manager, was able to pull together. The big savings had been
realized short of merger. But the ICC accepted all the railroads' studies and
claims, never raising questions on its own. When problems developed after
merger, the ICC never investigated to know what questions to ask in the
future that other railroads might profit by the mistakes. So much for the
effectiveness of regulation.

Immediately after the merger, other railroads began delivering cars bound for points on either the Erie or Lackawanna at random, to any point they chose on the merged system. It saved them a few petty dollars to make one delivery instead of two, but it brought the newly merged company to the brink of chaos. Erie clerks did not know the routings of former Lackawanna cars and vice versa, so shipments were lost.[52] Shippers put up with that only once and the railroad industry was the loser. So much for the willingness of railroads to help each other stem the motor carrier onslaught.

The State of New Jersey let Erie Lackawanna wallow in its commuter burden until the eleventh hour. Maybe managements before White had failed to make the facts plain enough, but it was more likely the politicians had chosen to ignore them. For example, listen to the state senators discuss the matter in hearings in 1965:

Sen. Ozzard: I would interject at this point, Sen. Stamler and Sen. Hillary, that if we take over the passenger service and the freight service is profitable, that the railroad might assist us very easily through increased taxes.

Sen. Hillary: That was on my mind, too.[53]

The same was true for Hudson County taxes, finally reduced under similar duress. And this was true as well for New York's full crew law that required on every train a crew whose size was apropos to the technology of the year the law was passed (1913). So much for the help states could give to railroads they said were essential to their economies.

If Erie and Lackawanna had made an honest mistake in the panacea mentality of the 1950s in thinking merger would solve more fundamental problems, other roads in later mergers had Erie Lackawanna as an example and should not have fallen into the same pit. They deceived themselves and the public, deliberately or not, into believing it was a cure. The evidence contradicted what they had already decided was good so they ignored the evidence. So much for the sagacity of corporate management, which still loved the old social-Darwinistic notion that ability alone got them where they were.

If there were any validity to merger, and that was a big if, it should have included all "natural partners." That was a little hard to define, but in this case would have probably brought together the Lackawanna and Lehigh Valley that were parallel east of Buffalo, the Nickel Plate and the Wabash that were parallel west of there, and the Erie that was parallel to them all. But such a merger could never be, first because the Pennsylvania Railroad would not permit it, and second because capital would not permit it. Security holders cared nothing about the industry in which they had invested, only about their interest and dividends. They were so jealous of losing a point or two, so concerned that every penny of nineteenth-century debt be paid in full that they would not consider the long-run salvation of a beleaguered industry. So much for the resolve of capital to help itself. It was self-destructive, not quite in the same way Marx had predicted, but self-destructive all the same.

And in the old Lackawanna Terminal at Buffalo, the vandals had scrawled their dirty slogans, the marble stairs had been smashed beyond recognition, blizzards whistled through the broken windows, and the bodies of dead rats and pigeons began to collect on the floors and on the counters where once tickets were sold for a ride on the *Phoebe Snow*—an apocalyptic vision of the future of private enterprise.

CHAPTER 6

Chessie and Norfolk & Western Restructure the East; 1961

On March 18, 1960, Stuart Saunders made the first carefully hedged announcement that his Norfolk & Western would merge with the Nickel Plate. A month later (April 28), Robert Bedingfield was covering the Chesapeake & Ohio's annual stockholders' meeting for the *New York Times* when a remark by President Walter Tuohy set him hurrying to a telephone. Calling other railroad presidents, he deduced that C&O was seeking an affiliation with the Baltimore & Ohio, and on page 1 the next morning, the *Times* had itself a scoop. The following November, the Pennsylvania announced it would seek absolute control of the Lehigh Valley. So before the ink was dry on the Erie Lackawanna merger, the entire railroad net in the Northeast was up for grabs.

Ever since the first Penn Central announcement in 1957, the air around eastern railroad headquarters had crackled with intrigue. After the board meeting of the Association of American Railroads in January 1958, Howard Simpson of the B&O had casually mentioned to Walter Tuohy of the C&O that their railroads "ought to get together."[1] The C&O, in the meantime, had extended casual feelers to the Nickel Plate. The B&O was in contact with Nickel Plate as well, even going so far as to invite NKP financial officers to Baltimore. But, as Simpson ruefully explained, the Nickel Plate men "put on their double bifocals when they looked at our financial reports."[2] All this had taken place before the "outer seven" conferences in 1958. Shortly after the Penn-Central negotiations fell through in February 1959, Alfred Perlman of the New York Central spoke to Tuohy about consolidation, but added that Central would need time to complete its modernization program and could not be ready to merge with anyone for five years.[3]

Nickel Plate was a jewel. It was an important railroad, but not so large as to be overwhelming. It had well-diversified traffic, it was independent, and it was profitable. That made it the keystone of eastern mergers. It was not strange, therefore, that it should be visited by an emissary from Roanoke, from the most profitable railroad in the nation, the Norfolk & Western. The N&W's Stuart Saunders was bullish on mergers. The splash he made in the Virginian coup brought him to prominence in the first place. In November 1959 he met with Nickel Plate Chairman Lynn White and its president, Felix

Hales. The bargaining was intense; no formal agreement had been reached at the time of the March 18 announcement. A serious obstacle was the fact that the two railroads did not connect anywhere. There was talk the Nickel Plate might extend its Fort Wayne-Muncie line into Cincinnati, or that it might acquire the Detroit, Toledo & Ironton road. At any rate, the First Boston Company was asked to work out a stock exchange ratio and formal resolutions were adopted in May.[4] But those who knew railroads were certain the Pennsylvania Railroad had the power to control the N&W, whether it was technically true or not. As Pennsylvania had grabbed off the independent Virginian, so it would now grab off the independent Nickel Plate. Everything that followed was in light of that one salient fact—the N&W merger was part of the Pennsylvania's thrust for absolute hegemony in the East.

1

Whether, on January 7, 1960, anyone at the C&O knew about the N&W's plans is not clear. No one at the Central did. It was less than a year since Perlman said the Central was not interested in merger for five years, but on that day there was a meeting of Perlman, Tuohy, Cyrus Eaton, and Allan P. Kirby to discuss the general trend of mergers.[5] The four men were old acquaintances. Kirby was Robert Young's old bankroller and the chairman of Alleghany Corporation, which controlled the Central. Eaton was a coal magnate and long-time associate of Young (he succeeded Young to the C&O chairmanship in 1954) who had continued Young's flair for controversy by his public admiration of the Soviet Union. Tuohy had been the C&O's aggressive vice president for coal traffic, and Young had raised him to the presidency in 1948. He was one of the few railroaders who continued to express an admiration for Young into the 1960s.[6] In 1954, at the height of Young's proxy battle for the Central, Tuohy had been sent to Denver as Young's personal emissary to Alfred Perlman, then the executive vice-president of the Rio Grande, to convince him to come to the Central.[7] But the four were no longer as close as they once had been and nothing concrete came of the meeting.

Perlman read of the N&W's March 18 announcement while vacationing at Palm Beach. He was alarmed and called Tuohy, who had little to offer that was reassuring. "I knew of this, Al," said Tuohy, "I knew of this before. I couldn't tell you because of confidences with Bill Daly of the Nickel Plate who is a friend of ours and who had had negotiations with the C&O." As Tuohy described the conversation, "Al said, 'Well I think this is very important and I think you and Howard [Simpson] and I ought to get together as soon as we can.'"[8] Tuohy and Simpson were already planning to have dinner and Perlman was invited to join. He couldn't make it, but a few days later dropped in unannounced at Tuohy's office in Cleveland. Tuohy was out of town, so he talked to Cyrus Eaton, who said the C&O was probably more interested in diversification outside of railroading rather than mergers within.[9]

Tuohy and Simpson had dinner as planned at the Statler Hilton in Washington on March 29, 1960. Tuohy said the C&O was ready to move ahead with consolidation at once and that if an agreement could not be reached quickly, it had other prospects under consideration. The C&O was interested only in control of the B&O, not a merger, and would not assume B&O debt. Furthermore, it could not wait for extensive "studies." In April, they met twice again to discuss exchange ratios.[10]

It was at that juncture that the *New York Times* broke the story. In piecing it together, reporter Bedingfield had called the Central. Perlman was "not in" and the company had "no comment." But Simpson chattered like a magpie. News that B&O had such a wealthy suitor would boost the price of its stock and improve its exchange ratio. Two weeks later, C&O made a firm offer, on the condition that it get a commitment for 80 percent of the B&O's outstanding stock, the amount needed to file a consolidated balance sheet with the Internal Revenue Service (meaning B&O losses could reduce C&O taxes). The B&O accepted on May 17, 1960.

The next evening, Presidents Perlman, Simpson, and Tuohy met for dinner in Washington. It was the first Perlman knew of it; releases had gone to the press and Central had been left out.[11] The following week, at a crowded and panicky meeting of Central stockholders at the Palace Theater in Albany, Perlman said he had been assured by Tuohy and Simpson that three-way talks would be held. In Cleveland, Tuohy said he was not altogether opposed to talks with the Central, but the B&O board said it was opposed. On June 12, under pressure to make good on his bluff, Perlman requested the ICC make a general investigation of mergers to see if they were in the public interest. Said one railroad president to Robert Bedingfield, "It's the first time I ever heard *him* talk about the public interest." Another said it was "sour grapes. . . . Perlman was asleep at the switch when C&O and B&O moved without his permission."[12]

Perlman and Simpson had lunch together on June 16 and Simpson was urged to disavow the C&O offer. But Perlman could make no firm counter offer. A week later, the Central board met in a stormy six-hour session to debate what it could afford to do. Four days later, it made an offer: one and one-half shares of Central plus $9 in cash for each share of B&O until it had 1,550,000 shares or 60 percent of the B&O's voting stock. Based on the previous day's closing price, that was about $42.50 a share. The C&O's offer was about $35, but C&O was paying dividends of $4 a year with ease, while Central was having a hard time paying $1. But Wall Street observers seemed to agree that the Central's offer was attractive and would probably keep the C&O from getting its 80 percent or maybe even 51 percent. They wondered how a railroad like the Central, which had asked the government for a guarantee on a loan for $40 million because it could not raise the money, could spend $13 million in cash for another railroad. The same day the offer was made, the commission announced it would not grant the Central's request for a comprehensive investigation of mergers.[13]

By July, the scene had shifted to Switzerland. A large block of B&O stock, perhaps 40 percent of it, was held through Swiss banks, which alone knew the names of the owners. Walter Grant of the Central and E. Bates McKee of Bache & Company flew to Zurich to recommend the Central offer. Then, Walter Tuohy and C&O vice president John Kusik flew over on a similar mission. On August 13, the bankers endorsed C&O. "I don't know who misled them," said Perlman, who flew back and thought he persuaded them to remain neutral. But the general director of the Credit Suisse, J.J. Kurz, said that was not so—customers were urged to make up their own minds, but if they asked for advice, they were told C&O. "Frankly, we don't see what grounds Mr. Perlman has for his neutrality statement." But Central was able to produce a telegram from the Bank Hoffman, a small bank, not a major broker of B&O shares, giving it unequivocal support.[14]

Howard Simpson, in the meantime, began to get disillusioned with the C&O and suggested three-way merger talks would be a good idea after all. Tuohy demurred, but Perlman thought it was a great idea and appointed his vice president, John Kennefick, to supervise the project. Having displeased the C&O, Simpson conveniently left for his vacation. On his return, he gave a luncheon for Tuohy and Perlman which lasted four hours, but the impasse remained. *Trains* rated it one of the social and strategic failures of the season, "its words lost in the roar of jets leaving Idlewild for Switzerland."[15]

When the C&O offer expired in September, only 29 percent of the B&O stockholders had accepted, but the C&O thanked them anyway for their "hearty response" and announced the offer would be extended for a while longer. Simpson was furious. If C&O sought a merger rather than control, it would not need 80 percent. He was afraid control would guarantee the B&O nothing and that C&O could loot and leave it helpless. So Tuohy dispatched to Simpson what *Trains* called a "Dear Howard" letter, in which he offered to investigate the possibility of a complete merger. The two men were supposed to meet in New York at the Eastern Railroad Presidents' Conference and later at a board meeting of the Richmond, Fredericksburg & Potomac Railroad, of which both were directors. At the last minute, Simpson canceled. On September 21, the B&O board voted to begin merger studies with the Central.

The C&O was always B&O's more desirable partner and studies predicted $23 million savings from a merger. But C&O only wanted control, and that promised savings of only $10 million. Control would give C&O

the benefit of B&O's lucrative routes, but offer B&O no security in return. The B&O had turned to the Central in desperation. Why had B&O been so outspokenly favorable to the C&O in the first place? "They forced us," said B&O general counsel Jervis Langdon. "They threatened to cancel their offer unless we gave in absolutely, without reservation."[16] Naturally, B&O shareholders were intrigued by visions of fat C&O dividends; at the stockholders' meeting, one of them said he was amazed at the company's change of heart. "You are charging the C&O management with complete bad faith," said one. In so many words, Simpson said yes. "They have talked merger to the public and stockholders, but have not come through with an offer."[17]

The C&O was stamping the B&O stock tendered to it, which meant that it remained committed to the C&O even if it changed hands. The Central was not stamping, and unlike the C&O, which published running tallies of acceptances, would not reveal how many shares were committed to it. It was thought to have no more than 20 percent. At a stormy stockholders' meeting in Albany, Perlman was questioned about the B&O, about passenger losses, and about certain unpleasant developments within Alleghany Corporation.[18] He would not discuss any of it. Aboard the *Empire State Express* returning to New York, the Central's officers read in the evening paper that C&O had invited B&O shareholders to a series of weekend parties and champagne balls at its posh watering hole, the Greenbrier, at White Sulphur Springs.[19]

On December 15, 1960, C&O announced it had 53 percent of B&O's stock tendered to it and stamped. But on December 23, there was a startling offer for a block of 75,000 B&O shares at $47 a share. The price that day was $37.25. Trading in B&O was temporarily halted. "We were convinced," said Walter Tuohy, "that Central or Alleghany was buying on the open market."[20] On January 17, at 9:15 A.M., Walter Grant of the Central offered $46 a share for a block of 50,000 B&O shares. Its price at the moment was $34.50. At 11:15, the party called back to say the C&O had offered a better price.[21] The next day, B&O shot up six and one-eighth points, and the morning after that jumped another four points immediately after the opening bell. By mid-morning it was twelve points over its low of the previous day. At 11:15, with a flood of sell orders pouring in as B&O holders rushed to unload at high prices, trading was suspended. Central was purchasing any share, stamped or not; even if it were stamped, C&O could not vote if it were in Central hands. Shortly before trading was suspended, the stamped shares actually commanded a higher price than the unstamped.[22]

When it was all over, Kirby said Alleghany bought to protect its interest in Central. Central said it bought to protect its position in eastern mergers. The C&O said it bought in response to Central. Central and Alleghany had paid $13 million for 369,775 shares, while for $29 million, C&O got 489,720 shares, which together with its remaining stamped shares gave it 64 percent.[23] However, even as the final exchange offer expired at midnight, on February 2, 1961, the morning papers carried full-page advertisements by the C&O to B&O stockholders, deceptively titled "Merger at Midnight." It told B&O stockholders they would be "connecting up with financial strength and earning power. Act now. If your B&O shares are held by your bank or broker, call them and have them sent to the C&O exchange agent, Morgan Guaranty Trust Company." The C&O wanted the B&O very, very much.

Triumphant, the C&O prepared to send its case to the commission. Wyer, Dick & Company made formal studies, like those for Erie Lackawanna. In March, C&O said it was also buying Western Maryland; it already had 7.31 percent, which complemented a 42.8 percent interest owned by the B&O.[24] The State of Maryland sold $18 million in bonds to expand general cargo facilities at Baltimore, and thus encourage the C&O-B&O relationship. Defeated, with no merger partner in sight, the Central flailed about helplessly. In April, it submitted a rather embarrassing petition for inclusion in the N&W-Nickel Plate merger, and then issued a series of "white papers" to explain its behavior.

2

Wall Street had been treated to another railroad spectacular. As it reached its climax in the fall of 1960, there came two bolts of lightning from Penn Center in Philadelphia. First, the Pennsylvania would sell its Sandusky line through central Ohio to the N&W, thus providing the necessary connection with the Nickel Plate, and it would permit the N&W to lease the Wabash and integrate it into the N&W system. Second, the Pennsylvania itself would seek absolute control of the Lehigh Valley. The operating results of the Lehigh had been so bad that it was practically a moribund railroad, but it was a dagger pointed at the heart of Erie Lackawanna. To the Central, it was the realization of an ancient nightmare, a Wabash-Lehigh east-west route under Pennsylvania influence that bypassed the Pittsburgh bottleneck, a violation of the "Agreement of 1941."

The Pennsylvania probably got a blacker eye than it deserved in the Lehigh affair, for Lehigh was the one banging on the door. It was desperate. Few railroads had performed so poorly in the recession and had themselves so thoroughly to blame. Once one of the jewels of the anthracite kingdom, it was a victim of overly conservative management. For example, as general merchandise delivered from western connections came to replace anthracite as its principal traffic, it failed to remedy its deficiencies in the Buffalo terminal, where connections to the Wabash required a 40-mile detour through Niagara Falls, and connection with the Nickel Plate required a seven-mile, five-hour ramble through the warehouse district, crossing the New York Central mainline at grade.[25] Lehigh never purchased enough freight cars and ran an annual car rental deficit of $1 million. It reduced its bonded indebtedness in the mid-1950s, but did so out of cash; when revenue dropped in the 1958 recession its cash position was dangerously low. One consultant said they had made a "bad guess" in counting on continued prosperity.[26] The company had been slow to adopt piggyback or radio communication and never experimented with ideas such as guaranteed rates that excited railroading in the 1950s.

It might have been the road's lackluster management, but every coordination project that might help the Lehigh but hurt the Pennsylvania always fell through. From Wilkes-Barre to the sea, the Lehigh and Jersey Central were parallel, often adjacent, neither carrying a fraction of its capacity since the demise of anthracite. But neither ever had the nerve to go through with the most obvious coordination project in the East.[27] (Jersey Central, it will be recalled, was peripherally in the B&O sphere.) Lehigh and Erie Lackawanna were almost duplicate railroads east of Buffalo. At the time Erie and Lackawanna were negotiating their merger, they had thought of bringing the Lehigh in but nothing came of it.

By the end of 1959, when it was clear the Lehigh was in trouble and was not going to be invited to any of the eastern mergers, its president, Cedric Major, arranged a series of meetings with Walter Tuohy of the C&O, Felix Hales of the Nickel Plate, and Stuart Saunders of the N&W, to suggest they include Lehigh in their plans. They all turned him down. Discussions with the Wabash were more hopeful and in the early summer of 1960 joint studies were authorized. It was never clear what the influence of the Pennsylvania was, but once Wabash got its invitation from the N&W, talks with the Lehigh ended.

In mid-September, Major asked James Symes of the Pennsylvania for an appointment to discuss merger. The meeting was unproductive, but Major's board told him to try harder. So there were more meetings, and on October 14, Symes called to say the Pennsylvania was prepared to seek stock control. It drove a hard bargain over the exchange ratio, and the longer the haggling went on, the more the position of the Lehigh deteriorated. In November, Symes made a final, take-it-or-leave-it offer, and after a tumultuous meeting of the Lehigh board, it was accepted.[28]

The ICC would want to know how stock control would save the Lehigh from bankruptcy, so there had to be some kind of report to show them. Lehigh could not afford professional consultants and the Pennsylvania never liked them. It sent two of its vice-presidents, Walter Patchell of the operating department and Fred Carpi of the traffic department, to do the job. The Patchell-Carpi studies envisioned annual savings of $6 million, mostly by having Pennsylvania staff assume the duties of Lehigh management. There would be savings from yard coordination at Buffalo and from abandonment of lighterage operations at Communipaw Terminal (Jersey City). Lehigh could abandon its shops at Sayre, Pennsylvania, and the

Pennsylvania would take over all locomotive repair. The studies first drew a pessimistic picture of Lehigh's future traffic potential (to explain why it needed help) and then said the future was bright (to explain why the Pennsylvania should be interested). Pennsylvania Railroad geologists would be sent to study mineral deposits along the Lehigh at some indefinite time in the future.[29] The studies were not comprehensive, concrete, or convincing.

To everyone but the Pennsylvania's lawyers, it seemed obvious the Lehigh and N&W cases were related and that the Pennsylvania was finally moving to consolidate the empire it created in the 1920s. Symes was candid: the Pennsylvania had opposed the ICC's plan of the 1920s because it was a "squeeze play." "It's a matter of known fact," he said, "that the Pennsylvania acquired ownership in the Lehigh Valley to protect itself in the matter of mergers in eastern territory."[30] Erie Lackawanna was determined to force the Pennsylvania to reveal its ultimate design and wondered if it had not deliberately abetted the Lehigh's troubles in order to accomplish its goals more cheaply. There was no obvious proof but there was a lot of circumstantial evidence that pointed in that direction.

For example, there had been a strange little affair over trackage rights. The Pennsylvania wanted to abandon its rambling branch up the Genessee Valley into Rochester and serve the city out of Buffalo instead, over Lehigh trackage. It would have saved the Pennsylvania money and produced extra revenue for the Lehigh, but the two roads could not agree on terms. It was odd that Erie Lackawanna had been able to negotiate minor trackage agreements with both the Lehigh and the Pennsylvania, but two roads with a strong interest in each other could not. Testimony indicated the Pennsylvania had demanded more favorable terms; the question was why, when it had such a strong financial interest in the Lehigh. Perry Shoemaker said he was "shocked," and a Lehigh man said, "we just thought they wanted too much of the pie, that's all."[31]

More serious was why the Pennsylvania waited so long to protect its investment. The Lehigh had been in a downward spiral for two years, but only when it was approaching its death throes was there an effort to ram the case through the regulatory process. Opposition was silenced with spectres of bankruptcy and interveners given no time to prepare their cases. The implication was that Lehigh had deliberately been left to wallow until it was helpless, but then the Pennsylvania had to move with haste before insolvency sank its equity altogether.

Trying to prove that this was part of the Pennsylvania's plan of conquest involved fishing in circumstantial evidence. First, there was the obvious stock ownership—33 percent of the N&W and absolute control of the Wabash. Together, the Wabash and the Pennsylvania Company owned 44.4 percent of the Lehigh and had made additional purchases late in 1959, after the Lehigh entered its tailspin but before it begged to be taken in. That was why EL and others thought the N&W and Lehigh cases ought to be discussed together. Symes refused. "If all these railroads are going to come down here and oppose every little consolidation or control, that is the best way of wrecking the whole [merger] thing that I know of."[32]

In the midst of the hearing, Symes mentioned, perhaps let slip, that the Pennsylvania would equip the Lehigh with centralized traffic control (CTC), an expensive signal system that would permit the operation of more trains. However, passenger trains were gone and through freights were down to four a day each way between Jersey City and Buffalo; with Fred Carpi's traffic study giving little hope of an upturn, the CTC hardly seemed necessary, unless someone high in the Pennsylvania anticipated a major increase. The EL was fascinated; it suspected the traffic would come from the Wabash in diversions from them. For their part, the Pennsylvania's lawyers acted as if a cat had been let out of the bag and were frantic to get it back in. Was it not true, they asked Perry Shoemaker, that Symes only "guessed" CTC would be installed. "I have known Mr. Symes for many years," said Shoemaker, "and I have a great respect for his guesses."[33]

In the midst of the hearing, Robert Bedingfield wrote a story for the *New York Times* in which he said:

Mr. Symes envisages for the Pennsylvania a series of consolidations in the next five years. He foresees in the same period, combinations of other eastern railroads that may leave his system with only one or at most two competitors in its territory. There are 34 today.[34]

Two days before that, the *Times* had run another story whose source was "a railroader close to the Pennsylvania scene." The reason for the interest in the Lehigh Valley, "which has little freight and no passengers," was to restore its position in the N&W. Its ownership of N&W stock was diluted from 45 percent to 33 percent when N&W absorbed the Virginian. With N&W stock selling over 100, direct acquisition of more was impossible. But it was believed N&W would need a route from Buffalo to New York, and at that time Pennsylvania could trade the Lehigh for N&W stock. It was an interesting speculation and no one particularly denied it. Nor did the Pennsylvania retract or clarify the statement about "a series of consolidations."

Erie Lackawanna, with the most to lose, had put forward a proposal of its own, a three-way merger of itself, Lehigh, and Pennsylvania, and Wyer, Dick & Company was hired to make a study. Neither Lehigh nor Pennsylvania would cooperate, so they had to resort to public information, clandestine interviews with Lehigh employees, and photographs of Lehigh facilities (which must have been through very long telephoto lenses, for as every railroad fan knows, the Lehigh Valley always had a pathological fear of photographers).

Despite the handicap, a report was assembled that was more sophisticated than the Patchell-Carpi studies. Savings would be substantial; virtually the whole Lehigh and Erie mainlines could be single-tracked and downgraded. It noted some savings the Patchell-Carpi studies had overlooked and pointed out some errors in Patchell's calculations.[35] The EL ran a big risk exposing this. Proper channels dictated that it make its proposal privately, probably over lunch, where no records were kept and when it was turned down, forgotten. Such a report presented James Symes with a terrible dilemma. To accept would turn a minor case into a major realignment of railroads; to reject was to repudiate the merger savings he was so fond of crowing about.

Bankruptcy was a pretty bad thing, was it not? asked the Pennsylvania. The EL had to agree, for it was a likely candidate. Did Erie know that Lehigh shippers were getting nervous about the railroad's ability to provide service? Bethlehem Steel, for example, noted that Lehigh was constantly unable to supply adequate gondola cars and that its entire traffic policy was up for revision as a result.[36] If EL forced a delay, it would be responsible for the debacle. (The EL thought it was interesting that the lawyer who testified for Bethlehem formerly worked for the Pennsylvania.) Besides, was not EL a big, hulking liability that would threaten the solvency of anyone who tried to help it? On the stand, William Wyer was asked:

Q: Is the Lehigh Valley headed for bankruptcy if the Pennsylvania doesn't get control?

A: I think it probably is, yes.

Q: What is your opinion as to where the Erie Lackawanna is headed?

A: Well, I think it is on the same road, but not as far down the road.

Q: Even though it is currently losing money at three times the rate of the Lehigh Valley, you don't think it is headed for the drain as fast?

A: No.[37]

It was the first time anyone had mentioned the drain.

3

Hearings in the C&O-B&O case got under way in June 1961. The principal argument of the C&O had a familiar ring: unless a favorable decision were reached immediately, B&O would be in bankruptcy. Only the know-how and credit of the C&O could save it. Part of this was true. The B&O was having difficulties.

The cataclysmic descent of the Baltimore & Ohio began in the third week of October 1957. From a 1956 high of $465 million, gross revenues fell to $359 million by 1961, and that year, the net operating loss was $31 million, the worst showing of any railroad. The effects of recession were compounded because the B&O was in the midst of capital improvement projects that had already consumed large amounts of cash, but had no earning value until they were completed. Some, like the new Hawkins Point Marine Terminal in Baltimore, were well enough along that they continued to receive funds. Others had to be canceled, such as the half-completed yard at Cumberland, Maryland, and the new coal docks at Curtis Bay (Baltimore). Low tunnel clearances on the main line across West Virginia made the use of piggyback equipment impossible. "Here we were, the shortest route between Baltimore and St. Louis," said Jervis Langdon, "and we were not competitive because we couldn't handle the equipment."[38] Yet plans to raise the clearances had to be canceled and a million dollars worth of bulldozers bought for the purpose were useless.

There were other projects that needed attention they could not be given. Most of the mechanical interlockers and semaphores installed between 1900 and 1923 needed immediate replacement, as did thousands of angle bars installed during World War II when there were restrictions on their size and steel content. Much of the track was due for reballasting, especially in the mountain areas where heavy sanding by the locomotives and leaking coal dust contaminated it, shortening the life of rails and ties. Most of the early FT-model diesel locomotives were at the end of their service life, as was more than half the freight-car fleet. Twenty-six percent of its 86,000 cars were bad-ordered (inoperable) by 1960, and hundreds with antique Duryea underframes could never be repaired.[39]

To cut costs, the passenger service was hacked to bits and the traffic department dismembered. John Kerslake, vice president for traffic, told how it took place.

Q: Are your sales people effective?

A: . . . the officers are stripped of help. We don't have enough clerks.

Q: When was the last general reduction?

A: We are having them all the time. The last one was last week.

Q: Was it a general one?

A: No, but it was substantial. We didn't furlough anyone, we retired them. Not that I didn't think we should fill their jobs. We just couldn't afford it.

Q: When was the last general reduction?

A: About 18 months ago. . . . Some of them were furloughed and some were retired. . . . Over the last six months we have cut our traffic force, I would say, 34 or 35 percent.[40]

Like the Lehigh, the B&O had tried to repurchase its outstanding debt ๅut of cash. In 1955, it had refunded a number of debt issues into a single consolidated mortgage which enabled it to reduce fixed charges by $2 million. But one of the series of bonds had found no buyers; left as a floating supply on the market, the price deteriorated. It meant the B&O had exhausted its credit. "I am not sure that if the B&O wanted to borrow any sizable amount of money, such as $50 million, they could do it on any basis," said Winthrop Lenz of Merrill, Lynch. "The Chase Manhattan, which has the existing loan, is practically on 24-hour call, they are so worried what may happen to this railroad."

Q: Would it be desirable to pay 10% or 15% for improvements that would pay for themselves in 3 years?

A: It would destroy what little credit is left. Bonds now selling in the 80s would sink to the 50s.[41]

Why should a railroad with these terrible problems be such a desirable merger partner? Despite the grim picture the B&O's problems were temporary. Recessions were bad for everyone, but there were better and there were worse times to be caught in one, and B&O had been caught at the worst. It was a highly leveraged company, meaning the bulk of its capitalization was in funded dubt. Thus in good times fixed charges were a small part of high profits; in bad times they might be overwhelming. In other words, the B&O ought to snap back as soon as the recession was over. Besides, it had taken $27 million of extraordinary write-offs, which made the 1961 results look worse than they really were.[42]

As in the Erie Lackawanna merger, a C&O-B&O combination would permit almost no abandonment of lines and rather minimal consolidation of yards. In fact, C&O advertised it as an end-to-end combination, apparently anticipating more problem from the trustbusters than from those who would criticize it for doing nothing to streamline the railroad plant. Even if the two roads looked parallel on the map, competition was not going to be reduced. Both hauled coal, for example, but the B&O's was mostly high-volatile coal used in steam plants, while the C&O's was low-volatile, used for coking. The B&O's automobile traffic came from St. Louis and Ohio, the C&O's from Michigan. The B&O's steel traffic came from Pittsburgh and eastern Ohio, the C&O's from Buffalo, Detroit, and Chicago. The B&O's chemical traffic came from Cincinnati and points in Illinois and Maryland, the C&O's from Niagara Falls, Charleston, and Ontario points. In the traffic of food products, paper, scrap iron, soda, glass, pipe fittings, and fluxing stone, each railroad served substantially different customers.

Hardly, countered the New York Central. Make a list of the 60 largest customers of the Central, C&O, and B&O, it said, and 15 of them would appear on all three lists—Allied Chemical, Armco Steel, Bethlehem Steel,

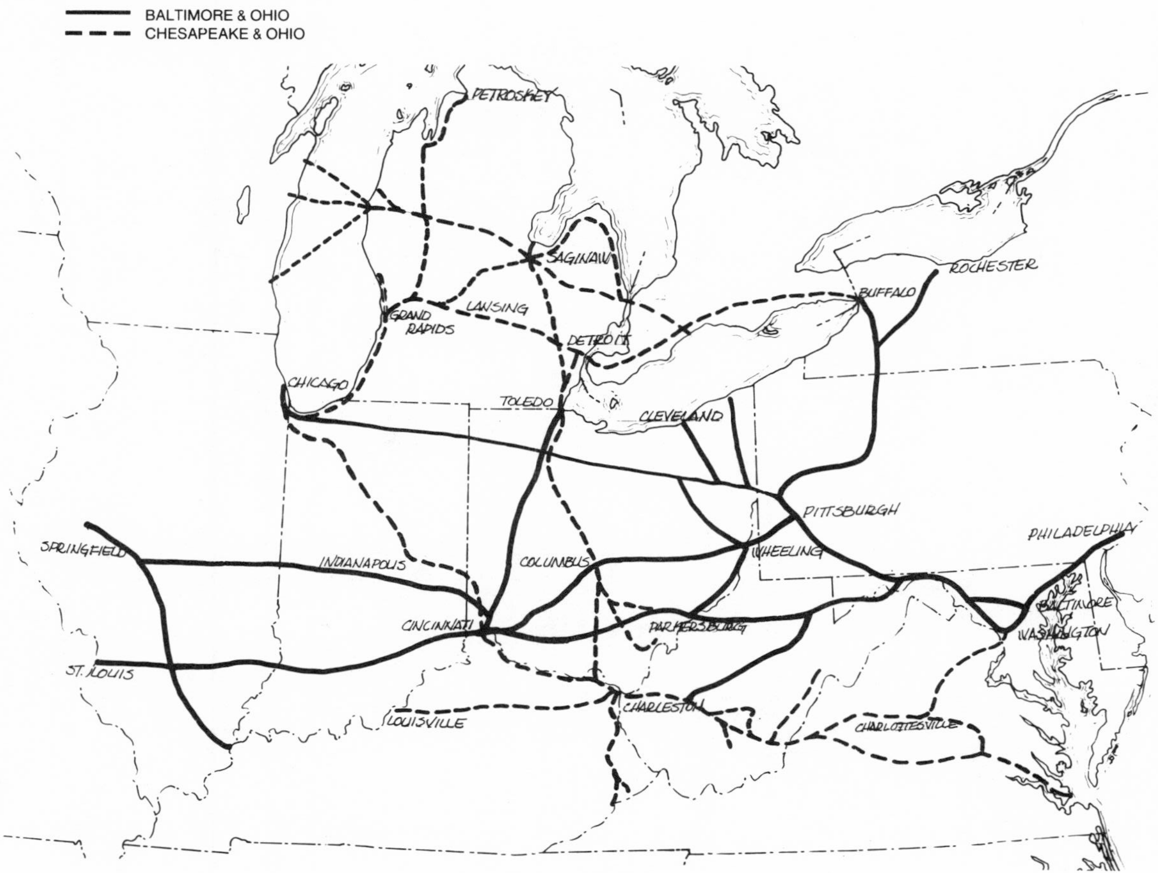

MAP 18: The C&O-B&O

BALTIMORE & OHIO
CHESAPEAKE & OHIO

ROCHESTER
BUFFALO
PHILADELPHIA
BALTIMORE
WASHINGTON
PITTSBURGH
CHARLOTTESVILLE
WHEELING
CLEVELAND
PARKERSBURG
DETROIT
SAGINAW
TOLEDO
COLUMBUS
CHARLESTON
PETROSKEY
LANSING
GRAND RAPIDS
CINCINNATI
LOUISVILLE
CHICAGO
INDIANAPOLIS
SPRINGFIELD
ST. LOUIS

Continental Can, Detroit Edison, Dow Chemical, DuPont Chemical, Eastern Gas & Fuel, General Motors, Jones & Laughlin, Owens-Illinois, Republic Steel, Union Carbide, the U.S. government, and Youngstown Sheet & Tube. That was competition.

The C&O said control would produce great savings. "Hardly," said the Central. The C&O's Wyer Report claimed only $13 million a year, not a lot for railroads that size.[43] If "savings" was the name of the game, much greater savings could be obtained from a three-way merger with the Central. The C&O said studies would take too long and the B&O would probably collapse. "We will make the studies," said the Central. "How can you afford studies like that?" asked C&O. "We thought [you] were poor." "We have enough to see that the public interest is considered," said the Central.[44]

"Savings" could come from strange places that outsiders never thought of. For example, there was an innocent-looking item in the C&O study called "pooling of freight equipment." The C&O supposedly had 9,914 extra freight cars, including 4,109 hopper cars (C&O called them coal cars), which could be used to ease B&O's car shortage. Exactly how it was determined the cars were surplus was beyond comprehension; the man who made the study in the first place couldn't explain it in cross-examination. Nevertheless, having determined that 4,109 coal cars were surplus, C&O leased 7,500 of them to the B&O, even though Howard Simpson had told his stockholders that B&O was not short of cars. The C&O was being paid for this, of course. Said Arthur Winn of the New York Port Authority: "The B&O needs 5,000 cars and the C&O gives them 7,500 for $7.5 million in rental. The profits were already rolling in."[45]

The C&O promised that it would underwrite the remainder of B&O's improvement program. It would not loan the money directly, but would guarantee loans. This was the single most powerful reason to approve control. But what would compel the C&O to do as it promised? It was not a charity. Presumably it acted in its own interest. The C&O said it would never have invested so heavily if it did not intend to protect that investment by rehabilitating the B&O. But when Walter Tuohy said he had committed $24 million to the B&O with no assurance the C&O or its stockholders would ever see it again, the opposition was incredulous. Had not the C&O once had heavy investments in the Erie and the Chicago & Eastern Illinois, and had it not refused them credit and let them go into bankruptcy? Dr. John Frederick of the University of Maryland, offering scholarly sanction of the C&O's plan, did not know about this. "Then how are you so certain, Doctor, that it will help, if you haven't explored the history of the C&O's past actions?"[46] Walter Tuohy said he felt no compulsion to rescue two of the railroads controlled by the B&O—Reading and Jersey Central. Why was it so interested in salvaging the B&O and throwing the others to the wolves? The C&O's distinction between philanthropy and motivating self-interest seemed a little muddy.

Finally, the C&O promised the B&O its miraculous know-how, what it believed was the managerial excellence that had made it rich. The C&O had invested its profits wisely in an impressive assemblage of young graduates. It had engineers to study railroad operations, geologists to locate and develop coal deposits along its line, efficiency experts to streamline its business methods, and even a department of golf, headed by Sammy Snead, headquartered at the Greenbrier, to sell coal to visiting Japanese industrialists (although the golfers had just returned from Japan without selling a single carload).[47] More successful were the recent demonstrations by fuel engineers of the efficiency of coal at certain government installations that were about to convert to gas, and their work with electric utilities in planning facilities that took best advantage of the burning qualities of C&O coal.[48]

There was a certain smugness about the C&O people, perhaps a remnant of the swaggering regime of Robert Young, that did not seem to characterize other successful railroads such as the N&W, for example. A witness from the Pittsburgh & Lake Erie Railroad said that C&O men ought to be proud of their fine accomplishments, just as P&LE people were proud. "But we know," he said, "that it is in large part our favorable position for moving bulk commodities. . . . I observe no deficiencies in the B&O management that require C&O know-how."[49] It was true that C&O's cost for locomotive repair was about two-thirds that of the B&O and its cost for track maintenance was well below the national average. Yet its passenger deficit was virtually out of control. It had no electronic yards; it had lagged in the development of piggyback; and its coal cars averaged only 16 round trips a year from mine to delivery, barely more than a trip a month.[50]

Q: What are those magic procedures you are going to give the B&O?

A: Did you say magic?

Q: Well, I assume they are going to be magic.[51]

None of this was going to endear the C&O to B&O men. C.E. Bertrand, B&O vice president for operations, saw it this way:

Q: Do you assert the B&O is an unsafe railroad?

A: No, we maintain safety.

Q: Do you feel yourself qualified to run it?

A: Yes.

Q: Do you need C&O direction?

A: No. I need money.[52]

John Barriger had been involved in consolidation matters since before most of the men at the hearing had their first Lionel. Now, as president of the Pittsburgh & Lake Erie, he was not impressed with what the younger men had wrought. The C&O-B&O was a bad combination because it was end-to-end. Such affiliations could reduce expenses by only 10 percent at most (and he had plenty of historical evidence to prove it). Their principal effect was to damage competition, and they did not provide any of the text-book justifications, like concentrating traffic in longer, more frequent trains, or the downgrading of excess track. Even if such affiliations were coupled with extensive improvement programs, they could never solve the fundamental problems of excess capacity and declining traffic volume. As for the C&O's generosity in helping weak railroads, it had never been generous before. Robert Young, for example, used to like to brag that C&O had saved the Nickel Plate from bankruptcy in 1941, when NKP couldn't meet a maturing bond issue. He never added that the funds came from the Reconstruction Finance Corporation. Barriger knew. He had been the chief of the railroad bureau of the RFC that authorized the loan.

He talked with depth and ease on all phases of railroading and pre-sented sophisticated exhibits such as a logarithmic chart of the peaks and valleys of competitive commodity shipments. He knew everyone at the hear-ing; he even knew many of their fathers. He told C&O counsel Edward Wheeler how he had worked with his father, Burton K. Wheeler of Mon-tana, in shaping the Transportation Act of 1940, and what the law had in-tended was nothing like the proposal before them. To some he was an eccentric grandfather taking the juniors by the hand. But he was not reminiscing about the way trains used to be. His history was vital, the past speaking directly to the present. And unlike so many, he even had a sense of humor:

Q: Have you ever worked for the C&O?

A: No. Are you offering me a job? I've been quite a boomer, you know. Maybe after this is over, I'll need one.[53]

Central pursued its case throughout the fall of 1961. It demanded and was granted hearings on the road in Boston, Syracuse, Detroit, Indian-apolis, Cleveland, and Chicago. Hearings finally ended back in Washing-ton on October 9. The very next day, hearings began on the N&W-Nickel Plate merger. Many of the people who had taken part in the one would take part in the other, and were in a state of exhaustion.

4

As the law read, railroads could not be compelled to merge, but if a merger were sought and a third road could demonstrate that its inclusion was required by the public interest, it could be required as a condition of approval. Whether the ICC was ready to face up to it or not, the *Chessie* and the N&W cases were going to restructure all of northeastern railroading. If they were approved, the New York Central, the Erie Lackawanna, and every smaller road in the East, whether financially strong or not, would be surrounded by these new, powerful combines. If this weakened them to the point where they could no longer provide adequate transportation, the economic fate of states, ports, and industries would be in mortal danger. So every railroad in the region had an immediate interest. The case became so weighted down with the concerns of third parties, the question of whether this particular merger had merit became secondary. In fact, the only protestants to attack it on its merit were a small group of communities on the St. Louis Line of the Nickel Plate.

At first perusal, the N&W's case looked impressive. Its studies were suitably dazzling, with tallies that anticipated savings of $27 million a year.[54] But like the studies before them, it was the company's word and nobody could get the information to challenge it. Stuart Saunders ticked off examples of improved freight schedules—fifteen hours faster for certain traffic moving east out of Chicago, and twelve to fifteen hours faster for traffic from the Southwest to points east of Buffalo. Total train mileage would be reduced by 1.3 million miles a year. Eventually, Examiner Lester Conley would recite these same examples in his report, and the commission would accept them as evidence the merger served the public interest "beyond question."[55]

Combining the Nickel Plate and Wabash always made good sense. Two railroads could hardly complement each other more. They were parallel and one's weakness was the other's strength. From Chicago to Buffalo, the Wabash was a poor railroad, with its ferry problems at Detroit and its trackage rights over the Canadian National, while the Nickel Plate was flat and fast. But southwest, toward St. Louis where the Wabash was a powerhouse, Nickel Plate was an undulating line built originally to narrow-guage standards. Every one of Saunders's examples of improved service had to do with Wabash and Nickel Plate, not N&W. The 15-hour reduction in Chicago-Buffalo schedules, for example, was nothing more than rerouting Wabash traffic over the Nickel Plate. "The public" was already getting those faster schedules from the Nickel Plate without a merger. It was just a little example of how the dramatic statement could be quite hollow.

The N&W was the dubious addition. It was true that traffic that once moved through the Port of New York was moving through Hampton

Roads, particularly midwestern grain. Cargill and Continental Grain were already sending most of their export through Norfolk without a railroad merger.[56] But dragging midwestern commodities up to Bellevue, Ohio, then dropping them straight south to the Ohio River, then over the backbone of the Alleghenies to Virginia tidewater was not a historic route. There would be no reduction of mileage or concentration of traffic; even duplicate shops were to be maintained—one in Roanoke and another in the Wabash-NKP heartland. It was in N&W's corporate interest to diversify out of coal and to have single-line distribution for its coal in the Midwest, as C&O got when it took over the Pere Marquette.[57] But corporate and public interest were not the same. When the hearing was over, the ICC had no firm evidence this combination was going to improve service to the public. It was, said Commissioner William Tucker in his stinging dissent, "a wholly inadequate record."

Exactly what constituted the public interest was an old debate that was not going to be settled here. Who was the public? Who spoke for it? How were conflicting interests among individuals within it to be reconciled? The ICC, following the precedent of the *New York Central Securities* case, accepted an affirmation by shippers and local communities as a sufficient demonstration, provided there were no equivalent objections.

The N&W then brought in several dozen shippers. The exercise proved that a self-selected sample of highly coached traffic managers, speaking in the private interest of their companies, and closely guarded by N&W counsel, did not prove a thing. Some thought the merger would improve their supply of cars, particularly air-slide grain cars. "Has it been indicated the merged system will acquire new grain cars?" The answer was no.[58] Some thought it would improve service. Was it deficient now? No.[59] Some thought it would increase transit privileges. Had they had assurances? No.[60] Some thought it would reduce rates. Had they been told so? No.[61] Some said single-line service would be an improvement over the present interchange. Was interline service of the N&W or Nickel Plate poor? No. In fact, it was better than the single-line service of some other carriers.[62] Others admitted that after making their glittering generalities, their distribution patterns would not change as a result of merger.[63]

Nearly all of the shippers indicated railroads were collapsing and only merger could save them. They had read about troubled railroads in the paper, or a daughter had said how positively decrepit the passenger train was when she went off to school. Their ill-informed or deliberately misleading comments implied that N&W was going to be among the first to go. A typical exchange:

Q: When you say "the increasingly apparent financial and competitive deterioration of the nation's railroads must be halted," do you include the Erie Lackawanna?

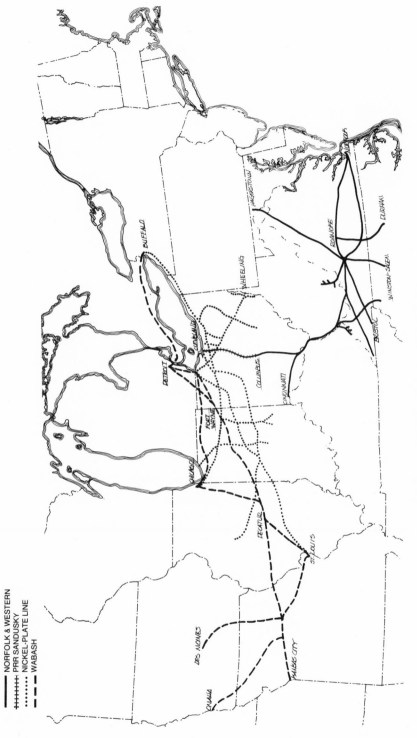

NORFOLK & WESTERN
PRR SANDUSKY
NICKEL-PLATE LINE
WABASH

BUFFALO

HAGERSTOWN

WHEELING

ROANOKE

DURHAM

BRISTOL

WINSTON-SALEM

CLEVELAND

COLUMBUS

CINCINNATI

DETROIT

FORT WAYNE

CHICAGO

DECATUR

ST. LOUIS

DES MOINES

KANSAS CITY

OMAHA

MAP 19:   *The Norfolk & Western-Nickel Plate Merger*

A: Oh, I am not qualified to comment on the financial or competitive state of Erie Lackawanna.[64]

This kind of testimony and cross-examination went on for days and days.

Governor Nelson Rockefeller had bumptiously arrived at the C&O-B&O hearing to offer his observations. The New York Central served New York State, so he was opposed to the C&O-B&O combination until they took the Central in. Since the governor always liked to think positively, he offered a three-point program that he thought would better solve railroad problems: (1) create a federal department of transportation, (2) repeal the 10 percent tax on passenger tickets, and (3) take a coordinated approach to mergers.[65] It was easy to sneer at the governor's simplification, and he nearly got himself politely excused as an incompetent witness. He understood, however, that the Port of New York was in trouble and that in addition to its labor and cost problems every one of the railroads to the interior that served it exclusively was in trouble. If all the midwestern carriers linked up with roads serving the Virginia ports, it could be the *coup de grâce* for New York. That was why, in the N&W case, New York and the New York Port Authority defended Erie Lackawanna.

The N&W mustered political celebrities of its own. Governors Barron of West Virginia and Combes of Kentucky each made perfunctory appearances. Terry Sanford of North Carolina couldn't make it; he sent a substitute who was abysmally ill informed. (He said single-line service was a good thing, then didn't seem to know what it was.[66] But the star performance was left to Governor J. Lindsay Almond of Virginia. "I have heard no opposition from any representative source in Virginia," he stated. Naturally not. Virginia could come out of this the big winner without risking anything. Having just returned from Brazil, Uruguay, and Argentina, Almond volunteered the following:

While I do not want to make invidious comparisons, I think it is general knowledge the deplorable state of railroad transportation in those countries owned by the government, and in my judgment, without undue criticism of our great South American neighbors, the situation is deplorable.[67]

Railroads, he continued, were "absolutely essential in peace and direly essential in war. In my judgment, the only answer is for these railroads to merge, to meet the age of progressive automation in which we find ourselves."

The N&W merger could do for Virginia what the opening of the Erie Canal did for New York in 1825—raise it head-and-shoulders above its rivals. When the governor was asked about the devastating effects this might have on other states and ports, he said, "Well, the attitude of Virginia has always been one of live and let live. I cannot conceive of any serious impact to other transportation systems outside the areas of this merger." When the situation was explained to him, he answered, "I cannot accept your hypothesis. However, the attitude of Virginia would not change because of its faith in the American system of freedom of enterprise and fair competition in all areas of industrial endeavor."[68]

Do politicians take their inconsistencies seriously? Government ownership was not remotely an issue for N&W or Nickel Plate, but it conceivably was for the railroads being deliberately excluded. If preservation of private enterprise was of overriding importance, then Governor Almond was acting as the handmaiden of Stuart Saunders in hastening its destruction for others. To affirm his belief in private endeavor, the governor said the State of Virginia would build new dock facilities at Hampton Roads to help the N&W. In contrast, and to their sorrow, the supposedly wild-spending states of New York and New Jersey were taxing their railroads and did not provide them with state-built dock facilities. The question of who were the real liberals and who were the real conservatives was always ambiguous.

Back when the N&W proposal was first announced, Erie Lackawanna perceived it as the most serious threat to its existence. Its own merger was as yet undigested, yet it felt compelled to devote the energies of its executive and legal talents to fight what it assumed was encirclement by the Pennsylvania. Therefore, it had made an elaborate study of a four-way merger including it and all the partners of the N&W scheme which foresaw $34 million in annual savings and an electronic classification yard at Huntington, Indiana, its junction with the Wabash.[69]

This was an acute embarrassment to Stuart Saunders. By including EL, he could justify his merger as a means of building a better railroad system. Excluding it opened him to the charge that his merger was designed to increase dividends to the rich, while ruining a railroad on which industries and jobs depended. It was unlikely, however, that N&W security holders would approve a merger with EL, whether Saunders wanted it or not, because its outstanding debt was so huge. If the commission should require inclusion, there would be no merger at all. Saunders's dilemma was obvious.

He swung into the kind of action he loved best. On October 12, 1961, EL signed an agreement whereby it withdrew from the case. In return, Nickel Plate would immediately join EL in building the new electronic Bison Yard at Buffalo, sharing the construction costs and ensuring that EL would be the route of preference for Nickel Plate interchange.[70] Then, upon consumation of the N&W-Nickel Plate merger, N&W and EL would begin good-faith consultation to see if "some form of affiliation would be mutually advantageous." Disputes could be submitted to an arbiter, but they would be limited only to the question of whether each was acting in good faith. A failure of either party to reach an agreement would not be evidence of a lack of good faith. Any agreements had to be submitted to the security holders of each company. If either should enter bankruptcy, the agreement could be canceled unilaterally. But to show its good faith, N&W promised to buy $1.5 million of EL securities.[71]

The man who negotiated this for EL, former Erie President Paul Johnson, gave no hint that his company may have made a poor deal:

Q: Will you agree, sir, that $1½ million of EL securities is not a significant proportion of ownership?

A: To a man brought up on the Erie Railroad, it's a lot of dollars.[72]

Others were less sanguine. Erie stockholders, for example, wired the ICC not to let their company withdraw; whatever it was doing was not in their interest. Having permitted the withdrawal, even the examiner had second thoughts that he may have made a mistake.[73] New York and the New York Port Authority continued to fight EL's battle in the belief that it was unwilling or unable to fight itself. Said Austin Tobin of the Port Authority:

A: I am singularly unimpressed with the agreement of October 12, 1961, and to my mind it is a very flimsy piece of tissue paper indeed, and I see no commitment on the part of anyone to do anything that really means anything.

Q: (by John Fishwick of the N&W) Is it your objection as to whether we will negotiate in good faith?

A: No, you are pledged to do that. We think if the heart were there, it could be done now.[74]

Stuart Saunders explained it this way:

Q: (by the examiner) Did your agreement with the Erie Lackawanna require stockholder approval?

A: No.

Q: But a merger would?

A: Yes.

Q: Then your contract with Erie Lackawanna is meaningless?

A: Oh, no. I am shocked to hear you say that.

Q: What did you contract to do with them?

A: We will sit down in good faith.

Q: There remains the possibility that nothing will be accomplished?

A: Yes.

Q: And the ICC is asked to consider this proposed merger on the basis that Erie Lackawanna may be left out in the cold and might not be included in any arrangement that will provide security for Erie Lackawanna or the public? Is that what you are proposing?

A: No, sir. I have already stated this before. We think and we hope we can work out an arrangement. But it is absolutely certain that if we don't go that way, nothing is going to be done. . . . We are not going to accept the Erie Lackawanna regardless of what the Commission says. . . . We are not going to do it. So you don't accomplish a thing. . . . Mr. Examiner, I cannot state too strongly on the record, we will not accept an order of the Commission to make us take the Erie Lackawanna. We cannot do it.

Q: Under any arrangement?

A: No, sir. And furthermore, the Commission has not the authority to require it.

Q: So what you are suggesting . . . is a take it or leave it proposition?

A: I have said that flatly, and we think it is in the public interest.[75]

This was the way Stuart Saunders liked to do business. He abhorred confrontation that splashed corporate secrets all over the public record, the way Central and C&O had gone after each other. He liked to deal behind closed doors, and he wanted mergers very much. He had demonstrated his technique in the Virginian, and he had only begun in this one.

Labor got an attrition agreement, somewhat modified from the Virginian case. It withdrew its opposition.[76] Little Akron, Canton & Youngstown was promised N&W would seek to control it. It would complement the merger in a minor way, but its tax base was too high for outright absorption. Besides, Saunders said the "rubber people" liked having it more or less independent. It withdrew.[77] The Pittsburgh & West Virginia received the promise of a lease. It was a healthy property as long as the Alphabet Route was a going concern. It withdrew.[78]

The Western Maryland was a little tough; being in the C&O-B&O sphere, it could not make a similar deal and the Maryland Port Authority was giving it some backbone. Would not the N&W solicit against the Alphabet Route for its own long haul to Norfolk? The N&W said no, not necessarily. Nickel Plate already had so many satisfied customers on the Alphabet Route that it would not care to risk losing the business altogether. There were hints it had promised transit privileges to certain large shippers if they would choose Norfolk over Baltimore. But the P&WV lease, plus a written promise to actively solicit for the Alphabet Route, seemed to be satisfactory. Baltimore and the Western Maryland withdrew.[79]

New York Central had been fairly quiet ever since the hearing began. It was still fighting for inclusion in the C&O-B&O, but from mid-autumn on, rumors were rife that Penn Central talks had resumed. This was confirmed on January 12, 1962, when Pennsylvania and New York Central signed a formal merger agreement. On January 15, Central withdrew from the N&W case, on January 17, from the Lehigh case, and on January 29, from C&O-B&O. Had the high command of the Pennsylvania, including Stuart Saunders, who was a PRR director, now silenced the last railroad opposition? Only the New York people and those troublesome communities down in the Nickel Plate boondocks stood in the way of total N&W victory. Everyone knew the commission never said no when powerful opposition was absent.

5

In the middle of the brawl for the B&O, when Alfred Perlman realized the Central was probably going to lose, he raised a very serious question that was embarrassing to every railroad with merger on its mind. If the well-off roads grabbed up only those pieces of the national system that struck their fancy, what was going to happen to the leftovers? The commission had to be made to see through the cries of imminent nationalization by roads that were well-off. The best way, Perlman said, was to combine the dockets, to hear all the cases together on a consolidated record. Then there could be no choice but to insist a home be found for everyone. Otherwise, a lot of innocent people—all those whose jobs depended on the leftovers and the industries they served—were going to be hurt. "The continuation of the present piecemeal approach," he said, "will result in a chaotic situation based on the survival of the fittest."

"When the 1957 Penn-Central talks collapsed," said *Trains*, "Al Perlman asked eastern presidents to review the whole merger question and produce a logical, voluntary blueprint that would . . . reduce railroading's cost, preserve essential competition, and ensure that the stronger did not get stronger while the weak got weaker. . . . Railroading is vulnerable to a charge of lack of statesmanship when the president of the number two road in the nation feels obliged to call in the regulators to keep order."[80]

The predator roads—the Pennsylvania, the N&W, and the C&O—would hear none of this. It was planned consolidation, they said, and planning was discredited. They offered no suggestion of what was to become of the leftovers—the Central, the Erie Lackawanna, and the New England roads—but insisted that what they wanted to do *and only what they wanted to do* was in the public interest.

The ICC was helpless. It knew it had failed in the 1920s. Hesitation would be denounced as obstructionism. Besides, there were on the commission honest men who still believed railroad executives' talk about savings and the dangers of imminent bankruptcy. To combine dockets would delay all decisions, in which time the weakest components might drop over the brink and the commission would be blamed. If a combined docket became too complicated and encumbered with take-it-or-leave-it conditions, the strong roads would just walk away. There would be no consolidation and the commission would be blamed. Yet the failure to combine dockets eventually made the Penn Central merger inevitable, for if there were going to be any mergers, the New York Central was far too important to be left out. The Penn Central monstrosity brought down the whole structure of eastern railroading and the commission was blamed.

By the end of 1961, the Lehigh Valley affair was moving rapidly toward a denouement. The Lehigh was going broke. Besides, long before oral arguments were presented to the commission, a strange thing happened. All the opposition just melted away.

Erie Lackawanna had its vague promise to be included in the N&W. The Central had its agreement with the Pennsylvania. The *New York Times* was naive on what had happened. "The merger-minded eastern railroads had finally settled family squabbles," it said, and implied all would turn out well.[81]

Late in 1961, the Kennedy Administration became alarmed about the Pennsylvania's ultimate designs and the failure of anything to stand in its way. Attorney General Robert Kennedy had the Justice Department's antitrust division investigate. In February 1962, it filed a preliminary brief in the N&W case in which it attempted to show the Pennsylvania did control the N&W. Justice's work had been hindered by the refusal of Wyer, Dick & Company or Coverdale & Colpitts to cooperate; they would not risk angering their corporate clients. Congress was slower to react, but a few senators were beginning to speak out. The consensus seemed to be that the ICC ought to wait before approving any consolidation until other government agencies could sort the thing out.

Yet on April 4, 1962, the commission let the Pennsylvania take control of the Lehigh, even though it was well known that President Kennedy was preparing a message on transportation for delivery to Congress the following week. The timing of the decision and its importance to the Pennsylvania empire made it disturbingly significant. Neither presidential nor congressional opinion seemed to bother the ICC, and the old charge that the agency was dominated by the most powerful in the industry it was supposed to regulate was given a new lease on credibility. Late that summer, James Symes suggested that in the event of a Penn Central merger, the Lehigh might be sold to the C&O-B&O, presumably on a *quid pro quo* basis, to give it an entry to New York. But the *Chessie* System was not interested, and the forlorn Lehigh Valley, eventually engulfed by the Penn Central, was left to twist slowly in the wind. For all the inflated claims of salvation through control, all that could be said about the Lehigh in the prosperous 1960s was that it survived. Tonnage and revenue declined steadily. At Batavia, New York, where once the *Black Diamond* had flashed on its last sprint into Buffalo, weeds grew on a decaying roadbed. Pennsylvania did keep true to one promise: it did not let the Lehigh become insolvent. Bankruptcy did come, on July 24, 1970, thirty-three days after the Penn Central itself had entered the courts.

CHAPTER 7

Preliminary Moves in the West; 1960-1962

Railroading in the West faced a different set of economic circumstances than in the East. In the first place, distances were long, which gave the rails a cost advantage over motor carrier competition and kept traffic, even high-rated perishables, securely bound to the rails. Second, the West was growing in population, production, and consumption at a faster rate than the East, frequently at the East's expense, so there was more market for the western roads to exploit. Finally, and because the West's economic development came late, western roads never invested in the expensive dead ends that littered eastern railroading—branches to carry resort-bound passengers, multiple tracks, fancy passenger terminal-mausoleums, and commuter operations. (The only commuter service west of Chicago was the Southern Pacific's comparatively modest one on the San Francisco Peninsula.)

When it came to consolidation, the West had a special problem. A look at a map showed a dense, spaghetti-like network across the flat prairies dominated by the grain-hauling roads known as the grangers. But the mountains and the deserts beyond were pierced by less than a dozen routes controlled by half a dozen carriers. Grain hauling was seasonal business for the grangers and the traffic fed them by the transcontinental roads was very important. Some of the transcontinentals, notably the Santa Fe, had their own entrances to the midwestern gateways and so turned little traffic over to the hungry grangers. The transcontinentals (all except the Milwaukee Road, which was really a granger road with a line to the Pacific) were financially strong and eager to move into granger country, but on their own terms. The perennial question was how to match transcontinentals and grangers so as not to have a lot of starving grangers left over. Ripley had had a hard time with it and so had the commission in its plans of the 1920s. One breakthrough had been the creation of a new transcontinental in 1934 with the completion of the Dotsero Cutoff of the Denver & Rio Grande Western with Reconstruction Finance Corporation funds. This forty-one-mile line linked the old Denver & Salt Lake line, with its six-mile

Moffat Tunnel under the Continental Divide, with the Rio Grande's main-line, opening a transcontinental route through Denver for the first time and providing lines like the Rock Island and the Burlington with a share of the transcontinental traffic moving over the central route.

1

Just as the Pennsylvania had used the consolidation provisions of the Transportation Act of 1920 to acquire an empire in the East, so the Southern Pacific had used them to acquire one in the West. By so doing, it had gone far to insure that it could veto any future consolidation there, just as the Pennsylvania could in the East.

First, it got control of the Central Pacific, that western half of the first transcontinental. Union Pacific didn't let it go without a fight and was powerful enough to extract guarantees that SP would not use that control to divert California traffic away from the UP at Ogden.[1] Next, SP took control of the El Paso & Southwestern, which originated a lot of mineral traffic on its line between Tucson and El Paso, and also provided a connection between the SP at El Paso and the Rock Island at Tucumcari.[2] But the SP's great coup was control of the Cotton Belt (the St. Louis-South-western), which gave it direct entry to St. Louis.

Cotton Belt was a poverty-stricken little southwestern line. Leonor Loree, veteran of the abortive "fifth system" schemes in the East during the 1920s, had once tried to merge it with the other weak sisters of the southwest, the Katy and the Kansas City Southern.[3] When that failed, SP saw a cheap way to get direct access to a major midwestern gateway. The route, via Corsicana, Texas, was 400 miles longer than the route via Tucumcari and the Rock Island. The SP never said a word about the cost of rolling freight those extra miles, and when asked it said such costs were impossible to determine. But when it was trying to extract higher payments from the American Fruit Growers Car Line, it had calculated with unflinching assurance that its costs were 3.026 mills per ton mile. At that rate, the extra cost for the Corsicanna route was about $55 a car, plus $32 to return the empty. Eventually, that was bound to be passed on to consumers.

Bringing the SP into St. Louis via the Cotton Belt inflicted damage on the Rock Island, which had now lost both the El Paso Line's mineral traffic as well as the SP's transcontinental traffic. It also hurt the Missouri Pacific, whose affiliate Texas & Pacific had been another favorite route of the SP into the St. Louis terminals. But the ICC saw control as a way to save the wheezing Cotton Belt, which SP admittedly turned into a first-class railroad.[4] For the SP, this had been done on the cheap, through stock control.

When all these acquisitions were completed, the giant was quiet, content to terminate 74 percent and originate 63 percent of California's traffic.[5] Then, in 1961, it shook western railroading like a California earthquake.

2

The intended victim was the Western Pacific, the last of the transcontinentals (completed in November 1909), once a weak stringer line in the hostile domain of the Southern Pacific but more recently a successful little company that had won attention, regionally and nationally, for good service and good dividends. The purpose of the incursion, not said in so many words, was to wipe out this embarrassing competition for the SP and re-create its monopoly dominance of old. No case illustrated the real motive behind the merger movement more starkly than this.

In some ways, Western Pacific was superior to the SP's Central Pacific line. Its route through the Feather River Canyon crested the Sierras a full 1,000 feet lower than the SP at Donner Pass. By running a tight ship, particularly since World War II, and by being innovative, WP had managed to win a secure niche in traffic moving over the central route. Most of it was turned over to the Denver & Rio Grande at Salt Lake City, which in turn passed it on to the Missouri Pacific at Pueblo, and the Burlington and Rock Island at Denver, roughly in that order. Thus if Western Pacific should come under Southern Pacific domination, it would send reverberations on roads reaching all the way to Chicago.

For many years, the Southern Pacific had enjoyed a monopoly of railroad traffic between the Bay Area and the Columbia River, the so-called Shasta Route. In 1930 and 1931, the Great Northern had extended a line southward and the Western Pacific northward to a meeting at Bieber, California.[6] Being east of the Shasta Route, it was nicknamed the Inside Gateway. It was more circuitous than the Shasta, but again, by running a tight ship and being innovative both in service and rate-making, it had developed a loyal following. In the meantime, the powerful Santa Fe, itself a transcontinental road well entrenched in southern California and up the San Joaquin Valley, needed more complete access to industrial parks in the Bay Area and the north. Relationships with the Western Pacific could not really be intimate, as both were competitors for transcontinental traffic; up against the power of the Southern Pacific, however, they had found a number of broad areas for cooperation, particularly on traffic coming down the Inside Gateway. It was obvious why the once weak and despised Western Pacific should now be sought by the Southern Pacific. Control would also cripple competition from two of its most powerful transcontinental adversaries, Great Northern and Santa Fe.

Without warning in September 1960, Southern Pacific began to buy Western Pacific stock. It moved with lightning speed and had 182,000 shares, or about 10 percent, within five weeks. On October 12, Donald Russell of the SP telephoned F.B. Whitman of the WP to request the *pro forma* information required by the ICC for filing an application for control. It was the first Whitman knew of what had happened.[7]

It can only be guessed what anger and frustration reigned at WP those October days. It did not want to be controlled or consolidated. It was a strong railroad with operating ratio low, net income high, fixed charges under control, morale top rate. It could field a super passenger train, the *California Zephyr,* with style and pride, the way it could field super freight service, every bit the equal of the mighty Southern Pacific. It was proof that a railroad did not have to be large to be successful. Indeed, with better operating results than the Southern Pacific, it was an indicator that medium size might be preferable. Perhaps that was why it was such an affront to the giants. It thrived on competition; it paid dividends while competing. It epitomized, in those days, the best of American capitalism.

On October 25, the Santa Fe announced that in the past two weeks it had also acquired WP shares and filed for control. It confessed it was only reacting to the SP. It did not even seem to take the "studies" it made of possible coordination projects very seriously.[8] Most of what the two roads could coordinate, they already had. Great Northern backed the Santa Fe, while Union Pacific backed the Southern Pacific, both with further stock purchases.

At first, Western Pacific fought back. Its board resolved that control by the SP was contrary to the best interests of shareholders, employees, and public, and demanded that Donald Russell be subpoenaed for oral interrogation.[9] But with the filing of Santa Fe's counter-application, it seemed to moderate and take the naive position that ensnared many others: that the commission's only choice was between the SP or the Santa Fe and that continued independence was probably out.

It was awesome how thoroughly the SP and Santa Fe strong-armed support for their proposals. Said one group of southern California cities (that eventually backed the Santa Fe): "Seldom have our chambers been flattered with the attention and effort that was expended by both roads to acquire support in this proceeding." The SP convinced dozens of shippers, city and town councils, and chambers of commerce not just to write letters but to file pleas of intervention. Each was identically worded, indicating they were railroad-inspired and railroad-written. Imagine what happened in a case like this: The California distribution manager for Armstrong Cork wrote a letter to the commission praising competition. "In areas where the Southern Pacific has competition," he said, "we find

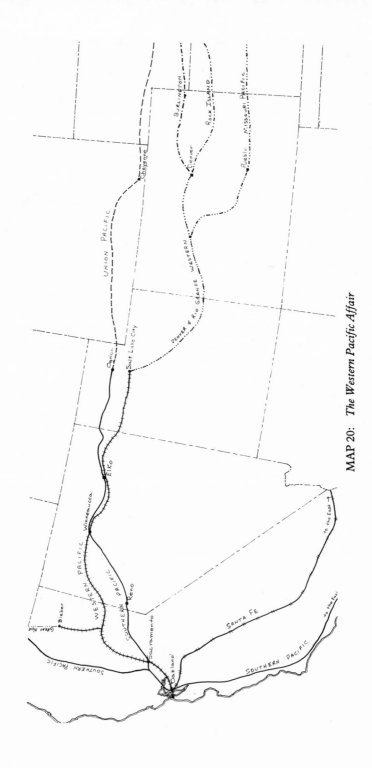

MAP 20: *The Western Pacific Affair*

our customers receive better service not only from competing lines, but from the Southern Pacific as well. . . . Generally speaking, we get better help from railroads like Western Pacific." Later, he wrote back a frantic letter, stressing the first had been written as an individual, not as a representative of his company, even though it had been on its letterhead.

On further consideration of this entire matter, I do not believe that I have sufficiently strong feelings on this subject that I would want my comments to influence the thinking of the Commission. . . . I would appreciate your returning my letter of December 22 and deleting my name as an interested party in these proceedings.

It would likewise be appreciated if the California Public Utilities Commission and the Western Pacific Railroad would return their copies of this same letter.[10]

Southern Pacific claimed, or tried to, that control would permit coordination that would substantially increase efficiency. If that seemed laudable, these projects were in fact quite modest. The two railroads' mainlines were nearly adjacent for 178 miles between Alazon, Nevada (near Wells), and Weso (near Winnemucca), and the two tracks had been operated as a single double-tracked railroad since 1924 (the WP eastbound, the SP westbound). The SP had in one recent year (1959) a small increment of eastbound over westbound cars, the WP the reverse. "The handling of these cars on an exchange basis would result in *substantial* savings in operating and investment costs" (emphasis mine). That was project 1. Project 2 involved SP traffic from the Ogden gateway to Oregon destinations which could use a segment of WP track between Weso and Flanigan, Nevada, permitting the abandonment of 53 miles of SP line. Finally, there would be certain "coordinations" between Stockton and Oakland in the area where WP originated and delivered most of its traffic.[11] That was all there was to the original SP case. Later, it found several more things to add to the list, implying that the desire came first, the rationalization second.

Donald Russell insisted control would have "no substantial effect on the competition Southern Pacific is today encountering in providing transportation service." He insisted railroads, including his, were down for the count and had no choice but to unite against nonrail carriers. "If such measures are carried out, I foresee a good future for railroads; if they are not, I can foresee only a continued shrinkage in the railroads' share of total transportation."[12]

It was the danger of extending reasoning, with some validity in some parts of the country, to an area where it had no validity at all. Southern Pacific's traffic was increasing, not decreasing, including its tonnage of high-rate commodities. By American standards its traffic was dense. Its profits were high. It seemed to have no trouble attracting capital. Russell seemed to be saying that we must reduce railroad capacity so that we will not have to reduce railroad capacity. It sounded like that crazy logic that came out of the Vietnam War: we had to destroy a village in order to save it.

In January 1961, the Department of Justice (Eisenhower's Justice) intervened in opposition to both applications on the grounds that control by either SP or Santa Fe would be in violation of the Clayton Act. Justice thought control was an especially cheap way to get rid of competition. A merger, at least, would force the predator roads to pay a decent price for WP securities. The department's debut in the rail merger movement was a rather crude exercise, its typed briefs looking sloppy beside the elaborate printed entries of the state public service commissions, but its efforts would gain in sophistication as time went on. Like the ICC, it was learning.

Hearings went on through most of 1961. Examiner Paul Albus recommended for the Santa Fe, but a majority of the commission thought neither railroad had made much of a case. It threw out both applications. Those close to the commission, however, insisted it was not because both proposals were so utterly devoid of merit, but because the commission, which usually bent as the powerful wished it to bend, happened to get caught between two equally powerful forces.

3

Three times the Northern Lines, James J. Hill's old Northern Securities empire, the Great Northern, the Northern Pacific, and the Burlington, had tried to merge, and three times they had been denied.[13] On February 17, 1961, the fourth attempt was formally launched with petitions to the ICC. It was four years since they had put out their first preliminary feelers and three years after their Wyer Report was completed. Of the intense negotiation that had gone on behind closed doors, the public would get only an occasional glimpse. No merger proposal to date stirred as much public opposition as this one, a clamor that finally forced the attention of the federal government. It would take nine years for the matter to be settled, and even then the bitterness would linger on. But the empire Hill and Morgan had put together was not to be denied. With each setback to its plans, it had come back again and again until the other side caved in. This was the blockbuster merger to date.

Back in the 1920s, neither the Ripley Plan nor the ICC's tentative plan recommended a consolidation of the Northerns. Since the *Northern Securities* decision in 1904, a new factor had entered into railroading in the Northwest, namely, the Pacific Extension of the Milwaukee Road. Completed in 1909 after horrifying cost overruns, it was virtually a duplicate of the Northern Pacific. Even as the last spike was driven, work was nearing completion on the Panama Canal, promoted by coastal interests to smash the transcontinental rate structure.[14] The Northerns closed all gateways to the new railroad west of the Twin Cities, which meant that any traffic solicited by the Milwaukee bound for a GN or NP siding, even in Seattle, had to be handed over to them at the Mississippi. For all these reasons, traffic on the new line never came up to expectations. The GN, NP, and the Union Pacific (which entered the region from the south) each handled about 30 percent of the Northwest's transcontinental business; the Milwaukee, a mere 12 percent, with one through freight a day generally sufficient for its needs over its magnificent right-of-way, 600 miles of it electrified.[15]

In the final settlement after the *Northern Securities* decisions, Great Northern and Northern Pacific were each allowed to keep a 48 percent interest in the Burlington. Around that, something of the old common interest remained intact. It was no big surprise that in the more favorable political climate of the 1920s, fearing that a final plan might forever separate them from each other and force one of them to take the unwanted Milwaukee Road, GN and NP should return to the commission and ask to have the *Northern Securities* decision reversed. It was the most sophisticated merger case the commission had heard up to that time, a harbinger, a model, really, for cases to come. For the first time, consolidation was put forward as a prerequisite for operating efficiency. From Sand Point, Idaho, to Casselton, North Dakota, for example, the GN was 101 miles shorter than the NP. Rerouting NP traffic over the GN line would save 400 million ton miles a year. Rerouting GN traffic moving off the Burlington at Billings, Montana, would save another 107 million ton miles. For locomotive fuel, GN would have access to the sub-bituminous "Rosebud" coal abundant on NP lands. Altogether, the savings were estimated at more than $10 million a year, quite a bit in 1925 dollars.[16]

The ICC was convinced and said the merger could go through—if the Burlington was divested entirely. Whatever breast-beating took place among the railroads' executives when they met in the offices of J.P. Morgan & Company in New York, they finally decided not to accept the commission's offer. The ICC paired NP and GN in its final plan, and left the Burlington and Milwaukee each to head up independent systems. In the real world, the status quo of the *Northern Securities* settlement remained intact—GN and NP independent, both under the protective benevolence of J.P. Morgan & Company, and each with a 48 percent interest in the Burlington.

In 1961, when the Northerns returned to the commission, their case for improved efficiency through merger was now standard thinking. It was as

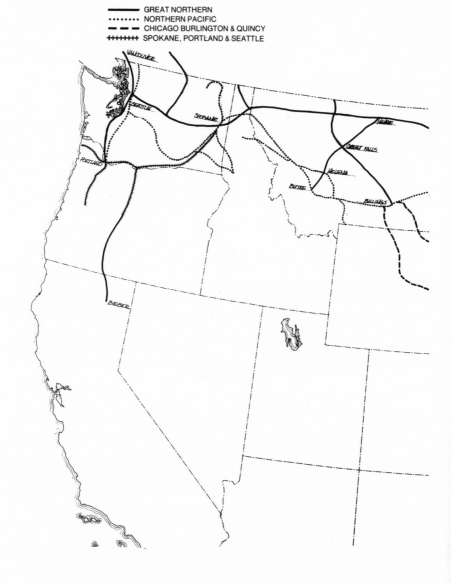

LEGEND:
- ——— GREAT NORTHERN
- ••••••• NORTHERN PACIFIC
- – – – CHICAGO BURLINGTON & QUINCY
- +++++++ SPOKANE, PORTLAND & SEATTLE

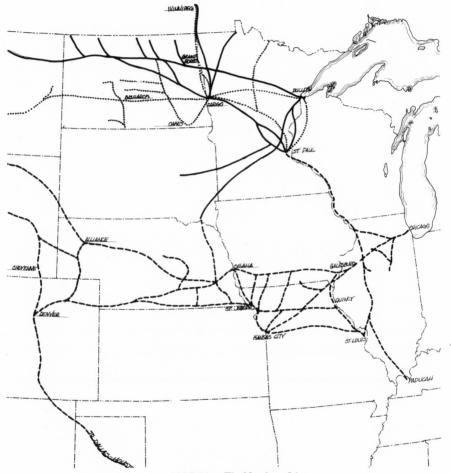

MAP 21: *The Northern Lines*

good, or as shallow, as the cases recently gone before. All components of the combination were financially strong and paying dividends, though operating revenues and ton miles were only holding steady and had been especially disappointing for the Burlington since the war. But they insisted there was no hope for survival except in retrenchment. They must save money, cut costs, reduce plant—like an elderly person fearing the bank account would run out.

Wyer estimated $46 million in savings and even the ICC commissioners who opposed the merger acknowledged $29 million.[17] If that money could be used for better purposes than unnecessary duplication, the public would have much to gain. Four areas of increased efficiency were the core of the railroads' case—transit privileges, car supply, improved service, and capital investment. Shipper after shipper testified the merger was good because of these things.

Yet even on its foundations, the case for merger began to teeter. On the matter of transit privileges, the railroads had a good point. Being able to stop a shipment en route for storage or processing, without losing the through rate, or being able to pick up grain from several points to form a carload for rate purposes, gave a tremendous flexibility to agri-business operations. Because the privileges involved higher costs to the railroads, they were always limited to the railroad that originally granted them. They were usually not granted at all when there was no competition to force them. There was the possibility this merger would open vast new transit and routing gateways all over the West.

On car supply, the crucial fact was that even while paying dividends, and despite recurring car shortages, car ownership of the Northern Lines had decreased. There was no indication anywhere on the record that this was going to change. What had been implied was that Burlington shippers would have access to NP cars, and NP shippers to GN cars, and so on, a play-off that was cynical at best. These implied promises apparently included private-owner refrigerator cars over which the railroads supposedly had no control.[18]

On the matter of improved service, one story revealed a lot. The railroads had insisted it was impossible to speed transcontinental freight schedules without a merger (which would permit routing over the best segments of GN and NP). However, when the Milwaukee Road speeded its schedules in 1964, the Northerns promptly followed suit, cutting as much as eighteen hours off Twin Cities-Seattle times (though admittedly with lighter trains, requiring more trains to do the work).

As for capital investment, there was nothing deficient about the Northerns as they were. They had the latest of everything and had shown no difficulty in raising the money to buy it. Admittedly, a return of 4–5 percent was not as good as some other industries, but not as bad as some, either.

They probably could not raise capital for extremely costly innovations, like electrification, or major new line construction (though given their retrenchment mentality, that was unlikely). While $13 million savings meant the difference between meeting fixed charges or not meeting them to Erie Lackawanna, $46 million meant mostly higher dividends here. Again, there was no promise on the record that these companies would make any investment beyond the cost of plant contraction necessary to effect the merger.

Furthermore, the way in which the case was presented cast doubt on its credibility. Day after day, shippers would take the stand and present the same four points, usually in the same order, often using identical phrases; coincidentally, these were the very phrases used in *Consolidation*, *Key to Transportation Progress*, the little booklet distributed by the railroads. "Around these four cornerstones," said the Minnesota Railroad and Warehouse Commission, "the entire structure of the applicants' case was built."

There was not a deviation as witness after witness paraded to the stand, monotonously told his story on direct, stood cross-examination showing the utter lack of facts he had available to him when he came to his conclusion, and then departed from his moment of glory.[19]

So much for the positive side of the case. On the negative side, the big question was why merger was necessary in the first place. The most significant areas for saving, as described by Wyer, could be carried out short of this drastic, irreversible act. Predicted savings at common points, for example, were so spectacular, particularly at the Twin Cities, it would have seemed independent roads would have wanted to carry them out—if they really expected the savings they said they did. The railroads greeted the suggestion with indifference, dismissing it as the wishful thinking of people who didn't understand the business. But it stood as *prima facie* evidence that they were crying wolf when they predicted calamity if they could not merge. Several commissioners thought so and flatly subtracted $5.25 million from the Wyer studies as savings that did not require a merger to realize. After all, when Erie and Lackawanna were really in trouble, they made coordination work.

But the big question was always competition. The point the Northerns were trying to make was that competition between railroads no longer mattered—it was all against trucks. They convinced only the true believers. Many of their own witnesses, shippers of heavy extractive and agricultural commodities over one of the longest rail hauls anywhere in the world, said 80 percent, even 100 percent, of their shipments were by rail and economically had to be by rail. "We are competing with the Northern Pacific as vigorously as we know how," said John Budd of the GN. "Great Northern is

Northern Pacific's most aggressive competitor,'' said Robert Macfarlane of the NP.[20]

"The consolidation of these two great corporations will unavoidably result in giving the defendant a monopoly . . . against which public regulations will be but a feeble protection,'' said the Supreme Court in 1896, sentiments that many thought still applied.[21] The railroads rushed out an exhibit that a majority of the commission thought misleading which showed that of the 4,479 stations on the Northern Lines, only 141 of them (3.14 percent) which already had competition would lose it. The problem was that numbers of country stations were meaningless; competition was moving the same commodities over the same route—in this case, Puget Sound to the Head-of-Lakes.[22] If competition was not important, what was the need for the exhibit?

Besides, the Milwaukee Road, in the Northerns' own neighborhood, offered a pretty good example of how competition worked. It was the one that initiated faster schedules. It initiated piggyback (adopting the New York Central's flexi-van system). It was the first to cut rates on Montana grain. Always, the Northerns followed. The Department of Justice cited eleven cases where when Milwaukee initiated, Northerns followed.[23] One shipper of lignite in North Dakota had a choice of NP or the Soo Line. Only the Soo would regularly supply adequate cars, even though it was financially the weaker of the two carriers.[24] The leaner and hungrier the competitor, the more likely it was to offer the shipper the service he needed. Making the Northerns more solidly entrenched was not a likely way to increase their efficiency or their capital investment. Summing up a consensus that was growing across the Northwest, the Department of Justice said the merger proposal came just when the railroads were beginning to break away from their worst shortcoming, noncompetitiveness and inflexible rate-making, just when the public was beginning to enjoy the fruits of competition.

To William Quinn of the Milwaukee, the options for his road were few. Given what seemed to be the inexorable tide of consolidation, flat-out opposition was not likely to stop the merger. A demand for inclusion might leave it as firmly out in the cold as Erie Lackawanna. So he supported the merger, provided that certain demands were met. He wanted 11 gateways opened up west of the Twin Cities, so Milwaukee could get its maximum haul on all traffic. He wanted trackage rights from Portland to the British Columbia border to enable him to participate in north-south movements along the coast and to generate traffic for the main line.

His reasoning was this: With a 1.2 percent return on investment, Milwaukee was not likely to pull off many more coups like speeded schedules. At the present competitive balance, it would die a slow, agonizing death. Therefore, approve the merger, grant the conditions, and at least the line would have a chance to pull itself up on its own. If that seemed reasonable, economist Leon Keyserling thought it was like having Ford and General Motors merge and say they would still have competition from the few Packard dealers left around. After William Quinn joined the enemy as president of the Burlington, his successor, Curtiss Crippen, had serious doubts about this strategy. While the Northerns claimed the Milwaukee's proposals would cost them $20 million in revenue, he thought they would produce little more than $8 million for his road; since the new traffic would add to costs, he thought the gains would be a "wash." Besides, Soo Line claimed that it would be ruined if Milwaukee got those conditions.[25]

One issue came up in the Northern Lines' merger that seemed to be unique, at least in its intensity and the bitterness it caused, but it raised deep questions about ICC procedure that touched all the mergers. It concerned the fairness and impartiality of the hearing examiner. Could a system where all evidence was taken by a single person who took no part in the final decision produce an adequate result?

The ICC examiners were hired from the civil service list, and after a training period were generally assigned to cases by rotation, although exceptions were made when a particularly sensitive or complex case was coming up. From the moment the first correspondence came in, especially the amount relayed through congressmen and the White House, it was clear this case was going to touch a few political nerves. It was unfortunate, therefore, that the man whose name came up was one with no experience in railroad cases. Since retirement from the army, Robert Murphy had dealt entirely with motor carrier affairs. Second, and whether this was known at first is not clear, he was an impatient man, intolerant of repetition and intolerant of incompetence or unfamiliarity with the rules. To some, he came across as just plain biased in favor of merger and against all who opposed it. "Applicants' counsel were treated with normal courtesy," said Paul Rasmussen of the Minnesota Railroad and Warehouse Commission, "but opposition counsel were always put on the defensive . . . reminded that repetition would not be countenanced. He allowed petitions in support of the merger at all stages of the hearing, but when it came to petitions in opposition, a different rule was followed, and the attorney in opposition was put through the ordeal of explaining the nature of the petition, the nature of the organization supporting it, and so on."

It is known to the opposition counsel, and I personally observed that the legal staff of the applicants were extremely disturbed by the tendency on the part of the examiner to show prejudice in their behalf. There was every indication that they counseled with him and urged that he reverse his rulings, because they were apprehensive that if he did not do so, bias and prejudice would be so conspicuous that on appeal to the courts, the protestants might prevail to such an extent the entire proceeding would be discarded.[26]

These were very serious charges, especially when it was realized the examiner sat alone in deciding the direction the record would take and in compiling the recommended report to the commission. While in a routine rate case he might do little more than chair a meeting, in a complex merger case he constantly made on-the-spot decisions of major consequence. It was a lot of power to put in the hands of an inexperienced bureaucrat.

In Murphy's defense, the case was long and repetitive; shippers, chambers of commerce, cities and counties, trade union locals, all had the right to say the same things, over and over. Hearings were held all over the West, far from the comforts of Washington, and living out of suitcases day after day got on everyone's nerves. Some shippers reflected on the Seattle hearings, which seemed to emerge as the most controversial of all: "There was no unfairness by the examiner. He was firm and decisive, and at times abrupt and curt. He reversed himself after reconsideration when he felt a previous spontaneous ruling was wrong, but he did give every party a full right to present his case."[27] Even the Milwaukee Road, with a tremendous stake in the proceeding, said it received a fair hearing.

But affidavits filed by the Department of Justice told a different story. Two of its field men talked privately with Murphy on November 5, 1964, when the hearings were nearly wrapped up. Here are some of the examiner's remarks:

When a person went to a doctor to have an ailment analyzed, that person didn't question the doctor's judgment, but accepted his advice . . . and if I went to a dentist to have my teeth fixed, I would place the care of my teeth in his hands and not question his judgment. . . . Finally, we must have the same confidence in the applicants' witnesses.

These railroads should merge because the railroads in the Northwest are in the shadows of the New England roads and if they don't merge, the same thing is going to happen to them that happened to the New England roads.

How could witnesses scheduled to testify at Spokane possibly be harmed when the applicant railroads have offered assurance that no one will be adversely affected?

You don't think I'm going to sit on this hard bench for six months and listen to witnesses who do not understand what it's all about?[28]

Later, said the investigators, Murphy added that "he could not understand why people would oppose a rail merger." This, said the Department of Justice, showed a "shocking, extreme and undisciplined personal bias in favor of the merger." The examiner pictures himself and the ICC as the sick patient, it said, needing ministrations from the railroads. But the ICC is supposed to probe; the public looks to it to do that. Bitter experiences with the abuses of industry experts who, through the years, sought rail consolidation in their own interests, was what gave rise to regulation in the first place.[29]

The credibility of the entire proceeding was now in considerable doubt. Major layoffs were anticipated—more than 8,000 jobs—with the most severe cuts at Auburn, Washington, and Livingston, Montana, the sites of major NP facilities. Elected officials in the Northwest were very responsive to labor.[30] The Railway Labor Executives' Association no longer claimed to defend merely the parochial interests of labor but attacked mergers as threats to competitive enterprise, to the long-run vitality of railroads, and to capitalism itself; they buttressed these attacks with briefs that were disturbingly eloquent. The Department of Justice, whose sloppy incursions into the Western Pacific and Seaboard-Coast Line cases invited contempt, had at last found its voice and its commitment. For a time, it kept alive the illusion that regulatory hearings were not just closed affairs for vested interests, but peoples' courts, dedicated to getting to the bottom of things. All the states served by the Northerns except Missouri and Nebraska either opposed the merger or approved only with heavy conditions to protect their industries and citizens.[31] The Minnesota Railroad and Warehouse Commission led the attack. In a state where the fires of prairie radicalism could still burn as brightly as they had in the 1870s, one could hear the voices of Grangermen and Alliancemen thundering down through the ages.

In the rising clamor, Congress could not turn a deaf ear.

CHAPTER 8

Congress Listens and the Commission Acts; 1962-1964

By April of 1962, feelings on merger seemed to have changed. Just a year before, it had been the salvation of railroading. The only opponent willing to advertise its opposition was labor, and since it had been smeared with the irrelevant featherbed epithet, its opinions were discredited. The largely indifferent public had bought the railroads' rationale with hardly a second thought.

But somehow things had turned out all wrong. The principle of merger seemed to rest on a foundation that didn't quite square with the facts. It was supposed to make railroads healthy so they could provide better service; it seemed only to be making them bigger, though probably not richer, with nothing in it for the public. Antimerger sentiment flamed across the Northwest. Hearings on the Penn Central were to begin in August, and most of the New York delegation in the House had come out against it.[1] Six other major cases were approaching their final stages of presentation before the ICC, each of them swirling with controversy.

On April 4, 1962, the ICC approved Pennsylvania control of the Lehigh Valley. To some, this was the signal that the commission was unable or unwilling to stop the mergers, or even consider them properly. Did it not understand this case was linked to all the others in the East? Did it not understand that by committing this one irreversible act, all the others might have to follow, each one closing the noose still further until the ultimate debacle was inevitable? If the public remained indifferent or ignorant, Congress, at least, seemed to notice that something was not functioning at the ICC.

Commissioner William Tucker, who would soon reveal his membership in the antimerger camp of the ICC, sent up an early warning. Contrary to some popular misconceptions, he told an audience at Boston University that the ICC did not decide these cases as a matter of whim but as a matter of law.[2] The law (section 5 of the Interstate Commerce Act as revised in the Transportation Act of 1940) directed the commission to approve mergers that were *consistent* with the public interest. That was quite different from the Transportation Act of 1920, which had restricted approval to mergers that *promoted* the public interest. Despite the seemingly neutral language of the 1940 act, its legislative history indicated a desire to encourage consolidation. Therefore, all the railroads had to show was that, on balance, their merger would not be harmful. The law had been passed in the wake of a depression when there did seem to be surplus plant in all industries, when plant contraction still seemed like a good idea. Furthermore, the 1940 act virtually eliminated any government or public input into the planning of consolidation.[3] But if times and needs had changed, Congress and Congress alone could change the law and give the ICC new direction.

1

President Kennedy recognized the inadequacy of the existing law. His message to Congress on April 5, 1962, the day after the Lehigh decision, called for sweeping new transportation legislation. He wanted transportation to remain privately owned, unsubsidized, "operating under the incentives of private profit and the checks of competition."[4] Those who had already characterized Kennedy as a screaming economic collectivist had not listened very closely.

His suggestions were, on the whole, remarkably pro-railroad. At least, they included a number of things the Association of American Railroads had been asking for—an end to minimum rate regulation, a free hand to institute intermodal (piggyback and container) routes and rates, and an end to subsidies for trunk airlines and user charges on government-maintained facilities, notably waterways and air traffic control. As for merger, he said, "this administration has a responsibility to recommend more specific guidelines than are now available, and more specific procedures for applying them." He assigned an interagency task force, with representatives from the Commerce, Justice, and Labor departments and the Council of Economic Advisors, to examine each merger to be sure competition, efficient services, and labor welfare were maintained. He chose Clarence D. Martin, undersecretary of commerce for transportation, to head it. The task force held its first exploratory meeting in late May, eventually submitted a report that echoed the president's ideas but otherwise retraced conventional ground, and was never heard of again.[5] So much for President Kennedy.

Congress showed no great alacrity to act on any of the president's suggestions, but Estes Kefauver of Tennessee, former presidential hopeful on the populist side of the latter-day New Dealers, introduced a bill to put a moratorium on mergers until December 31, 1963. It was offered as an amendment to the Clayton Act, which meant hearings would be conducted by his own antitrust subcommittee. Mergers that did not reduce competition and would therefore not come under the Clayton Act would not be affected. Mergers of roads with less than $200 million in gross assets or in bankruptcy were specifically exempted.

The purpose was to give the president's task force time to make its study and Congress time to contemplate it. Since most of the major cases before the ICC still needed briefs, examiners' reports, and exceptions (rebuttal briefs), and since each commissioner had to digest all the testimony (running 10,000 to 20,000 pages per case) plus the briefs and the exhibits, it was not likely this bill was going to delay mergers very much. Therfore, having no practical effect, its purpose was really to test political winds. Opponents affirmed their faith in the ICC, believed things had been studied to death already, and thought the matter should be considered by the Commerce Committee, not a subcommittee of Judiciary. It was a partisan split, the Democrats lining up behind Kefauver, the Republicans behind the opposition.

A wide cross section of experts was summoned, including railroad executives,[6] labor leaders,[7] representatives of state utility commissions,[8] the ICC and its staff, and scholars, some of them employed by particular interest groups and representing the gamut of opinion.[9] Everyone who testified came across well. Some thought it was inappropriate of Paul Rasmussen of the Minnesota Railroad and Warehouse Commission to bring up the grisly details of the examiner's deportment in the *Northern Lines* case, especially since he did it with such fervor. He and Senator Hruska (R-Nebr.) had an unpleasant exchange over that, which eventually boiled down to whether it was best to let railroads do as they pleased. James Symes and Estes Kefauver also came to verbal blows. Symes said a Penn Central merger would not diminish competition, and Kefauver grilled him on why, if that were true, he opposed the bill, since Penn Central would therefore be exempt. Those were the only dramatic moments, but there was substance, and that was what mattered.

The pro-merger forces were led by James Symes of the Pennsylvania and Professor Merrill J. Roberts of the University of Pittsburgh, testifying for the Association of American Railroads. They argued that the railroads' financial position was serious because the railroads were not sharing in the expansion of the national economy. The situation varied from carrier to carrier, but overall, their return on investment was pitifully low, the lowest of any major industry except commercial air transport.[10] Even if the railroads' method of calculating return was open to question, the trend was unmistakably downward.[11] As a result, the railroads were unable to attract capital. The new interstate highways, for example, were going to be technologically more advanced rights-of-way than the nineteenth-century rail lines, wiping out some of the railroads' advantage of greater ton-mile efficiency. Railroads needed capital to stay abreast. Merger would increase profits that would help build capital reserves, and for the first time in a long time, railroads might become an attractive investment. There was nothing evil about profit. The purpose of mergers was not to reduce rates. That would be a paltry, short-run gain for the public compared to a revitalization of the capital structure.

Furthermore, if railroads were to continue as private enterprises, they could not underwrite social goals such as unnecessary employment or the maintenance of certain passenger services, especially those designed to maintain the vitality of urban centers. Ultimately, most long-run social goals would best be served by a slimmer, more healthy railroad system. The Kilday Report, for example, openly feared the railroads were not adequate for defense needs and recommended not the saving of every branch line but concentration of traffic on fewer, first-class lines (as in the Soviet Union).[12] Any change as big as the railroad mergers was bound to hurt some while it helped others. It was unreasonable to expect immediate benefits to flow to everyone. But on balance and in the long run, they would permit economies of density and economies of scale.

Symes limited his remarks to the Northeast, bluntly dissociating himself from the controversial mergers in the South and West. He pointed out that the eastern railroads had not even been earning enough to pay income taxes. The reason was the deteriorating traffic volume, and the blame went to Congress for creating a monumental oversupply of transport facilities, now topped off with the St. Lawrence Seaway and the Interstate Highway System. It had not necessarily made the carriers using those facilities profitable, but it had gutted the eastern railroads. Many of those roads' lines were built to serve the light manufacturing that once dotted the countryside, sometimes sending branches up both sides of a given valley. It was not retrenchment to trade in this nineteenth-century investment for new, needed investment. Soundly conceived mergers were the best means. "I think," Symes said,

there is only one danger of monopoly in railroad transportation, and it is this. Many railroads cannot long survive present conditions as private enterprise. Today in the East, we are actually looking down the road to nationalization. To my mind, that is the most dangerous monopoly of them all, a subsidized national railroad system. One railroad, the New Haven, has already gone into bankruptcy and others are close behind. A series of bankrupticies in the railroad industry could very well cause the nationalization of all roads. Unless railroads in deep trouble, such as the major ones in the East, are permitted to use the self-help which the Senate subcommittee urged on us four years ago, the public is likely to see the very ultimate in monopoly in transportation, namely, government ownership and operation.[13]

However, Symes raised as many questions as he tried to answer. He did not mention that railroads had survived bankruptcies before—waves of them—without nationalization. Was merger necessary to abandon branch lines? Was it even a way to abandon branch lines? It had not been so for Erie Lackawanna. Why were the railroads that Symes himself cited as the weakest not being invited to mergers—like the New Haven? (Even George Harrison of the Brotherhood of Railway and Airline Clerks, a man not frequently given to favorable talk on mergers, thought some consolidation might be necessary in New England.) And what about Symes's favorite phrase—he used it often—"soundly conceived mergers?" What was a soundly conceived merger? He offered no definition, but seemed to take it for granted that if management planned it, it was soundly conceived. Some people thought the eastern mergers were the result of an accidental chain reaction, and elsewhere, merely an effort to reduce competition and fix prices. Unfortunately, neither the senators nor their staff counsel were familiar enough with the story to ask the right questions.

These questions weighed heavily on Professor William Leonard of Hofstra College, whose *Railroad Consolidation Under the Transportation Act of 1920* was still the standard history of the subject. He believed in consolidation, the Albert Cummins-Joseph Eastman style of planned consolidation. He thought it dangerous that capital should be the only planner, with no input from users, labor, or the public. He thought some of the proposals before the commission were pretty bad ones, and the commission was not getting good information. It relied mostly on opposing railroads, which had high-priced legal firms and came only to get concessions, then faded away without a trace. A fact—Paul Rasmussen of the Minnesota R&W Commission brought it up, and it was repeated many times without challenge—was that the Northern Lines budgeted $5 million to get their merger approved. That was for legal fees, transcript and stenographic costs, and the like. On the other side, it looked like this:

In the State of Minnesota, there is a revolving fund controlled by the legislative advisory committee, made up of the governor, two members of the senate and two members of the house. We found it necessary to go before this committee and request $5,000 be allocated to our commission in order that we could participate in the Northern Lines' proceeding. At the end of a 3-month period, the money was spent, and we had to ask for an additional $5,000 to carry on for the next 3 months, and as of this June 26, I will have to appear before this same body and request another $3,000 or $4,000 in order to continue.

At the present time, there are about 12,000 pages of testimony, 60 cents a page. That transcript would cost the state at present $7,200. There will probably be about 20,000 pages, about $12,000. You try and go before a state appropriation committee and get $12,000 for a possible need in connection with purchasing a transcript.[14]

Eventually, the Milwaukee Road let the State of Minnesota use its transcript.

Things were no better at the Department of Justice. Lee Loevinger testified that for five railroad merger cases and the *American-Eastern Airlines* case they had available only six lawyers.

Senator Kefauver: Frankly, half a dozen lawyers for all those mergers looks like spreading it mighty thin.

Mr. Loevinger: They are spread mighty thin, Senator.[15]

Into this void of public input swept the determined vested interests. Said Professor Leonard:

The present rash of rail mergers has reached what might be termed the peril point, where there will be real damage done to competition and the adequacy of rail service to the public unless the federal government acts in a broad and statesmanlike fashion. . . . I urge Congress to assume leadership in this matter . . . and not wait until we have giant rail systems crushing smaller and weaker lines in their territory, or until one large combination dominates the country.[16]

The ICC, which was now under attack, sent three of its members—chairman Rupert Murphy, Kenneth Tuggle, and William Tucker. Tuggle had spoken favorably of mergers in the past and Tucker had sounded that early alarm over the need for new legislation, but it was not known at the time that these men represented opposite poles regarding mergers. People forgot that commissioners, like everyone else, disagreed. But these men were agreed that the ICC was equipped to do the job properly and that input should come from sources other than railroads. When, for example, all the opposing railroads withdrew from the *N&W-Nickel Plate* case, they ordered their Bureau of Inquiry and Compliance into the case to develop the record. The bureau had already begun a study on its own and would be assuming a larger role in future cases.[17] Furthermore, ICC procedures were neither sacred nor cast in concrete. They could, and would, be modified to meet situations. It was inappropriate for any of them to comment on particular mergers they would have to decide, but they assured the subcommittee they knew what was going on, had good staff input, knew which cases were related to which, had legal precedents for determining public interest, and could tell who was exaggerating and who was bluffing. In short, they had things under control. Unhappily, the clanking Lehigh Valley decision coming the day before the president's message did not enhance the commissioners' credibility.

Labor led off for the antimerger forces. Railroads were financially strong, it said. Most were paying dividends. They had been able to reduce their outstanding funded debt, even in the recent years they claimed were so bad. Their earnings and net incomes were as high as they had been in the late 1940s and far higher than in the 1930s, when things were much bleaker than they had ever been since. Merger was not necessary then and it was not now. Railroads and banks represented a web of interlocking interests, and as in the days of *Northern Securities,* the banks stood to make the real profits from these mergers by selling and manipulating the securities necessary to finance them.[18] There was no evidence that any of the alleged savings had ever been brought down to net in mergers of earlier years. The public would pay in the form of reduced service and reduced employment (which in turn, reduced consumer spending). Even national defense would be jeopardized, according to Gen. James Van Fleet in his article "Rail Transport and the Winning of War."[19] Finally, the public should not have to pay for the fact that many individual roads were managed by wretchedly incompetent people. (If they were well managed, for example, how could General Motors report a half-billion dollar profit on sales of $2.5 billion in diesel locomotives?)[20] That was the reason, said George Harrison, for the railroads' hysterical screams for greater speed in processing these applications. They knew they had to strike while the recession was on. They would never get away with it otherwise.

For the first time since the Clayton Act era, the antimerger side had strong intellectual expression. Professor John Meyer of Harvard put it this way: mergers treated a symptom, not a cause. Traffic volume was the real problem and merger could do nothing about that. He had helped to set the field of economic history ablaze with his econometric study (with A. Conrad) "The Economics of Slavery in the Ante Bellum South." He had done some econometric studies of railroads as well and found that in the absence of competition, costs always tended to rise to the level permitted by earnings. Competitive innovation nearly always came from the smaller, less-entrenched railroad. Furthermore, with increasing size, railroads experienced clear and measurable difficulties in managing their unwieldy organizations. It was not an accident that well-managed, compact companies were turning in the best records in the industry—the Western Pacific and the Frisco, for example. "A great deal of wishful thinking would appear to exist in both transportation and banking circles on the beneficial effects that might be achieved from merger."[21]

There was no point, Meyer thought, in blaming railroad management. They had to meet weekly payrolls and were therefore prone to grasp at straws. They could not be expected to do long-range planning. But among the private reasons for merger, not often talked about, was the desire of well-managed roads to cash in on their managerial skills by taking over badly managed ones. Railroading was remarkable, he thought, for the mediocrity of its management, rather typical of heavily regulated industries where there was little room for innovation. Innovators got frustrated and tended not to stick around. A wider dispersion of good management, he thought, was the greatest benefit that could come from the mergers.

He was worried, however. The experience of other countries was that the creation of huge regional systems that turned out to be inherently inefficient was an evolutionary step *toward* nationalization. Professor James Nelson of Washington State agreed. If the giants began to falter, nothing could save them. Certainly the mechanics and, therefore, the attractiveness of national operation would be greatly simplified by the mergers.

No presentation at the hearing, in fact, nothing that had been said or written about consolidation since the days of Joseph Eastman, was as far-reaching in its implication as the paper presented by Kent Healy of Yale titled "The Effects of Scale in the Railroad Industry." It had been published the year before in pamphlet form by Yale and received limited circulation. Since it used sophisticated techniques of partial correlation analysis, it was probable that many of those who tried to read it couldn't understand it. But its conclusions were diametrically opposed to the traditional thinking of the past fifty years, and they were buttressed with evidence far more powerful than the guesses and hopes on which the conventional thinking was based.

He had taken all the class I railroads and eliminated certain special cases, namely, short-haul roads (Reading, Maine Central, Chicago & Eastern Illinois), roads where passenger traffic constituted more than 55 percent of train miles (New Haven, Boston & Maine, Jersey Central, Lackawanna, Long Island, and Florida East Coast), industrially owned roads (Duluth, Missabe & Iron Range, Bessemer & Lake Erie), and predominantly coal roads (Norfolk & Western, Chesapeake & Ohio, Western Maryland, Virginian). Then he ranked the thirty-seven remaining roads by size according to the number of employees. These were plotted on scatter charts measuring such variables as administrative expense, transportation expense, wage rates, and capital requirements per unit of output. Standard deviations were calculated to measure how much above or below the norm a road stood. There were differences between regions (the adverse effects sometimes not setting in for western roads until a larger scale was attained). If the New York Central and the Pennsylvania were removed, the trend was still the same.

It showed that for railroads with more than 10,000 employees, there were *no further economies of scale to be obtained* from increasing size, and for roads with over 19,000 employees, *positive diseconomies set in*. The larger roads required higher wages and higher transportation expenses and earned lower rates of return per unit of output than medium-sized roads. Only in administrative expense did unit cost seem to decrease with larger size. At the same time, there was no relationship between traffic density and capital requirements, and at densities over $50,000 revenue per mile, wages and transportation expenses increased per unit of output. Since the number of employees seemed to be crucial, the evidence suggested that the reason for this was the inability of management to oversee the larger organizations. In short, both economies of density and economies of scale *would not materialize* in the larger mergers. The companies would be worse off than they were before.[22]

No one who had committed himself to consolidation liked Professor Healy's conclusions, but no one was equipped to challenge them. Senator Hruska chided him for taking so long to complete his study (two years). "We are going to do our study in two weeks," he said. "We are much more expeditious than you." Regardless, with the publication of this paper, the case for railroad consolidation was in shambles.

The last day of the hearing was devoted to one of the most eloquent and most curious presentations to date. It was by Leon Keyserling, economist and former chairman of President Truman's Council of Economic Advisors. He was now a paid consultant for the Railway Labor Executives' Association, which had just published in pamphlet form the study on which his testimony was based, *The Move Toward Railroad Mergers, A Great National Problem.* At first glance, it looked like a sophomoric conglomeration of whizbang graphs illustrating a variety of national economic statistics. There were little drawings of smiling people in overalls, happy farmers with pitchforks, cornucopias, and so forth. But when what he was trying to say was understood, it was the most refreshing breeze to come out of railroading since the Burlington's *Zephyr* in 1934. It was not based on any of the complicated techniques of the Healy study. The fact that it seemed insightful only underscored how totally the railroads' pessimism had captured everyone's minds.

After nearly a decade of pre-Keynesian economic policy, Keyserling said, the national economy had failed to grow at the pace it should have. But with agressive, full-employment policies, the American economy was going to take off in the 1960s. Railroads had a bad break since World War II, when they had to adjust to the presence of new forms of transportation which could do certain jobs better. But their ton-miles, the measurement of work actually performed, were not significantly lower than at any other time in their history, and for some roads, were at their highest level ever. Admittedly, much of that was low-value commodities, so these high tonnage levels could not always be translated into net income. However, the period of difficulty was largely behind. In the next ten years, the need would not be for contraction of railroad capacity, but for expansion. Railroads handled 563 billion ton-miles in 1961. By 1970, he predicted, they would handle 820 billion. (They actually reached 764 billion in 1970, 851 billion in 1973.) All this talk of duplicate facilities was based on an unwarranted pessimism that would be disastrous if carried out. Since the historic record of cartels was always one of investment contraction, he was convinced the best way to insure the necessary expansion in the future was the preservation of vigorous competition. The fastest road to nationalization was cartelization.

Did that seem ironic? Business executives who had fortressed themselves in expense-accounted, fringe-benefited, mini-welfare states called corporations, were afraid of competition, anticipated recession, and preoccupied themselves with visions of decline and bankruptcy. They had no faith in freely competitive enterprise. Labor, which had so frequently been tarred-and-feathered as a fellow traveler, believed in competition, had faith in private enterprise, and looked forward to the future—if business could deliver the leadership which, in railroading, it had failed to do so far.

Everyone, it was said, looked good at the hearing—except the senators. Estes Kefauver had done his homework. His cross-examination was generally to the point, though in his effort to avoid discussion of particular mergers he failed to pin anyone down. Roman Hruska had also come prepared and took an active part. He and Kefauver were poles apart, but no points would have been satisfactorily clarified without their conflicting views. Philip Hart (D-Mich.) was a freshman that session. Perhaps that excused his lack of familiarity with the subject. Everett Dirksen (R-Ill.) came in occasionally, siding with Hruska in opposition to the bill, and contributing bits of Dirkseniana along the way. The others, Carroll (D-Colo.), Dodd (D-Conn.), Long (D-Mo.), and Wiley (R-Wis.), took no active part. Estes Kefauver alone had the interest, or the courtesy, to listen to Leon Keyserling. Even the subcommittee could not really grapple with the tough problems. It could hardly be expected that the full Congress would.

The Kefauver bill was never reported out of committee. It died at the end of the session and was not renewed. Congress did not deal further with railroad consolidation until the debacle, and then it was too late. The railroads had thrown down a terrible gauntlet: mess up our consolidation, and if we go bankrupt, you will be to blame. Maybe Congress was frightened. Perhaps it was too busy supervising the Vietnam War, or enacting Kennedy's other economic and social legislation. Railroad executives were acting in their own interest, as they should have been expected to act. The ICC was going to try to enforce the law as Congress had written it, trying to adjust its ambiguities as best it could. Everyone was trying to do his job except Congress. If either the railroads or the ICC needed further legal guidance, it was up to Congress to provide it. However, it would or could not. Instead, it demonstrated a horrifying lack of expertise, lack of interest, and lack of leadership. The ball was fumbled right there.

2

President Kennedy's first announcement of the presence of Soviet missiles in Cuba came on the evening of October 22, 1962. The nation was stunned and frightened, and by nightfall the next day, many Americans expected to be at war, or dead.

It so happened that oral argument on the C&O-B&O case was scheduled for the next day. Jervis Langdon, now president of the B&O, took the unusual step of delivering his company's summation himself. If we go to war, he told the commissioners, the men and women of the B&O were ready to do their part. But it was going to be close. Just a few more months at its present rate of deterioration, and the B&O would not be able to fight a war. Control by C&O was essential, immediately. The B&O could not survive without the freight cars, the capital improvements, the financial security. Commissioners were as scared that day as everyone else. Some think that single bravura performance dispelled all remaining doubt in their minds. The C&O-B&O merger was approved on December 17, 1962.[23]

The ICC is a very public body. It keeps few secrets, its records are open, and it has a very adequate staff that will produce them quickly, for anyone, on request. However, between oral argument and final decision there is a blind spot in commission proceedings, when the commissioners debate among themselves, off the record, free from the shackling rules of evidence. It had to be that way if there was to be meaningful give-and-take. There are some who think the real history of the mergers is locked up in the private files of the commissioners.

Vice-Chairman Abe MacGregor Goff wrote the majority opinion. The weight each man gave to various arguments, the points he thought strong or weak, will never be known. The collective wisdom boiled down to a full acceptance of the railroads' case and a rejection of all the opposition. (The contention of the New York Port Authority, for example, that diversion from the Central would bring that road to its knees, was dismissed as having "no weight"—with no further explanation.) The B&O *was* in mortal danger, they said, and C&O control *would* save it. Perhaps there could ideally be better combinations, but—a bird in the hand, and so forth. The commission was aware the case had been less than watertight, for the report was peppered with little phrases of doubt. But on the whole, it was reluctantly persuaded the C&O had behaved honorably, that it would rehabilitate the B&O, and that alleged savings were real. But the decision was not unanimous.

"I do not agree that these applications should be approved on this record at this time," began Commissioner William H. Tucker in his long and eloquent dissent. In the first place, the case was much too weak, like that interminable testimony on car supply (for example, how the C&O was going to lease cars to the B&O to ease its shortages). It was a short-run solution to a short-run problem, perhaps even a nonexistent problem at that.

The evidence consists of impressive *post hoc* rationalizations prepared by a corps of engineers, economists, accountants and traffic and financial experts employed to justify a prior managerial decision. Neither the examiner, nor any interested party to the proceeding, public or private, was endowed with the peculiar knowledge and the ample resources to challenge evidence of this character. The necessary findings could have been made if the general public had been represented by members of the Commission's staff and consultants retained by the Commission. We shall never know the answer . . . because the Commission's role has been passive from beginning to end. No such passive attitude existed half a century ago when the Commission retained Mr. (later Mr. Justice) Louis Brandeis as its special counsel in the *Five Per Cent* case of 1914.[24]

Tucker found it incredible that the majority should trust to the C&O's self-interest to rehabilitate the B&O when the historic record of aid by parent roads was so abysmally poor. Nothing indicated the B&O was in so much trouble that a decision could not wait until an adequate record was developed. The B&O's own president said it would operate in the black in 1962, and at the very least, the commission ought to consider its good financial showing in the first three quarters of 1962.

The stakes were high. This was the first of a series of cases that would reshape the eastern railroads. These cases were related. Each would affect the other. They could not be decided in isolation.

In a narrow, literal sense, the transaction proposed is the control of the B&O by the C&O. What these parties actually propose, however, is to become one of the giant rail systems of the East. The proposed three-rail system . . . presents one fundamental issue: What kind of railroad system should the present generation leave to the generations that follow? If there are any who maintain that only the owners are empowered to shape the device, I need only say that the properties have been duly entailed, first by the states and later by the Interstate Commerce Act. The answer provided by the Commission majority seems to be that whatever the carriers prove to be good for themselves is good for the country.[25]

Tucker was joined in his dissent by Charles A. Webb and in part by John W. Bush. They alone saw where this decision was going to lead, and were afraid, for the future of railroads and the future of the commission. "The decision to isolate this case from the others," they said, "is going to haunt the Commission for many days to come if the Central, and to a lesser extent, the N&W, are not allowed to strengthen their lines in the remaining 'merger' cases." Railroads knew this. That was precisely why they engaged in a "reciprocity of silence." They must not impede C&O-B&O, so C&O-B&O would not impede them.

If the Commission is going to open the gates on all eastern merger applications so each successive one becomes one of the basic reasons for requiring approval of the next . . . we may end up as the creators of another Frankenstein's monster far more ruinous than its fictional counterpart.[26]

Labor had been responsible for revealing many of the gaping ambiguities in the C&O-B&O record. Disappointed by the commission's decision, given hope by Tucker's and Webb's dissent, labor led the tattered forces of the remaining opponents to court. But the courts, both the district court and on appeal all the way to the Supreme Court, refused to consider the merits of the case and limited themselves only to questions of ICC procedure. Affirmation of the method was affirmation of the decision. The Supreme Court upheld the lower court and the ICC in October 1963.[27] Consolidation would go forward.

With that decision, there came an end to labor's antimerger press campaign. It had been going on since 1959 and had been limited mostly to labor publications. Consolidation was the big news on the front page of every railroad labor journal, most of it straightforward reporting on the fights among the railroads with emphasis on the role of bankers and fat cats. Headlines were delightfully inflammatory; the cartoons could have come out of Kansas in the days of less-corn-and-more-hell populism. But if its ultimate purpose was political, it had failed, for Congress sat as sphinxlike as ever. So now, with defeat by the Court, it was all over.

3

In later years, things were pretty much out in the open. When a Norfolk & Western official was asked, for example, why his company had not protested the Penn Central merger in the early period, in light of how vigorously it protested later on, he answered bluntly: we couldn't; they controlled us. That question alone came to dominate the N&W-Nickel Plate merger: did the Pennsylvania control the N&W? It was common knowledge that Pennsylvania owned about 33 percent of N&W's outstanding stock. It was common knowledge that four Pennsylvania men, James Symes, David Bevan (vice president for finance), and past presidents Walter S. Franklin and Martin Clement, sat on the N&W board of directors, while N&W President Stuart Saunders sat on the Pennsylvania board. It was obvious the N&W-Nickel Plate merger required at least the Pennsylvania's blessing, for the decisions to lease the Wabash and sell the Sandusky line were ones only the Pennsylvania could make. Still, everyone connected with either company vigorously denied having the power to control.

Throughout the hearings, Examiner Lester Conley made it clear he was aware of the situation and kept asking embarrassing questions. Where did the N&W hold its board meetings? (Philadelphia.) Were N&W affairs or Penn Central merger affairs discussed at a particular meeting of the Pennsylvania board? (Saunders: "I don't know. I purposely stayed away.") Regarding Saunders's concurrent directorships of the Pennsylvania and N&W:

Q: I would assume, sir, by your occupying those two very distinguished positions on two different railroads it would indicate that there is a relationship between those two roads? Am I correct in that?

A: It doesn't necessarily indicate that.[28]

With no time to spare, the Department of Justice gathered the dozens of scraps of evidence that were strewn liberally about and wove them into a meaningful whole. On countless occasions in the past, it said, the Pennsylvania or its officials acknowledged the power to control the N&W—in its official history, the *Centennial History of the Pennsylvania Railroad*, in statements by A.J. County in the consolidation planning of the 1920s, in statements before the Wheeler Committee in 1938, and in statements under oath in various court proceedings. Threats of antitrust action would occasionally frighten it into selling a few shares, but it would always buy them back when the threat had passed, either directly or through Kuhn, Loeb & Company. In the period after 1938, Pennsylvania cast sometimes as many as 62.5 percent of the votes for N&W directorships and never less than 50 percent. Even in 1960, after the Virginian had been absorbed and Pennsylvania holdings diluted, it still cast 37.5 percent of the votes. Prior to the Virginian absorption, no other stockholder owned more than 2.2 percent of N&W's stock, the wide distribution giving the Pennsylvania a disproportionate clout in company affairs. Since Virginia law required approval by two-thirds of the holders of each issue of stock for certain kinds of corporate transactions, including merger, the Pennsylvania had an effective veto even after the Virginian was taken in. Pennsylvania held a quarter, sometimes more than a third of N&W directorships, and always a quarter to half of the seats on the executive committee. Room 1034 of Penn Center Plaza in Philadelphia, in the midst of PRR executive offices, was inscribed as the office of the president of the N&W Railway and was adjacent to the offices of Walter Franklin and Martin Clement. On December 28, 1960, the PRR board of directors had passed a formal resolution saying it approved, authorized, and consented to a merger of the N&W and Nickel Plate.[29]

Tie all of that together, said Justice, and it constitutes effective control, especially in light of the legal precedent set in the *Rochester Telephone* case (in which the court directed the extent of control be determined not by artificial tests but by the special circumstances of each case).[30] And in the offices of the Pennsylvania Railroad, the danger signals were recognized immediately. Previously silent before the ICC in the big eastern mergers, it quickly filed a petition to intervene "as a precautionary measure."

Looking back, this may have been the ultimate test of the commission's mettle. It had come out of the C&O-B&O case looking pathetically prorailroad, accepting at face value the little technical points raised by railroad attorneys and ignoring the broad, regional issues that seemed so obvious to everyone else. David Bevan raised a last-ditch technicality in this case, the kind on which the commission seemed so prone to stumble. The PRR's N&W holdings were divided between the PRR itself and the Pennsylvania Company; they could, therefore, not be treated as a single block, and could not constitute control. Yet if these bald-faced denials of control or influence were to go unchallenged, there would be many who would give up hope on the ICC, convinced it was either in collusion with the powerful companies it was supposed to regulate, or frightened of them.

So it may have come as a surprise in some quarters when it turned out the ICC did have mettle. The press release went out on April 17, 1963. Examiner Conley found the PRR had the power to control the N&W and he recommended that full divestiture be required as a condition of merger. Admittedly, there were problems. Three hundred million dollars worth of stock could not suddenly be dumped without severe dislocations to securities markets, and besides, much of it was already pledged as collateral for various loans. But confidential memoranda that have been released since then indicate the Pennsylvania took this very seriously and immediately began to cast about for other high-yield investments.[31]

The commission approved the N&W-Nickel Plate merger on July 13, 1964, Tucker alone dissenting on the merits of the case. As before, he thought the railroads had failed to make a positive case for consolidation. He thought the record inadequate, the need for great hurry spurious, and protection for other railroads, Erie Lackawanna in particular, inadequate.

The N&W, however, had not come through as unscathed as the C&O. Appendix O required the record be kept open for five years, in which time Erie Lackawanna, Delaware & Hudson, and Boston & Maine could petition for inclusion. In the meantime, and until such time as Pennsylvania influence was entirely gone from the N&W, the newly merged company was ordered to solicit traffic through the Buffalo gateway for Erie Lackawanna. Consummation of any part of the merger constituted irrevocable assent to these conditions.[32] Furthermore, the Pennsylvania was given ninety days to submit its plan for complete financial and managerial divestiture.

Now the awful decision lay with the Pennsylvania—a dilemma largely of its own making. Should it stick with the N&W and $11 million in annual dividends that in a few recent years were the only thing that kept it in the black? If it did, it would bring the eastern mergers to a halt. Or should it cast its lot with the New York Central? There was no positive assurance that the Penn Central merger would be approved. One can only imagine the breast-beating that must have gone on in Penn Center Plaza those summer days of 1964. There were only ninety days to reach a decision.

CHAPTER 9

The Rise of the Penn Central; 1961-1966

In June 1964, the Boston & Maine filed for the discontinuance of all passenger service, bringing to a head the impending railroad disaster in New England. In 1958, when Congress gave the ICC jurisdiction over passenger service, it had in mind the branch-line locals that state public service commissions, under heavy down-home political pressure, had required to ply their lonely journeys. That was why the law limited discontinuance to those trains that were not required by the public convenience and necessity *and* which constituted a burden on interstate commerce. The B&M was going broke and passenger trains were believed to be the cause; hence, they were a burden on interstate commerce. But they were well patronized and there was no substitute rail service; thus they were required by the public convenience and necessity. It was a situation the law could not cope with and new legislation was in order. Then the State of Massachusetts came to the rescue of the Boston commuter service and the ICC found a way to skeletonize the rest.[1] So once again, Congress was saved from having to come to grips with the problem.

Knowledgeable people looked at the B&M, at the short hauls, the branch lines, and the shift of New England manufacturing to light-weight, high-value electronics, more susceptible to truck competition than the textiles of old, and wondered if getting rid of the passenger trains was going to help. Wasn't merger a good idea? If it was a panacea for everyone else, why had the New England roads been so totally excluded?

1

On October 11, 1965, the New Haven posted discontinuance notices for all its 273 daily interstate passenger trains.[2] These trains were required by the public necessity; even the private automobile could not substitute for the work they performed, not without tripling turnpike mileage and parking space. The need for relief was not to avoid bankruptcy—that had already come in 1961 thanks to Hurricane Diane in 1955 and the opening of the

Connecticut Turnpike in 1959. It was to forestall an operating breakdown. Maintenance was so badly deferred, rolling stock in so shocking a state of disrepair, and morale so low that safety could no longer be guaranteed on the high-speed, high-density routes. Shortly, it would be impossible to put a train over the line. There was no way to avoid the New England crisis now. It was a time-bomb in the lap of the ICC.

Tucker and Webb had seen it coming as early as the C&O-B&O decision. Without dwelling on New England in particular, they recognized that among the eastern railroads, there were some losers and some winners. The strong roads, so eager to pluck off the winners, would eventually have to face up to the losers. The case-by-case approach was going to drop them all on the final merger. This was why they regarded James Symes's talk of "balanced competitive systems" and "soundly conceived mergers" as silly hypocrisy. Symes did not advertise it, but he also saw the situation coming. Actually, he could not even pretend to ignore it, since Governor Powell of New Hampshire had summoned him and Alfred Perlman to Concord in 1961 and told them they had better come up with a convincing proposal or New Hampshire would do everything in its power to wreck their merger.[3]

The three-system East, the so-called Symes Plan of C&O-B&O, N&W, and Penn Central, could digest New England only by neutralizing it. All the New England roads, including the Central's Boston & Albany, would be dumped into a New England terminal railroad. To that end, Symes offered the Lehigh Valley to the C&O-B&O at scrap value, for it was the only one of the big three without access to the New England lines. It was a way of saying that C&O was expected to take some responsibility. Unhappily, C&O had no interest in New England and knew the Lehigh Valley had never been competitive to New England points anyway.[4] But a minor setback must never stand in the way of a brave idea and, besides, the terminal railroad had plenty of proponents in New England. One was E. Spencer Miller of the Maine Central who had sparkplugged that conclave of New England railroad officials back in 1959. Those talks had broken off, but the study that had been commissioned from the J.G. White and Arthur D. Little firms of Boston was complete and offered dozens of suggestions for coordination.

A stumbling block had always been the New York Central presence in New England in the form of the Boston & Albany. Alfred Perlman said that whenever he approached B&M people on the possibility of coordination, B&M's Pat McGuiness would just say, "Why don't you rip up the B&A?" and drop the subject.[5] The B&A lost money by itself, but it was a valuable feeder to the Central system as a whole. As the New England crisis loomed, Symes may have given Perlman a hard push to get out of the region, but there were signs the Central itself was getting weary of New England's over-meddling politicians whom Perlman thought were responsible for bringing on their own railroad crisis. The State of Massachusetts, for example, refused to let the B&A install centralized traffic control and rip up one of the two tracks, even though CTC worked everywhere else on the system. He had no respect for politicians who had threatened to cut off all state aid to New Haven passenger services if it tried to abandon any of its unused branches. Nor did he respect New Haven management, for while pleading for more traffic, it had failed to exploit its grandfather rights to blanket southern New England with coordinated highway services.[6] But regardless of his opinions, it was vital to James Symes and the Penn Central merger plan that the idea of a terminal railroad be kept alive.

In case the idea sounded progressive, a bit of history was sufficient antidote. In early New England, the railroad had followed rather than created industrial development, hence an abnormal number of branch lines.[7] Trickles of freight filtered through dozens of gateways rather than trainloads through a few of them. In the early twentieth century, much of the tonnage was within the region, which meant an unusually short haul. Even for traffic originating west of the Hudson River, nearly half of it (41.5 percent) had a total haul of less than 150 miles and required an average of three terminal handlings. Short hauls, terminal handling, and branch lines all contributed to an abysmally slow service. It took three days for a car to move 40 miles from Nashua to Beverly in 1920, five days for the 165 miles from Nashua to Meriden, three days for the 66 miles from Bridgeport to Windsor Locks. This ghastly inability to move the traffic was a major cause of the operating breakdown during World War I, which saw, for example, an embargo on all interchange with the B&M two out of every three days between 1916 and 1918. Most of this information was made public in the *New England Division* case of 1921, at the dawn of the motor carrier age.[8] It showed a classic vulnerability to motor carrier competition.

Following the Morgan-Mellen debacle on the New Haven, New England political and commercial interests developed a remarkable insularity and wanted the trunk lines expelled from the region altogether. A committee of New England governors, the Storrow Committee, was adamant for home rule, even though the only private source of funds for capital improvement was the trunkline railroads. With the greatest of caution, in 1923, they suggested some kind of public aid as preferable to domination from the outside. (Remember, this proposal for "socialization" was in the wake of the Plumb Plan hysteria, which made it quite remarkable.)

Actually, the issue of outside control was academic in the early 1920s. The New Haven and the B&M had such a low rate of return, no one was interested. Only when that rate improved at the end of the decade did the Pennsylvania make its rapid moves on the New Haven. In 1931, another committee of New England governors again recommended—rather hysterically—the expulsion of the Pennsylvania and the creation of an all-New

England terminal road. Interestingly, the fact that portions of the New England system were controlled by the New York Central and the Canadian National did not seem to matter as long as the Pennsylvania was driven out. This committee, like the Storrow Committee before it, put tremendous emphasis on maintaining coastwise steamer competition, even if it forced rail rates up to keep the ocean service alive. But the coastwise steamers were dying. Said Professor James Nelson, keeping them alive sacrificed the substance of competition for the form. It must remind one, he said, of the tales of ghost ships with ghost crews condemned to ply the seven seas forever without cargo and without destination.[9] It meant that on the eve of the motor truck onslaught, New England railroads were vulnerable from the standpoint of rates as well as service.

In that governors' committee of 1931, only the Rhode Island delegation perceived the implication. In their dissenting report, they rejected the idea of a terminal railroad and favored affiliation with the trunks. If the trunk-lines were shut out, what would stop them from using some kind of truck distribution to reach their destination, bypassing the New England roads altogether? They even used the word "container," quite novel in 1931.

There were remarkable service improvements in the years that followed. In the 1920s, it took the B&M eighty-three hours to deliver cars from Boston to the New York Central at Rotterdam Junction (near Schenectady). By the 1930s, it advertised fourth-morning delivery all the way to Chicago, third-morning delivery by the 1950s, and second-morning delivery by the 1960s. (Boston-Chicago schedules via the Canadian Pacific were still seventy-seven hours in 1965, the reason for the diminishing importance of the Canadian connections.) The New Haven had pioneered the piggyback concept in the 1930s and had filed the petitions to the ICC that opened up vast new opportunities for piggyback service and rate-making in 1954.[10] Many customers, who had that classic pattern of New England distribution —bulk commodities in by rail, finished goods out by truck—liked the new Plan I piggyback introduced that year by which trailers were hauled at a uniform rate and moved on a motor-carrier bill-of-lading. But as if to underscore the dire predictions of the Rhode Islanders in 1931, the two major trunks, Central and Pennsylvania, refused to give the New Haven much cooperation. Central did not introduce piggyback until 1958, and then only a flexi-van service that was incompatible with anything the New Haven offered. As late as 1961, piggyback interchange with the Pennsylvania required a costly over-the-road haul through the city streets of New York, encouraging shippers to take delivery directly from the PRR at Kearny, New Jersey.[11] Both bypassed a New Haven line haul. That was precisely why the idea of a terminal railroad was a bad one and why another conference of New England governors in 1963 recommended for trunkline affiliation.

So once again, the proponents of mergers were fighting on the wrong side of the economic fence. Alfred Perlman would stand in front of a hearing examiner and say with a straight face that he saw no way a Penn Central merger could hurt the New Haven, even though one of its principal justifications was to reroute all former PRR traffic bound for New England via Albany and the B&A.[12] No one else had the nerve to be that smug. Hotboxes, derailments, and electrical fires were all common on the New Haven now. Both New Haven and B&M were unilaterally settling *per diem* (car rental) accounts at $2 a day instead of the usual $2.88, a short-run saving that ran a terrible risk of retaliation and back indemnities. A B&M official almost bragged how his road had resourcefully created its own cash flow— by holding bills forty-five days or more before paying them—a cash flow that could have a short period of success.[13]

Someone had to take responsibility for the mess. Public ownership was still anathema to almost everyone. The very man with the greatest reason to recommend it for the New Haven, James Symes, had trapped himself. How could he say nationalization was the worst possible thing for his road and the best possible thing for somebody else's? So just as it was beginning to sink in that the Pennsylvania was going to be stripped of the Norfolk & Western, the likelihood that it would inherit the New Haven began to dawn. The *New Haven Discontinuance* case would be the vehicle that would tie the fortunes of the New Haven and the Penn Central together, to the death.

2

Penn Central was the big merger. If it had been a success, all the mergers would have been judged successful. It ended in disaster and discredited them all. When at last the debacle lay exposed, it seemed that other roads were lucky merely to have survived their mergers. For Penn Central, merger was not the only cause of what happened. Historic problems came welling up out of the past; unanticipated problems of the national economy swirled about the top; and a certain corporate petrification was apparent long before the merger took place. But one salient lesson emerged: no amount of regulation, short of dictatorial control that no one wanted, could save an industry from its own foolishness. It had set itself on merger, even when there were plenty of warnings that it was not the solution to the problems of Penn or Central. The clues were all there, on the record, but they were so obfuscated by management, so buried in procedural verbiage, so clouded with the selfish demands of everyone else, it would have taken a clairvoyant ICC to spot those clues as controlling.

James Symes took personal credit for conceiving the Penn Central merger.[14] In the first throes of the 1957 recession, it was a bold idea. He believed in mergers, even when the recession passed, even when serious

nothing more than a stopgap to gain time (for what was not clear). Other men had built the railroad; still other men had built the Horseshoe Curve and tunneled under the Hudson River; still others had electrified it; still others had dieselized it. The merger would be his monument, for the enduring glory of the Pennsylvania Railroad. He took a humiliating rebuff from the Central when it broke off the first merger talks in 1959, but he forgave it the moment it again showed interest. His board of directors, successful corporate men though strangely docile, never questioned him. Only one of his subordinates seems to have raised a doubt—David Bevan, who incidentally was passed over to succeed Symes in favor of the N&W's Stuart Saunders, the man with the demonstrated ability to get a merger through. Perhaps if James Symes had remained at the helm through the critical days of the merged railroad, there would have been no debacle; perhaps he was the last of the great men of the Pennsylvania Railroad.

What enthusiasm ever existed at the New York Central died with Robert Young. Alfred Perlman never wanted a merger, not with the PRR, nor did the technology-and-computer-oriented management team he put together after Young's death. It was never clear why. Some thought he disliked Symes. Others thought he had been snubbed by the Protestant-establishment condescension of the PRR hierarchy. Some thought he thought the PRR management was incompetent. Some thought he wanted to rebuild the Central first. Some thought he thought the merger would flop. He kept changing his stories and the press kept embellishing them with rumors that most likely did not come out of thin air.

He broke off the talks in 1959. He said he realized the Pennsylvania held all the trumps the day of the N&W-Nickel Plate announcement and that he had no choice but deal with them the day the C&O got more than 50 percent of the B&O.[15] Perlman was supremely confident that he could single-handedly build the Central into something great, although the goal was more elusive than it had been for him on the compact Denver & Rio Grande. But if everyone else was merging (and diverting traffic), he had no choice. So he telephoned Symes in September 1961 to see if the offer was still good. It was an inauspicious way to begin the greatest railroad merger in American history.

When Perlman called, Symes had no hesitation. Within a month, studies of both operations and finances were under way. On November 14, 1961, Symes and Perlman went to Washington for a private conference with the ICC commissioners. "I have good news for you," said Symes. "Pennsylvania and New York Central are going to merge."[16] Such a conference was not unusual for big cases, although it did indicate that certain people had an access denied others. The stock exchange ratio was executed in January and ratified by stockholders the following May. In the meantime, there were the Kefauver hearings and the business of running two troubled railroads. Perhaps there just never was time to step back and rethink things coolly.

3

It is often forgotten in the grand sweep of the disaster that lay ahead that the concept of Penn Central had a more logical rationale than any of the other mergers. Each of the two greatest railroads in the East was to be redesigned into speciality roads, doing those tasks it was able to do best.

Squarely in the path of the Pennsylvania Railroad lay the backbone of the Appalachian Mountains, a defiant wall astride its mainline. On the 924 miles from Chicago to New York, 25 percent had grades greater than 0.5 percent, and on the tortuous passage from Johnstown to Altoona, around that engineering feat known as the Horseshoe Curve, 36 miles were on grades in excess of 1 percent. It was a dangerous bottleneck where trains required long helpers and where maintenance crews had to walk the track daily on this most vulnerable mainline in America. Stephen Meader spun a yarn about it in *Long Trains Roll*, where German saboteurs infiltrate the crews that guided the squealing, smoking trains down the mountainside, filling secret notebooks with the vital statistics of this jugular of the American war machine. It was railroading that made the pulse beat fast. It was railroading that kept efficiency low and costs high.

If all railroads were operated as one, no dispatcher would make New York- or New England-bound merchandise and perishables climb that mountain. He would wing them eastward over the New York Central's water-level route that paralleled lakes and rivers along nearly its entire length, with only 16 of its 949 miles from New York to Chicago on grades over 0.5 percent. Yet as long as these roads were separate, the vast traffic-generating mechanism that was known as the Pennsylvania Railroad had no choice but to send it up and over the curve. The situation was even more absurd for New England traffic, which the Pennsylvania hauled to the heart of the New Jersey waterfront, loaded on car floats frequently delayed because of heavy fog across the headlands, and ferried to the New Haven's Bay Ridge Yard on Long Island, there to be reassembled into trains for dispatch across the Hell Gate. From the west, it should have rolled over the water-level route through Buffalo and Syracuse; from the south it should have gone directly from the PRR to the Central's River Division, all to converge at Selkirk Yard just south of Albany, and there to be reassembled for New England destinations—free of ferries, free of fogs, free of labor disruptions on the waterfront. Merger would allow that magnificent transportation mechanism known as the water-level route to realize its full potential. Selkirk would be the heart of the new system. From an operating standpoint, the merger would succeed or fail on Selkirk.

Some said this would gut rail service across Pennsylvania, but such was not the case at all. The trains that would be diverted did not serve Pennsylvania; they just passed through it. The PRR mainline would be cleared for the job it really needed to do, supplying the industrial complexes of Philadelphia and Baltimore and down the lower Delaware and Schuylkill Valleys. The NYC traffic bound for these destinations would no longer have to wend its way over the difficult Clearfield District through the wilds of northeastern Pennsylvania, but would take the mainline.

No other merger rested on this kind of plant rationalization. What community-of-interest had tried to create just before the antitrust hysteria, and enlightened public servants from Albert Cummins to Louis Brandeis to Walker Hines to Joseph Eastman had dreamed of, would now be realized in the Penn Central merger.

The Pennsylvania and the New York Central had come out of the 1950s badly shaken but apparently intact. As the merger made its way through the regulatory process in the early 1960s, revenues climbed back and then exceeded their prerecession levels. Operating costs were kept in line. The operating ratio remained disappointing, but there were plenty of roads doing worse. Money was still being put back into the railroad ($1.5 billion between 1957 and 1968). Pennsylvania put a lot into Conway Yard near Pittsburgh, the operating heart of the railroad. Central installed an entire series of electronic yards at Buffalo, Detroit, Youngstown, Elkhart, and Indianapolis, and was planning another at Syracuse. Despite the plowback, there was money to extinguish some debt and reduce fixed charges. The Central in particular earned a reputation as a bold experimenter in marketing techniques, particularly in the area of pricing. The final results of all this were not spectacular, as their return on invested capital remained a dismal 1 percent or less. However, it was known these roads had terrible passenger losses they presumably could not help, and their part of the country was not growing as fast as other parts. At least until 1966, there was nothing alarming in their performance. If a merger did bring an approximation of the expected $81 million in annual savings, along with the formidable advantages of combined sales forces and combined routings, it seemed reasonable to think all might turn out well.

Yet even in this rosy picture there were some terrifying flaws. By most measurements, productivity on these two roads was stagnant. With a greater volume of business, and in a period of dollar inflation, how could costs be held in line unless severe cuts were being made somewhere where it didn't show? In maintenance, for example. Symes confessed it on the first day of the hearing; his road had accumulated $304 million in deferred maintenance and as a matter of policy was shrinking plant to avoid the purchase of new material. Could it mean that despite a few showy improvements, these roads were slipping into obsolescence? Why was only New York Central mentioned for innovative services and marketing techniques? Did it mean two managements were developing very different ideas on how to run a railroad? Why were dividends being paid, even when maintenance was being neglected and there was virtually no net income on the bottom line? The Pennsylvania had a high accident rate and unusual amounts of track under slow-orders—both signs of advanced stages of poor maintenance. Pennsylvania also had a fearsome amount of bad-ordered equipment—15 percent of its freight car fleet and 20 percent of its locomotive fleet in 1963. Both roads had a poor record of equipment and labor utilization, plus an unusually high frequency of shipper complaints—all signs of inadequate management.[17] Until 1966, the seriousness of this was hard to discern, for good trends were mixed with the bad. Only when the 1967 statistics were in, in early 1968 just as the merger took place, was it apparent these railroads were dying.

In the conventional thinking of the 1950s, this may have spelled a classic case for merger. But by the time Penn Central came up for judgment, conventional thinking was in deep trouble, especially from the Healy hypothesis of diseconomies and management inadequacy. Once a merger was carried out, there was no going back. If management had misdiagnosed its ills, if merger was a mistake and the giant began to falter, government would be all that could save it. What the ICC was asked to determine in this case had shifted almost imperceptibility from previous cases. It no longer had to simply find out what the merger would accomplish and who would be helped or hurt by it, but whether or not it was the correct medicine for the most fundamental of railroad ills. Then how was it that in a year of hearings conducted all over the Northeast, with 25,000 pages of testimony plus another 100,000 pages of briefs, exhibits, and correspondence, the really important things could slip by?

In the first place, the railroads' operating studies were largely irrelevant. They concentrated only on the grand sweep of traffic rerouting, differing markedly from the Wyer Reports of other mergers and creating a dazzling and dangerous illusion of comprehensiveness. Walter Patchell of the Pennsylvania, who was in charge of studies, stood cross-examination for two weeks and seemed to defend them brilliantly. Some of his exhibits were a little obscure or a little technical, lacking something, perhaps, in the way of concrete decisions. Compared to the studies presented in other cases, there was no reason to think these were any more deficient. No one before had asked the railroads to explain exactly how they were going to carry out their merger—what would be done first, who would do it, who would instruct the others in what they were supposed to do? It was assumed executives would not be where they were if they did not know how to execute.

Looking back, Central and Penn probably did themselves a great disservice by relying entirely on expertise from within, for they were not only limited by the intellectual capacities of men already imbued with a company's way of doing things, but they had no one to arbitrate disputes. The studies, it turned out, did not go beyond the theoretical level. Whenever NYC or PRR teams disagreed on a particular item, it was left unresolved. Later investigations revealed glimpses of this—a memo from a PRR executive, for example, who returned from a vacation to find mountains of technical data piled on his desk. "I am searching desperately for some concrete evidence of progress," he wrote, "completed projects, approved networks, etc.—but finding little. Nevertheless, everyone seems to be working very hard, and I am sure there is as much progress being made as can be expected at this time."[18]

The *Wall Street Journal* had already spilled the beans on the chaos at Erie Lackawanna, and that was a smaller and more manageable property. Erie Lackawanna witnesses were even forced to say—on the Penn Central record—that their merger had produced few of the savings anticipated.[19] When Fred Carpi, PRR vice-president for sales, was asked to give a single example of more efficient routing, he chose traffic from Buffalo to Rochester, where the Central had a direct line and Penn was extraordinarily circuitous. He admitted the PRR didn't get much of the business—just a few cars when both shippers and receivers had sidings on the line. Everyone was appalled that it got any with schedules so slow. "I have a couple of oxen down on the farm," said one of the lawyers, "and I think they can beat that schedule from Buffalo to Rochester." What was astounding was that when asked to give one example, that was all Carpi could think of.[20] Still, no one really picked this up and pursued it.

R.F. Ventrella, Michigan representative for the Brotherhood of Maintenance of Way Employees, gave one of the most incisive—and prophetic—comments of the hearing:

. . . As to merger, we have heard here this morning, and we have heard at Kalamazoo . . . shippers and a lot of others testifying in behalf of merger, and it was all guesswork of what can happen. Nobody knows. I don't believe the railroad companies themselves can testify to what will actually happen.[21]

He was very humble, not encumbered with a law degree, he said, and he didn't always know what they were talking about. The technicians, he thought, had a language all their own, so ordinary people couldn't understand them. He hoped they could understand each other. "I would advise the ICC to look back and get all the facts of the mergers they have approved, and see what the result was."[22] But it slipped by—just another labor guy who didn't understand what it was like to run big corporations.

Six years passed between the time the first studies were presented to the commission and their implementation. They were updated and refined, resulting finally in the Master Operating Plan, but that document was never distributed to the general managers before the merger; when it was, afterward, it proved to be of no help.[23] Every study of the Penn Central disaster agreed that premerger planning was woefully inadequate and that it was the direct cause of the operating breakdown after merger. But in all the hearings, no one asked the right questions.

Another reason the hearings missed the mark was because the merger's opponents were interested only in how their ox was going to be gored. Once again, it showed how dangerous it was for the commission to rely on adversaries to develop the case. Opposing railroads never fought the Penn Central idea on its merits, but only to see that the merged railroad cared for their problems. New Haven demanded inclusion. So did Erie Lackawanna, Delaware & Hudson, and Boston & Maine *if* they were not taken into the N&W. Western Maryland wanted its friendly connection, the Pittsburgh & Lake Erie, detached from the New York Central before merger. Monon wanted out of a contract for using the Indianapolis passenger terminal. Chicago & Eastern Illinois wanted to make sure its rental for trackage rights over the NYC didn't increase. Chicago & North Western wanted better interchange arrangements at Chicago. State authorities defended client railroads—Maryland, the Western Maryland; New York and New Jersey, the Erie Lackawanna; Massachusetts, New Hampshire, Rhode Island, and Connecticut, the New Haven.

The situation of the New Haven was critical from the start. Its most important connection, the Pennsylvania, was going to divert traffic to the hostile New York Central. Yes, we solicit against the New Haven, said NYC Vice President A.E. Baylis. We solicit against them on every plan of piggyback service, and their service is so bad, we get the business. Yes, we refuse to interchange certain types of specialty cars with them because we prefer the business to go to our own customers. Any routing conditions the commission might impose will be meaningless when we get to their customers and sell our superior service. The N&W took the Virginian traffic away from the Central, despite conditions, and Erie took the Lackawanna traffic. Now it's our turn.[24]

Considering that this involved brother railroads in an industry that chose to represent itself as besieged from without, some of the remarks by Penn and Central executives were shockingly arrogant. For example, Alfred Perlman on the New Haven:

Q: Do you believe the New Haven would be competitively disadvantaged by the formation of the proposed Penn-Central system?

A: No.

Q: You testified that Central would be hurt by C&O-B&O?

A: That was entirely different. . . .

Q: You find nothing in the relations of the Pennsylvania and the New York Central which would cause you to believe there would be any disadvantage to the New Haven?

A: None at all.[25]

Or Fred Carpi on the Erie Lackawanna:

Q: Let us test your judgment. The Erie, based on the figures given here, last year lost something like $25 million. I ask you to assume in the next two years it only loses $15 million a year. Your testimony is that the Erie Lackawanna can continue to provide good, strong, competitive service losing money like that?

A: Sure.

Q: If that is so, Mr. Carpi, why can't the Pennsylvania Railroad and why can't the New York Central keep doing a splendid job for the public losing Niagaras of dollars in the same way?

A: Why should we?[26]

If railroad executives sometimes looked bad, politicians could look worse. A few, like Congressman William Ryan of New York City, spoke with dignity and eloquence. He was sympathetic to the railroads' problems, he said, but he thought they had been crying for more opportunity to compete and that's what the president's message had offered them. Now, they just seemed to want less. As he saw it, merger would simply require more regulation to replace the lost competition.[27]

Others were neither eloquent nor enlightening. Mayor Hugh Addonizio of Newark, for example, thought the Pennsylvania should help out with Newark's urban renewal problems before it was allowed to merge and was angry that it had not established a passenger stop at South Newark.[28] Congressman Thaddeus Dulski of Buffalo never bothered to find out what different groups of people in his constituency thought of merger (shippers, for instance) but instead talked only to labor. He knew nothing about railroads—had not even heard of the Nickel Plate or whether it served Buffalo. Finally, he settled on what he apparently thought was a substantive issue—the PRR's passenger service out of Buffalo. He thought it was inadequate. The railroad scheduled a train into the capital every day at 8:30 A.M., with bedroom and breakfast service, but Congressman Dulski only used it when the airports were snowbound, which was when everyone else wanted to use it, which was why he had been unable to get space, which was why he was mad.[29]

Milton J. Shapp appeared *pro bono publico*. That was all anyone could think to call it; he hadn't been elected to anything yet, so he represented only himself. He was going to make the merger into a hot political issue in the hopes it might land him Hugh Scott's senate seat or the Pennsylvania governorship (which it finally did, in 1970). He was a millionaire (in television antennas) and spent a good part of his fortune on the case. He stuck with it from beginning to end, with a higher caliber of input than most politicians. Unhappily, he latched onto an unimportant facet of the case and simply wouldn't let go. The merger, he said, would be the greatest disaster to Pennsylvania since the Erie Canal; it would "penalize today's citizens and future generations of unborn citizens, condemning them to a loss of opportunity, low wages and poor education," simply because thirty-one trains were going to be diverted from the PRR mainline to the water-level route. He was not dissuaded by the fact that these trains only passed through the state, clogging Pennsylvania rails for Pennsylvania commerce. It was his straw horse, and he rode it right into political prominence.

The Railway Labor Executives' Association, through its attorney, William Mahoney, put on a thoughtful case with no banker-baiting and no political posturing, but like the rest, it missed the boat. It was based on the Keyserling hypothesis that railroads needed to expand to meet the needs of an expanding economy. Keyserling himself came and presented testimony for five days in April 1963, much as he presented it before the Kefauver Committee. It was reasonable and intelligent. But the railroad thought it was expanding. In the 1963 annual report, PRR stockholders were told the railroad "had entered a progressive phase of restored financial health and growth." Perlman thought he was expanding and bragged about it in the pamphlet, *A Decade of Progress on the New York Central, 1954-1964*. Unfortunately, these investments weren't producing anything on the bottom line because these were not sound railroads. The Northern Lines liked to portray themselves as being worse off than they were; they needed a blast of the Keyserling hypothesis. The PRR and the NYC were diseased railroads frantically trying to portray themselves better than they were; the Healy hypothesis of diseconomies would have been a more fruitful line of inquiry.

No one really pursued the Healy hypothesis, however. Without being asked, James Symes felt compelled to answer it in his opening remarks. He pointed out that both PRR and NYC had more employees during World War II than the two companies together would have now, so there was no danger of unmanageability. (Professor James Nelson asked the significant question in his New England study: to what extent did their previous large and perhaps unmanageable size contribute to their subsequent decline?) Perlman became vicious when the subject was brought up—that "nonsensical idea," he said, was thought up by a man who had never run a business in his life. (Healy had been a classmate of Perlman's at MIT.)[30] The reactions of both men signified that the Healy hypothesis cut close.

The most controversial case came from an unexpected quarter, the

Pennsylvania Federation of Labor, represented by Albert Brandon of Pittsburgh. His technique was to fire verbal shotguns at key witnesses to see if anything stuck. Not much did. But his questions were based on scraps of evidence—hearsay from the men he represented, for example, or rumors that appeared in the press—and one came away with the feeling that where there was that much smoke, there might be fire.

You say, he asked James Symes, the PRR suffers from a heavy tax burden. Is it not true that in the State of Pennsylvania it pays no property taxes except in the cities of Philadelphia and Pittsburgh, and then only within the 1905 boundaries of those cities? It was true. You say you suffer from politically motivated regulation, but have you ever been denied permission to remove a passenger train by the Pennsylvania Public Utilities Commission? No, they hadn't. Has the PUC ever denied you a rate change in Pennsylvania? No, they hadn't. You say you are discriminated against, but do not the bus companies and streetcar lines have to go before the same PUC when they want to curtail service? Symes didn't know.

Was it true the Pennsylvania's policy of favoring *ex parte* rate increases was costing it a lot of business? No. You lost seven cars a week from the Iron City Breweries in Pittsburgh to Fairmont, West Virginia? Symes didn't know. What else was lost? He didn't know. Your list of the ten largest stockholders of the PRR is mostly brokerage houses—anonymous street names—holding stock for somebody else. So we don't really know who owns these railroads, do we? No. On your railroad, you delegate a lot of authority to the comptroller's office. Is it true that he determines the amount to be spent on maintenance? At that, Symes got huffy. "I see all these railroad lawyers coming around here, and not one of them is opposing the merger," he said. Brandon shot back, "Maybe it's because they're all afraid."[31]

Brandon played with Perlman, too, and extracted a few spontaneous insights into the inner sanctum of the New York Central. You mean, he asked, that after Robert Young waged an expensive proxy fight, he turned around and gave you full control of the railroad? "He certainly did," said Perlman, "the chief financial officer even reported directly to me." Who is Mr. Allan P. Kirby (one of Perlman's directors and Young's old bankroller at Alleghany)? "Mr. A.P. Kirby is an industrialist or financier or whatever the heck you want to call him. I don't know, he's got a lot of money, anyway." In the first Penn Central talks, Mr. Barriger did most of the studies for you, did he not? No, but he helped. In those studies, did not Mr. Barriger indicate a low opinion of PRR management? No. REPEAT: "You are telling me that Mr. Barriger did not indicate to you a very low opinion of the competency of Pennsylvania Railroad management?"

"He did not."

Does the Pennsylvania have better equipment than you? Perlman didn't know; he thought their equipment was all right. "Well, Mr. Barriger found out for you, didn't he?"

"He did not."

"And so from November 1957, to January 8, 1959, you had under active exploration a merger between the Pennsylvania and the New York Central, and you never got a written report of it?"

"That's just what I said three times before."[32]

Neither Brandon nor Mahoney believed that, and wanted to see those earlier studies, which they never got.

4

James Symes was past retirement age and in 1963 stepped down as chairman. Stuart Saunders took over on October 1, 1963, the day before the hearings closed, apparently with an understanding to get the merger through. So he began to work the magic he had worked in the Virginian and Nickel Plate mergers. One by one, the opposition either disappeared or radically softened its attack. He was a most remarkable man and it was a virtuoso performance. His technique was to be generous to his adversary, too generous, perhaps, for any railroad but the coal-rich N&W. If generosity failed, he would turn on a little social charm, or a little political pressure, just the right combination in the right places; it usually softened the ground nicely.

He was known for his attrition agreements with labor and so it was presumed Penn Central would get an attrition agreement. Exactly how it transpired, or how tough was the bargaining, was never known. Labor knew Saunders wanted to deal and they knew the minimum he was good for, so they tried, and got, a little more. The Luna-Saunders Attrition Agreement was executed on May 20, 1964. It was essentially the same as the agreements Saunders made in the Virginian and Nickel Plate mergers, except that it applied to *all employees on the date the agreement was signed.* Thus, on merger day, February 1, 1968, Penn Central had to take back into its employ every person who had worked for it since May of 1964. The ICC hearings were reopened to review this. Saunders said it would be cheaper for the company than the *New Orleans* conditions, and it would give management a free hand to transfer people from one point to another as needed (although he implied there would be transfers across seniority and craft lines, which the labor lawyers firmly scotched). But Saunders's testimony lacked comprehension and fell apart on cross-examination. It was doubtful if he understood—or cared—about mundane issues such as how to calculate the rate of attrition or how this agreement was going to work out at the bottom levels.[33] The important thing to him was that labor and its political allies had been silenced.

On the day Saunders took the chairmanship, the previously dormant Justice Department read a statement at the hearings announcing its complete opposition to the merger—on its merits, on its destructiveness to competition, and on the harm it would do innocent parties. It preferred a four-system East, so in case things didn't work out, there would still be maneuvering room for more mergers. Drew Pearson later implied it was all to save "the Kennedy family's favorite railroad," the New Haven. It was Justice's timing that was so curious. It had been unusually quiet in the case until the day before hearings closed, and put no witnesses on the stand. But its record in the mergers had been spotty anyway. Only in the politically sensitive *Northern Lines* case had it shown real backbone. The rumor still circulated that in addition to the conservative influences of Father Joe, the Kennedys were going out of their way not to appear antibusiness after the confrontation with United States Steel in the spring of 1962. Nevertheless, Justice reiterated its total opposition in its brief of June 1964.

With that in mind, negotiation with the New Haven's trustees for inclusion in the Penn Central began on June 16, 1964. No one but Saunders showed any enthusiasm for it. Perlman was opposed and so was James Symes, who remained on the PRR board. Symes also opposed the attrition settlement and a wide gulf apparently opened between him and his former protégé. Determined to extract the best price they could, the New Haven's trustees were prepared with some tough bargaining tools, including a study by Wyer that showed the property was capable of generating income for fixed charges. The first sessions began with book value as a starting point, but different methods of calculation by the two sides led to a wide impasse, Penn Central claiming $41 million as a fair price, the New Haven insisting on $84 million.

In July, the ICC approved the N&W-Nickel Plate merger, giving the Pennsylvania ninety days to make up its mind on divestiture. Saunders now had to have the most concrete assurances that the Penn Central merger would go through, and a meeting was arranged with Attorney General Robert Kennedy on August 24, 1964. Kennedy would be leaving office shortly. He could not bind his successor to a course of action, and it would be unseemly to retreat so soon from positions taken on the June brief. But an understanding was reached: he would recommend to his successor that if the ICC approved the merger, and if terms were reached to include the New Haven that were acceptable to its trustees, Justice would withdraw. Two weeks later, Kennedy had left office; Nicholas Katzenbach became attorney general, and he confirmed to Saunders that he concurred in Kennedy's decision. Saunders kept Katzenbach informed of developments with the New Haven at meetings the following January and again in April; both times, the attorney general reconfirmed the understanding.[34]

Beginning in September of 1964, however, the New Haven trustees introduced the concept of liquidation value as a means of determining fair price, which was considerably in excess of book value. Perlman was annoyed; liquidation value had been a fiasco in settling the affairs of the Ontario & Western, he said, and virtually precluded that anyone would want to continue to run it. Nevertheless, on the basis of liquidation value, the New Haven trustees demanded $161 million. Penn Central reluctantly offered $128 million, and the trustees accepted immediately. The agreement was signed January 5, 1966. This included operation of the freight service only; exactly what was going to happen to the passengers was not clear. The feeling among the financial people at Penn Central was that the New Haven had made a pretty good deal. In place of a cadaverous railroad running up annual deficits of $15 million, they would get 95,000 shares of Penn Central stock, $23 million in Penn Central bonds, and $8 million in cash.[35] So the most serious obstacle to the merger was cleared. Connecticut, Massachusetts, New York, and Rhode Island continued to plump for the inclusion of the passenger service, but the New England opposition had been mostly defused.

Other critical opposition vanished as well—New Jersey, Pennsylvania, and the City of Philadelphia. Governor David Lawrence of Pennsylvania had instigated the original opposition. When William Scranton took over in 1964, he was willing to reach an understanding—no more opposition in return for guarantees of service at the Port of Philadelphia. It was never clear what promise New Jersey Deputy Attorney General William Gural got in return for that state's withdrawal. Reporters Joseph Daughen and Peter Binzen, in their *Wreck of the Penn Central*, implied Saunders had simply dangled the railroad's traditional Republicanism to Scranton and his personal Democratic orientation to the New Jerseyites. Democratic Mayor James Tate of Philadelphia had been adamant in his initial opposition, fearing not only the port might suffer, but that the company's main offices would be moved to New York, with a massive loss of jobs and prestige for the city. But the mayor had a dramatic change of heart and Saunders thanked him for his "support in the most glowing terms."[36] Daughen and Binzen said the mayor admitted he had found Saunders "most persuasive."

Milton Shapp was in a more delicate position, politically. He had assumed the railroad's old-line Republicanism could be converted into an issue for the Democrats, but he had not counted on Saunders, an active Democrat, having close relations with President Johnson. Former Governor Lawrence apparently underwent his conversion on the merger after Johnson brought him to Washington as chairman of the Committee on Equal Opportunity in Housing, and he apparently began to influence Democratic party circles back home. Shapp did manage to get the gubernatorial nomination in 1966, but Johnson sent up Secretary of Commerce John Connors to campaign for him, and Connors kicked things off by saying the merger would be good for Pennsylvania and for the nation. Then Walter Annenberg, a Republican but nevertheless a Saunders intimate and PRR director, brought the full weight of his near monopoly of Philadelphia communications to bear against Shapp—*The Philadelphia Inquirer*, the *Philadelphia Evening Bulletin*, and WFIL-TV. He told *Philadelphia Magazine* that Shapp was using the merger as his *schtick* (publicity gimmick) and he didn't like anybody using Saunders or the PRR that way. In April, Saunders brought Arthur B. Krim, finance chairman of the Democratic National Committee, to Philadelphia, and arranged a luncheon, just the three of them, at the Warwick Hotel. As Shapp told Daughen and Binzen, Krim said bluntly the president favored the merger. Saunders said if he (Shapp) would drop his opposition, his political campaign would receive a large contribution, and so would the DNC, which was what seemed to interest Krim.[37]

But to his credit, Shapp did not back down. It was he who uncovered one of the most haunting pieces of evidence to come out of the proceeding, for it gave not only a disturbing insight into the mentality of the men who guided the merger, but foreshadowed what was to come. In his effort to placate political opposition in cities across Pennsylvania, Saunders had made a series of speeches to city councils and civic groups. He had apparently been at his persuasive best, since most of them dropped their opposition. But at New Castle, he had held up two unwieldy volumes, Joseph McCarthy-style, and said they contained new data on the operational plan of the merger that the ICC didn't even know about. "We have taken every department, every operation of our railroad, we've studied 43 different railroad yards—none of this was done in 1961—as to how we are actually going to operate this railroad."[38] That was almost an admission that the ICC had been deceived. Should it not at least take a look at these alleged new studies, to see what the railroad did, or did not, know about what it was doing? Shapp thought so, but the railroads replied that it was "just a study of implementation . . . nothing of substance." So whatever was in those two volumes, or was not in them, was never known.

5

In its handling of the N&W-Nickel Plate announcement, the ICC had received a very black eye. The case had been decided on June 24, 1964, but was not made public until July 13. In the interim, word leaked out that set off a last minute speculative rush in Nickel Plate securities.[39] This kind of gaffe was common at other agencies, but a rarity at the ICC. It was most important that it not happen again. Still, it was almost impossible to stop rumors, especially when the commission was sitting on so many controversial cases, and when so many people, from eleven commissioners and their secretaries and staff to typists and printers, all knew about it. As early as November 19, 1964, for example, Drew Pearson wrote in his *Washington Merry-Go-Round* that "you can write it down that the biggest railroad merger in history . . . will soon be given the green light."

The Pennsylvania went ahead and agreed to divest the N&W, and the N&W stock was put in trust as a preliminary step. So the N&W-Nickel Plate merger was consummated October 15, 1964. Wabash president Herman Pevler, another PRR-system man, had already taken over as president, succeeding Stuart Saunders. As far as anyone outside the company knew, the merger went smoothly. Only the Erie Lackawanna business seemed to cast a shadow over its horizon.

For the big three cases before the commission in the spring of 1966, the Northern Lines and Penn Central mergers and the New Haven discontinuances, the evidence was in, the examiners' reports complete, and oral arguments finished. When the commissioners began their private deliberations and it was seen how the decisions were probably going to go, it became apparent that a single strand of reasoning entwined them all. As such, they ought to be handed down together so everyone would see the logic. On April 25, 1966, a press release explained that in two days, on April 27, three of the most far-reaching decisions in recent ICC history would be rendered simultaneously. Preparations were elaborate. Microphones and a battery of press telephones were installed. Special pre-announcement briefings for the press began at 9:30 A.M. and the official announcement at noon was to be coordinated with a statement by Senator Edward Kennedy, directed primarily at New Englanders. And so, at noon on M-Day as it came to be called, the blows fell:

1. By a six-to-five vote, the Northern Lines' merger was denied.
2. The New Haven was permitted to drop twenty-one of the thirty-seven trains on the Shore Line, and nineteen of the thirty-seven trains on the Springfield Line. All other trains, including commuter trains, were to remain in operation.
3. By a unanimous eleven-to-zero vote, the Penn-Central merger was approved, to include all of the services of the New Haven Railroad.

Webb's majority report in the *Northern Lines* case concluded that a need for merger had not been demonstrated and that it would violate the antitrust laws and be harmful to other railroads. The dissenters (Tuggle, Freas, Walrath, Murphy, and Goff) seemed astonished that a merger had been turned down. If the majority thought it was protecting the Milwaukee Road, they said, preserving the status quo was no way to do it.

Penn Central was approved *only* because it was the *only* way to take care of the New Haven. That was why it passed and the Northerns' did not. Even so, approval was given only on the condition that Erie Lackawanna, Delaware & Hudson, and Boston & Maine be indemnified for losses from diversion (Appendix G). Reimbursement was to be based on a complicated formula and would end upon the inclusion of those roads in the N&W system.[40] The commission believed it had dispatched its duties and even put out a little brochure to pat itself on the back for the "uncommonly accurate reporting of the complex issues" of M-Day.

But it was not over. In June, the Norfolk & Western, previously silent in the *Penn Central* case, petitioned that it be reopened. Its statement was a brutal denunciation of the Pennsylvania Railroad. Among other allegations, it said that despite the trusteeship of the PRR's N&W stock, it still had the power to control N&W indirectly by its influence over the trustees, including private meetings with them for the purpose of giving them instructions. It further believed the PRR was going directly to N&W stockholders in an effort to turn them against certain policies of N&W management.[41] In light of this, the ICC postponed the effective date of merger from August 12, 1966, to September 30. Erie Lackawanna, D&H, and B&M were on their way to court anyway over the issues of indemnity and inclusion if the ICC didn't reopen the case immediately. In July, at what was probably the merger's most sensitive moment, New York Central petitioned to discontinue all passenger service, bringing instant wrath upon its head from labor and political and public sources. Was it stupidity, or was it the Central's own way of derailing the merger? On September 8, 1966, civil suits were filed to block Penn Central.

In July and August, the Northern Lines petitioned for reconsideration. Oregon, South Dakota, and Iowa changed their former opposition to approval. The Milwaukee Road and the Chicago & North Western announced the Northerns had capitulated to all of their traffic and gateway demands. Various labor unions notified the commission that they were in the process of working out attrition agreements, which once upon a time the Northerns had sworn they would never accept. Labor was expected to withdraw its opposition shortly.

Everything had been settled. Nothing had been settled.

CHAPTER 10

The Emergence of Four Southern Giants; 1960-1976

If nothing was settled outside the South, it was being nicely settled within. Southern railroads had an easier time with mergers than the rest of the country, not through any particular virtue, but largely because of lucky circumstance. In the end, the region had four comparatively well-balanced systems, all of them either financially strong or potentially so. The Southern Railway and the Seaboard Coast Line-Louisville & Nashville systems came to dominate the coastal plain and the mountains, with feeders to the midwestern gateways at Chicago, St. Louis, Memphis, and New Orleans. West of the mountains, the Mississippi Valley and the cotton Southwest came under the sway of the Missouri Pacific and the Illinois Central Gulf.[1]

The process exacted a price in terms of the credibility of management, of the ICC, and of the principle of consolidation itself. How well these entrenched cartels would serve the South remained to be seen. But for the time being, consolidation seemed to have succeeded in spite of itself—in spite of itself because the first big merger, Seaboard-Coast Line, the key merger that made it possible for all the others to group themselves so neatly, required that two of the most successfully competing roads in the nation join together, eliminating that competition, with no visible compensating benefit for the public.

Like western roads, southern roads were in a region of expanding industry. Their hauls were generally long, including passenger hauls, and they were free of commuter burdens. Though the southern states had experienced the full blast of antirailroad populism in the 1890s, the tax structure was lenient toward railroads and was nothing like the burdens imposed by New York or New Jersey, for example. Southern politicians were usually cordial, perhaps too cordial, to all big corporate interests, including railroads.

But like the East, southern railroads had undergone a change in traffic patterns that had caused peculiar, if less devastating, stresses. Until World War II, the southern economy was mostly agricultural and the railroads were built to serve that agriculture with a myriad of criss-crossing branches.

As agricultural processing moved south and hauls of raw products became shorter and hence susceptible to truck competition, a lot of branchline trackage was rendered more or less obsolete. Citrus, for example, was once shipped by rail as fresh fruit from all over Florida, but now was shipped as frozen concentrate from a few key plants. However, unlike the East, southern carriers had found more satisfactory replacements for the traffic they lost such as phosphates out of central Florida. At least the bigger southern carriers were all quite profitable.

1

In July of 1960, when merger was still a hot, and as yet untarnished topic in railroading, two of the most prosperous of the southern carriers, the Atlantic Coast Line and the Seaboard Air Line, summoned three hundred of their officers and stockholders to the Hotel Robert Meyer in Jacksonville to tell them about the merger they had planned. After each delegate received his "Your Plan for Progress" kit, John Smith of the Seaboard got up to tell how it all came about. It was after the Smathers Committee hearings in 1958, he said. Everyone had testified about the railroads' terrible problems. We thought Congress was going to come through with help, but it was soon evident we were going to have to help ourselves. It happened over luncheon one day shortly afterward with Thomas Rice of the ACL. "I don't know who originated it, but it was a simultaneous acceptance of merger."[2]

Then Rice took the podium. He told of the hard time he had finding the appropriate way to describe the new day that would soon be dawning. "Ceiling unlimited" had come to his mind. So had "the sky's the limit." "We can sit here and dream for hours and be unable to foresee what is possible under a happy union of these railroads that have run side by side."

I'll tell a little story. I've told it to these Coast Line folks, but I'd like to tell it for the benefit of the Seaboard becaue I think it is so appropriate when you think of what this merger can mean. During World War II, there was a little boy standing in a field near London on a heavy foggy day with his hands held in front of him, with a string going up in the fog, and an American Army officer walked by and said, "Son, what are you doing?" and he said, "I am flying a kite," and the officer said, "Well, why are you doing that, you can't see it?" and the boy replied, "No, mister, but I can feel the pull." And I hope that as you gentlemen sit here for the next two days and listen to some of these talks in the planning of this merger, that you can feel the pull, and you will go away from here as enthusiastic and as jubilant over the possibilities and the opportunities as I am. Thank you so much.[3]

That story probably told more about the motivation of this merger than all the statistics presented to the ICC. For of all the major mergers, none raised more controversy simply on its merit than this one. The justification rested on what was now the standard litany: (1) parallel railroads were duplicates and wasteful, (2) railroads were failing and going to be nationalized if they did not merge, and (3) the elimination of competition was not important. Nowhere was the justification more inapplicable to the situation at hand.

The reader should beware of a time warp. In unraveling the complicated story of mergers, it has been necessary to jump back and forth from the early 1960s to the late 1960s. The Seaboard-Coast Line merger was conceived in the late 1950s, testimony was taken in 1961, and approval was given in December 1963. This made it a contemporary of the *C&O-B&O* case. It is possible that had it come later, after the precedent of a denial as in the *Northern Lines* case, and after thinking on consolidation had become more sophisticated, it would never have passed. But in 1963, a majority of the ICC accepted its transparent justification, reciting some of the most obvious items in its report. But it left the commission divided and the merit of merger swirling in controversy.

To look at the map, Seaboard and Coast Line seemed as parallel and as duplicate as two railroads could be, their routes entwining from Richmond to south Florida. If one believed that railroad traffic was declining in the face of truck competition, then it seemed superficially reasonable that two railroads were not necessary. That was implied to dozens of shippers and political figures who found it plausible and never investigated further. But nothing in the railroad presentation indicated they were going to abandon one of them. The Wyer studies anticipated that only 20 percent of the $39 million savings would come from duplicate lines, and marked only a few segments as potentially redundant. For their part, the railroads did not file a single abandonment application, indicating they were reluctant to go even that far. (Erie Lackawanna, for example, simultaneously filed applications to abandon all of the lines declared surplus in their Wyer Report with the merger application.)

The crucial fact was that tonnage was increasing on these two railroads, not decreasing. Whether that could be translated into net income was another matter, but it did indicate the need for physical capacity was not diminishing. The assertion on the record that these railroads operated at only 25 percent of capacity was wholly unsupported. "The term capacity remains undefined," said dissenting commissioners Tucker and Webb. "The figure is therefore meaningless, phony. It dangles in mid air. Of all the straws clutched at by the Commission to justify this merger, this is the most fragile."

The railroads said they would go broke if they did not merge. To demonstrate this, they told the ICC, and the ICC accepted, that the GNP was rising faster than railroad revenues; that railroads' proportion of intercity tonnage was declining; that from twenty-one selected cities, trucks now carried twenty-five million tons of freight a year while the railroads carried only twenty-two million; that the Florida citrus crop, the Georgia peach crop, and the Alabama potato crop no longer moved by rail; and that railroads, which in 1950 carried twice as many passengers to Florida as the airlines, carried only 40 percent as many in 1958.[4]

This said only what people knew already; in a rapidly expanding economy since World War II, newer forms of transportation had grown faster than railroads and some types of traffic no longer moved by rail. It did not say whether railroads had found new traffic to replace what they lost or whether they were earning profits from what they continued to carry. The fact was that even in the recession of the later 1950s, ton-miles continued to increase for these two railroads, gross revenues were down only slightly (6 percent for the ACL, 1 percent for the SAL), net income was the highest ever, and dividends were strong. They had grown steadily in all measurements except passenger traffic right up to the recession and continued to grow after it was over. In other words, an argument that may have had some validity elsewhere in the country, had none here.

The price was going to be high. Eighty-eight counties in six states would lose all railroad competition. Hardest hit were the coastal low country and Florida where, except for the nearly branchless Florida East Coast, there would be no other railroads south of Jacksonville. Make a list of the ten top commodities carried by each railroad, said commissioners Tucker and Webb, and they will be identical, right down to the tenth item. That's competition.

It seemed you either believed railroads still competed with each other or you did not, and for those who shared the crying-towel mentality of the 1950s, who had watched the trucks get the citrus and the peaches, no further explanation was necessary. But one item in the railroads' case revealed a lot, and not what it was intended to reveal. Their tonnage of phosphates had increased over the years, and being heavy and bulky, was generally considered captive to the rails. But from at least one point, Mulberry, Florida, trucks had managed to win a share of the traffic—and forced rail rates down in the process. This was supposed to show how railroads were losing on all fronts against hopeless odds. What in fact it showed was that railroads, thinking they had the traffic captive, had overpriced their services. Higher-cost trucking firms had called their bluff, and railroads now had to compete. Nothing implied they were losing money at the new competitive rate. But they did not want to compete; they were afraid of it.

In fact, said Tucker and Webb, "the history of these two railroads' operations reads like a summary of the fruits of competition." The majority could not minimize the loss of competition by peppering their report with phrases like "relatively moderate," or "inconsequential," or "not substantial." The majority said they relied on the judgment of the many shippers who testified in favor of merger. But, pointed out Tucker and Webb, testimony was mixed, *pro* and *con*. Most of those who favored merger recited the same information in the same phrases, indicating it was prepared for them by the railroads. The commission could not rely on a "Gallup poll of indoctrinated shippers."

Three of the big paper companies, Union Bag-Camp Paper, St. Joe Paper, and St. Regis Paper, made extensive presentations on the importance of competition. The majority of the commission recognized this by specifically giving the Southern Railway the right to serve the St. Regis plant at Quinlan, Florida. That not only showed how contradictory was the thinking of the majority, but raised the most serious question of why a giant shipper was able to extract concessions denied smaller ones. The ICC, said Tucker and Webb, "conceived 76 years ago in the sweat and tears of the Granger Movement, finds today that there is a great public benefit in the ability of shippers to deal with one railroad rather than two. *Sic transit gloria mundi.* "[5]

The case raised terrible questions about the validity of studies. Wyer's report was similar to the one for Erie Lackawanna, with about the same strengths and weaknesses. As before, none of it could be disproved in cross-examination, since no one could get the information to challenge it, but it couldn't be proved, either. The ACL, who presented this study as the best technical advice procurable, had once called a similar report by Wyer "superficial," "erroneous," "biased," "unsound," and "a euphonic fantasy." That report (which recommended ACL not be allowed to control the Florida East Coast) was criticized by the examiner for basing its conclusion on a single year's data, and the ACL had concurred. But the Seaboard-Coast Line studies were also based on a single year's data, and this was now claimed to be the only valid way.[6] The same was true for the diversion studies presented by various railroads. Methods of calculation varied widely. Some took random samples over a long period of time; others took car-by-car samples for a short period. Some measured traffic only through certain gateways; others measured only selected commodities. Discrepancies were so wide that credibility was lost. Tucker and Webb said what no one had dared say before, officially, that the known guarantor of good service, competition, was going to be replaced by a possible $20 million in savings "that had been whipped together by paid consultants to justify a merger that management had already decided on."

Another terrible question was the role of the Mercantile-Safe Deposit Trust Company of Baltimore. It owned 56 percent of the ACL Company, the holding company that controlled the ACL and the Louisville & Nashville Railroads. Some, among them W.P. Kennedy of the Brotherhood of Railroad Trainmen, suspected Mercantile's president, Thomas B. Butler,

MAP 22: *The Family Lines*

was the prime mover behind the merger. What was remarkable was that under the plan of merger, Mercantile would retain control of the combined railroad (and the L&N) even though its client, the ACL, had lower earnings, a poorer record of maintenance, and a poorer debt-equity ratio. Said the Florida East Coast, "there is an epidemic of railroad mergers that appears to be threatening the traditional reluctance of the American people to permit huge combinations of financial and industrial interests."[7]

Yet another terrible question was the role of the state in promoting these new cartels. At the meeting in Jacksonville, the two railroads had almost bragged about how they were going to "lay the groundwork" for political support. The letter of the governor of South Carolina was the most comprehensive, but was otherwise typical. It read like a summary of the fallacies on which the merger rested.

I am aware . . . of the problems that confront the railroads, not only in the Southeast but in the nation. I am aware that these problems cannot and should not be solved by government subsidy, but must be and will be solved by the railroads themselves through carefully formulated plans such as the proposed merger of these two fine lines. In fact, as I read the Smathers Committee report of 1958, railroads generally are urged to consider mergers where possible as a step in their program of self-help. It is patently illogical and uneconomical for two railroads to have parallel lines and a duplication of services. . . .

It is equally patent that a strong and healthy transportation system will result from this merger, will add much to the continued growth of our state and the South.

I heartily endorse the merger . . . as a courageous and progressive step on the part of these two railroads to meet and solve their own problems without depending on government financial subsidy or hand out.[8]

Was one of these "uneconomical" railroads going to be dispensed with? Of course not. They were much too busy for that. Was it "patently illogical" to have parallel railroads when both were earning money and paying dividends? Not by any normal definition of capitalism. Was it patently obvious that merger would create a strong transportation system? It hadn't been proven by experience and it certainly was not obvious if you believed, as many southerners claimed to, in free competitive markets.

The governor's letter was a dreadful example of how vulnerable the non-railroad amateur was to skillful propaganda. It also exhibited one of the least edifying traits of what southerners like to call conservatism and what others might call national-socialism—a faith in the integrity of the powerful, a lack of respect for competition, and a ready willingness to use the offices of the state to eliminate that competition. It would not be the last example of this in the history of railroad mergers.

Amidst the controversy, the two railroads clamored to get the regulatory process over with so they could merge. It had taken them two years to prepare their own case, but they objected strenuously that others should have as much as four months. Little Florida East Coast pointed out that its small legal department was already taken up with other matters that could not, on a moment's notice, be laid aside. "It is most doubtful," said the Southern, "that savings of $38.7 million can be achieved without violent and far-reaching impact on the transportation service of the area."[9] It demanded the work sheets and engineering data of the Wyer Reports, and never got them, on the grounds it would delay things. Nowhere had the demand for speed been more exposed as a guise to shroud the deficiencies of the case.

It was remarkable, thought dissenters Tucker and Webb, for the majority of the commission to fly so blatantly in the face of the president's message, in which he asked that competition be maintained. It was also remarkable in light of the Supreme Court decision, just handed down, that held competition a desirable goal (in banking).[10] They thought the commission's confidence in its ability to provide, through regulation, the checks and balances that would no longer be provided by competition was wishful thinking.

"In viewing the unfolding rail merger scene, one cannot fail to be impressed with the aura of inevitability that hovers over the subject. . . . By this decision, the Commission has given consolidation a virtually unobstructed green light. . . . After this current wave of unification has receded, some merged companies will no doubt, in turn, seek to combine with other merged companies."

I do not suggest that the undesirable consequences of this merger will be experienced overnight. The merged company will enjoy for a time the enlightened management of the separate companies. Competitive instincts will not atrophy immediately. The aggrandizement spawned by monopoly is likely to develop by imperceptible degrees.[11]

Florida East Coast and most of the other opponents went to court seeking to have the commission's order enjoined. They convinced a circuit court that insufficient weight and improper interpretation had been given the antitrust laws, following much the same legal reasoning as Tucker and Webb. But the Supreme Court did not agree. The commission, it thought, had placed a correct interpretation on the *McLean* decision.[12] So if Congress did not change the law, there was no legal defense against the mergers. They would go through exactly as management planned them.

Yet somehow, something didn't quite fit. It would seem from the foregoing that under the sugary New South gentility of the Jacksonville meeting, these were ruthless monopolists in collusion with bankers, bent on deceiving the commission and the public in order to gorge themselves on profits extracted from helpless shippers, consumers, and workers. But they weren't people like that. They ran two of the most magnificent railroads in the land and provided some of the most outstanding service. They deserved the highest accolades in capitalism's hall of fame for running a tight ship under difficult conditions and earning a merited profit. So why spoil it with this pathetic case for merger?

The clue was in a few remarks by L.S. Jeffords, an ACL vice president, to the Jacksonville meeting.

Looking at the merger from a purely selfish standpoint, I would view it as a necessity for survival's sake, if nothing else.

We are competing against each other when we should be fighting the common enemy.

Now let us consider the merger from an individual point of view. What is more to be desired than the achievement of security?[13]

Notice the cold-war imagery of "survival" and "common enemy." Notice the elevation of security as the most important goal in life. In railroad affairs as in world affairs, the enemy was at the gate. Communism lurked. Nationalization was communism. Any price must be paid to save the nation from that. Who knew better how to do it than the American businessman?

This was a generation of men who began their careers in the depression, who reached their prime in the era of cold-war McCarthyism. This was the terrible legacy. They were scared.

2

With all its flaws, there was one powerfully compensating factor to the Seaboard-Coast Line merger, though it was never mentioned in the ICC's report. Southern Railway had applied to control the Central of Georgia, a marginal earner that was already showing signs it could no longer raise the capital to make the improvements needed to remain competitive. The application was submitted in August 1960, a month after Seaboard-Coast Line, and made its way through the regulatory process at about the same time. Central's traffic and administrative functions would be taken over by Southern, and there would be complete coordination at common points. By and large, the case stirred a minimum of controversy. The routes of the two railroads complemented each other, and Central would have a home. In like manner, the Southern would also acquire the Savannah & Atlanta, the Georgia & Florida, the Pidcock Lines, and the Norfolk Southern.[14]

The significance was that a merged Seaboard-Coast Line would be balanced by a stronger Southern. Hence, there were a number of provisions in the Seaboard-Coast Line decision specifically designed to strengthen the Southern Railway. Through no design that anyone was willing to admit to, and in spite of the myriad of unresolved issues that still surrounded the SCL

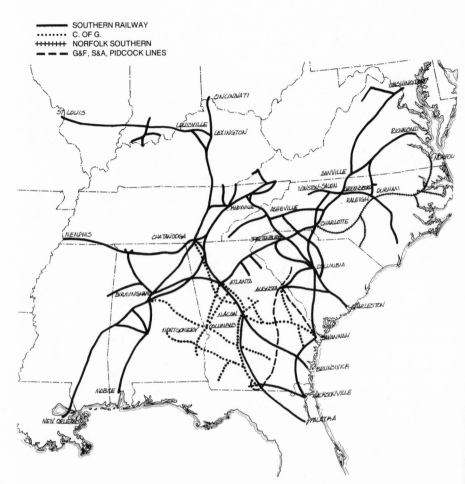

SOUTHERN RAILWAY
C. OF G.
NORFOLK SOUTHERN
G&F, S&A, PIDCOCK LINES

WASHINGTON

ST. LOUIS
CINCINNATI
RICHMOND
LOUISVILLE
LEXINGTON
NORFOLK
DANVILLE
WINSTON-SALEM
GREENSBORO
DURHAM
KNOXVILLE
ASHEVILLE
RALEIGH
MEMPHIS
CHATTANOOGA
CHARLOTTE
SPARTENBURG
COLUMBIA
ATLANTA
BIRMINGHAM
AUGUSTA
CHARLESTON
MACON
MONTGOMERY
COLUMBUS
SAVANNAH
BRUNSWICK
MOBILE
JACKSONVILLE
NEW ORLEANS
PALATKA

MAP 23: *The Southern Railway Expansion.*

merger, consolidation was beginning to restructure the rail system of the South into a few strong, competitively balanced systems the Progressives of long ago had dreamed of.

Tucker and Webb didn't think it was going to work. In the face of the great "rail duopoly," they said, a duopoly which controlled 89 percent of the South's mileage, the handful of remaining independents would be "little more than pilot fish." Furthermore, it was "not prudent to assume the Southern will always be a vigorous competitor for the merged company; that it will not join it in a cozy cartel. Two can tango. It is much harder for three."

Unhappily, the *Southern-Central* case was engulfed in another controversy that overshadowed everything else. Even the good consolidation extracted its pound of flesh from labor. Attrition conditions were labor's objective in all mergers, but since the Supreme Court had specifically ruled they were not required by law (in the case growing out of the Erie Lackawanna merger), labor had no recourse if it could not negotiate them privately.[15] But the *New Orleans* conditions, which were imposed by law, were getting a little creaky, and the Railway Labor Executives' Association sought clarification.

First, the *New Orleans* conditions failed to take into account a number of new situations that had arisen. One was an inclusion of fringe benefits—hospitalization, medical-surgical, life insurance, and vacation rights. Another was protection against job losses that were the result of capital improvements that could not have been made without merger.

Second, they had been difficult and unpleasant to implement. The mere act of imposing them only began the process. Specific implementing agreements had to be worked out with each lodge. Senior men who were going to be affected would use their seniority to bump junior men, so a single dislocation might set off a chain reaction affecting a dozen or more people. The one that ultimately got the boot was one with so little seniority, the *New Orleans* conditions offered little protection. Disputes, and they were many, went to arbitration panels. If they were the best machinery around, they were far from perfect. Commission files were filled with pathetic letters from employees who felt they had been let down by everyone. In several cases, companies had denied a particular improvement was the result of consolidation, placing the burden of proof on the employee. It was not known how many suffered in silence, unable to afford the price of American justice.

Furthermore, even the possibility of litigation had been largely sealed off in three companion cases growing out of the L&N-NC&StL merger, which held disputes matters for arbitration boards, not judicial review.[16] Another decision ruled that neither individuals nor an individual union could block a merger by refusing to negotiate implementing agreements.[17] Years later, the Court would open a slender avenue of redress by ruling in the *Nemitz* case that an implementing agreement which did not meet the minimum protective standards could be litigated by an individual employee. But even that concession was wrung by the slimmest of margins. Three justices dissented, and two Nixon appointees, Powell and Rehnquist, had not yet taken their seats.[18].

If the RLEA had asked for clarification, it had not bargained for what it got. The commission rewrote all the protective conditions from scratch, apparently in the hope of updating and simplifying them. The objective was laudable enough. Just to understand the *New Orleans* conditions, one had to have a complete command of the *Oklahoma* and *North Western* conditions which preceded them, plus the Harrington Amendment and its legislative history, plus the Washington Agreement. The very facet of a merger that most people needed a lawyer to figure out for them was the one that most needed to be understood by hundreds of individuals who did not have private counsel. But the new code, the *Southern-Central* conditions, was drawn up by ICC staff with no supervision (some thought) from the commissioners and with no input from company lawyers. Codifying a complex body of common law was tricky business. For example, just mention of the Washington Agreement meant invoking dozens of decisions, interpretations, and conventions about that agreement that had grown up over twenty-five years' experience, whereas to write into a code what the Washington Agreement said, or what one bureaucrat thought it said, invited some very serious omissions. Regardless, the commission plunged ahead.[19]

The Southern would have had little interest in a declining property like the Central unless it could convert its obsolescent, labor-intensive operation into a productive, technology-intensive one like its own. But it had given some early warnings that it did not intend to be generous with the men displaced. It had calculated the cost of labor protection on the basis of the obsolete *North Western* conditions and seemed enraged when the examiner suggested the *New Orleans* conditions would be imposed. It claimed, rather hysterically, that this would cost it $20 million. The commission said flatly this dire prediction was unwarranted. Based on the number of men the company said would be affected, it had never cost any carrier that much before—unless the company was not telling the truth about the number of men involved.

After the new *Southern-Central* conditions were issued, the company asked for some declaratory rulings on how the commission would rule if it were an arbitration board. It was not one, and should have treated this request with caution. Arbitration boards were not bound by the rules of evidence and it was regarded as crippling to their work if they were locked in by interpretations arrived at elsewhere. Furthermore, the commission could not even pretend to act like an arbitration board if it did not have the full particulars of a case. The company offered some scenarios. Suppose, at some future date, it built an electronic classification yard at Macon, Georgia, a point served by both the Southern and the Central. Could an arbitration board rule it was the result of control, entitling displaced employees to protection? Suppose it built an electronic yard at St. Louis? Could a board say that was made possible by savings derived from Central control?

The commission said frankly it thought these "horror" scenarios were unreasonable. As for determining whether a certain capital improvement was the result of consolidation, it thought arbitration boards were equipped to handle that, "although with regard to the St. Louis yard, we cannot conceive that an employee would be successful." It thought—and it said this several times—that the company was unduly mistrustful of arbitration boards. "The railroad industry generally has accepted them as a reasonable method for settling disputes of this nature, and we are not appraised of any situation where this has resulted in harassment or injustices to the railroads."

Commissioner Webb was not so sanguine. He sensed the *Southern-Central* conditions had been a mistake and suspected the company was laying a trap. "These opposing ideas cannot be reconciled by sprinkling comments throughout the report to the effect the applicant is unduly mistrustful of arbitration. . . . The befuddlement of all could not be more complete."

The week after the Southern received this unclear clarification, it dismissed 1,500 Central of Georgia men without previous notice, without implementing agreements, without attempting to merge rosters, and with the extent of their protective benefits in doubt. Some, but not all, were offered lump-sum settlements if they signed a release excusing the company from all further obligation, and were threatened with a menial job on a distant part of the system if they refused. If they turned that down, they were eliminated from all protection. Older men were offered jobs they could no longer physically perform, and when they could not, were dismissed. No Southern Railway employees were affected; the burden fell entirely on Central men. In that way, the number of men involved was kept low. It was the worst instance of labor relations to come out of the merger movement. Southern was a signatory of the Washington Agreement, but it chose not to honor its contract, taking the narrow view that the new *Southern-Central* conditions were its only obligation. To save a few dollars, morality had been thrown to the winds.

The trouble seemed to lie in the fact the new conditions did not include certain clauses from the Washington Agreement, notably clause 4 (requiring ninety-day written notice of contemplated changes), clause 5 (requiring the merging of seniority rosters), and clause 9 (permitting a lump-sum separation allowance in lieu of a coordination allowance). The *New Orleans* conditions included all of this simply by citing the Washington Agreement. Omitting a reference to that document opened the door to an interpretation that abided by the letter of the law but not its spirit. Of those 1,500 Central men dismissed, many were old, many were unskilled. They had been cast out without warning, some after many years of service, most with only the slightest idea of how seriously they had been wronged. They were unfortunate to live in states with some of the least adequate unemployment insurance systems. All the previous allegations of railroad greed paled beside this example of callousness.

The RLEA asked the Federal District Court in Richmond for a declaratory ruling on whether the *Southern-Central* conditions were valid. Management won the round—they were upheld.[20] But the commission was instantly uneasy over an interpretation of its new rules which held them and the Washington Agreement mutually exclusive. So it issued a new clarification, explaining it had always assumed the Washington Agreement would be honored by those who had signed it.[21] The Supreme Court thought this was still insufficient and remanded the whole case to the commission with orders to clear up the confusion once and for all. Litigation continued for three years, but the final report, on November 15, 1967, was a rare instance of commission anger toward a railroad carrier.

The Southern's own president, it said, had once testified he would honor the Washington Agreement. The railroad had then tricked the commission into clarifying certain aspects of its orders while leaving others vague. It read the law in a novel way that no one in the history of protective conditions had done before. It exhibited a "callous disregard for the established rights and interests of the employees of the Central of Georgia." Straightening the matter out was going to be costly, and that was too bad. Back indemnities would have to be paid. (Remember, it was now more than four years since the men were dismissed—merely contacting some of them was going to be difficult.) Then seniority rosters would have to be merged with the Southern, as they should have been in the first place, and that would involved a whole new category of men. Once that was done, said the commission, all employees were to receive the full protection of the *New Orleans* conditions *beginning the day the implementing agreements were signed.* As before, the railroad responded with hysterical claims that this would cost it $55 million and ruin it. But the commission was in no mood for crocodile tears. Referring to the railroad's behavior, it said:

Such a self-serving interpretation is totally inconsistent with the purpose of railroad labor law. . . . In relying upon an interpretation that most assuredly constituted a radical departure from past employee benefits, applicants willingly assumed certain risks of subsequent judicial reversal. . . . Applicants knew, or should have known, the frailty of their position.[22]

3

If a triangle were drawn with Chicago at the apex and a line from Pensacola to El Paso as a base, it would be filled by three dominant railroad empires—the Seaboard Coast Line-controlled Louisville & Nashville to the east, the Missouri Pacific to the west, and the Illinois Central Gulf up the middle. However, neither the L&N nor the MoPac quite reached Chicago; they required the little Chicago & Eastern Illinois to complete the crown of the triangle. Like a three-pronged wishbone, the C&EI extended southward from the Windy City, one prong to a connection with the L&N at the Ohio River, at Evansville, Indiana, one to the MoPac on the Mississippi River, at St. Louis, and the third, its own traffic generator, into "Little Egypt," the soft coal country of southern Illinois.

The C&EI was a free agent, and merger discussions of the past had seldom paired it with either the MoPac or the L&N. For years before 1920 it was controlled by the Frisco. The Pennsylvania coveted it as a Chicago-St. Louis link in the 1920s, but it eventually came within the Van Sweringen sphere. (The Vans let it go into bankruptcy in 1933.) The ICC's final plan of 1929 put it with the Chicago & North Western. In 1947, it had tentative three-way discussions with the Katy and the Chicago Great Western, and when the Katy backed out, made overtures to the Monon. Later it asked to be included in a C&O-B&O-Central combination if that should ever come about. So there seemed to be a historic instability to the C&EI that made many people assume it ought to be linked to someone else.

Despite that, it had seemed to prosper on its own. It was an early pioneer of piggyback. It had worked hard to market Illinois soft coal by quoting joint rates with water carriers, first through the Ohio River port of Joppa, Illinois, and then on the Great Lakes through Chicago. For its efforts, it had kept its operating ratio respectable and its net income adequate (though erratic). Passengers knew it for the Dixie Route trains that thundered down the Chicago-Evansville line to the L&N connection, often in multiple sections: the *Dixie Flyer,* the *Dixie Limited,* the *Dixie Mail,* the streamlined *Dixie Flagler,* the lovely and popular *Georgian-Hummingbird,* and its own local streamliners, the *Whippoorwill* and *Meadowlark.* It was never a compact hotshot like the Western Pacific, but it was not moribund, either.

The question—and it was subtle—was whether C&EI was better as an independent, ready to serve all connections, or affiliated with one of its principal connections. Like the B&O, the recession of the late 1950s hit it at a bad time, when it was in need of capital improvements—locomotives, freight cars, and bridges. The bridges were crucial. Even a troubled railroad can borrow money for rolling stock—the creditors can repossess it and sell it to someone else if the company can't pay. Fixed plant is another matter.

Several bridges on the Evansville line, notably the one over the Wabash River at Clinton, Indiana, were simply not strong enough to carry the new, heavy equipment being purchased by many railroads such as the "Big John" jumbo hoppers of the Southern Railway or the "Big Blues" of the L&N, 250,000 pounds apiece when fully loaded. If C&EI could not rebuild

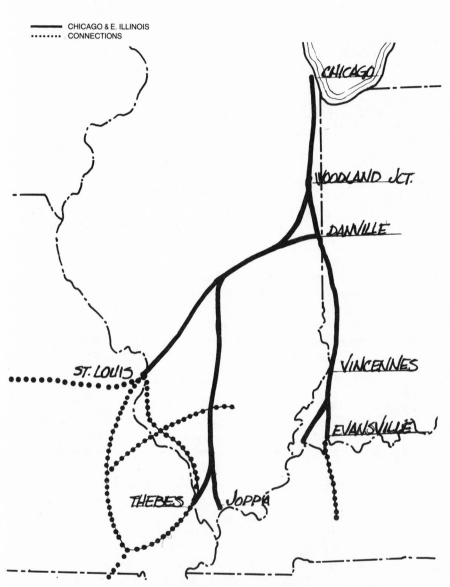

CHICAGO

WOODLAND JCT.

DANVILLE

ST. LOUIS

VINCENNES

EVANSVILLE

THEBES

JOPPA

MAP 24: *The Dismemberment of the Chicago & Eastern Illinois*

its bridges, it could not handle the cars; if it could not handle the cars, it would lose the traffic—like the Dow Chemical shipments from Freeport, Texas, to Midland, Michigan, five cars a day, $400 a car to the C&EI. The C&EI board recognized this could be a turning point. It was the very crisis that made it imperative for the B&O to lower its clearances on the Baltimore-St. Louis line. It was already believed some railroads, like the New Haven, the Lehigh Valley, the Jersey Central, and the Katy, had passed beyond this point of no return. By 1965, C&EI was able to finance improvements on its own by selling the bridges to insurance companies who contracted for the necessary work and leased them back. This involved an expenditure of only $3.7 million on the Wabash River bridge, for example, not much in terms of normal corporate borrowing. It indicated the C&EI had skated by its crisis on the thinnest of ice.[23]

Recognizing the peril of the point of no return, the C&EI's David Mathews began merger discussions with the MoPac in the spring of 1960, and Wyer, Dick & Company was asked to make studies. The railroad people at MoPac, like President Russell Dearmont, were enthusiastic, but money people, like the representatives of the Mississippi River Fuel Corporation that controlled MoPac, were not. They objected to taking responsibility for C&EI's debt, so would offer only stock control. Mathews, believing his railroad was worth a better deal than that, went to W.H. Kendall of the L&N, and Wyer studies were commissioned again. Confident that MoPac was out of the picture, L&N passed up an opportunity to buy a large block of C&EI securities, part of the estate of Henry Hammack, a Kansas City investor, when they went on the market in the spring of 1961. Over at MoPac, General Counsel Downing B. Jenks, who had previously been with the C&EI, knew that for certain kinds of transactions, including merger, approval was needed by two-thirds of the class A preferred stock. Acquisition of the Hammack shares would give MoPac veto power over any merger. It bought them.[24]

Whether that constituted the power to control—illegal, since the ICC had not given permission—was obscure. When the fire got hot, MoPac put the whole works in trust but continued to buy C&EI securities. The ICC's Bureau of Inquiry and Compliance and Commissioner Tucker thought the dealings were as shady as the Frisco's illegal efforts to control the Central of Georgia in the late 1950s, but the commission did not agree.

By this time, MoPac had applied to control the C&EI on the grounds that C&EI was hopelessly destitute and would collapse if MoPac aid were not forthcoming immediately. Questionable financial dealings, said the commision, need not be a bar to a consolidation that was otherwise in the public interest.[25]

The hearings were long. Illinois Central was especially bitter about this MoPac invasion of Chicago. That, plus litigation over the stock, postponed a decision into 1965. In that time, the C&EI failed to collapse according to MoPac's timetable. In fact, it bought new locomotives and cars, got its new bridges, and put a nice net income down on the bottom line. David Mathews was proud of his railroad and what he had done for it, and didn't want it swallowed up with anything as cheap as stock control. MoPac, he said, hired three of his young executives away at salaries he couldn't match, and such was the superior management MoPac now wanted to give back to save the railroad.[26]

It seemed incredible, therefore, that the ICC would cite the obvious imminence of C&EI collapse as reason to allow control. Admittedly, another benefit of control, improved freight schedules, was attractive. Eleven hours could be shaved off Los Angeles-Chicago schedules, fourteen off Dallas-Chicago, and twenty-three off Houston-Chicago, making MoPac-C&EI routes competitive with single-line routes, like Santa Fee, for the first time. But in 1958, on consultation with the MoPac, C&EI had begun similar services to the ones contemplated now, passing not through St. Louis, but through Thebes, Illinois, way down on the C&EI's Little Egypt line. Southbound traffic developed nicely, but northbound traffic off the MoPac failed to develop at all, and finally MoPac said it was due to an obscure clause in its trackage agreement with the Cotton Belt. Funny, thought Mathews, but there was no trouble with these trackage agreements now.[27]

The L&N had been electrified by the news of MoPac control; it immediately began retaliatory purchase of C&EI stock until it had enough to block MoPac control if it chose. But it supported MoPac as long as it could buy the C&EI line from Evansville to Woodland Junction, Illinois, with trackage rights into Chicago.

So the C&EI was pulled apart like a wishbone. Despite evidence to the contrary, the decision was predicated on the assumption C&EI could not survive alone. Only Commissioner Tucker thought the record said exactly the opposite. MoPac was required to submit annual reports on progress toward the goals of control. Needless to say, they looked very good. Physical improvements were made, new experiments with incentive rates were conducted, and traffic through the Thebes gateway developed very nicely, requiring three manifest freights a day by 1972.[28] As the life of the Dixie Route passenger trains flickered out one-by-one, Chicagoans were quite unaware when the last impediment was cleared and the L&N actually entered their city. That curious little entity, the Chicago & Eastern Illinois, was for all practical purposes gone.

4

The Illinois Central had not fared well in the mergers. It had intervened in the Seaboard-Coast Line merger to get the L&N detached from Coast Line control, and failed. It had watched the Southern-Central control with misgiving, as Central, a former subsidiary (in the 1920s), had been one of its principal connections (through Birmingham, Alabama). In the contest for C&EI, it had filed a counterpetition to take full control of C&EI itself, and when that failed, it took MoPac to court over its dubious dealings in C&EI securities.[29]

But at last, the IC found a merger mate, the Gulf, Mobile & Ohio, itself the product of successful mergers in the past. The GM&O never quite won the reputation of a hotshot among medium-sized roads, as did Western Pacific, for example, but it sometimes earned as much as 10 percent on investment and deserved more accolades than it got. It traveled the hill country of Mississippi, so bare that Larry Provo of the Chicago & North Western once remarked that "even a rabbit would have to pack a lunch." But its traffic grew in volume and dividends were regular. The growing importance of the Port of Mobile and national prosperity both helped, but GM&O was really testimony to the fact that medium-sized roads, well-managed and soundly financed, could hold their own against the entrenched giants.

For the GM&O, the giant in question was always the Illinois Central, which paralleled it from Chicago to the Gulf. The IC was also riding the crest of fortune. In 1966, the year the green diamond emblem was replaced by the split rail, it was not only a national leader in unit train operation, but had just earned its highest passenger revenues in a decade. As long as Wayne Johnston was chief executive, both freight and passengers were treated as though they were important. To him, good service meant profits, and both were a matter of honor. But for better or worse, he had turned his beautiful railroad into a diversified conglomerate, the Illinois Central Industries, following the lead of MSL Industries and Ben Heineman's Northwest Industries. It was bold and it was controversial. Would it protect the railroad against the wild fluctuations of the business cycle, or would it divert capital away from an industry that tended to be capital-starved? He also helped conceive the idea of a merger with the GM&O, though he died before the application was filed.

Merger was supposed to save $12 million a year, with the usual promises of better service. For the giant Crown Zellerbach installation at Bogalusa, Louisiana, this "improved" service meant one train a day instead of two. The studies were full of similar contradictions. One plan, to eliminate GM&O yards and switching crews at St. Louis and Chicago, was simply not possible if previous levels of service were to be maintained.[30] Out of hundreds of pages of exhibits and weeks of testimony, it was picky, perhaps, to focus on errors, but it was rather shocking at this late stage of the merger movement that underlying studies were prepared so sloppily. The blithe promises of savings and better service still did not rest on a firm factual foundation.

Were savings the real purpose on two dividend-paying railroads, or was it really a desire to eliminate competition? In the state of Mississippi, Illinois

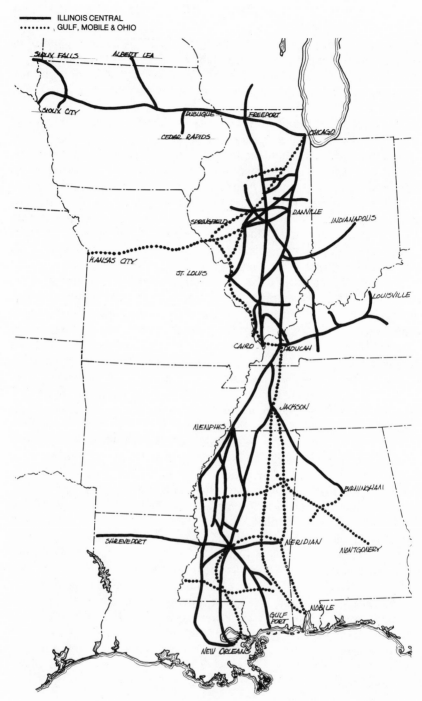

ILLINOIS CENTRAL
GULF, MOBILE & OHIO

SIOUX FALLS   ALBERT LEA

SIOUX CITY   DUBUQUE   FREEPORT   CHICAGO

CEDAR RAPIDS

SPRINGFIELD   DANVILLE   INDIANAPOLIS

KANSAS CITY

ST. LOUIS

LOUISVILLE

CAIRO   PADUCAH

JACKSON

MEMPHIS

BIRMINGHAM

SHREVEPORT   MERIDIAN

MONTGOMERY

MOBILE

GULF
PORT

NEW ORLEANS

MAP 25:   *The Illinois Central Gulf*

Central Gulf would be as close to a monopoly as Seaboard Coast Line was in Florida, but state politicians eagerly courted the IC's favor. The final merger agreement of December 28, 1967, was signed at the governor's mansion in Jackson, with both the incoming and outgoing governors looking on. After that, Governor John Bell Williams became one of the merger's most outspoken proponents, seeing it as a means to "strengthen our economy, broaden our trade horizons, and offer brighter opportunities for the future of our great state."[31] In contrast, the U.S. Department of Justice was unconditionally opposed. The IC and GM&O were each other's most serious competitors, it said, and other modes of transport could not be substituted for the services they performed. Projected savings, which amounted to 3.1 percent of combined revenues, did not warrant a structural change like merger, especially when each of the lines had accomplished more significant productivity gains than that in recent years, separately.

Unhappily, Justice and the State of Mississippi had things all mixed up. When Justice argued that other forms of transport could not be substituted for rail, it meant that bulk commodities could not be moved by truck. The IC and GM&O lay astride the Mississippi River system from one end to the other and got none of the subsidies that built dams and locks and dredged channels. Bulk commodities that were rail-bound elsewhere, across the Northwest, for example, were not so here. So it would have been reasonable for Justice to take a more continental viewpoint. The state, on the other hand, was responsible for the welfare of interior points, where there were no rivers and where rail competition was important. But the state, in this case, was "conservative," which meant it believed positive good came from making the powerful more powerful. Justice, at this juncture, was "liberal," meaning the motives of vested interests were open to suspicion. Neither was prone to let circumstances disturb them.

The IC kept reminding everyone that the law said a merger need only be *consistent* with the public interest; it did not need to *promote* it. But there was probably no need to get shrill. The arguments for merger in this case were no worse than the ones that prevailed before. The record indicated a merger was not needed. There were no guarantees it would result in improved service. But if everything worked out, it would save the companies a little money and that had always satisfied the commission before. The one nice thing about it was that Illinois Central Gulf would be roughly equal in size to the other southern systems and this gave the appearance there had been a plan for consolidation all along. The ICG graciously took in a number of faltering short lines in Mississippi—the Mississippi Central, the Columbus & Greenville, and the Bonhomie & Hattiesburg Southern. They said they could not survive alongside the merged giant. They couldn't survive within it, either. By 1975, shippers on the Columbus & Greenville, distraught about the prospect of wholesale abandonment, petitioned for, and got, the little railroad's independence back. Illinois Central Industries, the holding company, was declared a common carrier and subjected to full ICC regulation. Approval of the merger by the commission was unanimous, and last-minute litigation by the MoPac and the Kansas City Southern failed to halt its consummation in August 1972.

Merger was no panacea. The ICG's operating ratio tended to climb, and net income tended to fall, and the condition of track, even on the Chicago-New Orleans mainline, deteriorated badly. By the spring of 1977, rumors that Illinois Central Industries wanted to sell off the railroad operations were so rife, that ICG Chairman E.G. Hillman wrote a two-page piece in the *ICG News* to quash them—more or less. "What's in the long haul, in the merger program, or nationalization . . . who knows? What we do know is that the railroad is not currently for sale. . . ."[32] What life would have been like for the GM&O if it had remained independent can only be guessed; all that remained was David Morgan's moving obituary in *Trains:*

The Gulf, at least, won that "G" in ICG. A letter in a reporting mark, a word on a letterhead—that's more than marks the last mile of the Minneapolis & St. Louis or the Wabash, and so many more. . . . "G" in ICG—the late Ike Tigrett would have enjoyed that—hanging his road's signature on the name of the carrier that tried to derail him in 1940.

We Americans sympathize with the underdog, yet we applaud the success story. For a season in railroading, we had both under one banner—and that's what the "G" in ICG is all about.[33]

5

Two more items tidied up the South. At the end of August 1968, the Tennessee Central wound up its affairs and ceased operation. It was the only rail competition for the L&N at Nashville, and in years gone by had played a stormy role in Tennessee politics. Now it was bust, with no hope of reorganizing independently. The IC was interested in the western portion, from Hopkinsville, Kentucky, into Nashville, promising that city more effective competition than it had ever had. The L&N took the middle portions and Southern took the eastern end.[34] It was vaguely like vultures at the carcass, but there was no place for Tennessee Central in postmerger railroading.

Nor was there a place for the Monon. When the L&N took the Evansville line of the C&EI, the Monon apparently felt it needed to be included somewhere. Since its lines were almost entirely in Indiana, most consolidation thinking, from the Ripley Report on, assumed it would fit into one of the eastern systems. It was something of a tribute to the growing economic clout of the South that southern carriers now had the resources to invade trunkline territory. The L&N made a bid. Exactly why the Southern Railway was not interested was a matter of conjecture, since it was believed the Monon interchanged more traffic with the Southern than with the L&N.

It was hard to imagine that any sizable railroad should feel threatened by the loss of Monon interchange, but as the last of the buffer roads began to disappear, the scrambling of the great powers became intense. All the midwestern roads demanded something. The Milwaukee Road, for example, insisted its stringer line into the Indiana coal country would be rendered worthless without the neutral Monon connection. It demanded—and got—trackage rights into Louisville and a direct connection with the Southern Railway—over which Soo Line and Chicago & North Western were ready to go to court.[35]

The Monon had been at the point of no return back in 1946, a sick little railroad that seemed irreversibly run down. Then it got a new leader, John Barriger, who worked a magical rehabilitation. *Trains* was fascinated with the Monon success story in those years and did a series of feature articles on it. There was something heartwarming about an honestly run little railroad that fielded both freight and passenger trains in competition with the Pennsylvania and the New York Central and earned the loyalty of a generation of Indianians. Even its singing commercials were good:

> All across this great big nation,
> They're the epicures' sensation.
> Oh—those—wonderful Monon meals.

But that was in a day when Indiana was full of independent railroads, all feeding traffic to the Monon at dozens of junctions—plenty of alternatives, plenty of options. When they were gone, eliminated by the mergers, there was no place for a local road, even one that was well-run. Monon, the Hoosier Line, ceased to exist on July 31, 1971.

Life was not altogether happy for the remaining independents in the South. Florida East Coast had been wary ever since the first Seaboard-Coast Line application. It had demanded, and been refused, trackage rights to west Florida and the sole right to serve Fort Lauderdale and Miami. It became the favored connection of the Southern Railway, some thought virtually an extension of it, and interchange with the SCL dried up despite the protective conditions. In 1976, FEC filed a formal protest with the ICC against what it alleged was the SCL's blatant disregard of the conditions imposed in its merger.[36]

The Frisco seemed to do well as a bridge line between the southern and western roads where, thanks to the industrial expansion and population growth of both regions, traffic was considerable. It had discussed merger with the Southern; its most important single connection was the Santa Fe (with whom it had been affiliated in the nineteenth century and with whom many thought it ought to be affiliated again). In 1976, it began merger talks with the Burlington Northern.

Seaboard Coast Line, in the meantime, virtually merged with the L&N without ever going before the commission, by buying all the remaining outstanding stock. The ACL had controlled it since the turn of the century and had retained control after the SCL merger, despite protests from the Southern and the IC. After 1969, officers of the roads were practically interchangeable. Other ACL subsidiaries, the Clinchfield and the West Point Route, were brought under the SCL umbrella, now called the Family Lines.

Perhaps in retaliation, the Southern began merger talks with the Missouri Pacific in 1975, but a year later they were broken off for undisclosed reasons. It was believed MoPac had wanted a bigger share than the Southern thought it deserved. "They're a good railroad," one Southern spokesman is said to have remarked, "but they're not that good."[37]

So, as Commissioners Tucker and Webb had predicted, the merged giants were coming back to merge again. It seemed that once set in motion, the consolidation trend could not stop.

CHAPTER 11

Stalemate in the West;
1963-1976

For a railroader with a long memory, the Rock Island had always been a hard-luck road. At one time, it was expected to be one of the nation's great railroads. But it had failed to complete its lines to the Pacific in the nineteenth century, forever relegating itself to granger-road status. Mismanagement by the Moore-Reid syndicate before World War I condemned it to a sort of endemic financial anemia, much as the Morgan-Mellen experience had done for the New Haven. Strategic moves by the Southern Pacific in the 1920s, the purchase of the El Paso & Southwestern and particularly the Cotton Belt, reduced its transcontinental traffic through the Tucumcari gateway to a trickle.

To those with a shorter memory, however, the Rock seemed well enough adjusted to postwar realities. Its insolvency in the Depression had been rugged, but stripped of its old debt, it was able to dieselize and make capital improvements (such as the high bridge over the Cimarron that cut freight schedules by two hours). The *Rocket* streamliners that used to line up at La Salle Street Station in Chicago seemed to symbolize a healthy property with a touch of class.

No one really had a satisfying explanation for what went wrong. It was nothing dramatic, like Hurricane Diane was for the Lackawanna. The competition is formidable on the prairies, and as *Trains* explained, the Rock didn't go anywhere that somebody else didn't get there faster and straighter. After the 1958 recession, other railroads seemed to extricate themselves from the trap of stagnant revenues and escalating costs, but the Rock did not. The first net loss was not reported until 1965, although by then a cancerous undermaintenance had already infected the branches and was beginning to attack the trunk. Without capital investment, shippers left, just a few at first, but that reduced revenues, which further reduced investment, which drove away more shippers; suddenly, the railroad was at the point of no return without anyone being able to recall the turning point. It was a terrifying scenario, similar to what was, even then, happening to the pre-merger Penn Central. Some thought it might happen to all American railroads, with no one the wiser until it was too late.

It also happened that the Rock became the vortex of the most prolonged merger contest of all. Like its financial struggle, it started out routinely enough. Creditors of three of the big granger roads, the Rock, the Milwaukee, and the North Western, had summoned a meeting of presidents and made it clear they wanted consolidation. And so, in ordinary fashion, the Rock and the Milwaukee began talks, but they sputtered and fizzled. Then the Southern Pacific seemed to sense a bargain and hired Coverdale & Colpitts to do some studies. In early 1963, there was a flurry of portentious rumors from the West, and on February 28 the word was official that Union Pacific would seek to merge with the Rock, whereupon it would sell all RI lines south of Kansas City to the Southern Pacific. The Rock's management and largest stockholders approved of the deal, and so it was expected the rest of the stockholders would approve, like sheep, the way they always did.[1]

Then entered Ben Heineman of the Chicago & North Western—the lawyer who had made commuter trains pay. He had not been invited to the conclave of February 28, as he should have been, because his railroad could lose 157,000 cars a year in Union Pacific interchange at Omaha if UP should gain its own entrance into Chicago. There was no way North Western could allow this to happen as long as it was able to fight. Heineman made an offer, not to the UP or the Rock Island, but over their heads to Rock Island stockholders. For each share, he offered an exchange package of C&NW stock, C&NW bonds, and cash. Translated into dollars, it was worth considerably more than the market price of RI stock.[2] If all RI shareholders accepted, they would own about 50 percent of the North Western. It was an attractive deal that stunned the UP, for when shareholders were presented with real alternatives, they were not so easy to push around.

This was an earthquake to western railroading.

1. The Milwaukee could not tolerate a UP line into Chicago any more than the North Western, for it, too, fed at the trough of UP interchange at Omaha. It sided with the C&NW.
2. The Santa Fe could not tolerate the SP in Kansas City or Memphis. It supported C&NW so it could get RI's southern half.
3. Frisco could not tolerate the loss of its Santa Fe interchange if that should happen, so it backed SP.
4. Missouri Pacific could not tolerate the loss of SP interchange at El Paso, so it backed C&NW and demanded trackage rights over SP all the way to the Pacific coast.
5. The Rio Grande could not tolerate any further encirclement by the UP and demanded "affirmative relief," the right to buy the RI's lines from Denver to Omaha and Kansas City, including its Armourdale Yard complex at Kansas City.
6. The Burlington could not tolerate SP control of the RI's half of the Joint Texas Division (the old Burlington-Rock Island Railroad) between Fort Worth and Houston, and demanded full control by itself.

7. Kansas City Southern could not tolerate further encirclement by the SP, and demanded routes to Houston, Dallas-Fort Worth, and Chicago (and even began to plan schedules and solicit traffic).

8. Missouri-Kansas-Texas (Katy) could not tolerate any diversion by anyone, and demanded to be included in whatever plans were made.

In the midst of it all, Missouri Pacific bought three million shares (8 percent) of the larger Santa Fe and asked for stock control.

Union Pacific sent Wyer, Dick & Company to study the Rock, and the report was not encouraging. Shippers said the Rock Island service was a day slower than other lines. Congestion at major yards was serious. Tight curves and annoying grades had forced the Kansas City-St. Louis line out of active competition. Slow orders were spreading through the system—500 miles of them by 1967, 2,300 miles by 1970, including 1,800 miles of the mainline. Wyer said $23 million was needed immediately for fixed plant, another $107 million for rolling stock.[3] The UP could provide that kind of capital; C&NW could not. So it was a dilemma. The C&NW would cannibalize the Rock; UP would rebuild it, and in doing so, destroy the C&NW.

In November 1963, the Rock Island stockholders were supposed to meet to ratify management's plans. Merger with UP required approval by two-thirds of them. But the UP's campaign had not been going well. Nothing, for example, had been heard from the 25 percent of RI shares held anonymously in street names by the large brokerage houses. When the meeting was called to order, management did not have two-thirds of the proxies. Moments before voting was to begin, UP hurried in with a restraining order. With victory in its grasp, the C&NW, or parties thinking to help it, had committed a terrible gaffe. It had failed to register with the SEC a pamphlet mailed to RI shareholders pointing out the advantages of the C&NW offer.[4] That constituted an illegal solicitation of proxy. It was suggested the UP had done the same thing earlier, by placing unregistered advertisements in financial journals, but fairness was not the issue. There was nothing for the RI stockholders to do but go home. Ben Heineman was described as "shaken." In the meantime, the Rock's directors and the UP increased their holdings of RI stock. When the long-postponed vote was finally taken, the UP had it, with 78 percent.

So the *Rock Island* case was not really about the fate of the Rock Island but of the Chicago & North Western and all the other western roads. That had been the heart of the merger problem from the beginning, not what consolidation would do for the roads that merged, but what it would do to the ones that did not. Union Pacific, quite understandably, did not want to get into the seasonal, low-yield granger business any more than necessary, so it did not want the C&NW at any price even if it was UP's historic partner in the Overland Route. Rock Island offered it mainlines to key midwestern gateways with comparatively few granger branches, and it was cheap.

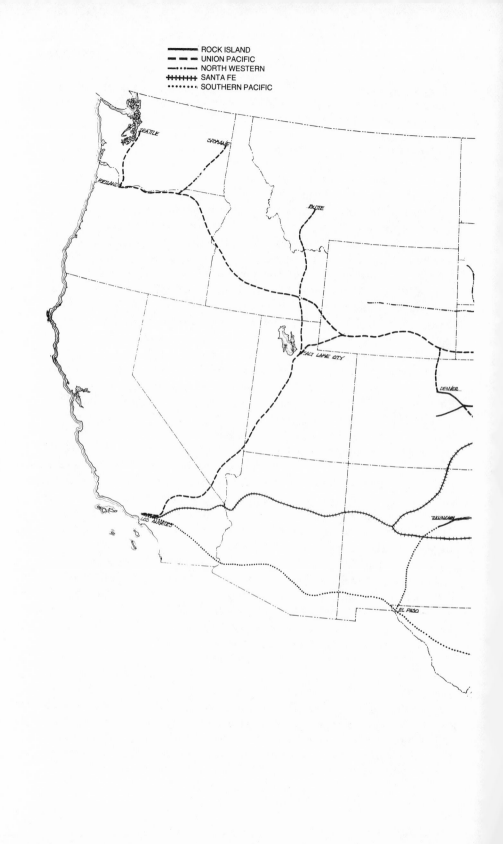

ROCK ISLAND
UNION PACIFIC
NORTH WESTERN
SANTA FE
SOUTHERN PACIFIC

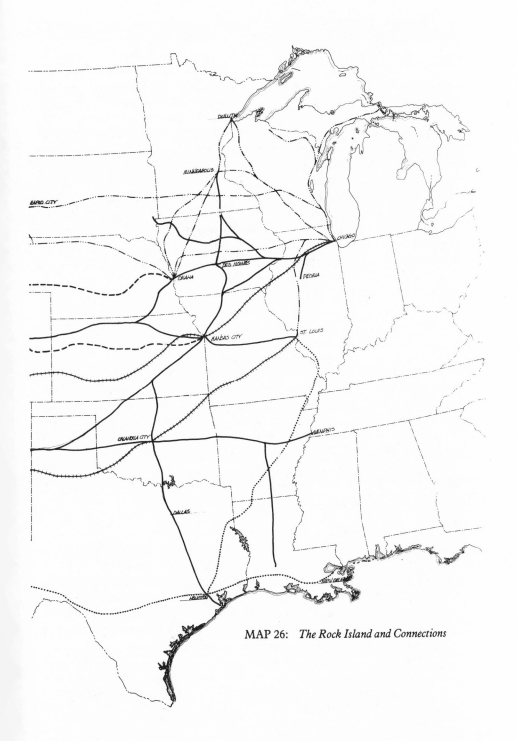

MAP 26:   *The Rock Island and Connections*

The bottom line for the C&NW was either a chance to remain a viable railroad or a decent price for its properties. If Ben Heineman was regarded in some quarters as a slick operator whose heart was in conglomerates, not railroads, all he asked from the railroad community now was concrete recognition of the true value he felt the C&NW had legitimately earned through its own efforts. In 1966, he offered to sell the C&NW to the UP (although the railroad's profitable chemical subsidiaries, acquired through the diversification program, were not included). When that was turned down, he said the C&NW was prepared to buy the UP, a deal that would include an exchange of stock that would leave UP shareholders in control of the C&NW. That was turned down. There were huddled meetings throughout 1966 and 1967 in Chicago, New York, and Pittsburgh, usually sponsored by Heineman and usually including Frank Barnett of the UP, Robert Lovett of the investment firm of Brown Brothers, Harriman Company, principal stockholder of the UP, Benjamin Biaggini of the Southern Pacific, and Ernest Marsh and John Reed of the Sante Fe. The best proposal they could make was a four-way joint control of the Rock Island, which satisfied no one.[5] The situation, in other words, was deadlocked.

1

For Ben Heineman, the Chicago Great Western was no substitute for the Rock Island, but it gave the C&NW a chance to show it was willing and able to take marginal carriers under its banner. The CGW merger had none of the strategic ramifications of the Rock Island; CGW was just not that important. The affair was dominated mostly by local issues, like the loss of employment at Oelwein, Iowa, Great Western's headquarters. In fact, Chicago Great Western was a classic example of what consolidation was supposed to correct, the absorption of poorly located lines by regional carriers who would keep the necessary parts and downgrade or abandon the rest.

What constituted an unnecessary railroad depended on who was talking. The Great Western's arrival in the 1880s was greeted frigidly by the prairie roads already operating because it was a rate-cutter, smashing the cozy price-fixing pools of the established lines. Even in the late 1940s, it was still reluctant to join the regional rate bureaus, whose purpose was also to fix prices. Circuitous or not, it had shown occasional signs of life in the 1950s and 1960s, for example, in the way it developed the Roseport Industrial Park south of the Twin Cities. But it got in the habit of running long, long freight trains behind six- or eight-unit diesels, providing shippers with once-a-day service they found inadequate. Its revenues declined every year after 1955, but costs increased. By the time of the C&NW offer, though not

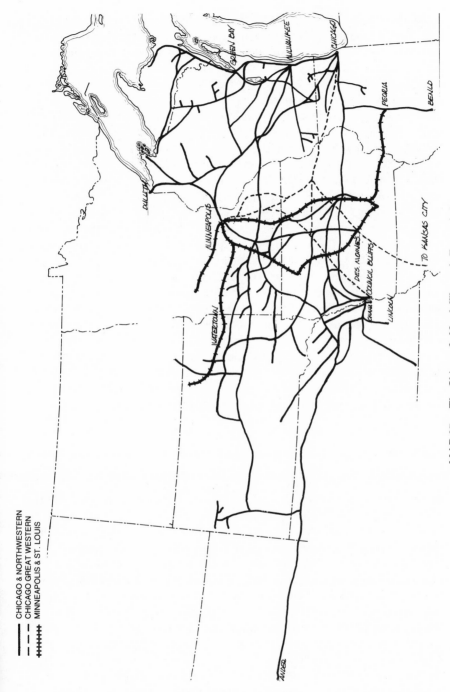

MAP 27: *The Chicago & North Western's Expansion*

insolvent, it was already at the point of no return—"serious financial problems with an inability to solve them internally," as the court would put it. Aware of what was happening, it sought merger partners beginning in the early 1960s; first the Rock Island, then a long-time favorite connection, the Soo Line, and finally the Frisco. The C&NW's offer in the summer of 1964 was apparently a happy surprise.

As always, the aggrieved party with the most persistence and ready funds to pursue that persistence, was another railroad, in this case, the Soo Line. Diversion studies reached their pinnacle of absurdity as the Soo claimed losses of $1.7 million, while the C&NW insisted that by its scientific calculation, Soo would only lose $13,000. In its approval of the merger, the commission threw up its hands and said the truth must lie somewhere between.[6] Soo went straight to court, a very friendly court, as it turned out, which said, quite properly, that its job was not to substitute its judgment for the commission's, even if it thought the commission's judgment was bad. It then proceeded to substitute its judgment for the commission's.

The court decided the *Great Western* case should have been combined with the *Rock Island* case. It thought Soo Line employees were entitled to job protection, and cited a precedent case it liked better for this than the one cited by the commission. It thought Soo should have access to Roseport. Finally, it said, the commission would have to come to grips with diversion; it could not just throw up its hands. So the case came back on remand. The commission complained testily, but thrashed around the diversion studies some more, and finally accepted the court's judgment in place of its own.[7] On July 1, 1968, the Chicago Great Western was no more.

2

The Chicago & North Western seemed to have a halo around its head in the mid-1960s. Under Heineman, a diversification program through the Northwest Industries holding company went well, even if a bid for the B.F. Goodrich Company fell through. Acquisitions in clothing (Fruit of the Loom, Union Underwear), shoes (Acme Boot), steel (Lone Star), and especially chemicals (Velsicol) paid off handsomely, if not directly to the railroad, at least in the enhanced prestige of its management. *Trains* thought it was a bad omen that Northwest Industries' 1968 annual report listed the railroad at the end, but the company explained that things were in alphabetical order and transportation came last. The railroad itself was never a strong earner, but it acted as if it were, buying the M&StL, merging with the CGW, and battling the Union Pacific in the biggest merger fight of the century. Its great success with commuter traffic, which contrasted sharply with the eastern roads' scramble for subsidies, made it something of a darling among laissez-fairists, and outside the commuter zone, shippers and competitors alike came to know it as a lean and often ruthless prowler for freight.

M-Day was in April 1966, after which the Northern Lines came to terms with their former adversaries, including both Milwaukee and North Western on the matter of routes and gateways across the Northwest. But the deal—that seems an appropriate term—was more extensive than that. If Milwaukee and North Western would bow gracefully out of the Northerns' merger, the Northerns would not interfere in a Milwaukee-North Western merger. There was even a rumor that Milwaukee and North Western promised the Northerns access to the industrial districts of the City of Milwaukee as part of the arrangement.[8] Exactly where relations between the Milwaukee and the North Western stood at the moment was not clear; on again-off again merger talk had been going on since the 1950s. At any rate, the settlement with the Northerns seemed to be the catalyst. North Western and Milwaukee would form a new company, temporarily dubbed the Chicago, Milwaukee & North Western Transportation Company. (Employees were asked to think up better names, like Trans-Midwest Lines, perhaps.) The C&NW would name eight of the fifteen directors, and ultimately, Northwest Industries would have control. Application was filed with the commission in June 1966.

Practically every western railroad took part. There were 19,000 pages of testimony, briefs were enormous, and yet the case never stirred the passion of the Northern Line's merger. Perhaps it was *déjà vu*; everyone was bored. Perhaps, deep in their hearts, they wished these two big marginal roads well, if not for altruistic reasons, then at least to keep them out of other people's mergers. Controversy seemed to settle on two nasty issues. One was the demand for the so-called Lyle condition, trackage rights for the Illinois Central from Lyle, Minnesota, to the suburbs of St. Paul, to replace the friendly connection it lost in the 1950s when the C&NW took over the Minneapolis & St. Louis. The Minnesota Railroad and Warehouse Commission took up the IC's cause, not for any love of a big railroad, but because it promised to give an advantage to some politically potent agribusiness shippers in southern Minnesota. As a general impression, its presentation smacked of populist stump-thumping. Arguments that held water when talking about technologically efficient dividend-paying railroads did not hold water when talking about marginal earners which were skidding in the same netherworld as the Rock Island. It showed once again how political bodies went to bat for their client-vested interests.

The other nasty issue was the demand of the Soo Line for full access to the industrial sidings of Milwaukee. It provided a close look at railroad competition in a major industrial center, and competition was a principal issue of consolidation. Milwaukee Road served 576 sidings in Milwaukee,

C&NW, 203. Reciprocal switching arrangements between them opened up most of these sidings to each other. The Milwaukee Road already extended trackage rights to the Soo Line, including those C&NW sidings to which it had rights. Soo was not allowed, however, to solicit traffic competitive with the Milwaukee Road, which included everything between Milwaukee and Chicago. The contract had just been renewed (in 1963) for twenty-five years, and Soo had no complaints about it then.

The Milwaukee Road handled 50.6 percent of all traffic in the city, C&NW 33 percent, Soo 5.4 percent, and via Lake Michigan car ferries, the C&O had 8 percent and the Grant Trunk Western 3 percent.[9] A merger not giving the Soo unrestricted access would virtually create a monopoly. In Florida and Mississippi they seemed to like railroad monopolies, but in Wisconsin they didn't. On the other hand, opening Milwaukee to the Soo would grant it the benefit of investments it never made and would wipe out one of the few trumps the Milwaukee Road and C&NW had. If shippers didn't like their service, said Milwaukee and C&NW, they could always short-haul them.

Over and over the issue was competition. Over and over, shippers testified they got better service, and often better rates, when there was more than one railroad. If they didn't get good service and good rates, they could and would take their business to the trucks. They testified that C&NW in particular was difficult to deal with. The Krause Milling Company in Milwaukee, for example, said Milwaukee Road would grant rates on corn from Iowa to Milwaukee that were competitive with rates to Chicago, but the C&NW would not. They had no idea why not; they just wouldn't. Others had similar stories. General Mills, Masonite, and Land O'Lakes Creameries described in vivid detail how service to their plants on the former Chicago Great Western deteriorated after merger.

Nevertheless, Examiner Henry Darmstadter recommended approval of the merger in December 1968. It was one of the most sophisticated merger reports to date, particularly in its analysis of the role of competition.[10]

But the merger itself came unraveled before the proceedings went any further. Some dissident Milwaukee Road stockholders accused their own company of selling out to the C&NW. Not only had Milwaukee turned in a better financial record than C&NW in 1967, entitling it to more favorable terms, they said, but its open-gateways deal with the Northern Lines would likely make it permanently the stronger. What's more, it had failed to inform its stockholders of the open gateways in its latest proxy solicitations, and for that indiscretion, they filed a class action suit.[11]

Meanwhile, the golden halo around Northwest Industries turned dime-store green. It reported a 50 percent drop in earnings in 1969 and omitted dividends in the last quarter of that year and the first quarter of 1970. That, plus the failure of its planned takeovers of B.F. Goodrich, Home Insurance, and Swift & Company sent the price of its stock tumbling from a 1968 high of $60.625 to a 1969 low of $10.625. The ICC recognized instantly that the original stock-exchange ratio was no longer valid and ordered hearings reopened. This was for the protection of Northwest as much as anyone, but the commission hinted broadly that it would declare Northwest a transportation company, like Illinois Central Industries, bringing it under full ICC regulation.[12]

Heineman told Curtiss Crippen of the Milwaukee Road that he was tired of the whole affair, but that under no circumstances would Northwest renegotiate the exchange ratio. If the Milwaukee wanted to buy the whole C&NW Railroad, it was for sale. It was rumored that Northwest Industries badly needed the tax loss that a sale of its railroad assets would produce. Since the Milwaukee didn't have the resources to purchase, the merger was off.

Reactions were bitter. Some accused the commission of meddling in internal affairs, like stock-exchange ratios, where it didn't belong. (That was not correct; it was required by law to make sure such transactions were fair. There were too many cases of manipulation in the old days, with helpless small-time security holders always winding up the losers, for it not to do so.) Some Milwaukee Road dissidents wanted to oust their own board for letting the deal fall through. (That group, incidentally, all speculators from outside the Milwaukee's service area, had also tried to oust the Boston & Maine's board under similar circumstances.)[13] Most criticism, however, fell on Ben Heineman, that he should have been allowed to dangle the Milwaukee Road for so long while the last hours of its strength ebbed away; that the time of so many people, and all the thousands of dollars spent on the proceeding could be thrown away when one man changed his mind.

3

The Northerns never denied their surprise at their setback on M-Day. But the alacrity with which they gave in to virtually all the demands of their adversaries—attrition conditions to labor, new gateways to other railroads —indicated the price they were willing to pay to get their merger. In the meantime, four commissioners had left the commission, including the Northerns' principal antagonists, Tucker and Webb. Perhaps the new commission would see things differently. Hearings were reopened, but were brief; there wasn't much left to say. The commission noted the new agreements did not change the factual basis of the matter, so could not be responsible for a reversal. The final report retraced the same ground as the first, issue by issue, approving what had previously been disapproved. The lesson? If one commission turns you down, wait for another. Only two

commissioners, Paul Tierney and Virginia Mae Brown, remained uncon-
vinced. Both believed, despite what the Milwaukee Road was now saying,
that a few gateways were not going to turn it into a viable railroad. At least,
said Tierney, we should wait until decisions are reached in the *Milwaukee-
North Western* and *Rock Island* cases. That did not mean combine cases,
but wait. Keep options open. But Tierney and Brown stood alone. The
Northern Lines' merger was approved on November 30, 1967.[14]

There were petitions for reconsideration. Injunctions were sought. All
were turned down. By one account, on the morning of May 10, 1968,
operators at company offices began answering phones with a cheery
"Burlington Northern," at least until 10 A.M., when Chief Justice Earl
Warren issued a restraining order. The GN's John Budd and NP's Louis
Menk had been sitting with the final papers before them. Menk complained
that the railroad was losing $100,000 a day by these interminable delays,
then clarified that what he meant was that the railroad was not getting
started on the work to achieve merger savings that might, someday, save
$100,000 a day. The change in emphasis was important, but most news-
papers picked it up the first way and never got around to the clarification.

Delay was all that was accomplished. The merger was upheld, first by a
three-judge panel, and on February 2, 1970, by the Supreme Court, 7–0.[15] It
was fourteen years after merger planning began, nine after it went to the
commission. Burlington Northern began operation on March 2, 1970.

4

Perhaps it was just sour grapes on the part of the North Western. It was
losing its fight for the Rock Island at the hands of the Union Pacific which,
by comparison, seemed so rich and well-connected. It was annoyed—and
suspicious—that Wayne Johnston kept the Illinois Central out of the *Rock
Island* case because he had this "philosophy of mergers" that railroads
ought not interfere in each other's merger plans, even though he pursued
the C&NW like a quarry over the "Lyle conditions" in the *Milwaukee-
North Western* case. So the C&NW brought forth sweeping allegations that
the Harriman family and the banking house of Brown Brothers, Harriman
Company still controlled the vast railroad empire that old E.H. Harriman
had put together at the turn of the century. The charges never quite stood
up but they triggered a lot of scrambling by a lot of people. It was a
shrouded glimpse of one of the forces—some people thought the real force
—that lay behind the mergers.

The extent of Harriman influence on the Union Pacific was not hard to
determine. E.H. Harriman had remained at the railroad's helm until 1909,
when he chose his attorney and personal friend Robert S. Lovett to succeed
him. Harriman's son Averell succeeded Lovett, Averell's brother Roland

succeeded Averell, Lovett's son Robert A. Lovett succeeded Roland. In 1967, Lovett was succeeded by Frank Barnett, the railroad's general counsel. Barnett had been a partner in the New York law firm of Clark, Carr & Ellis, which had long been associated with the Harrimans and the UP, the late G.A. Ellis having formerly been UP general counsel. Brown Brothers, Harriman, the investment firm, was successor to all the Harriman interest in the UP, approximately 350,000 shares, with the rest of the railroad's stock widely distributed among 103,000 shareholders. Three of its partners sat on the UP board—Roland Harriman, Robert A. Lovett, and Elbridge Gerry, a Harriman grandson. These three normally dominated the railroad's executive committee.

Harriman's original empire consisted of the Union Pacific, the Southern Pacific, and the Illinois Central. Antitrust action forced the sale of the SP holdings, but down through the years, UP kept roughly a 23 percent interest in the IC. When Wayne Johnston was president of the IC, he would say whenever a controversial matter was coming up that he had to "go and see the big brothers," meaning Brown Brothers, Harriman. Johnston was succeeded at his post by William B. Johnson, who C&NW alleged was handpicked by the resident partner of Brown Brothers, Harriman in Chicago, Stephen Y. Hord. Hord, said C&NW, short-circuited the IC's own search committee, and recommended Johnson even before the man had applied for the job. Johnson, who had spent his career at the Pennsylvania Railroad and then at Railway Express, was recommended to Hord by Frank Barnett. Barnett and Johnson went on fishing trips together, and Johnson regularly kept Barnett informed of IC activities, even though he, Johnson, knew this could be construed as improper. When asked about his relationship with Barnett, Johnson kept having lapses of memory—fifty, to be precise. The C&NW thought this raised "more than a lingering doubt" about illegal relationships between the two railroads and filed a motion for discovery with the ICC.[16] The Missouri Pacific and the Department of Justice joined the C&NW.

The Union Pacific hastily put its IC stock in a voting trust. As for the commission, it did not discount these charges, although previously, when the MoPac had complained about similar matters in retaliation for the IC's lawsuits in the Chicago & Eastern Illinois affair, the commission refused to go into a general investigation of "who owns the railroads." Without further investigation, it ordered IC, Illinois Central Industries, Union Pacific, and Brown Brothers, Harriman to make known the full extent of their interest in each other. The commission reserved jurisdiction to act on this information at a later date, if necessary. Within ten years after the IC-GM&O merger was completed, the Union Pacific was to divest itself of all interest in Illinois Central Gulf and Illinois Central Industries. So closed *l'affaire* Brown Brothers, Harriman.

5

For all of its massive volume, the *Rock Island* case boiled down to a series of violently conflicting studies on traffic diversion. They were the products of electronic computers—everyone had access to them now—and the computers made things hopelessly confused. They added enormous complexity which required exponentially more intricate cross-examination to clarify. Everyone selected a different method for making computation. Some took random samples. Some took "typical week" samples. Some did car-by-car analyses. Some included all traffic. Others excluded certain kinds of traffic, for reasons that constantly varied. Some used judgment early in their calculation, others not until the very end. The method chosen produced the results desired. The discrepancy between what one railroad said it would lose and what its opponent said it would lose ran between 200 percent and 2,000 percent. The ICC was under court order to take this seriously and try to reconcile it. It was not permitted to laugh.

Then came briefs that were enormous, running 1,000 pages each and more, with lovely charts and maps. They cost thousands of dollars and untold bureaucrat-hours to prepare, and then to read, and they did not clear the issues. The sheer inadequacy of the adversary system had come home to roost.

The man who wound up in charge, Administrative Law Judge Nathan Klitenic, did a yeoman job trying to sort it all out. His report was in three installments, running around 1,000 pages each. In the first (September 1971) he analyzed the nature of the railroads involved and their traffic patterns. In the second (March 1972) he discussed the demands of each, and the repercussions those demands would have on others. In the third (February 1973) he tried to come to grips with the traffic studies. It was a dreadfully difficult task.

In his third installment, Judge Klitenic recognized that either the applications had to be denied, or a major restructuring of the western railroads was necessary. There were no middle roads, most certainly not the Union Pacific's wish to have its merger with no strings attached. Perhaps it would have been wise to let the Rock Island go into receivership, but he rejected the idea, believing the ICC could not condemn a solvent carrier to a receivership that might end in liquidation. Given that, he introduced his groundbreaking theory. The very existence of independent midwestern granger roads was obsolete and was the cause of railroad problems in the West. The idea that a few transcontinentals should feed traffic to half a dozen of these roads, which in turn fed it to a few eastern trunks was, as he put it, as old-fashioned as the steam locomotive. So he rejected the North Western's bid for the Rock Island. It would go to the UP.

What followed was the most refreshing document of the merger movement. The railroads had asked for this. They had not shown an ounce of statesmanship in restructuring their strengths and weaknesses on their own. They had forced the ICC to do it for them. These were the strings he attached:

1. The Union Pacific must sell the southern portions of the Rock Island to the Southern Pacific.
2. The Southern Pacific must give trackage rights to the Santa Fe into St. Louis.
3. The Southern Pacific must sell to the Santa Fe the Rock Island line from Amarillo, Texas, to Memphis.
4. The Southern Pacific must give the Burlington Northern sole control of the Joint Texas Division, the old Burlington-Rock Island.
5. The Union Pacific must acquire the Chicago & North Western.
6. The Southern Pacific must sell and the Union Pacific must buy the Central Pacific.
7. The Santa Fe must acquire the Western Pacific, the Denver & Rio Grande, and the entire Missouri Pacific-Texas & Pacific.
8. The Texas & Pacific must sell and the Southern Pacific must buy the line from El Paso to Fort Worth.
9. The Southern Pacific must sell and the Santa Fe must buy the line from Klamath Falls, Oregon, to Flanigan, Nevada.
10. The Southern Pacific must acquire the Katy and the Kansas City Southern.
11. Holding companies, specifically the Union Pacific Company, the Southern Pacific Company, and Santa Fe Industries, shall be considered common carriers by rail and come within ICC jurisdiction.
12. The record shall be held open to determine whether the Milwaukee Road shall be included in the Union Pacific System.
13. The record shall be held open in order that the Frisco may be included in a system of its choice.

It took some study on the map before the sheer brilliance of this came clear. This was the blueprint for the competitively balanced systems that had eluded everyone since the time of Albert Cummins. There would be four railroads west of the Mississippi—the Burlington Northern, the Union Pacific, the Santa Fe, and the Southern Pacific (with Canadian Pacific's Soo Line on the periphery). Each would serve two of the four midwestern gateways—Chicago, St. Louis, Memphis, or New Orleans—and extend all the way to the Pacific coast. Each of the three corridors—northern, central, and southern—would have two major competitors, each with important areas of strength, but each with compensating weaknesses. In the north, for example, the UP (ex-Milwaukee Road) would be weaker than Burlington Northern, but would be balanced by a more complete network in the midwest. The UP would dominate the central corridor but the weaker Santa Fe (ex-Western Pacific-Rio Grande-MoPac) would have more complete feeder lines in California. No weak carriers would be left over, save perhaps the Soo Line. No one would have stringer lines deep into hostile territory that could never be viable.[17] Just as Professor Ripley had suggested in 1921, this

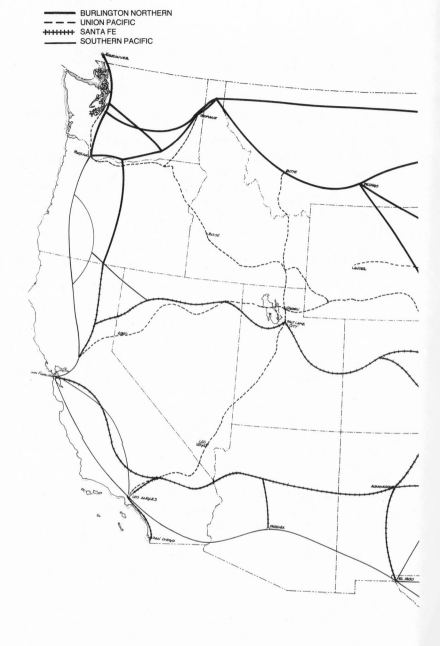

BURLINGTON NORTHERN
- - - UNION PACIFIC
++++++ SANTA FE
SOUTHERN PACIFIC

VANCOUVER

SPOKANE

PORTLAND

BUTTE

BILLINGS

BOISE

LANDER

OGDEN

SALT LAKE CITY

RENO

LAS VEGAS

SAN FRANCISCO

ALBUQUERQUE

LOS ANGELES

PHOENIX

SAN DIEGO

EL PASO

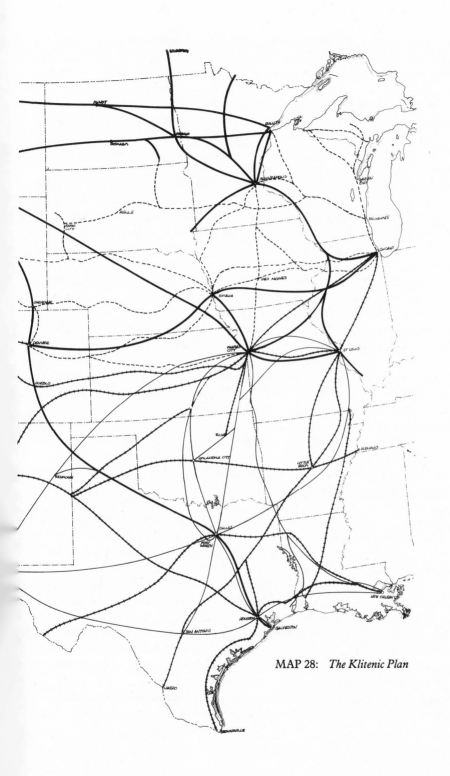

MAP 28: *The Klitenic Plan*

amazing balance was not possible without dismembering at least one of the existing major systems. Circumstances had cast the Rock Island as the blood sacrifice. There were many who would mourn its passing. But in an imperfect world, the Klitenic Plan was quite remarkable.

Perhaps the swiftness and hatefulness of the response from railroads was a measure of its brilliance. Only the North Western and the Milwaukee seemed to accept that what had happened was the logical result of greed and shortsightedness, but this was hardly the first time weaker roads sought solace from the commission. The strong roads rejected it *in toto.* The SP and UP, for example, filed exceptions that refuted every suggestion point by point. They would not be generous about anything. They would do nothing that was not unquestionably in their immediate corporate interest. It was a shockingly selfish response that seemed oblivious to political realities and long-run railroad problems. Santa Fe, SP, C&NW, MoPac, Rio Grande, and Soo asked to have the case dismissed immediately. Rock Island, which had been diddled by everyone for eleven years, was in no mood for that, and denounced their petition as the most "arrogant and cynical document ever filed with the Commission."

Some will argue the commission tried to reach too far. If it insisted on restructuring the western roads along the lines of the Klitenic Report, nothing was going to happen at all, because none of these people could be forced to do anything. If it were imperative to "save" the Rock Island from receivership, it would have to sacrifice the perfect plan. But the Rock had comparatively little funded debt, so merely protecting it from creditors would not stop the outward flow of cash. Receivership, therefore, would probably mean liquidation, at which point the commission could parcel out essential lines to various other roads in a way "consistent with public interest." Perhaps Amtrak, the National Railroad Passenger Corporation, would take the Chicago-Omaha mainline through Des Moines, for it was the superior passenger line in that corridor. Perhaps the "cram down" provisions of the bankruptcy act could be used to force reluctant parties to take their responsibility. Such an end for the Rock Island was a shame. It was steeped in the history of the American West. No one who had traveled the silvery *Rockets* could look on this without sadness.

So the ICC backed down and pushed the Klitenic Plan aside. The UP could have the northern Rock Island, SP the southern Rock Island. Rio Grande could have part of the western Rock Island, the line to Omaha but not to Kansas City because that would hurt the MoPac. (Rio Grande had previously offered to buy the MoPac's Kansas City-Pueblo line if it wanted to sell.) Burlington Northern was given several nice presents—access to industrial areas of Portland previously served only by UP, access to the Canadian Pacific over the UP subsidiary Spokane International, and sole control of the Joint Texas Division. Santa Fe would get the Rock Island's

Amarillo-Memphis line, but must also acquire the Katy, a booby prize beyond the point of no return.[18] To protect the midwestern bridge carriers (C&NW, Milwaukee, Frisco, KCS, and MoPac), the UP and SP were required to deliver as many carloads to them in interchange as they had in the past, for a period of five years. If traffic fell short, there was a formula for indemnification. If shipper routings made it difficult to comply, the railroads were to change those routings in order to do so. If the protected roads failed to provide adequate service, UP and SP could complain to the commission. Holding companies were to come under ICC regulation.

Commissioners Tuggle, Deason, and Clapp knew even this was too severe. It still asked the railroads to do what they didn't want to do. If the purpose was to save the Rock Island, it wouldn't work because the big railroads were still going to walk away. Commissioner Brown alone stood by the Klitenic Plan. She thought a grand opportunity to restructure the western railroads had been allowed to slip by. What was going to happen to the protected roads in five years when the protective period ran out? The majority opted for the middle ground that solved nothing.

Union Pacific, complaining loudly that businesses were not allowed to run their own affairs anymore, withdrew its merger offer entirely. The long case was over with nothing to show for it. Rock Island slipped rapidly to the brink. In February 1975, a last-ditch plan was put forth whereby the Rock's own employees would give it an "interest-free loan" in the form of a 10 percent pay cut. The unions agreed, but the rank and file did not. When the last appeal for a loan from the U.S. Railroad Administration failed, other roads began to refuse to settle interline accounts, the railroads' way of administering last rites. Bankruptcy came on March 17. An embargo on all shipments anticipated the closing of the railroad. Under ICC supervision, interested railroads were summoned to a meeting to parcel out the remains. The SP, for example, put in a bid for the Tucumcari-Kansas City line, complaining that it needed $100 million for rehabilitation. But the trustees said no. The price offered was too low. A kick of rigor mortis, perhaps. But some cash was found and the line did not shut down. By August, talks with the Missouri Pacific seemed to indicate another merger was in the offing, although that finally fell through.[19]

As for the North Western, it was the subject of a bold experiment in industrial organization. In July 1972, it was sold to its own employees, although only 1,000 of a total 14,000 actually bought stock, and most were executives. The new company took responsibility for its $400 million-plus debt, something Ben Heineman made sure of before he pulled Northwest Industries out. But the railroad had $900 million in assets and $300 million annual revenues, which seemed like enough security. Said Examiner Reidy, the move was "unprecedented and laden with unforeseen imperfections" but a worthwhile experiment in the financing of marginal operations nevertheless. He worried that if the owners should ever become disillusioned with management, they might ensnarl the whole railroad. "Plainly put," he said, "profits are readily attributed by the employee-investor to his own efforts and skill, whereas management is the logical one to blame for a loss."[20] But through 1977, at least, the experiment seemed to work, helped by the Soviet wheat deals and the long trainloads of interchange that continued to pass from the Union Pacific to the C&NW at Omaha.

The Burlington Northern regarded its merger as a success. Management profited from the mistakes of others by doing the premerger planning carefully and not merely cosmetically. Executive positions and the people to fill them, for example, were designated in advance, and that seemed to give jealousies time to cool before it really mattered. In *Fortune,* Rush Loving, Jr., would eventually write about BN as "the merger that worked." The company had a big boost from the environmental crusade that began about the time of its merger, later reinforced by the oil embargo of 1973, which made it profitable to mine low-sulphur coal on company land and transport it by rail. Even so, the merger was a shock that at first sent operating ratios climbing and shippers complaining. It was a shock that culminated with top-level management bundling all of its middle-level staff off to an isolated resort at Wickenburg, Arizona, and bluntly telling them to get a grip on themselves and their jobs before there was a disaster.[21]

But the merger had been predicated on the assumption—however tenuous —that it would not only strengthen the Northerns' ability to make capital improvements and compete with trucks but would strengthen rail competition by opening up new gateways to the Milwaukee Road. Therefore, an incident shortly after the merger was very disturbing. Certain shippers who had private sidings on BN lines were coerced to sign agreements saying they would use BN service exclusively, which eliminated any benefit the Milwaukee Road might get from the open gateways. It came to the attention of Richard McLaren in the antitrust division of Nixon's Justice Department, who obtained a consent judgment prohibiting the BN from enforcing these contracts.[22]

As for the Milwaukee Road, the new era of northwestern railroading seemed to begin with promise. The first Milwaukee Road trains into Portland received a gala reception from city fathers, and the railroad advertised its new gateways heavily. Tonnage on the transcontinental line increased handsomely for a while, a boon to railroad fans for it required calling out historic electric locomotives for service over the mountains. Not long afterward, Milwaukee Road entered Louisville over Monon trackage (following the Monon-Louisville & Nashville merger). That meant more celebrations and publicity, for shippers now had a single-line haul from the Ohio River to Puget Sound. For several years, the "creative crews" advertising campaign kept the railroad's name before shippers and the public.

But in the end, it couldn't face the formidable competition of the BN and the interstate highways. In its approval of the BN merger, the ICC held out the possibility that if worse came to worst, it would order BN to include the Milwaukee Road. As Milwaukee Road began to slip toward the point of no return, the time came for it to ask for its promised inclusion. The BN fought it vigorously, and the ICC was in a dilemma. Whether it ordered inclusion or not, the revived competition that was supposed to have been the justification of the BN merger was dead. The Milwaukee Road's pleas were turned down.

Despite this setback, Milwaukee Road had a will to survive. It turned to the old and effective expedient of coordination. In 1977, it began a line coordination with the Rock Island into Kansas City. It invited the C&NW to coordinate with it between Milwaukee and the Twin Cities, but it already shared a portion of those tracks with the BN, and BN refused to allow any new tenants. Likewise, BN refused to make any further coordinations with the Milwaukee Road in the Rocky Mountains or in the Midwest.

Under 1976 legislation, Milwaukee Road was able to sell senior preferred stock (called redeemable preference shares) to the Federal Railroad Administration in order to finance the rebuilding of the Milwaukee-Twin Cities line, which had not received high-standard maintenance since the 110 mph days of the early 1950s. If that made the federal government a major Milwaukee Road stockholder, that did not seem to matter to a railroad that could no longer sell securities to the public. And despite its woes, it lived up to its obligations under the Amtrak law to provide passenger service under contract for the National Railroad Passenger Corporation, better than most of the wealthy roads, with an overall on-time performance of more than 95 percent.

Yet in the age of consolidation, a shroud of enveloping loneliness seemed to descend on the Milwaukee Road, which was underscored by a poignant little note in *Trains:*

Asked if he would be attending an off-line railroad trade association convention in 1978, the Milwaukee Road department head parried the question. "I don't know; it's a long way, and I really don't have that much in common with most of those people. I mean the MoPacs and the Santa Fes don't talk our language."[23]

Was the country better off because the Northern Lines had had a merger that seemed to work, when the price was to leave the rail system in its region in more serious disarray than before? Perhaps it boiled down to which railroad you rooted for.

CHAPTER 12

The Eastern Inclusion Crisis; 1966-1968

Until the late 1960s, the ICC chairmanship was a rotating office which shortly after M-Day passed to the commission's chief dissident, William H. Tucker. Tucker, a Kennedy campaign organizer in Massachusetts in 1960 and a Kennedy appointee to the commission in 1961, had opposed the mergers, not because the idea was intrinsically bad, but because the railroads had planned them so badly. It was said that once the majority reached a decision he disagreed with, he never twitted them when events proved them wrong, and for that reason was able to impart some of his thinking on them.[1] He was a driving influence behind the denial of the Northern Lines' merger on M-Day. His colleague, Charles A. Webb, who had frequently joined him in dissent, held his tongue in the Penn Central decision. So Tucker alone, concurring separately, said in essence, I told you so. By approving the other eastern mergers without really thinking what it would do to the other railroads, the creation of this monstrosity was inevitable. Once C&O-B&O was approved, Penn Central had to be approved, for they were as interlocked as if they had been on a single docket.

Everyone said they assumed Penn Central was going to be unbelievably powerful. It was going to blanket the East. If there were such things as merger savings, and railroad men said they believed in them, Penn Central was going to have $60 or $70 million extra to play around with, to make capital investment that would drive them all to the wall. It would be the most powerful voice in statehouses and in Washington and would dominate the Association of American Railroads. Even the N&W and the C&O claimed to feel the hot breath of PC power. For the eastern outcasts, like Erie Lackawanna, it was overwhelming.

John Fishwick, general counsel of the N&W, saw the problem clearly. "For over a generation," he said, "we have had an eastern railroad problem that has been a source of concern and frustration for the industry and the public. Its symptoms are pockets of poverty in an age of plenty. Penn Central, with all its promise, is no answer to this. It will shift the woes of the New Haven to the Erie Lackawanna, the Delaware & Hudson, the Boston &

Maine and the Jersey Central."[2] These were the leftovers that had to be put somewhere. The much ballyhooed "three-system plan" had been no plan at all because it did not take them into account.

It was called the inclusion crisis. It was against the background of a Penn Central merger that was approved but not yet consummated. The question was, at what level could order be restored from the mess that had been made? Could private companies work it out, without government direction? Was a firm hand at the ICC going to do the trick? Or was it going to take more than that?

1

When Erie Lackawanna sealed its famous "Agreement of October 12" with the N&W, it gave no hint it was dissatisfied or had signed at the point of a loaded gun. Nickel Plate was to join in the construction of Bison Yard, and that was supposed to assure the continued flow of traffic over the old Lackawanna-Nickel Plate route. Ground was broken, construction began, and all seemed well.

Then, relations between EL and Nickel Plate turned ice cold. There was a persistent rumor around the Buffalo yards that NKP had tried to build a siding from the far end of the yard to a connection with the Lehigh Valley, a few hundred feet away, and EL said no. It was one reason why NKP might lose interest. It was committed to help pay for the yard but not necessarily to use it. When it opened, and for years afterward, there was not a Nickel Plate or N&W train in sight. Headquarters in Roanoke said only that Bison "wasn't working out." Years later, John Fishwick said the real reason was that Erie Lackawanna had kept them out (by refusing to negotiate proper labor agreements). After investing $7.5 million, it seemed incredible that would stand in its way.[3]

When Nickel Plate and Lehigh failed to get a connection by way of Bison, they went to the Pennsylvania, which had a spur line around the city outskirts. Trackage rights were arranged and approved by the ICC; soon, long freights began to roll over the "Abbott Road" interchange, 100 cars or more, usually behind NKP locomotives and always with NKP crews. It was a new run-through service from NKP's eastern marshaling point at Conneaut, Ohio, to the Lehigh's western one at Manchester, New York. Service began in February 1964 with one train each way and was so successful that a second was added in July, together averaging 200 cars a day eastbound, 160 westbound.[4] But it was against the law for Nickel Plate crews to operate on Lehigh trackage rights without authorization, and it was against the law not to have air brakes tested at the exact point where a train was received in interchange. So the folks at Erie Lackawanna hurried down to Abbott Road to catch this on their Kodaks.

Looking back, it was the Lehigh's laudable attempt to save itself. There was hardly a more pathetic railroad in the land. When quizzed on how sweet it must be inside the Pennsylvania empire, Lehigh's general manager H.C. Kohout, a former PRR man himself, shouted that they were getting nothing from the Pennsylvania. The PRR had given them no clue as to what it intended to do with them. They were just trying to run a railroad under very difficult circumstances. Everybody was up against the deadly competition of Al Perlman's New York Central, which had become particularly aggressive with the high-value, high-speed, high-rate commodities. The new run-through service allowed Lehigh to reduce terminal time in Buffalo by seven hours. Closing time for piggyback out of Oak Island Yard in Newark was competitive with New York Central and Erie Lackawanna for the first time ever. The reasons were complicated, but if crews were changed or air brakes tested in any other manner, the time advantage would be lost. They were negotiating with the unions to run crews through from Conneaut to Manchester, but so far, no agreement had been reached. The new, young management at the Lehigh wondered why something like this was not done years ago, but then, there were a lot of things about past Lehigh management it could wonder about.

Nickel Plate had gripes of its own. The old Lackawanna had been its right arm; the two roads had solicited traffic together. That meant the sales people at EL knew the NKP's customers, and went to them and tried to solicit business for EL's long haul. The NKP knew, for example, that some of their customers had been told by EL that NKP's service out of Buffalo wasn't what it used to be and that they ought to use EL's Hornell route instead. The NKP had approached EL on the possibility of run-through service, but EL was committed to Bison and wasn't interested. "We leaned over backwards for the Erie Lackawanna," said John Fitzpatrick of the NKP, admittedly for selfish reasons, because Lehigh service was so deficient. But it wasn't deficient anymore. A lot of it, said Fitzpatrick, was the persuasiveness of the Lehigh's young traffic man, George Wallace, who "was out making friends where the Lehigh was never known before, . . . and gee whiz, we wanted to be in their picture too." Both Lehigh and NKP were furious at the State of New Jersey, which admitted it was interested in EL profits only so it would not have to cough up subsidy for EL's suburban service.

Q: Would you oppose Erie Lackawanna if they cut five hours off their schedule?

A: No.

Q: But you are here opposing the Lehigh Valley for doing the same thing?

A: You didn't let me finish.

Q: No further questions.[5]

So much for the way it looked on that side. If you were an Erie Lackawanna man standing down there at Abbott Road in the chill of a Buffalo
autumn, you looked on this as the doom of your railroad. Nickel Plate was
about to merge with the N&W, which the Pennsylvania had been found to
control. Lehigh Valley was controlled by the PRR. Was the grand strategy
now coming clear? Was Lehigh going to be the N&W's route to New York
Harbor? The EL's merger had not been successful. Robert Fuller, the chairman of its executive committee, was saying so publicly. If it had no friendly
connection at Buffalo, then investment in Bison Yard had been a waste of
money. Appendix O to the N&W-NKP merger required N&W to solicit
preferentially for it, and this run-through service was not only a breach of
good faith but of ICC orders.

Is it not true, asked an EL attorney of the Lehigh's Kohout, that the more
traffic that is diverted from EL, the less it will be worth, and the less someone will have to pay for it? That someone, of course, was the N&W, already
under agreement to negotiate in good faith. That's not the point, said Kohout. Look at EL's debt—almost $320 million (counting equipment trusts)
and all of it due in the near future. Lehigh, he said, had only $70 million of
outstanding debt, with maturities spread evenly to the year 2000. "If the
N&W's objective is to reach the seaboard, they can do it a damn site easier
by acquiring the Lehigh Valley."[6]

Inclusion was the issue. Debt was the obstacle.

2

When Erie Lackawanna signed the Agreement of October 12, many observers thought it had been played for a fool. But its $320 million debt was
there for all to see. Certainly a sagacious businessman like Stuart Saunders
knew all about it. He wanted that agreement so badly, he practically
ordered poor old Paul Johnson of the Erie down to Washington to sign it
and deliver it to the ICC before the ink was dry. When the implication began to sink in—that N&W might be saddled with $320 million in obligations
—Saunders ordered a merger study put on his desk to see the extent of the
damage. H.L. Scott of the N&W and J.M. Moonshower of the EL worked
on it, and had a preliminary draft ready by August of 1963.[7] This coincided
with the nadir of EL's fortunes. The property was visibly decaying, the
treasury held $6 million of unpaid bills, and morale was at rock bottom. A
wave of derailments, the result of undermaintained plant, and rule infrac-
tions brought on by lax discipline were symptomatic of the whole mess.

In the meantime, Saunders left the N&W for the Pennsylvania. Pennsylvania divested the N&W, the N&W merged, and the Lehigh run-through
service began. With regard to EL, the silence from Roanoke was deafening.
So in August 1964, the EL board decided to do a little prodding. It didn't

say so in so many words, but the bottom line of its plan was to saddle the N&W with EL debt and leave EL stockholders in possession of $84 million of prime N&W bonds, at roughly $16.64 a share, a price Erie stock hadn't commanded since 1957. (Speculators immediately moved into EL stock—there was a 100 percent turnover in the calendar year 1965.)

In Roanoke, the idea met an icy reception. The N&W's new president, Herman Pevler, formerly of the Wabash, did nothing about it until the next spring, and then said only that things would have to be studied some more. The EL thought it could tell when somebody was stalling, especially when John Fishwick, N&W general counsel, told N&W stockholders at their annual meeting that EL had too much debt and would *never* find a home in N&W. Did that constitute a violation of the October 12 Agreement, a failure to exhibit good faith?[8] Fishwick said that as a prerequisite to further talks, EL would have to demonstrate it could help itself by slimming its long-distance passenger service and getting out of the commuter business altogether.

Meanwhile, Scott and Moonshower were proceeding with the studies, but not altogether harmoniously. Differences seemed to settle on: (a) the N&W's reluctance to make any capital outlays in order to integrate the Erie; and (b) its reluctance to admit that Erie lines west of Hornell had any value. When the studies were complete, there was renewed silence. On November 1, 1965, Scott arrived unexpectedly in Moonshower's office with a proposed report he wanted signed immediately so he could take it back to Roanoke that night. "I saw at a glance," said Moonshower, "that it was a major departure from our joint plan. It was little more than coordination. . . . I saw that he had signed it already. When I said three or four times that I would not sign, he said he would buy a razor and stay overnight or however long it took."[9]

If this seemed like *prima facie* evidence that N&W was not negotiating in good faith, there was another side to the story. In August 1965, the N&W negotiating committee confronted EL on its debt. Fishwick said simply that $270 million of non-equipment debt was absurd for a road of that size and earning power. It would have to be reduced to a $120-$140 million range, comparable to other railroads. The N&W, in other words, was not going to be made responsible for the profligacy of past Erie managements. Even Robert Fuller, chairman of the EL's executive committee, seemed aware that a major writedown would be necessary sooner or later. But the day of reckoning was at hand. The EL had barely made it past the maturity of $12 million of first consolidated mortgage bonds in 1964 and did so only by extending the maturity date to 1969 and paying double the interest. More issues were due in 1971 and 1973. This was on a railroad with net working capital that equaled less than a month's expenses. Neither N&W nor anyone else could take a risk like that. It's too bad, said John Fishwick. "Without all the debt, Erie would be valuable."

It was within the power of EL bondholders to do something about it. They included the most prestigious insurance companies in the land and Fuller made sure they understood the seriousness of the situation. But their response, on at least two occasions, was that they would rather see the company go under than have a writedown.[10] If that were the case, said John Fishwick, "there would be little possibility they would be agreeable to modify those securities after N&W had an $84 million investment to protect."

3

When the B&O became a part of the *Chessie* System, it brought with it a dowry of dubious distinction. It owned 43 percent of the outstanding stock of the Reading Company, and while it did not exercise formal control, its influence in the form of dual executives was great. Reading had one of the heaviest freight traffic densities in the nation—one of the heaviest passenger densities, too—but distances were short and it was not making much money. Reading controlled the Jersey Central, a giant terminal railroad, stripped of its anthracite but not of its commuters. It was losing money— lots of it. And then, there was the Western Maryland, which the B&O could not touch even though it owned 43 percent of the outstanding stock, because Clayton Act proceedings in the 1930s had forced that stock into a voting trust. Back then, it was practically an open-and-shut case. The WM and B&O tracks intertwined like snakes. Two more competitive railroads were hard to find. The C&O exhibited a peculiar passion for the WM and began buying WM stock on its own account even before it got control of the B&O. In the summer of 1964, B&O sought permission to exercise formal control. No interest whatsoever was expressed in Reading or Jersey Central.

In some respects, the idea made good sense. At Cumberland, Maryland, B&O already had a sophisticated yard for westbound traffic and WM facilities could become the equivalent for eastbound traffic. At Baltimore, the new automatic coal-loading piers at Curtis Bay needed the traffic of both roads to operate at peak efficiency. The WM had superior grades eastbound over the Alleghenies, the B&O westbound. Predicted savings came to $6.2 million, substantial for the size of Western Maryland.

In other respects, the proposal was merely in the corporate interest of the C&O-B&O. Not only did WM compete mile-for-mile with B&O, but it solicited freight from B&O's competitors—the Alphabet Route in connection with N&W lines and the Pittsburgh Dispatch Route in connection with the Pittsburgh & Lake Erie-New York Central lines. The C&O-B&O said there was no place for a little railroad like the WM now that mergers had surrounded it with hostile competitors. But WM was still very profitable, with a legion of satisfied customers. There was no sign that its traffic was threatened or that it was physically unable to do its work.[11]

When the case was laid out before the ICC, it struck some of the commissioners that a golden opportunity had unexpectedly come along. On the one hand, here was a consolidation that made good operating sense and one which the C&O—which had lots of money—wanted very, very much. On the other, here were two outcast roads, Reading and Jersey Central, which had to be found a home somewhere. So why not make the C&O take the outcasts as the price for getting the WM? Supposedly, a report along those lines was all written and ready to go. But shortly before it was to be released, news came of the impending default of the Jersey Central on government guaranteed loans. This changed the whole picture and only two commissioners, Tucker and Tierney, were left in the hardliners' camp. So the Western Maryland case passed and nothing had been done about the outcasts.

4

Early October 1964 was an exciting time at N&W headquarters in Roanoke. Would the Pennsylvania divest? Though he once argued before the ICC that the PRR did not have the power to control the N&W, John Fishwick now said: "The Pennsylvania always had a thumb, and I think anybody on the N&W knew the thumb would be exercised if we did anything they really didn't want us to. . . . In a great many areas, the N&W ran itself, but there was always—to use Justice Holmes's phrase—the brooding omnipresence in the sky."[12] He doubted seriously if the Pennsylvania ever really thought it could have the New York Central and the N&W too. "It was a risk they knew they were taking." But, he said, "I think they were playing for high stakes—domination of the East."[13] The Pennsylvania had ninety days to make up its mind about the N&W. The first of October came and went, and no word had come, so an N&W delegation paid them a visit. "We wanted them to divest," said Fishwick, "but there is no question it was their business judgment." We tried to tell them that "giving you half the East is alright, but at least give the rest of us the other half."[14]

At that same moment, the Western Maryland business was coming to a head. The C&O wanted to know what position the N&W was going to take, and that led to several meetings between the two roads. It was after one of those meetings, and just after the Pennsylvania decided to divest, that John Fishwick said:

This was going through my mind, and I woke up in the middle of the night and I kept turning this thing over, and finally the idea of a merger of the N&W and the C&O seemed like a good one.

The next morning I went to see Mr. Pevler, and with some trepidation, because it seemed like quite an idea in view of all the propaganda that had been spread about the other alignments, and I told him that it just seemed to me we were focusing on the Western Maryland problem and this didn't really solve the situation, and we ought to start talking.

Mr. Pevler seemed quite surprised, but then we talked about it, and a couple of days later, when we were driving over to the Greenbrier about the Western Maryland situation, we talked about it some more and agreed we ought to throw this idea out, and we did. When we did, it seemed to generate a spark, and then they picked up, and it didn't seem like such a radical idea.[15]

The idea was breathtaking. Fishwick assumed that sooner or later somebody was going to be made responsible for the outcast roads, and the rich roads, the N&W and C&O, were the likely candidates. Luckily, as it turned out, each of them had its own crosses to bear. A merger of the coal giants would have so much financial power, it alone could privately shoulder the burden of $650 million indebtedness and not wind up in receivership. So N&W-C&O was to be the vehicle to bring the outcasts home.

Even a company as powerful as this would have to be insulated from a risk of this size, so a holding company dubbed "Dereco" was to be the device. R.W. Presspritch Company, whom N&W trusted to keep the plan secret, was given the task of working out details. It was complicated. Nowhere, either in the ICC report or in the proxy material that went out to stockholders, was there an explanation understandable to reasonably intelligent people. It went like this: the outcast roads were to be merged into new outcast roads (thus the Erie Lackawanna Rail*road* would become the Erie Lackawanna Rail*way*). All the stock of the new railroad would be owned by Dereco, a holding company controlled by the N&W-C&O. Dereco would issue its own stock to the stockholders of the old railroads and in five years that Dereco stock would be convertible into N&W stock. It would permit the parent company to take advantage of tax loss carry-forwards, but if one of the small roads defaulted, the immediate strain would be on Dereco, not N&W-C&O. "We had to have the N&W-C&O merger to meet the onslaught of Penn Central," said Fishwick, "and we had these losers. They were having speculators move into their stocks and we felt we could not deal directly with them."[16]

These plans were being made in secret through the spring and summer of 1965, just when Erie Lackawanna was flailing about for inclusion on its own. The first public announcement was on August 31, 1965. The next day, EL and N&W delegations met again for another in their continuing round of talks, but this time, Walter Tuohy and Gregory Devine of the C&O were there. The EL was presented with the idea and the terms. "We asked," said Robert Fuller, "if the terms were take-it-or-leave-it. Mr. Pevler said they were. We asked Mr. Fishwick if the N&W would continue to bargain in good faith as required by Appendix O. He said the proposal for the N&W-C&O plan constituted compliance with the obligation and there was nothing more to negotiate."[17]

Fishwick was disappointed—and perturbed—at their reaction. "We were looking at this thing as a large sort of jigsaw puzzle. If we looked at each of the items separately, it wouldn't have been a workable deal for us, but looking at these things as part of a whole . . . we saw a great risk, but a great opportunity to do something that was good for us, but would also be in the public interest. . . . It was a program for hope. We had no studies. All we were saying was 'Let's take a guess as to what's really in it for us and for the Dereco people.'" He expected, he said, "the boards of the Dereco roads would jump up and say 'Hurray, we've found a saviour.'"[18]

Over at the Pennsylvania, they were furious. Fishwick had been a protégé of Stuart Saunders at the N&W. Now things had gone sour. "You're going to regret your action," Saunders was said to have told Fishwick when they met one day by chance at the ICC.[19]

5

The following month, Erie Lackawanna gave up on the N&W's good faith and asked to have the N&W merger case reopened for the purpose of requiring its inclusion. It had been given five years to ask for this, and N&W had been expressly warned that consummation of its merger constituted irrevocable assent to whatever settlement might result. The N&W insisted its Dereco proposal was the only means for this and a merger of the N&W and the C&O would have to come first. But merger talk no longer had its old magic, and N&W surmised, probably correctly, that there was a general lack of patience for the plight of the rich. Delaware & Hudson and Boston & Maine joined EL for the showdown.

The D&H's position was almost tragic. It was still profitable, in good physical condition, and a thoroughly desirable merger partner. But it was the rich kid in a very poor neighborhood. Two hundred miles separated it from the N&W, bridged only by the Erie Lackawanna. Unless EL could make itself acceptable for inclusion, D&H was sunk.

Time was working against it. Since the decline of anthracite, it depended almost entirely on bridge traffic. One of its most important connections was the PRR at Wilkes-Barre, Pennsylvania. Henceforth, that traffic would move into New England via Selkirk, bypassing the D&H. Even in the midst of national prosperity, and before the Penn Central onslaught, D&H had shown no capacity to grow. It desperately wanted control of the PRR's Wilkes-Barre line because it feared PC would downgrade it or even abandon it. If it could get a route over Penn Central trackage rights to Hagerstown, Maryland, it would have direct connection to the N&W. The N&W doubted the route would be a success and it would be in Penn Central's interest to delay and harass trains until it was not a viable service route.[20] So the D&H's plan for inclusion got a lukewarm reception.

The Boston & Maine's reception was as frozen as a New England winter. It had lost money every year since 1957, in substantial amounts, only some of which could be traced to passenger deficits. Its freight revenues had declined 30 percent since 1957, which B&M countered with boosterish projections of growth in New England in the next five years. But B&M had made similar projections in other cases, and N&W looked up its record. The B&M's "experience in crystal ball gazing has been calamitous," it concluded. "B&M has barely been able to predict revenues for three months let alone for five years."[21] Then, there were the huge blocks of B&M securities reaching maturity in the immediate future—$46.5 million in 1967 and $19 million in 1970. Both issues were already selling at substantial discounts, so refunding was out of the question.

As if that were not enough, there had been a distressing amount of speculation in B&M stock shortly before it petitioned for inclusion, much of it by the company's own officers, at prices only a fraction of what B&M claimed it was worth to the N&W.[22] A grand jury had just handed down a thirty-count indictment against B&M's president, former president, and other officers. The charge, though technically not embezzlement, was "improper sale at known, unadvertised prices to fraudulent middlemen with the defendants intending acquisition and retention of the proceeds." The president was eventually convicted of selling B&M passenger cars in this way and got eighteen months and a $5,000 fine. His executive committee expressed its "deepest respect and confidence in his ability," but stockholders were complaining about his $75,000 a year salary, and initiated seven civil suits over the profiteering.[23] In short, the waters around the B&M were so murky, the N&W could hardly be blamed for not wanting to go in.

In March 1966, N&W sent a special train to inspect the three roads first hand. Clarence Jackman, vice president of engineering for the C&O, was in charge. It traveled the EL mainline, stopping overnight at Youngstown, Binghamton, and Hoboken. It returned to Scranton, entered the D&H at Wilkes-Barre, spent a night at Albany, then went on to Montreal. It traveled the B&M from White River Junction to Springfield, then went to Boston and Portland, and returned through Lawrenceville to Mechanicville. The D&H returned it to Binghamton and the EL to Buffalo. The D&H got relatively high marks, though it was noted that virtually no new material had been installed since 1960. The B&M was described as "rundown." It had placed only a veneer of ballast on the mainline, and mud was already pumping through. Speed was 45 mph. The EL's maintenance had deteriorated badly since 1960. Less than a mile of new rail a year had been installed; 30 percent of the ties were rotted and speed on the mainline was 50 mph. "In summary," Jackman wrote, "EL has been held together for the past several years by the installation of used material made available through the retirement of track since the merger." On the three roads, 43 percent of their locomotive fleet was overage. Freight car fleets had been reduced 27 percent since 1960.[24] The B&M denounced the tour as a "whirl-wind." No one from the ICC was invited to go along.

The next move was up to security holders. If the poor roads had no debt and no fixed charges, they could earn money. So the question was how much debt would carry over. Put another way, it was how much the old security holders were going to lose. Four of EL's principal creditors, John Hancock Life, Prudential, Woodmen of America Life Insurance, and Aid Association for Lutherans, were ready for a showdown in the courts to get every cent. Was it ruthless greed? Or would some of the same people who would be hurt if EL shut down, be hurt more if their life insurance company got in straits by a forced writedown of serious proportions?

6

Ever since John Fishwick confessed the idea for an N&W-C&O merger came to him in the middle of the night, there had been a goodly number of guffaws. "About this dream or this vision of yours . . . ?" he was asked. "This was not a vision, as I tried to tell you," he said. "I was awake. It hap-pened to be in the middle of the night when I was thinking about this. It was my best attempt to be honest . . . and I resent it being called a vision."[25]

Still, there was plenty of room to be cynical about a combination of the nation's two most profitable railroads, especially on the grounds that it was somehow necessary for their survival. They had each cried wolf once before, on their first round of mergers. Back then, it was going to be a three-system East. That was managements' plan for a balanced railroad system. Now it was asserted Penn Central was going to create imbalance. But month after month, all through the Penn Central hearings, these two railroads had never said a word. The N&W pleaded the Pennsylvania had forced them to remain silent because it controlled them,[26] an admission that some promi-nent railroad leaders had lied about on the public record. The C&O had no excuse at all. If it were true that Penn Central was going to unbalance the East, then it had conspired with other railroads to deceive the ICC. There never had been a three-system plan at all. Managements had simply played it by ear, making up convenient rationales as circumstances came along. Practically any two railroads could rattle off a list of savings and service improvements that might come from merger, especially when nobody was going to check up on them.

That wasn't quite fair, said John Fishwick. Pennsylvania and New York Central were staggering giants in the early 1960s, and talk about a Penn Central merger wasn't really frightening back then. Now, they had "shifted from two sick railroads to two that were growing stronger, and this growth had been slow, but it was accelerating." Unlike N&W-C&O, Penn Central had the advantage of a balanced freight traffic, not dependent on coal. It would have better coverage of the region with greater ability to make through rates, extend transit privileges, and attract new industry. It alone had sufficient concentrations of traffic to justify large capital investment in railroad facilities.[27]

Take any of the indices that really count, said Robert Minor of the New York Central—net income, operating ratio, transportation ratio, carload traffic, fixed charges, passenger deficit—and Penn Central was going to be way behind the other two. Even though it was going to have routes across the industrial heartland superior to N&W-C&O, those roads were going to get more and more traffic because they alone could afford the specialized freight equipment. As to the super Penn Central service that was going to crush everyone else, train AJ-1, the Reading-Alphabet Route manifest out of Philadelphia every day at 7:35 P.M. already beat the Pennsylvania Railroad's best schedule to St. Louis by more than two hours. The whole purpose of the Penn Central merger was to balance the financial strength of the coal roads. Would PRR have divested the N&W if it thought N&W would seek to merge with the C&O? "I don't know," said John Fishwick, "I can't read their minds." But he didn't think they did it for any altruistic feelings toward the N&W. It was a business judgment, what they believed was best for them and their stockholders.[28]

Would not a merger of the N&W and C&O deliver dictatorial control over the transportation of coal into the hands of a single corporation? All private parties—shippers, receivers, and transporters—said no. The N&W and the C&O originated most of the coal, but they terminated only a portion of it, so Penn Central would remain very much in the coal business. Furthermore, N&W already dominated the low-volatile coal fields while C&O dominated the high-volatile ones. There was really no competition to begin with, so nothing could be lost. (The same argument had been used to justify C&O-B&O.) A number of the big producers, among them Island Creek Coal, Valley Camp Coal, and Southern Pocahontas, all said a merger would improve service. But every single state whose industry depended on the uninterrupted flow of coal from the Pocahontas fields felt a deep concern. Coal was more solidly bound to rail transportation than any other commodity, save perhaps iron ore. Once this near monopoly was created, there was no going back. Every public body thought it was unnecessary to play with dynamite like this.

The one great positive benefit the merger had to offer was a home for the Dereco Roads. Sometimes, the sincerity seemed doubtful:

Q: Would approval of these terms fulfill your obligation under Appendix 0?

A: Yes. If the Commission approved everything as we say, then we could merge and make an offer to the five, and if they didn't take it, we would have fulfilled our obligation. After all, nobody can make these railroads merge with us.[29]

But then, speculators were playing with the Dereco stocks and Penn Central would soon be breathing down all of their necks. The hearing examiner recommended approval of the N&W-C&O merger (on March 29, 1969). It was a long, straightforward report that laid out the case in detail for the commissioners. The ramifications were too deep to be prejudiced at a lower level.

7

Though they had insisted all along that they alone could plan the mergers, railroads were winding up the merger movement more divided, more mutually distrustful—even hateful—than before. They had failed to come up with a plan that met even their own needs, let alone their customers' or the public's. They had swept the ICC along with arguments of savings and service improvements that were significant only when taken in isolation. That led directly to the inclusion crisis. Even within its limited powers, the commission had failed to knock heads together and make the industry come up with a satisfactory solution. Congress sat on its thumbs, and now it was up to the courts.

In broad outline, there were three sets of cases—one to halt the Penn Central merger, one to force the N&W to take the Dereco roads, and one to force the Penn Central to take the New Haven—passengers, commuters, and all—going under the generic title "The Inclusion Cases." The first set began over Appendix G, the protective conditions imposed in the Penn Central merger for the benefit of the outcast roads, including the controversial indemnity payments. The protests came in such a chorus from everyone on all sides that the commission surmised it was the novelty of the conditions that had everyone spooked, rather than any demonstrable grievance. But it reopened the hearings anyway, noting that it believed the conditions were self-enforcing. Any attempt by Penn Central to frustrate the purposes of protection automatically invited terrible retribution by the ICC, to which consummation of the merger constituted irrevocable assent. So, it said, while the hearings went on, Penn Central could go ahead and merge, and everyone ought to be happy. But Erie Lackawanna's nerves were at hair-trigger edge. With N&W giving it the cold shoulder in the summer of 1966, with the brooding anticipation of a Penn Central about to blast it to oblivion, it led the pack to court.

The outcasts lost the first round in district court.

THE EASTERN INCLUSION CRISIS   259

We do not suggest that the country will perish if [PRR and NYC], which have lived apart for more than a century . . . must continue to do so pending reconsideration . . . . But what is in the public interest eventually is in the public interest now unless there are truly significant considerations on the other side. No suggestion has been made . . . by the plaintiffs of willingness to post a bond to indemnify PRR and NYC against loss from what may prove to be an unjustified postponement of the anticipated savings.[30]

That was October 4, 1966. On October 18, Supreme Court Justice Harlan granted a stay. Argument was held the following January and a decision handed down March 27. Harlan, Fortas, Stewart, and White upheld the lower court and the merger. But the majority found Appendix G neither self-enforcing nor adequate and ordered consummation delayed until it was reconsidered.

We do not believe this is too high a price to pay to make as certain as human ingenuity can devise, a just and reasonable disposition of this matter. After all, this is the largest railroad merger in our history and if not handled properly, could . . . irreparably injure the entire railroad system in the northeastern section of the country.[31]

Justice Douglas went much further than that. The decision in favor of a merger was irresponsible from the start, he said.

Now the "panic button" is being pushed and we, in turn, are being asked to act hurriedly and become the final instrument for foisting the new cartel upon the country.

What is the nature of this cartel? . . . Only one of the largest stockholders of the applicants is known. The remaining largest stockholders are brokerage houses and Swiss banks holding nominal title for their customers. The beneficial owners are unknown and apparently of no concern to the Commission.

. . . Nor did the Commission consider it relevant that, through interlocking directorates, the proposed directors of the merged company are the directors of . . . corporations which deal with the railroads, or that the control of the railroads is steadily being concentrated in the hands of banks, insurance companies and other large financial interests.

This merger, like the ones preceding it, apparently is a manipulation of financiers and not part of the regional planning which is the ultimate function of the Interstate Commerce Commission. Yet if the imprimateur of the Commission is to be put on the plans of the financiers, much more should be known about them.[32]

As for the problem at hand, he asked, if the Penn Central merger was justified on the grounds of saving the New Haven, why was it permissible to destroy the Erie Lackawanna and the rest of the outcasts?

Under court order for reconsideration, the commission decided it was time to bring the reopened N&W-Nickel Plate case to a conclusion. The N&W was ordered to take in EL, D&H, and B&M immediately, under the Dereco holding company plan, but without a prior merger with the C&O. Terms, including stock exchange ratios, were prescribed. The N&W went straight to District Court in Roanoke to have the order set aside, while Erie Lackawanna went to District Court in New York to have it enforced. In a combined decision, the commission was upheld.[33] The N&W was going to have a northeastern empire whether it wanted it or not.

On M-Day, the Penn Central had been required to take over the New Haven. Dickering over the terms had continued through the summer of 1966, during which time the New Haven was kept pasted together by various state subsidies, most of which were going to run out on January 1, 1967. After that date, cash began to hemorrhage at such a rate that by summer it would not even be possible to meet the payroll. But not all the bondholders were satisfied with the terms the trustees had made, and a pack of them, led by one Oscar Gruss, brought suit.[34] The haggling was bitter. Dissenters insisted a freight-only New Haven was capable of earning a return. On liquidation value of individual items of property, debate was contentious. Take the New Haven's forty parlor-bar cars, for example. The New Haven people said they were worth $23,000 apiece, based on recent auction prices for similar equipment. Ridiculous, said Penn Central. Those cars were at the end of their service life. There was no significant market for them anywhere in North America, and certainly not if all of them were dumped on the market at once. It offered $5,000 apiece, top.[35] While all this was going on, the hotboxes, the fires, the derailments, the power failures got worse on the New Haven. The ICC hurried its deliberations, winding them up in November 1967. But the derivative suits went on.

On January 15, 1968, the Supreme Court ended all debate on all issues. As for the dissenting New Haven bondholders:

While the rights of bondholders are entitled to respect they do not demand Procrustean measures. They certainly do not dictate that rail operations vital to the nation be jettisoned. . . . The public interest is not merely a pawn to be sacrificed for the protection of a class of security holders.[36]

Despite the ability of the privileged rich to keep these matters in almost endless litigation for their own benefit, capital was reminded that investment implied a risk and that those who put their money in the New Haven Railroad gambled and lost. Penn Central would acquire the assets of the New Haven for the $90 million package agreed upon (of which only $8 million was in cash, it should be remembered).

That was it. This final installment of the inclusion cases reaffirmed the N&W's obligation to pick up the three outcast roads, and the desirability of the Penn Central merger. Where railroads and commissions and congresses had failed to work a solution in eight years, the Supreme Court did it in one sweeping decision.

The N&W sent John Fishwick to head up the Erie Lackawanna. "Sending one of our top men to Cleveland to restore the Erie Lackawanna's earning power should be solid evidence we are dead serious about forming Dereco," said Herman Pevler, and noted that "I didn't tell Jack he had to go out there. I asked him if he wanted to go and he said he did." Fishwick knew that if he made a success of this booby prize, big things would open up for him in the N&W. It wasn't going to be easy. His family was less than eager to leave civilized Roanoke for the icy inconveniences of Cleveland, but he kept a stiff upper lip. "I'm selling my house in Roanoke. We're moving to Cleveland. . . . the job given me by the N&W is to look after the interests of the Erie, and it is my intention to make it the best competitor of the Penn Central and the N&W and the trucks and the waterways and do the best job I can for Erie Lackawanna and its security holders."[37]

As much as EL wanted into the N&W, there had been no love lost between the officers of the two companies. The N&W was sophisticated and computer-oriented; Erie was just plain old railroad. It was impossible to disguise the contempt of the N&W or the jealousy of the Erie. But the Dereco plan went ahead and the Erie Lackawanna Rail*road* reorganized as the Erie Lackawanna Rail*way* on April 1, 1968. The haggling over the Bison Yard at Buffalo finally ended. A Buffalo Terminal Division was established, including all the N&W and EL lines in the district. Not long afterward, arrangements were made for the C&O to use the yard as well, making it the focus of nearly all non-Penn Central activity in the city.[38] Delaware & Hudson joined Dereco the following June but the Boston & Maine held out for more money (which the Supreme Court made clear it was not going to get).

Penn Central was born at one minute past midnight, February 1, 1968. After daylight, the new board of directors gathered in Philadelphia for its first meeting and official photographs, everyone smiling as big and warm a smile as he could muster. There were press conferences later, with Penn Central flags flying high. Stuart Saunders and Alfred Perlman posed, smiling, in front of a Lionel boxcar all freshly painted with the new PC emblem. (The little toy car was green, but it was made expressly clear it was *not* the New York Central's old jade green.) "Long courtship makes for eternal bliss," said Stuart Saunders, noting the companies had taken advantage of the long delay in consummating merger to work out new studies so the merger would go more smoothly. There were going to be lots of new super unit-trains, and the Metroliners were going to be a great success.[39] Everything was going to be wonderful.

Stuart Saunders was on the cover of *Time* and was being named the *Saturday Review's* businessman of the year. David Bevan, the railroad's chief financial officer, whose job it was to get the credit from the banks to keep the merger afloat, was not on the new board, though he was on the Pennsylvania's old one. He was not asked to join in the happy photographs in front of the toy boxcar. He was mad. Perlman didn't stick around for the champagne toasts. He got on his railroad car and went back to New York. That was how the greatest adventure in modern railroad history began.

CHAPTER 13

The Fall of the Penn Central; 1968-1970

If there were ever to be a test of the validity of merger, Penn Central was going to be it. There might have been better ways for Penn and Central to solve their problems, but they had cast their lot with merger. Now, unlike the Northerns or Seaboard Coast Line, those savings had to be real, because the situation, especially on the Pennsylvania Railroad, was more desperate than anyone imagined.

The Pennsylvania Railroad, wrote David Bevan, its vice president for finance, in November 1967, requires average cash balances of $45-$50 million to cover normal activities. "We have not had balances in this area at any time this year, and at the end of October, our cash balance amounted to roughly $8,500,000." He pointed out that money had been borrowed just to maintain balances, that in spite of this, at the rate accounts were being drawn down, they would reach zero by the end of the year and be $22 million in the hole by February—which was the month that the merger was consummated.[1]

This growing financial paralysis seems to have been the reason it was decided to merge all the railroads' operations at once, without any further preparations, the moment permission was received. It was essential—at least for accounting purposes—to bring as much of the merger savings down to net as quickly as possible.

It should have been known from experience in previous mergers that other railroads would deliver cars to whichever yard, former PRR or former NYC, that pleased them. Waybills for those cars could wind up at the opposite yard, rendering cars effectively lost—"no bills" in railroad vernacular. No effort was made to train routing clerks in how to cope with this, nor to instruct them in the myriad of new routes and stations they were responsible for all over the Penn Central system. No time was taken to complete track connections or yard alterations before rerouting began.

Here, then, are some of the things that happened after a "soundly conceived" merger.

1

Construction of Selkirk Yard near Albany was begun before the merger. It was to be the focal point of the new railroad, where all traffic rerouted over the Water Level Route would funnel to New York City and New England. Twenty million dollars was budgeted for the project, but cost overruns exceeded 100 percent. By July of 1968, although only seventy of the ninety classification tracks were in place, the yard was ordered opened. No one dared tell management things weren't ready. Traffic poured in on clerks and crews that were unrehearsed, to a yard that was half complete. Lost, loaded cars wallowed at Selkirk sometimes up to twenty-seven days. Routing instructions changed almost weekly. As one set proved unworkable, new ones were issued. When one of the ICC's inspectors asked an employee what his instructions were, the reply was "yesterday's, today's, or tomorrow's? They're all different."[2] Meanwhile, fully staffed work trains were waiting to complete construction, but they couldn't get into the yard because the entrances were blocked in the crush of traffic. Hours were lost, sometimes entire days, and the very construction that would relieve congestion could not be finished.

All traffic delivered by the PRR on car floats to the New Haven's Bay Ridge Yard on Long Island was ordered rerouted through Selkirk. Lighterage operations in New York Harbor were expensive, so it was important in terms of "savings" to get Bay Ridge closed. That meant cars bound for destinations even in Brooklyn or Queens were sent all the way up to Albany and all the way back down the east bank of the Hudson for delays up to six days, thus aggravating the situation at Selkirk.

Nor was the River Division, the old West Shore Railroad up the Hudson, prepared for this new traffic. In the heyday of West Shore passenger traffic, it was double tracked, but in the 1950s, when traffic dwindled to three freights a day, it was reduced to single track without many passing sidings. No sidings were added after the merger, though the number of trains tripled and some of them were too long for the sidings anyway. Trains often had to wait "in the hole" more than six hours for trains in the opposite direction. Average over-the-road time, as calculated from the dispatcher's log, was six hours, eleven minutes for the 128 miles, but 13 percent of the trains took more than eleven hours and some as long as eighteen hours. Since crews were forbidden by law to work more than sixteen continuous hours, they sometimes had to "book-off" while en route, blocking the mainline while they rested. Police at Bogota, New Jersey, for example, had repeated complaints about diesel engines idling noisily all night in residential neighborhoods.

South of Alsen, New York, nine racks of new Cadillacs had flipped over on a broken rail; they lay beside the track in a mangled heap for eighteen months. Wrecked boxcars lay alongside the track at Lake Katrine, and at Esopus, and at Cornwall, and at West Point. Speed was 10 mph on the temporary track installed after each of these wrecks, but since the line was so congested, there was no "down time" for the work crews to get in to clean up the mess.[3]

At the time Bay Ridge was shut down, proper track connections between the River Division and the PRR's Waverly Yard in Newark had not been completed. In fact, they had not been started. Trains had to make a tortuous backup around Newark using a portion of Lehigh Valley trackage and crossing the main line of the Jersey Central at grade. Together with delays on the West Shore and at Selkirk, transit time to New England was increased by five to six days. Shippers were not pleased.

On the drawing boards in Philadelphia, Buffalo's Frontier Yard was supposed to have a capacity of 2,026 cars a day. But those familiar with it knew it began to get congested at 1,100 cars and could reasonably be expected to dispatch no more than 900 cars a day. A strong wind from the west could slow cars rolling over the hump and make even 900 a wishful figure. Frontier was never intended to handle industrial traffic, particularly for the Lackawanna steel district. Seneca Yard was to do that, but Seneca wasn't finished when former PRR yards were ordered closed and everything was dumped on Frontier. So Frontier broke down. Overflows were sent to other yards that were having their own problems.

At Toledo, the PRR's Outer Yard was closed in favor of the NYC's Stanley Yard. Before merger, Stanley was used for coal shipments; it was so deteriorated from this track-busting tonnage that Central had thought of closing it, especially when derailments began to average fifty a month. But in spite of that, Outer Yard was less efficient, switching an average of seventy-two cars per locomotive shift against eighty-three at Stanley. When Outer was closed and its crews moved to Stanley, efficiency there fell to forty-two cars per shift. A year later, in 1970, it was back up to fifty-seven cars, but that was because sales in the Toledo region had fallen by 30 percent, shippers having taken their business elsewhere. At Stanley, the weight scale broke and no one seemed able to find the funds to repair it. Cars that needed to be weighed had to be classified separately, taking up a whole track in the yard, then sent out to the half-abandoned Airline Yard nearby, weighed, and sent back and reclassified for a delay of three to four days.

The same thing happened at St. Louis. The PRR's Rose Lake Yard couldn't handle the combined load of two railroads, so some of the cars had to be taken back to the Central's old yard. That was the worst of both worlds, the expense of operating two yards, especially with one of them hopelessly congested. Cars for local points on the former NYC line between

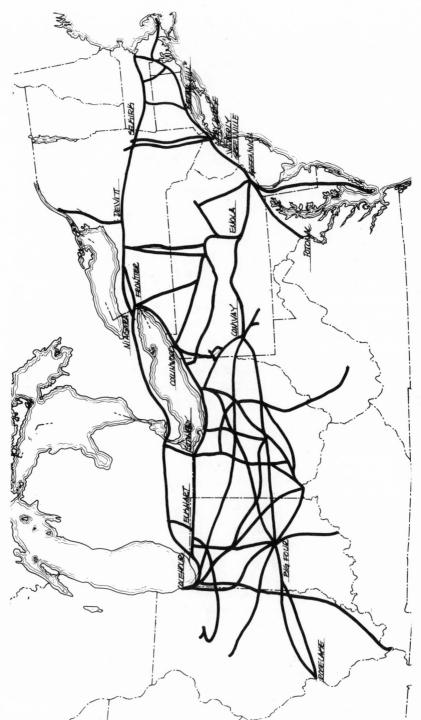

MAP 29: *The Penn Central Bottlenecks*

St. Louis and Indianapolis, which was to be downgraded in merger, were sent all the way to Indianapolis over the PRR line and then forwarded back in local trains, almost to St. Louis itself.

Before merger, NYC averaged one derailment a week in its St. Louis yard (average delay, three to four hours; average cost, $100). The PRR averaged two derailments a week (average delay, four hours; average cost, $470). Now, thanks to the magic of merger, there were four derailments a week with an average delay of seven hours at an average cost of $500.

The NYC's Big Four Yard at Indianapolis was to be the Selkirk of the West. Cars from all over the Midwest were to be gathered there, grouped into solid blocks for common destinations and dispatched often all the way to Selkirk. Premerger planning called for the installation of extra tracks when the PRR's Hawthorne Yard was closed, but a second study purported to show the extra tracks weren't necessary. "I was told by a Penn Central employee," said an ICC inspector, "that management didn't want to incur the extra expense, and the second study was tailored to fit that decision." The yard was so jammed with lost and misclassified cars that trains were backed up down the mainline waiting to get in. Sometimes, just to clear space, batches of cars were sent out to be classified somewhere else, and many had to be returned to Big Four to be handled again. It was a classic case of trying to force merger savings before it was practically possible to do so.

One story was typical of the lack of planning. The labor contract between the NYC and the Brotherhood of Locomotive Engineers required that seats in the locomotive cab be equipped with armrests. The PRR's agreement had no such requirement and its locomotives had no armrests. It was not long before NYC and PRR units funneled into Big Four and became mixed. Normally, they would be dispatched in rotation, so PRR engines were set out for NYC crews, and vice versa. But NYC crews stood on their rights and refused to operate units not properly equipped. That meant endless switching and turning, which added to the overall chaos. On one ICC inspection visit to the ready track (where locomotives waited for their next assignment) there were only PRR units and NYC crews available for service, so everything was at a standstill. These contract differences were common knowledge beforehand, said the inspector, and required only minor modifications, which were never performed. Add to that the shabby maintenance of the locomotive fleet, which put a lot of units out of service altogether, and the problem of power shortages became critical. In the third quarter of 1969, 624 trains were delayed for lack of power; in the fourth quarter, 1,817 trains; and in the first quarter of 1970, 2,993 trains.

The ICC inspectors watched the chaos at Big Four and surrounding territory, and thought these stories were typical:

1. One day at Terre Haute, there was a burst of activity to call a crew and locomotive to send out some badly delayed cars. When the crew reported for duty and the locomotive was attached, it was discovered no caboose would be available for several hours, until incoming trains arrived.

2. At Big Four, seventy-nine cars of coal for local delivery to the Indianapolis Union Railroad were reported arriving on the next train, and a local transfer crew and appropriate switching locomotive were called up. When the train arrived, it was not seventy-nine cars for local delivery, but 129 cars for Chicago. So the local crew was paid its day's wages and dismissed, and a road crew was called. Two hours later, the seventy-nine local cars showed up, and the same crew had to be recalled and paid a second day's wages.

3. One day at Big Four, there were 300 empty hopper cars clogging things up, waiting for dispatch over a single-track line to Ashby in southern Indiana. Two trains were ordered to forward them immediately, without taking into account the fact that three trains were already on their way up the single-track line that had only two passing sidings. The line was instantly jammed. Three of the trains suffered delays of more than six hours.

4. One day at Anderson, Indiana, nearly seventy loaded and badly delayed cars were waiting to be picked up by a passing train. Despite telephone calls, Big Four Yard had no idea when a train could be expected. Local people were frantically discussing what to do, when four locomotives and a caboose came rolling down the track. They tried to wave it down. The crew waved back, and rumbled on into the afternoon sun. The dispatcher at Big Four said another train might be along in four hours, but it would have room for only twenty cars.[4]

2

"Shippers are dissatisfied with our service," said a perceptive memo of November 1968. There followed a list of some of the railroad's most prestigious customers—Allied Chemical, International Paper, Uniroyal, Shell Oil, National Distillers, National Starch, Stauffer Chemical, Hooker Chemical, and the New York Perishable Dealers' Association. Complaints from each were attached. A year later, nothing had changed—a similar memo with similar attachments, only the list was longer. Kodak piggyback vans, for example, were missing connections at St. Louis 75 percent of the time on their way from Rochester to Dallas. More than 40 percent of St. Louis-New England traffic suffered delays of more than three days. "We have lost a sizeable amount of fresh meat traffic to Erie Lackawanna. Shippers have said it was the far greater reliability of their service."[5]

I keep getting reports of the success of our sales people, only to have the business taken away due to our poor service. Attached are two sheets of specific instances. It is by no means complete, as we don't always learn of lost traffic until long after the fact. This business listed represents $800,000 in revenue. Attachment showing Truc-

Train performance. Only two operated on an acceptable basis. Maximum weekly performance was 35 percent on time. Many cars of western perishables are being misclassified. During April, 200 cars were improperly blocked.[6]

In Cincinnati, Chevrolet was complaining, Delco was complaining, March Foods was complaining. Anchor-Hocking Glass reported 110 cars due but not delivered, thus disrupting their production. Thatcher Glass supplied empty bottles to Seagram, who then reloaded the cars with filled bottles. They required clean cars, and since the cleaning track was discontinued in a cost-cutting move, they couldn't get them. The business was diverted to trucks. Armco Steel reported no deliveries for five days in April 1968, causing a backup of 209 cars. Supervisors excused every charge as a special circumstance. Special circumstances were epidemic.

We always have published second morning delivery schedules to the East. It was always sent in two trains from Rose Lake to Enola and arrived in time for evening market trains.

It is now taking five days to move over the line. DuPont is complaining. Publicker is complaining. Rohm & Haas is complaining. Tenneco is complaining. The auto industry is complaining. These are just a few of the patrons who were promised good service when we merged, but instead, the service has deteriorated.[7]

Other railroads were getting annoyed. On run-through service with the Cotton Belt Railroad, cars were taking six to eleven days just to reach St. Louis. "We have lost a major amount of business between New Jersey and the West Coast," said the Cotton Belt. "Can you get it back?"

"Responsibility for this rests in your region," said headquarters to the local supervisors. "Our reputation with connections has suffered."

"My first reaction is that it's not that simple," came the reply. "On later reflection, I still think it's the same. . . . Let's wait and see what happens."[8]

Reluctantly, Cotton Belt and Missouri Pacific agreed to do some of Penn Central's blocking (grouping cars for common destinations), but PC still missed its principal MoPac connection three out of four days. "This is the record of BF-3," said headquarters to the officials at Rose Lake. "Needless to say, it isn't very good. Would you review your entire operation and hopefully show a marked improvement in the performance."[9]

Things were no better at Chicago. Following former NYC practice, trains from all over the East converged on Elkhart, Indiana, where they were broken down and regrouped. Shorter trains were dispatched directly to the yards of connecting roads in Chicago. But they were arriving late at Elkhart, frequently bunched up, clogging the yard. They were constantly missing the connecting trains of western roads, clogging their yards, and those roads began to get short-tempered in turn. "Eastbound deliveries are not being made properly to our yards," said a beleaguered local official. "Chicago & North Western is the worst offender. Illinois Central is also bad." A delegation from headquarters was dispatched to smooth things over with those roads. But a year later, Jervis Langdon of the Rock Island wrote Perlman:

Our Rock Island run-through must make Union Pacific connections. You are so late, we run a special make-up if there is any possibility we can overtake at North Platte [Nebraska]. If not, we add your cars to mail-express train 1, but even so, connections are terrible.[10]

By that time, Santa Fe and Milwaukee Road were also complaining.

Of seventy-one shippers contacted in Baltimore by ICC inspectors, five detected some improvement in service since merger, forty-three said it was worse, and twenty-two thought it was about the same, usually noting it was bad before. Chrysler and General Motors said they would divert if they could, but were stuck with sidings on the PC. Scott Paper, Philco, and Crown Cork had switched to motor transport. Downingtown Paper said that erratic deliveries of coal prompted it to convert to fuel oil. Lukens Steel switched to the Reading. Hotpoint switched to the Central States Dispatch (B&O) route. The Indiana Grain Cooperative switched 75 percent of their business to the N&W. Its new unit train to Baltimore would go B&O. Stokely-Van Camp had planned a new warehouse-distribution center on the PC but was going to build it on the N&W instead. "It took ten days for them to get one of our cars out of town," said Central Soya in Indianapolis, "then another 17 to get to Louisville. Then it was misplaced and returned to us, still full of feed. After that, we divert all we can. Even if service improves, we're not returning to Penn Central. Eighty-five percent of inbound traffic is now diverted and 100 percent of outbound."

1. At Indianapolis, Kroger Supermarkets advertised a special on fresh cantaloupes. The cars went to Pittsburgh instead, and by the time they got back, the fruit was rotten, a total loss of $9,000. Kroger thought the damage to its customer relations was "severe."
2. At Syracuse, a carload of live hogs was left in the yards over a hot summer week end with no provision to water them. On arrival, fifty-four of the animals were dead, the others unusable. "The carrier," said the shipper, "says the number of damage claims causes this kind of traffic to be a loser, but it seems to be the carrier's fault."
3. At Indianapolis, Stokely-Van Camp noted that a batch of cars of fresh fruit from California was misclassified as empties and sent back to California. Contents were a total loss and cannery production was disrupted.
4. Eli Lilly, the pharmaceutical manufacturer, noted that a carload of frozen animal glands from Davenport, Iowa, to Indianapolis, arrived twenty-seven days late and

thawed. Contents were described as an "unholy mess," and a total loss—
$15,000.[11]

At about this juncture, the advertising department wanted to kick off a new
campaign with a theme running: "Have you tried Penn Central service
lately?" The idea was not approved.

3

If you were a shipper and wanted information about your delayed
shipment, it was best to be patient. The railroad didn't answer its telephones. Kroger Supermarkets in Indianapolis said it took an average of
seven man-hours a day by its own staff to trace lost cars on the PC
Railroad. Allied Chemical thought it was no wonder: the Baltimore switch-
board had been taken out in a cost-cutting move. Customers were directed
to route calls through Philadelphia, but the railroad's operators up there
didn't know the Baltimore people or their numbers. Armstrong Cork said it
didn't care; when it wanted information, it called collect, person-to-person,
to either Bossler or Flannery at system headquarters. A New York shipper
noted that it took several days and many attempts to reach the New York
tariff office, which turned out not to have the information needed and suggested Erie Lackawanna might have it. Said an ICC inspector:

Nearly all shippers contacted said the attitude of station employees, which was none
too good prior to merger, became almost intolerable within a few months after the
merger. It was my experience when making agency checks, that these employees were
flooded with requests to trace delayed traffic. When this became almost impossible,
they had to face, day after day, irate shippers and receivers, and suffer the caustic
comments made toward them and their company. This, plus the failure of their
railroad to provide any semblance of the service they had known on their separate
lines prior to merger, dropped their morale to near zero. It was not confined to station employees, but happened to sales people, yard police, and any other department
that had contact with the general public.[12]

Even shippers were probably unaware of how totally management had lost
control of car-tracing. In one test, the computers were asked, on the basis of
existing data, to locate twenty cars known to be on the system. They couldn't
find any of them.

One of the first revelations after the debacle was that the two railroads
had incompatible computer systems. Both used IBM 360s, but NYC fed
information with punch cards while PRR used punched tapes. So the systems could not exchange information, talk to each other, as it were. It
looked all the worse because this hardware had been purchased after the de-

cision to merge. Two railroads could not agree even in a sensitive area that provided car-tracing, billing, and statistical data for management. Some suggested this was a cause of bankruptcy. As the railroad strangled with lost cars, with customers deserting in droves, it was a matter that demanded investigation.

Both railroads used essentially the same method of car-tracing. A complete report showing every car on the system was prepared by computer between 3 and 5 A.M. and delivered to management at 5:30 A.M. It was possible to get selective updates every two hours. It had been fairly sophisticated computer technology when it was developed in 1959, and had been improved since then, especially with the installation of the 360s. But unlike newer systems being used on other railroads, it had a fundamental fault in that it could not detect errors that might be fed into it, even to the basic logic of car movements. If erroneous data was entered into the system, it stayed there. Data could be checked to see if it was consistent within itself, but not to see if it was consistent with previously reported data.

Before the merger, both PRR and NYC computer people were aware of these shortcomings and agreed new systems were in order. But they couldn't agree on which one, so decisions were postponed. While Southern Railway and Southern Pacific, for example, went ahead with new sophisticated systems, NYC and PRR stagnated, and on merger day had to struggle to make the old systems function at all.

The breakdown of the computer billing system not only irritated customers, who didn't need further irritation, but it meant the railroad was not getting timely payment of accounts receivable. The NYC's old TAC (Treasury Accounting Control) system was abandoned in favor of the PRR's SRA (Station Revenue Accounting) system, which was too bad, for while TAC gave weekly reports and showed every account unpaid over eight working days as delinquent, SRA gave only monthly reports. It required a large amount of manual preparation and contained only minimal controls on accuracy and adequacy of information fed into it. There was no way to insure that all movements got into the billing system. It could not provide information to sales people so they could resolve customer problems.

At the start of an audit in March 1968, there were at Detroit, for example, 140 unidentified checks on hand, amounting to $306,768 in revenue. By May, only eighty-three had been identified, and the remainder, some of them up to five months old, included one check for $32,158. Machine errors were found in 104 items, totaling $45,875 in collectible revenue. Twenty-three more bills, totaling $97,938 in collectible revenue, had incorrect due dates. Collection would be delayed at least a day. On hand in excess of forty-eight hours were 1,490 statements with unbilled revenue of $372,000.

In Chicago, an auditor found a file cabinet of shipping orders for which switching bills had not been prepared. These were a month old and totaled $10,000 in revenue. After preparing the remittance of January 13, 1969, said the auditors, there were still on hand twenty-three checks totaling $7,125. Auditors found serious arrears of unanswered correspondence on the coal desk, the rate desk, and the cashier's desk. Across the system, unsettled accounts went from $57 million shortly after the merger to $87 million in January of 1970, to $101 million in March 1970.

"In freight billing," concluded the ICC inspectors, "delay in forwarding the data to the billing centers and inexperienced personnel at the billing centers were the primary cause of the problem." At Indianapolis, which had not been a billing center before merger, it was necessary to bring in billing clerks from other parts of the system. Eighty jobs were authorized, but only twenty people actually transferred, the rest preferring a lump-sum severance. About 60 percent of the people working in that office were hired off the street. So there were only twenty experienced people to handle accounts that amounted to $100,000 a day, and functions such as corrections, revisions, and overdue notices were dispensed with.

Errors were common. "Patrons get no bills, or wrong bills, or pay their bills and get threatened with legal action for non-payment because it was entered in the wrong account. Agents are continually trying to assist patrons in obtaining correction and relief from these errors, and it is frustrating when they can't get it." Auditors noted that examples of triplicate billing resulted in "stronger than normal commentary from the most reputable of patrons." The ICC concluded: "The present system is totally dependent on the quality performance of agreement personnel. Management control over the quality and promptness of rendering bills to patrons is too late in the system and otherwise inadequate."

Agreement employees can be no better than the management that directs them. Firm lines of authority were never laid down at the bottom levels. Hence, auditors noted, station agents in charge of accounts reported to trainmasters, who were operating men responsible for moving trains. Trainmasters frequently neither understood nor appreciated the importance of paperwork. At Niagara Falls, New York, the agent was made to do the trainmaster's operating reports, to the neglect of agency work. At Watertown, New York, he was being used as an extra brakeman, found by auditors riding atop boxcars. "We found poor morale existing throughout most of the agencies. It was primarily the result of recent budget cuts being applied to personnel performing functions related to revenue processing or revenue control at the agency level."

Even the computer reports that management needed for effective control and budgeting failed because they were studded with errors, which led either to wrong decisions or false hopes. Inspectors again cited the lack of training at the bottom. One inspector visited the office of Jonathan O'Herron, for example, an executive vice president. On his desk, he found confidential memos describing the programmed reduction of forces from 95,000 to 91,000 in the next year (1970), yet employment charts also on his desk showed employment rising from 94,000 in mid-February 1969 to 95,772 in mid-June. "The confidential memo painted a rosy picture while the house was burning down."

"If you looked at the 'T' report this morning [a major report on train movements]," said Vice President David Smucker, "you would wonder what happened to the Pennsylvania Railroad." Information was missing, sometimes from whole regions in the old PRR areas. The information that was there was unreliable. An ICC inspector at Chicago explained that for years, "the FT-3 Report on the PRR was known to be less than factual, since it was believed by personnel to be the basis for the elimination of yard crews. Yardmasters would add a few hundred cars, trainmasters some more, and so false figures were made up to compare with past false figures."

An example of how good ideas came to naught was the DICCS (demurrage inventory car control system). Cars delivered to a customer's siding had to be unloaded in a specified time or else the customer owed a fee (demurrage) for every day the car remained unavailable for reloading. Also, if switching movements were performed within a plant, the customer had to pay. Both were important sources of revenue. Previously, clerks had to check each individual siding, but DICCS provided a simple method for conductors on the switching runs to record the information and feed it into the teletype. However, the conductors were never taught how to do it, or what, precisely, constituted a demurrage day, or what constituted a chargeable switching move; so the record was incomplete, with many cars omitted. At Toledo, for example, $3,812 was collected in June 1967 for demurrage, while in June 1970, for approximately the same work, only $1,601 was collected. Many of the clerks, rather than checking for errors themselves, let the customers find them, which they did. Forty percent of demurrage bills were being returned for correction.

The mere fact that computers couldn't talk to each other was not that serious. At worst [said inspectors] it should have meant that two telephone calls might be necessary to get any given information. Long delays in transit, mis-delivery of cars, improper blocking of trains, mis-routing and congested yards, were not the computers' fault. It was only the recorder of information. Problems of computer incompatibility, when examined, usually revealed it was other problems underneath. Such fault as there was seems to have been the inability of field personnel to report information, due to their inexperience, or the fact that their attentions were constantly being diverted elsewhere. The system depended absolutely on operational personnel giving it the right unput. They were so harassed, or so inexperienced, the information didn't get in, or it was the wrong information.[13]

4

The Luna-Saunders Agreement of 1964 required the railroad to provide a job for everyone who worked for it from the day the agreement was signed until the merger. No one dreamed it was going to take four years to consummate. Many people were hired during that time, and many were laid off, but on merger day, jobs had to be offered to all of them; 2,967 accepted, and the railroad was saddled with what appeared to be an impossible burden. Some observers thought labor had outsmarted itself, for assuming it really wanted long-run job security, sticking a troubled railroad with this was foolish. E. Clayton Gengras, an insurance executive and PC director, said the Luna-Saunders Agreement was the merger's "death warrant." However, total employment fell in the year of merger (from 106,000 to 102,000) despite the people taken back.

The railroad, while pleading poverty, never missed a dividend. Its officers were receiving fat salaries ($279,000 for Saunders in 1970, for example, including benefits). There were all the little things that stuck in peoples' craws, like Saunders's chauffeured limousine and his memberships in Philadelphia's fancy clubs. Anyone who did not see the Luna-Saunders Agreement as part of a broad class confrontation, American-style, was missing the point. Furthermore, management had caved in on this agreement, or at least Saunders had. It was unlikely the ICC would ever have imposed labor conditions that severe. It never had before.

To the end, Saunders insisted it was a good agreement. The big thing the railroad got out of it was the right to transfer employees wherever they were needed. As in previous mergers, however, many refused to transfer, their loyalty being to their profession or their locality, not necessarily the company. Then the railroad had to pay them lump-sum separation allowances. In 1969, 61 percent of all trainmasters, 81 percent of all transportation superintendents, and 44 percent of all division superintendents had been at their jobs less than one year. It was a Herculean task to work out implementing agreements in dozens of overlapping seniority districts, where tiny differences in work rules made for endless confusion. In 1964, the railroads estimated the cost of their labor agreement at $78 million over eight years, based on wage scales of the early 1960s which were never updated. By the end of only 18 months after merger, $64.7 million had already been spent, not the only merger estimate to turn out very wrong.

Regardless, the extra employees taken back were a fact of life and might have been a valuable resource. There was plenty of work that needed doing.

But they were wasted, swamped in a sea of declining productivity. There were shortages of clerks and telephone operators, of freight-car repairmen and crews. Up to a quarter of the late trains in 1969 were delayed because of the unavailability of crews.

Knowing that x number of employees would have to be taken back on merger day, a special fund was established to which their pay would be charged. It would show as a nonrecurring expense of merger and not as an operating expense. Thus, it made the railroad's financial statement look better if as much were charged to that fund as possible. Actually, only a little over half the people expected to return came back. They were identified as recalled labor, used different-colored time cards and were ordered to be kept idle or assigned to make-work projects "such as cleaning up facilities that would not otherwise be cleaned, and so forth."

"Recalled employees do not, in fact, stand around idle," said field inspectors of company auditors Peat, Marwick & Mitchell. "All are given work and are integrated into regular work teams, especially at Altoona, which has the greatest number of recalled employees. . . . In our audit work thus far, we have made visits to the shops, and from visual observation, could not distinguish regular workers from recalled personnel. All seemed to be doing the same work." When the ICC's Bureau of Enforcement visited Altoona in January of 1971, it was told by the local supervisor that there were no nonproductive employees at Altoona and never had been. "Those called back were put to work. Wages of 767 men were charged against the special account. While the time-cards of these employees designated them as non-productive employees, they performed productive functions on car lines and in normal shop activities." When recalled men were transferred to the active labor pool, substitutes were added to the recalled status, so eager was the railroad to keep a full contingent in that category.[14]

By 1970, 59 percent of PC revenue was paid in wages (versus 44 percent for all class I railroads). Overtime was 12 percent of gross payroll, double what it had been for PRR and NYC in 1960. Productivity per employee was 87 percent of the class I railroad average.[15] An ICC inspector calculated that if it had remained close to the class I average, PC would have saved $377 million in wages, plus an additional 15 percent in fringe benefit costs.

This did not excuse labor for the excessive crews required in three important PC states (New York, Ohio, and Indiana) or the work rules (sometimes deservedly called the featherbed rules) that may also have forced unnecessary man-hours on the railroad. Every person of an anti-union persuasion will introduce these factors at this point in the debate. But all other railroads had to cope with them, and did so with varying degrees of success. They were not germane to the special problems of PC or of merger. Again, management had failed to manage, and merger had made the situation worse.

The problem of poor morale ran deep, and its origins antedated the merger. Again, the cause seemed to flow from management. One story illustrated the frustration of the men on the trains: a passenger conductor on a train that was late, without heat, with patrons standing in the aisles because seats and windows were broken, with the bathrooms leaking smelly fluids, with passengers venting their frustrations viciously on the conductor and his crew, broke down and wept at the end of the run. "They expect me to do a job, and send me out with tools like this."

Part of the problem could be seen in the horrifying gap of employees in the bracket of five to fifteen years' experience. Young men who hired out for the railroad, which had few rewards and no job security, were not prone to stick around. So the railroad was deprived of the service of many who struck that balance between adequate experience and youthful enthusiasm. Here is how the process took place.

A young man anxious to do a good job in his first real employment hired out for the New York Central at Niagara Falls in 1960. He was hired, not by management, but by senior agreement employees, who set his work assignments and schedules. So it was with them, and not management, that he had to curry favor. He was trained entirely by agreement personnel, whose morale, even at that time, was none too good. They taught him all the tricks of shortcutting work and expected him to shortcut just like they did. Though trained only to be a car-checker in the yards, he was put to work at preparing cars for clearance through customs at the Canadian border and at car-tracing, which meant direct contact with shippers and the public. Only once did anyone from "management" visit the yard office—a perspiring young business-school graduate visibly different from everyone else because he wore a necktie. He spent about a week going over papers. He spoke to no one. No one spoke to him. The brotherhoods had regular lodge meetings where deep loyalties quickly developed. Management's only contact with most employees was the innocuous house organ, *The Headlight*. The young man soon found there was no point in going out of his way to do a good job. There was no one from management to see or hear. Agreement employees didn't like it. Advancement for them came only with seniority, which rewarded those who kept their mouths and their minds shut. So he left the New York Central, like everyone else his age who had pride of workmanship and who demanded recognition for it. It was a sloppy operation, without leadership, where management had abdicated its authority to workers' soviets in a way that few leaders of American unionism had ever foreseen or wanted.

In 1970, in singling out Niagara Falls, along with Kalamazoo, Michigan, as the two most incompetently run stations on the system, ICC inspectors noted that even the most rudimentary custodial services would boost morale. They noted the hundreds of cars moving on illegal "memo" way-bills through these yards (which left no duplicate record in case car and waybill should become separated)—the result of lax discipline. They noted the extraordinary number of mistakes and omissions in yard records, made by incompetent or untrained personnel, and recommended complete audits of these stations.[16] For anyone who had worked there, the revelations were no surprise. The rot had been creeping in for a long time.

5

Also, at the time of the collapse, it was believed that antagonism between New York Central people (the Green Team, so named for the Central's jade-green boxcars) and the Pennsylvania people (the Red Team, after the Pennsy's Tuscan red passenger cars) was responsible for the debacle. In Pittsburgh, where the PRR was overwhelmingly dominant, or in Detroit, where NYC was dominant, ICC inspectors thought antagonism was minimal. Surprisingly, given the chaos at Rose Lake, rivalry seemed under control there. Even at York, Pennsylvania, deep in PRR country, agent Bill Athey reported that the only NYC man stationed around there was trainmaster Bill Armand, "a gentleman all the way around and very respected."

Elsewhere, a Green Team-Red Team antagonism was apparently real and may have wrecked the railroad. Rumors of similar divisions in other mergers smoldered—lots of smoke but never quite a fire. This time, the human side of merger could not be ignored.

At the employee level, it seemed to be petty but ran deep. Despite all the time prior to merger when labor agreements could have been worked out, few of them were. In Chicago, only yardmasters and company police had reached accord. Everyone else was still working under old agreements that preserved minor contractual differences. For example, explained a local supervisor, employee A is a former NYC clerk in an office with employee B of the PRR. Both held identical positions and are called up for jury duty. The railroad pays employee A full salary because of her previous agreement with the Central but pays B nothing. Imagine how they are polarized.

Former NYC and former PRR passenger train crews were laid over in Chicago. The NYC men were put up at the Fort Dearborn Hotel while the PRR crews went to the commissary in the 16th Street yards or were bunked in the basement of Union Station. Ironically, said ICC inspectors, "both crews claim it constituted favorable treatment of the other."

At lower and middle-management levels, the rivalry was poisonous. "It wasn't a merger," was a common remark, reported ICC inspectors. "The so-and-sos took us over, and the so-and-sos get all the choice assignments." Reported another inspector, "I found the relationship after the merger between employees of the former PRR and the former NYC to be strained and suspicious. You always heard derogatory remarks about the other group. I have been seriously questioned by the officers of both former Penn and former Central as to the competency of officers and employees of the opposite railroad. I was always told that bankruptcy was caused by the Penn or Central people, depending on who I was talking to."

"The policy of mixing officers," he continued, "however well-intentioned, meant that a Central man always reported to a Pennsylvania man who always reported to a Central man. They did not understand each other, or if they did, were at odds with the instructions or the procedures. The tendency of a supervisor was to bypass his superior to get the ear of a friend from his road. So countermanding orders were frequent, with ill feeling all around. Pennsylvania people ate lunch with other Pennsylvania people, and so forth. The feeling was that 'we were doing all right until the red side (or green side) took us over.'"

A shipper of fresh meat at Albany said he had been visited by three salesmen for the PC Trail-Van service. During the course of conversation, he said, each of them made it crystal clear that they were all New York Central men.

At Philadelphia, a former Central trainmaster was brought to the PRR's prestigious Greenwich Yard. Another Central man was made superintendent of the district. An ICC inspector noted that not one PRR trainmaster had a good word for the superintendent and that he was said to show extreme partiality to the NYC trainmaster. When that trainmaster needed extra cars, he got them on orders from the superintendent, even if the PRR trainmasters didn't have enough for regular evening placements. They believed the Green Team would bend over backward to keep each other from looking bad.

Every merger disturbed top-level management, for everyone wondered what it was going to do to his career. The longer merger was postponed, the more corrosive was the effect. Neither NYC nor PRR designated who would hold the top posts in each department until the merger actually took place. If the merger didn't come off, it could damage a man's authority with his subordinates if it were known he had been passed over. So, on merger day, the assignments fell across senior management with surprise and shock. Except in the financial area, which was all Red Team, it looked as if Red and Green had been spread fairly evenly through the top ranks. Regardless, the Green Team believed the Red Team held the real power, and much of the young and aggressive management that Perlman had assembled panicked and fled. Wayne Hoffman went to Flying Tiger. John Kennefick went to Union Pacific. Walter Grant went to Consolidated Edison. Nearly 100 of the Central's marketing staff were gone by 1970.

Rivalries that smoldered in other mergers apparently set off explosion after explosion at Penn Central that paralyzed decision-making. Some of the evidence is hearsay, and must be used with caution. It was collected by reporters, and some of it may be self-serving to the Green Team, which increasingly gave the impression the New York Central would have survived if it had not been swallowed up by the monumental incompetency of the Pennsylvania Railroad.

What was known was that Red and Green teams had found it almost impossible to reach any agreements of significance prior to merger. A key issue was the inability to reconcile the decentralized organization of the PRR with the top-down organization of NYC. Upon merger, said ICC inspectors, rather than adopt one system or the other, lines of authority just got muddled. On the PRR, for example, budgets were worked out at lower levels and passed upward for review. On the NYC, they were handed down from above. After merger, both systems were used, both ineffectively.

It showed up in two very different philosophies of railroading. The Red Team saw the railroad as a mover of volume. The entire rate structure of the PRR was designed to encourage movement—essentially low rates for minimal service. Marketing research existed only to justify prices, not determine them. It was an old-fashioned vision of railroading. Perlman and his Green Team, on the other hand, were business school graduates, steeped in new marketing techniques. Relatively high prices were charged for providing the shipper with precisely the service he wanted, which had been, after all, the key to motor-carrier success. They were interested only in traffic that made money for the railroad. They were prepared to work closely with the shipper and buy new equipment if necessary. The Red Team acted as if every shipment had jolly well better fit in a plain old boxcar.[17]

This was not a difference visible to the general public and, in fact, the new marketing philosophy was relatively new even to the Central, dating from the early post-Young years. Perlman's forces had to fight against older, entrenched forces, and were hostile to any attempt by the Red Team to undo their work. That led to one of the top-level confrontations that rocked the railroad, between Perlman and the Red Team's vice president for sales, Henry W. Large. At a sales staff meeting in Tarrytown, New York, early in 1969, for which Large had worked hard preparing sessions, Perlman delivered a blistering diatribe against the low-rate philosophy and against Large personally.[18] Daughen and Binzen in the *Wreck of the Penn Central* described it as a brass-knuckled attack which the Red Team received in stunned silence. Later, when Perlman was again urging Saunders to dump Large, Saunders (according to Rush Loving, Jr., in *Fortune*) said, "You just don't like Henry Large."

"I do like Henry Large," said Perlman. "He's a great big lovable Saint Bernard. No one can help but like him. But he's giving away the railroad."

"But shippers like him," countered Saunders.

"Well, who doesn't like Santa Claus?" Perlman replied.

Perlman didn't get along with another Red Team senior vice president, David Smucker, described as an autocratic PRR traditionalist, known as

"Mother Smucker" to some of his subordinates. The two men apparently just hated each other. "You run a wooden-wheeled railroad," Perlman is said to have told Smucker shortly before the merger. Perlman didn't think Smucker was out on the road enough and didn't show enough enthusiasm. Several of the sources for Rush Loving, Jr., and Daughen and Binzen thought it was a personal vendetta and that Perlman was unable to adjust to being number two under Saunders. Pushing Saunders to purge the Red Team became a fixation. At any rate, Smucker was kicked out and replaced by the Green Team's R.G. (Mike) Flannery. But Smucker's own swan song was a famous memo of November 13, 1969, in which he delineated the extent of the operating disaster to Saunders, and blamed it on Perlman.[19] It was no matter. Saunders was already looking for Perlman's replacement and even entertained Louis Menk of the Burlington for that purpose.

At the very top, Stuart Saunders was chairman and chief executive officer. Perlman was president and chief administrative officer. Saunders set for himself the job of attending to finances, diversification, politics. Perlman's job was to run the railroad. The twain never met—much. It was as if, at the very top, there were two separate spheres to the Penn Central that never communicated nor shared common goals, but each with access to friendly ears on the board of directors. Perhaps, if there had been plenty of money to run the railroad, paths would not have had to cross. But Perlman, at least, never thought Saunders gave him enough money or enough authority.

Saunders was outwardly cool. He despised physical activity the way he seemed to despise being bothered with details of railroad operation. His sport was bridge. Asked if he enjoyed it, he said, "I play to win."[20] He would not deign to ride his own commuter trains to work, but went by limousine instead, a trait that did not endear him to the riders of the red rattlers. He was a patron of the Philadelphia arts, a member of many clubs, including the very exclusive Philadelphia Club. Saunders was never critical of Perlman in public. Before a Senate investigating committee, he said:[21]

Mr. Perlman and I—I have the highest regard for him and I think he is an excellent operating man, and I have no great difficulty getting along with him. We don't want rubber stamps or men that don't have convictions at the top of this railroad. We had disagreements and that is natural. But they weren't of any critical nature and Mr. Perlman had complete authority to do whatever he wanted to do and he is an excellent railroad man.[22]

Perlman, in contrast, seemed to have a steely hatred for Saunders, or at least he was more open about it. "Mr. Saunders came from one of the wealthiest railroads in the country, and his outlook on problems may be entirely different from mine," he told a Senate investigating committee. "A lot of people say, 'Well, here are two men of different philosophies.' Well, sure, when a man comes from one side of the tracks he may have a different philosophy from the other.''[23]

Q: (by Senator Hartke) Mr. Saunders . . . left the impression, at least with this Senator, that you had complete authority to run the operation and you were given everything you needed to run it. Is that true?

A: It was not true.

Q: In other words, it was not true in personnel, was it?

A: No, sir.

Q: Was it true in regard to money for these projects you were talking about?

A: No, sir.[24]

There was something, not only about Perlman, but about the whole Green Team—smugness, perhaps, or a sense of superiority—that seemed to pervade their whole relationship with the Red Team. Wayne Hoffman, the one who went to Flying Tiger, told Daughen and Binzen: "I had no regard for PRR management or their philosophy. I felt they had to be changed." Robert Odell, a PC director and former NYC director, told the board in a highly charged meeting of November 26, 1969:

As to some background, the New York Central was in excellent condition before merger. . . . To say that the merger has been a tragic mistake to date is an understatement. Central had a smooth-running official organization with teams of capable and enthusiastic executives. Discord among management or directors was practically non-existent. Many of the outstanding executives resigned because they correctly anticipated the existing discord in Pennsylvania management would be increased after merger.[25]

He called the NYC "depression-proof," meaning the new marketing techniques had made it less reliant on commodities whose volume fluctuated wildly in recession. "Depression-proof" was Perlman's term. Statistics bear out that Central was a better-run railroad, but not that it was really depression-proof. But the Green Team never got over the feeling that once they had known a great railroad, and the Red Team had wrecked it.
There was something deeper to this rivalry. The PRR's leadership had been a self-perpetuating elite since the railroad's founding in the 1840s. The NYC had gone through a revolution in the Robert Young proxy fight of 1954 which severed relations with the Vanderbilts and their self-perpetuating management. The PRR's senior officers were mostly in their late fifties or early sixties, had spent their whole career with the PRR or its affiliates,

lived in the plush western suburbs of Philadelphia, were members of the city's social elite, including its prestigious clubs, and were Protestant and Republican (except Saunders, a Democrat because of his Virginia origin). Concluded a Senate investigating team:

It appears that the Pennsylvania Railroad responded substantially to the people its management met socially. Its direction was determined more by the social ethos of Philadelphia and its own traditions than by the demands of the market or the concepts of the business community at large.[26]

The Green Team had been assembled by Perlman from careers in other companies, sometimes other industries. They were in their forties or early fifties, lived in respectable suburbs of New York but were not part of the city's social elite, and were more mixed, religiously and ethnically. Perlman was Jewish in an industry a Senate investigation said was "not known for its tolerance." One Green Team executive of Irish extraction told Daughen and Binzen, "I was brought up to hate Protestants and the Pennsylvania Railroad. After this [merger] I've got to love them both."

The effect of these differences is impossible to measure; some people would like to discount them. But there are some who believe they were the single most important reason these two companies should never have merged in the first place.

6

At the time Penn Central collapsed, press attention focused on its investments outside of railroading. Some of them were inexplicably bizarre. They were supposed to bring money in to the railroad; instead, they had seemed to drain cash away. The mere spectacle of the stuffy Pennsylvania Railroad wheeling and dealing with Dallas banks and Florida land developers was remarkable. On top of that, there were executive-suite intrigues, unaccounted funds, posh sauna baths, buxom blondes, and lots of wretchedly bad judgment. Naturally, it made good copy.

Once it was clear the PRR would have to divest itself of the N&W, it had to decide what to do with its last great liquid asset. There were some who suggested it ought to be used to pay off the company's debt, freeing about $40 million a year in fixed charges for investment in the railroad. Most of that $40 million in fixed charges went to the banks and insurance companies on the railroad's board of directors. They agreed with Stuart Saunders and David Bevan that putting money in the railroad was like putting it in 1 percent securities; the dividend-paying N&W securities should be replaced by investments paying as equally high a return.

This was more than a simple conflict of interest for the railroad's directors. It struck at the foundation of corporate morality. Was it right to take money from a capital-starved railroad and put it into businesses unrelated to it, or into the industries or territory it served? Was there no moral obligation for railroaders to run railroads? If they were going to milk the railroad of its credit and its good name, were they not hastening the day when the government would have to take it over? It has occurred to some people that there may have been those associated with the Penn Central who were not pained to see the railroad crash in flames, as long as they could keep their high-yield investments outside of railroading—which is approximately what happened.

If these people did not realize what they were doing, why did they hedge these investments carefully in holding companies, so that in case the railroad fell, the investments would be beyond the court's reach? If they had a clear conscience, why did they take out an insurance policy for $10 million with Lloyds of London to protect themselves from breach-of-trust lawsuits?[27] If they were proceeding competently, why did they mislead their own directors on the profitability of these investments? If they were doing this honorably, why did some of them (not Stuart Saunders or Alfred Perlman or any of the Green Team) use inside information to profit themselves by buying and selling shares in the same companies as the railroad?[28] Milton Shapp related a little vignette to Daughen and Binzen that seemed to sum it all up.

There's no doubt that Saunders wanted to get out of the railroad business, even during the merger controversy. I've been at several parties with him where he had a few drinks, and he was always talking about Litton Industries and how Litton and these other conglomerates had cash coming in and were putting it to good use, getting good returns. He said he wanted to keep the money for real estate investments instead of putting it in the fucking railroad. That's what he said, the fucking railroad.[29]

Both the merger partners had been in business other than railroads for years, mostly real estate on lands adjacent to railroad operations. The PRR had the Penn Center complex in Philadelphia and Madison Square Garden in New York; NYC virtually owned New York's Park Avenue as far south as Forty-second Street, for that had been the railroad's right-of-way until the tracks were put underground when Grand Central was built in 1913. On that land were office buildings and five hotels. Investments after 1963 were different in that they required an outlay of cash, and except for Buckeye, a pipeline laid along some PRR right-of-way, and Strick, the manufacturer of the containers used in NYC's flexi-van service, had nothing to do with railroad operations.

Paying for these acquisitions was not as easy as it looked. The N&W stock, with a market value of $289 million, gave the illusion of a large reserve, but since much of it was pledged as collateral on loans, it could not be sold immediately. That which was sold netted only $37.6 million for the railroad. The sale of the Long Island Railroad to New York State for $65 million actually netted more. The rest of the $201 million sunk into diversification was borrowed. Any dividends the railroad might receive from subsidiaries had to be balanced against the fixed charges it paid out on these loans.[30] The railroad, in other words, was gambling with borrowed money.

If the diversification program had been a roaring success, there may never have been a fuss. Overall, it was a fiasco. Strick and Buckeye apparently turned out fairly well and made regular contributions to consolidated net income. Arvida Corporation was a Florida land-development operation with choice holdings in the Miami and Sarasota areas. It was building condominium complexes on the beaches and was already getting into environmental troubles, especially in Sarasota, for its sub-sea level sewage systems. It paid dividends to the railroad amounting to about 2 percent a year. Great Southwest Corporation was developing industrial land around Dallas and the "Six Flags" amusement parks in Georgia and Texas. Macco Realty Company, later merged with Great Southwest, developed residential land around Los Angeles. Neither paid a single cash dividend to the railroad. Senator Hartke and others were incredulous that a supposedly sagacious businessman like Saunders was so nonchalant about what was going on.[31]

Q: You have the Great Southwest Corporation on page 77?

A: Yes.

Q: Does it show a loss of $330,473 for 1968?

A: This—see, the Great Southwest has a number of subsidiary companies. This only includes part of it. If you look at the annual report to stockholders, and what reflects there, through earnings, the Great Southwest Corporation and consolidated subsidiaries—and the figures that I gave you are the consolidated earnings and they are the only things that count.

. . . .

Q: Let's go through a couple more, and then I have a question. Do you want to comment on the system's investment in Capistrano Highlands?

A: That's nothing but a subsidiary of Macco Corporation.

Q: Losses to the extent of $740,000?

A: Macco Corporation is a corporation that has some 40,000 acres of land in California. Very fine property. And they have a number of—

Q: Very fine property, right?

A: Yes.

. . . .

Q: What about the Great Southwest Golf Club, Inc.? Assets of $2 million and a
$120,000 loss in 1968?

A: . . . Now you can go through and pick out individual companies and find this.

. . . .

Q: Now L-A-G-U-N-A, how do you pronounce that?

A: Laguna.

Q: The Laguna. They had assets of $2 million and a loss of $286,000. Pent Land
Home, assets of $26.8 million, losses of $142,000. Another one here, total of $5
million in assets, losses of $187,000. . . . You needed cash in hand, I think, more
than these losses, right?

A: But if we were going to sell anything, what we ought to sell is Great Southwest
Corporation, not these little nits and lice.

There was a reason why companies like Arvida and Great Southwest
should be attracted to the railroad. There were advantages in being linked
up with a transportation company whose securities were regulated by the
ICC and therefore not subject to the full disclosure laws of the Securities
and Exchange Commission. Financial people had known of this for some
time. When, after the PC merger, the railroad holdings of Alleghany
Corporation fell to less than 22 percent of its assets, and the ICC revoked its
status as a common carrier, it hastily bought a motor carrier, Jones Motor
Freight Lines, to have its ICC regulation restored.[32]

But why the railroad was attracted in return was a tougher question,
especially since the return from these companies was about the same as
from the railroad. There was no conclusive answer, but there was circumstantial evidence to which both the House Banking Committee and Senate
Commerce Committee investigations gave a great deal of weight.

David Bevan's good friend was Charles J. (Charlie) Hodge, who formerly
worked for the Army as a general and now was chairman of the executive
committee of Glore, Forgan & Company, investment bankers and brokers.
Hodge helped arrange the early acquisition of Buckeye Pipeline, and otherwise cultivated a close relationship with the railroad's officers. He staged an
elaborate dinner party at the Links Club for Saunders in 1963 with a guest
list mostly of prominent bankers.[33] He arranged a gala trip to Europe for
Saunders and his wife in 1965. The relationship of Hodge and Bevan grew
warmer, particularly through a fishing club known as the Silverfish, whose

membership consisted of twelve men mostly from the financial world. In that way, Hodge and Glore, Forgan & Company became virtually the sole financial advisor to the PRR and later to the PC. Hodge was an ardent promoter of the land company deals, and his company received large brokerage fees in the transactions.

The significance was that because of this social relationship, objectivity in making investments may have been obscured. It may have been further obscured by Penphil, an investment club composed mostly of members of the Silverfish. Members put up only around $16,000 (which later prompted Bevan to testify that it was only "a very small affair"). But much more was borrowed from the Chemical Bank, which made loans to the group at the prime rate, largely on the railroad's credit and compensating balances. Penphil invested in companies in which the railroad had an interest (and often shortly before the railroad increased its investments). Bevan and Hodge made all the decisions regarding the placement of Penphil investments. So the possibility of trading on insider information, and of conflict-of-interest, was great.[34]

Of all the railroad's investments, none was more strange than Executive Jet Aviation, an air shuttle service. It was illegal for the railroad to control anything engaged in commercial aviation, but the PRR said it thought that (a) investment solely in nonvoting securities of EJA would insulate it from criminal charges, or (b) the Civil Aeronautics Board would rule in its favor, or (c) Congress would act in its favor. In fact, the CAB ruled against the PRR (and fined it $65,000 to make sure the point was clear) after which the railroad continued to bankroll Executive Jet.[35]

Executive Jet had ambitions to become a big airline, but it wasn't making any money and the railroad kept coughing up cash. The company's founder and president, O.J. (Dick) Lassiter, formerly an Air Force general, piled up around $50,000 in annual expense accounts. As readers of *Car and Driver* discovered in April 1970, he frequently escorted one Linda Vaughan on these junkets, while she was on assignment for the Hurst Performance Products Company, a purveyor of racing car accessories. (She was known in the trade as Miss Hurst Golden Shifter, and her job was to ride around automobile race tracks on a large replica of a floor-mounted gear shift lever.) She got a ten-carat diamond from Lassiter before she was dumped for new girl friends. There was also enough money in the EJA till for a deluxe gymnasium-sauna complex, with one Wally Soga as head karate instructor. Even the droll House Banking Committee was tempted to burlesque this one by calling it the "Saga of Soga."[36]

That committee, in fact, was so gleefully appalled by the rot it had uncovered at Executive Jet that it spent 93 pages documenting it with memos, testimony, and tabulations. Needless to say, the details have only been touched on here. How was it that a man such as David Bevan, supposedly having financial acumen, would pour $20 million of railroad money into this thing, even after the CAB ruling? The question, said House investigators, cries out for an answer.

They thought a document known as the Ricciardi deposition was the clue. J.H. Ricciardi had been hired as a kind of social director for EJA, had been fired, and had sued for recovery of salary. In a deposition in that suit, Ricciardi asserted that he had arranged trips for David Bevan and Charlie Hodge, and provided them, on more than one occasion, with female companionship. Later, in a deposition of his own, Lassiter asserted that he believed Bevan and Hodge felt threatened by public disclosure of certain activities, and directed investigators to the Ricciardi deposition. Bevan denied everything, and whether or not there were females, at least some evidence seems to indicate that most of the money had been squandered before Ricciardi ever came on the scene. But the House investigation concluded: "Under the circumstances, consideration must be given to the possibility that public revelation of certain personal activities that might have been extremely embarrassing to Bevan, is inevitably linked to the question of why Bevan acted in the strange way he did throughout the deteriorating Executive Jet catastrophe."[37]

7

To focus on Executive Jet, however, was to exaggerate the losses of diversification. Overall, the program was breaking even, not hemorrhaging cash like the railroad. At worst, it preoccupied the attention of management at a time when it was desperately needed elsewhere. But on the balance sheets, it was deceptive enough to fool the board of directors and mesmerize management.

Statistically, it appeared that in the five-year period 1964-1969, diversification had earned a net return of $146 million. But included in that figure was $115 million of "undistributed earnings," which were funds the subsidiaries had not declared as dividends, which meant they did not flow upward to the railroad. In fact, by the time fixed charges on money borrowed for diversification were subtracted, only $19.9 million flowed upward to the railroad. That was a rate of return of 14.27 percent in five years, or 2.85 percent a year.

Stating these earnings in the more exaggerated form was part of a deliberate policy called "earnings maximization," or what one memo referred to as "imaginative accounting."[38] Bevan described it this way in a memo to Saunders on November 21, 1966, claiming the idea was basically Saunders's own:

1. A policy may be instituted for attempting to keep as far as possible net income and cash flow as closely together as possible without regard to what the immediate effect is on earnings. Up to several years ago, this was basically the policy pursued by the Pennsylvania Railroad.

2. The policy may be instituted for maximizing earnings to the greatest extent possible within the limits of good accounting practices. In the last several years, this has been done on the Pennsylvania in accordance with your expressed desires. It does mean, however, that we tend to create a wider and wider difference as between reported income and cash flow. Today, the cash flow of the Pennsylvania Railroad is substantially less than its reported income.[39]

Specific examples were difficult to explain without excessive detail. Two should suffice:

1. When the real estate subsidiaries sold parcels of land, customers normally made only a down payment, the rest due over a period of time. Two methods of accounting could be used. One recorded a profit on an installment basis, only as cash was received. On that basis, Great Southwest and Macco together earned $9.4 million in 1968. The other approach recorded the entire profit in the period in which the sale was made, regardless of the amount of money received. That was how PC chose to record it, and on that basis, they appeared to earn $30.7 million.

2. Penn Central and the Baltimore & Ohio each owned 50 percent of the Washington Terminal Company, which owned Washington Union Station. In 1969, the station was leased to the Department of the Interior and the Washington Terminal Company was liquidated. This had to show on the railroads' books as something, even though it represented no cash income. The B&O chose to represent its share of the station at the conservative book value (representing the original cost of construction)—$3.1 million. The PC represented it at its appraised value, a sum that would not be realized for many years under the lease, if ever—$13.7 million. Even a lowly stockholder who happened to own shares of both PC and B&O caught this huge discrepancy and wondered about it.[40]

There was good reason why Saunders wanted earnings maximized when he arrived at the PRR, even if he hesitated to use that phrase. The stock exchange ratio with the NYC was 1 share PRR to 1.3 shares NYC. But the decline in PRR earnings would probably have required the renegotiating of this delicate matter had there not been a way to cosmetically inflate the PRR's earnings. Bevan added, in a memo of November 21, 1966:

Over the short term today, the New York Central earnings as reported are much more real and tangible from the standpoint of an ability to pay dividends than are those of the Pennsylvania. Virtually all of their earnings are actually available for the payment of dividends. . . . On the other hand, much of the Pennsylvania Railroad's income is in the form of income of subsidiary companies which in turn, have their own requirements for the plough back of money.[41]

After the merger, the greater the earnings on the bottom line, the better the credit of the railroad. For a railroad living on borrowed money, this was important. It lulled the board of directors into thinking all was well—probably the most serious consequence of earnings maximization. So the policy was continued.

When Saunders wanted something from the government such as a loan guaranty, it was important to be able to show the railroad down on its luck. "I think," he wrote in 1969, "our picture is bleak enough to achieve most of the results we need from the point of view of legislation and regulatory agencies. . . . If we go too far in this regard, we get ourselves in greater trouble so far as financing is concerned."[42]

In front of creditors, an absolutely rosy picture was essential. That was why the railroad continued to pay dividends, even as it hurtled toward bankruptcy. Perhaps Saunders was overly solicitous of stockholders, but he was gambling that somehow a confident front could be maintained, even in front of all the creditors sitting on the board, until problems somehow took care of themselves. But as time went on, even the puffery written for annual reports was peppered with phrases like "uphill fight" and "adverse conditions."

Finally, at the terrible meeting of the finance committee on May 27, 1970, the information could no longer be withheld. Cash losses for 1968 had actually been $140 million; for 1969, $220 million; for the first quarter of 1970, $100 million. Since the merger, $993 million had been borrowed, of which only $240 million had been repaid.

Up to this time, the full board acted as if it was unaware of what was going on. Actually, it couldn't have been completely unaware, certainly not after Alfred Perlman was sacked in September 1969 by Saunders, without consulting the full board, and replaced by Paul Gorman of Western Electric. But only one director, Robert Odell, formerly a Central director, was willing to probe the gangrene. He was aware of the financial situation of the railroad, and of Great Southwest-Macco. It was not just insult but bad judgment that he was not consulted on a multi-million dollar purchase of land by Macco within twenty miles of his home in Los Angeles—land that was purchased without even Penn Central being consulted. He warned Saunders that Great Southwest-Macco, by not consulting its principal owners, may have broken the law. Saunders was upset and sought legal advice, which confirmed that Odell was right. So Saunders went shopping among lawyers until he got the opinion he wanted. In another "Dear Stuart" letter, Odell warned that self-serving legal advice was not fooling anyone and was typical of management's high-handedness.[43] It was no surprise to Robert Odell that a few months later Great Southwest-Macco was forced to write down two-thirds of its assets for a $130 million paper loss.

At the PC board meeting in November 1969, Odell offered a resolution to restructure management, giving power of both operations and finances to the president and designating Alfred Perlman as the man to fill that post. The minutes of the meeting read as follows:

The chairman of the board thereupon asked if the motion were seconded. There was no second. The board then unanimously adopted a motion that Mr. Odell be thanked for his interest in the company's affairs and that his motion be tabled.[44]

Once upon a time, thrifty little investors put their tiny savings into shares of stock that built great corporations. They became part owners, and management was merely the hired men running the shop. Everyone knew, by the twentieth century, that stockholders no longer played an active role in company affairs—if they didn't like the way it was being run, they normally sold their shares rather than fight. But at least it was thought the board of directors, who represented mostly the large creditors, would keep an eye on management for the benefit of investors generally. The Penn Central affair was the first real indication of how totally the board-of-director system had broken down. These men, executives in their own right, usually for large banks and insurance companies, were each directors for several corporations. It was prestige, and it was that vital interlock by which capital maintained a tight control over capitalism. They were preoccupied, spread too thin, perhaps even lacking guts, and they failed to do the job they were supposed to for the railroad. Management was left with no watchdogs at all. Like most powerful individuals and institutions with no watchdogs watching, it was tempted by secrecy and arrogance. The breakdown helped to ruin two railroads and damaged the credibility of capitalism.

8

The final descent into the abyss began in April 1970. Bevan knew there were going to be substantial debt maturities that year—$100 million of them—and by March it was clear the only way they could be met was to borrow more money. He suggested a new issue, $100 million of Pennsylvania Company debentures. Saunders, the board's finance committee, and the ICC all seemed receptive.

That was in late March, and Saunders and Bevan must have had an inkling of what the first quarter earnings report was going to look like. The railroad was still awash in problems, aggravated by a brutal winter which saw Selkirk and Frontier closed for days on end in January, with temperatures averaging 22.3 degrees below normal, with more than $8 million spent on snow removal. But when the quarterly report came out on April 22, it was a shocker even to those expecting the worst. Losses from railroad operations were $102 million. That was more than $1 million a day. Saunders hurried off to Washington, hat in hand, to talk things over.

At 10.5 percent, it was hoped the debentures would still be attractive. But when the prospectus came out in mid-May, it contained, in the small print at the back, a notation that killed it instantly. Between April 22 and May 8, it said, "maturities and payments of commercial paper exceeded sales of commercial paper by $41.3 million." That was it. It was like a run on the bank. The railroad was sinking and the rats were fleeing. There was no further chance that funds could be raised privately. On May 28, the news came over the Dow-Jones wire at about 1:20 P.M.: "The Penn Central today withdrew its proposed offering of $100 million in debenture bonds. No reason was given." There had already been massive sales of stock by financial institutions represented on the company's board, prompting more than casual speculation that bankers had freely traded on insider information.[45] The rush to sell continued.

Walter Wriston at the First National City Bank of New York, the bank most deeply involved in the PC revolving credit loan of $300 million the year before, was furious. How could his bank have gotten so enmeshed unless somebody had not been telling the truth? Who was to blame? He summoned both Saunders and Bevan to New York separately and was not impressed with their explanations. Others were beginning to suggest it was time for a change of management, but Wriston was apparently the chief protagonist.

Perlman was unaware of any of this. Since he had been kicked upstairs to the meaningless position of vice chairman (until his employment contract ran out in November 1970), he had been under a kind of house arrest, whiling away his hours in the New York office, consulted on nothing. Bevan and Saunders apparently each thought the bankers were talking about firing the other, and that his own position was safe.

Daughen and Binzen wrote a moving account of the last hours of the old management. At a special board meeting on June 8, Paul Gorman began with a statement that the banks' willingness to loan money, even under a federal guarantee, depended, among other things, on the reorganization of top management. The officers left the room. A motion was made to fire Perlman and Bevan and kick Saunders upstairs, stripped of power. There was discussion. Some thought Saunders ought to go as well. Director William Day, president of the Pennsylvania Banking & Trust Company and a member of the same Philadelphia clubs as Saunders, kept murmuring, "oh no, oh no." Gorman was summoned. Should Saunders go or not? The answer was "go." The resolution was unanimous. The meeting adjourned while a delegation went to tell the three officers they had been fired.[46]

The Nixon administration desperately did not want the worst business failure in American history during its tenure. Its worst fear was a Wall Street panic, and a bankruptcy of this magnitude could easily trigger one. Secretary of Transportation John Volpe worked on a loan guarantee for $200 million from Congress. Senator Hugh Scott, Attorney General John Mitchell, Federal Reserve Board Chairman Arthur Burns, Secretary of the Treasury David Kennedy, and Secretary of Commerce Maurice Stans all pitched in to help get the loan. The greatest hope was pinned on the Pentagon that an arrangement might be made under the Defense Production Act of 1950.

But the skeletons would not stay in the closet. Two hundred million dollars wasn't going to be enough; at least another $500 million was needed to rehabilitate the railroad. Undersecretary of Transportation James Beggs admitted to a closed-door session of the House Defense Appropriations Subcommittee that the $200 million was only the first installment on a planned salvage package of $750 million. The only security was accounts receivable, the weakest of all collateral, because the rest of the railroad's assets were pledged. Assistant Secretary of Defense Barry Shillito weakly admitted there was no contingency plan in case the railroad defaulted, but added the government was not expecting to have to make good on this loan. "An endorser never does," shot back one of the congressmen. Where was this money going to go? Most of it, it turned out, was not going to the railroad, but to bail out security holders, including $60 million to Swiss banks. Penn Central was a client of Nixon's and Mitchell's former New York law firm. It was alleged that at least one cabinet member, perhaps more, had personal commitments to Great Southwest. And the Pentagon, while it insisted Penn Central service was essential to the national defense, was huffing and puffing about being railroaded into the railroad business.

Jack Anderson's *Washington Merry-Go-Round* got hold of the secret testimony and published some of the choicer morsels. Congressman Wright Patman, at the helm of the House Banking Committee and perhaps the last of the old railroad-baiting populists in Congress, had plunged into an investigation of alleged insider trading in Penn Central securities and had already fished up political dynamite. He just smiled and rubbed his chin at the administration's frantic pleas to help the big bankers with fat salaries who had gambled and lost on Penn Central. The fact that the railroad's real estate holdings were put carefully beyond the reach of a bankruptcy court and the fact that the discredited officers were getting very fancy pensions ($125,000 a year for Saunders, for example) were fatally damaging as far as politics were concerned. The fact that bankruptcy would not mean the trains would stop running punctured the defense argument. The politics were overwhelming. The rich could not beg for money from average folks when their own nests were so snugly feathered. There would be no loan.

There was, at the close of business on Friday, June 19, approximately $7 million in PC bank balances. The payroll on the next Tuesday was $12 million and on Thursday, another $8 million. By the end of the week, nearly $10 million in commercial paper was due for redemption. The board met in special session on Sunday, June 21. A motion to file under section 77 of the Bankruptcy Act carried unanimously. It was hoped that by taking this action on a Sunday, the financial markets would have a night to think it over before they panicked.

On Monday morning, Wall Street was described as "shaken" but there was no panic. The discredited officers continued to get their pension checks, but some banks refused to cash PC payroll checks for the men and women who had slugged it out all week trying to keep the trains rolling.

Mike Flannery, it was said, was just beginning to solve the railroad's computer and operational problems as the house came down in flames. Perlman, when his contract with PC expired, went out to San Francisco to begin a new career, at age sixty-eight, as president of the Western Pacific. Flannery, his loyal lieutenant from the heady days of the marketing revolution at the New York Central, went with him. Saunders's peace was punctuated with summonses to testify. He wound up as a consultant to coal producers in Richmond, Virginia. Bevan was indicted for multiple counts of misappropriation of funds, and was released on $50,000 bail. He pleaded innocent. Rumors of possible criminal charges against Saunders were persistent. In 1974, he signed a consent decree (neither an admission nor denial of guilt) on allegations by the SEC that he conspired to withhold vital information and defraud the public by misrepresenting the railroad's true financial condition.[47] A year after Penn Central's fall, Congress bailed out Lockheed Aircraft when it came to similar grief with a $250 million loan guarantee.

As for the merger, it had been the most miserable fiasco in American business. Later, there came a terse announcement from Roanoke that Norfolk & Western and Chesapeake & Ohio had suspended merger discussions indefinitely. The credibility of merger was gone.

CHAPTER **14**

The Coming of Conrail;
1970-1976

The East was a railroad graveyard.

1. Jersey Central succumbed in 1967 to the paralysis of labor-intensive terminal operations in high-tax territory, without the benefit of a long rail haul.
2. Boston & Maine defaulted an interest installment of its 5 percent first mortgage bonds, and in March 1970, was dragged forcibly to court by four nervous creditors.[1]
3. Penn Central fell in June 1970.
4. Lehigh Valley, dependent on Penn Central for advances that were no longer forthcoming, fell in July 1970.
5. Reading fell in November 1971, thanks largely to environmental concerns over high-sulphur coal that slashed coal tonnage 66 percent between 1967 and 1972, with the most severe decline beginning in the spring of 1971.[2]
6. Erie Lackawanna fell in June 1972 after all its troubles, done in at last by Hurricane Agnes, which tore out 135 miles of the mainline between Elmira and Salamanca, New York, including 11 bridges. The N&W, which controlled it through the Dereco holding company, did nothing. "It grabs my gut to have to vote to do this," said John Fishwick. It happened just when it looked as though EL, under the N&W umbrella, was going to be the Cinderella of the East.[3]

The list of corpses was remarkable in that it included every railroad that had not been invited to a merger, or had taken part in a weak-sister merger. Obviously, the economics of the Northeast was no longer hospitable to railroading. Merger did not cause the situation; it was to have been the solution. It had failed. The postmortem on Penn Central continued for several years, and there was never a consensus. The merger debacle had aggravated a bad situation in which the Pennsylvania Railroad, at least, was probably headed for bankruptcy anyway. Debate was on whether the merger or the bad situation deserved the most emphasis. Certainly, Penn Central could not be held responsible for the bankruptcies of the others.

1

Or could it? It hadn't helped. Delaware & Hudson, for example, had survived as a solvent railroad, but not by a comfortable margin. It used to receive 100,000 cars a year from the PRR at Wilkes-Barre, Pennsylvania, which it forwarded to New England and Canada. The PC rerouted as much of this traffic as it could through Selkirk, and the more traffic volume fell on the Wilkes-Barre line, the more PC justified curtailments of service. By 1971, PC and D&H exchanged only 54,000 cars. Then Hurricane Agnes obliterated the Wilkes-Barre line and PC was in no hurry to repair it. In fact, it wanted to abandon it. It was odd, said D&H President Bruce Sterzing, that D&H could lose traffic like this and still manage to make money, while the more PC gained, the more money it lost.[4]

In a similar way, EL, B&M, and Reading all felt the PC's death clutches. At one time, for example, Maybrook Yard in eastern New York had been the bustling interchange between the Erie and the New Haven. The EL traffic through Maybrook increased steadily through the 1960s and represented 10 percent of EL's gross revenue. When PC took over the New Haven, it immediately changed schedules so as to add a whole day to traffic moving through Maybrook. The PC trainmasters were warned they must expedite traffic through Selkirk so as to outperform EL at all cost. We must "get the long haul to Chicago instead of only to Maybrook," said one of its confidential memos.[5] Maybrook traffic fell 30 percent in six months. The ICC reminded PC it was obligated under Appendix G (to its merger approval) to solicit *for* the outcast roads, not against them, under pain of terrible indemnities.[6] But PC let the key bridge on the Maybrook line over the Hudson River at Poughkeepsie deteriorate until it could accommodate only short trains, and only at funeral-train speeds. Then, one spring day in 1973, the bridge burned and the Maybrook gateway died.

The day the bridge burned, everyone on the little Lehigh & Hudson River Railroad tried to keep a stiff upper lip but it was tough. The life of this little, first-class shortline depended on Maybrook and the bridge. For years, it had gathered cars from the Lehigh Valley, the Pennsylvania, the old Lackawanna, the Alphabet Route, and the Central States Dispatch Route, and forwarded them to Maybrook and the New Haven connection. Now it was all over. Already in receivership, there was no point even trying to reorganize without the bridge.[7]

The railroad village of Maybrook is quiet now. The rails of the once mighty yard are still in place, but they are rusty underneath the wild flowers that have reclaimed the cindery soil. Not a single freight car is in sight, and the only sounds are the crickets and the birds that nest in the abandoned round house. A fading "no parking" sign flaps aimlessly beside the greasing pit and ready track, where the locomotives of five railroads had gathered

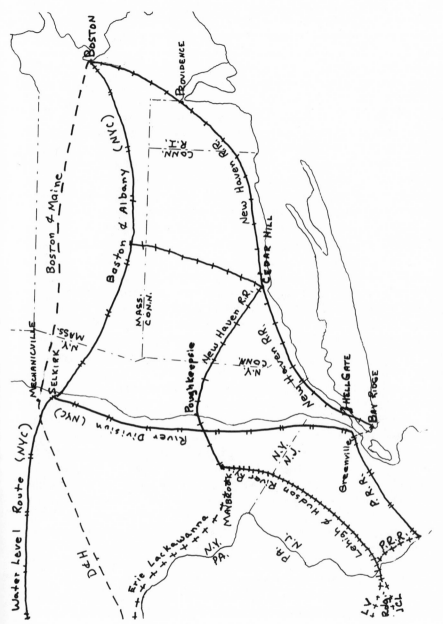

MAP 30: *The Poughkeepsie Bridge and Other Entrances to Southern New England*

not so long before. If Maybrook had been obsolete, this would be only a sad footnote. But it was the most efficient route into southern New England. It was a situation that was being duplicated at other routes and junctions. Such was the mischief the mergers had wrought.

2

Bankruptcies were nothing new to railroads. They had survived them before—waves of them. Assuming the railroad was serving a useful purpose and was physically sound, bankruptcy meant only that the court would order a controlled reduction of its debt. With fixed charges thus reduced, it could make money again. But from the start, there was something ominous about the northeastern crisis, particularly for the Penn Central. Even without the obligation to pay its fixed charges, it was losing Niagaras of money—$237 million in 1970, $180 million in 1971, $105 million in 1972. Each successive reduction of the loss seemed like a laudable achievement, but it was still unlike anything railroading had seen before. And most serious of all, the track continued to deteriorate. Wrecks were common now and sometimes involved jumbo tank cars carrying highly explosive chemicals. People with homes near the tracks had good reason to be scared. Speed, even on main lines across Ohio and Indiana that carried passenger trains, had to be reduced to 10 mph for long stretches. This was looking less like an ordinary receivership and more like a terminal liquidation.

Judge John Fullam was put in charge of the PC reorganization (and subsequently of the Lehigh Valley and Reading reorganizations as well). A liberal on civil rights, and an unsuccessful candidate for a congressional seat from Bucks County, Pennsylvania, he was described as a no-nonsense guy, but was thought to have only a limited familiarity with corporate affairs. For trustees, he appointed Jervis Langdon, former president of the B&O (of "missile crisis" fame in the C&O-B&O case) who at the moment was the $100,000-a-year trouble-shooting president of the near-bankrupt Rock Island; Willard Wirtz, former secretary of labor under Kennedy and Johnson; George Baker, retired dean of the Harvard Business School; and Richard Bond, retired head of Wanamaker's Department Stores and a Philadelphia socialite.[8] Paul Gorman, the man who replaced Perlman, left the railroad soon after the bankruptcy, and William Moore, crack vice-president of the aggressive Southern Railway, was brought in. Moore spent sixty days touring the system. "We're broke," he told employees, "and we need your help making this railroad run." He slimmed down the bureaucracy at headquarters and made the lax supervisory staff shape up. He helped to track down the $4 million of PC money that previous management had let disappear without a trace into a Liechtenstein bank, and the

352 boxcars a midwestern shortline had stolen, repainted, and rented back to PC. But in the end, he was defeated like all the rest, leaving Langdon as the chief operating officer.[9]

At first, it seemed as if the railroad could be reorganized in a few easy steps. First, to show how thoroughly the trustees went about their work, the railroad's historical memorabilia was auctioned off at a sad little affair at the Thirtieth Street Station in Philadelphia, including the carved oak clock from the Newark station and the railroad's library. More substantive was the effort to get more freight. An aggressive sales campaign was mounted, which was laudable enough, except that more traffic seemed to be coming from the other bankrupt roads than from trucks.

Next, the passenger trains had to be dumped. Early in 1970, PC petitioned to discontinue all passenger service west of Buffalo and Harrisburg.[10] Petitions on these trains could have been filed as early as 1958, but only now were the losses discovered to be unbearable. There was, in other words, something vaguely contrived about this maneuver—not that some of the trains weren't losers, just that petitioning them all at once smacked of a gimmick to get publicity.

The ploy worked. Congress panicked, and the result was the Amtrak law that established the National Railroad Passenger Corporation, which took over the operation of nearly all noncommuter passenger services in the United States on May 1, 1971. But that did not silence Penn Central. It was unique in that more than half of Amtrak's trains operated over its rails, chiefly in the Washington-Boston corridor. The corridor was unique in that it was the only mainline in the country devoted primarily to passenger service. So the fees paid to railroads who operated Amtrak trains may not have fully compensated PC.

Next, the trustees determined that 10,000 miles of line, or about half the railroad, no longer served useful or profitable purposes.[11] Some segments were put up for abandonment immediately. Most remained as a kind of vague package deal, the new panacea for the revitalization of the railroad. As with the merger panacea years before, a crying-towel campaign was launched (which the business press eagerly picked up) to impress the public that the regulators were at fault for forcing the railroad to keep these branches long after their usefulness was ended.

The fact was, these branches served shippers and communities, and their loss threatened a loss of jobs for the employees of those shippers. None of these people had been given notice that their rail service was in jeopardy until the railroad suddenly messed up its affairs. Some had recently been encouraged to build or expand facilities along these very lines by the railroad. Of course it was mandatory that the regulators take careful scrutiny of every one of these segments before the railroad left the industrial geography of the Northeast in shambles.[12] Piggyback and container service probably would render some of these lines obsolete someday, but premature abandonment could preclude development of heavy, rail-dependent industries. Besides, these branches were valuable feeders for the mainlines. Abandoning them today could be a reason to abandon the mainlines tomorrow. There were already plenty of railroaders who wanted to get their railroads out of railroading. Among the most prominent defenders of the abandonment scheme was the Department of Transportation, including both of Nixon's secretaries of transportation, John Volpe and Claude Brinigar, who had close connections either to highway projects or oil interests. The implications of this should not have been taken lightly.

From the beginning of the merger movement, railroad men had led the public to believe the mergers were going to be the vehicles for the elimination of these "duplicate lines," but the mergers had accomplished nothing of the sort. These lines could not all have become losers overnight. So the abandonment scheme also had a contrived quality, like the passenger discontinuance scheme—a gimmick to precipitate a crisis.

Next, the trustees wanted to renegotiate all contracts with labor, not just the Luna-Saunders Agreement, but all work rules in general. There had been a phenomenal wage settlement in 1972 that provided a 42 percent wage increase over forty-two months. Whether or not it was deserved, it came during the Nixon administration's wage-price controls and was approved by the pay board unanimously. Federal guidelines allowed a maximum increase of only 5.5 percent unless existing wage scales were clearly out of line with other industries. Even the private-industry representative on the pay board, Virgil Day, a vice president of General Electric, publicly defended the 42 percent settlement as proper.[13]

Of course, this made PC's reorganization more difficult. It had to improve productivity fast. Its record at this was the worst of any major railroad in the country. If wage increases were the catalyst that finally forced action, they were a blessing in disguise.[14]

In management's defense, the Luna-Saunders Agreement, at least on paper, had been overly generous. It went beyond the legitimate purpose of easing the transition from a productive job in railroading to a productive job at something else. It was—on paper—privately financed welfare-for-life to those whose jobs had been rendered permanently obsolete. No enterprise, public or private, could be saddled with that kind of unproductivity and produce beneficial results at the other end. As for the work rules problem, this is not the place to discuss a complicated issue that had been brewing for a long time. Seven government studies agreed that existing work rules forced railroads to hire unnecessary labor.[15] The Penn Central, in other words, was not just barking at a straw man.

But there was another side to the story. Fair or not, all railroads operated under essentially the same rules. It was not labor's fault that PC had failed to make use of its manpower to its best advantage. Second, the Luna-Saunders Agreement was outrageous on paper only, for as was discussed in the last chapter, the railroad was using recalled labor in productive functions. Finally, the railroad was not so poor that it was time to beg from its employees. Railroad credit had been used for nonrailroad acquisitions that were beyond the jurisdiction of the bankruptcy court because they were neatly protected by the device of the holding company. The capitalists, in other words, had saved the juicy plums for themselves and were telling labor it had to make sacrifices to keep the dross afloat. As long as the executives, who had provided such remarkably bad leadership so far, got big fat salaries and pensions, labor felt no compulsion to make things easier.

Labor was not rigid on the work rules question, either. The Brotherhood of Railway and Airline Clerks, for example, negotiated several changes the railroads had been seeking for a long time, but PC chose not to take advantage of this, which prompted President L.E. Dennis to read a scathing denunciation of PC ineptitude before the House Commerce Committee in 1973.[16] Al Chesser of the United Transportation Union (successor to many of the operating brotherhoods) indicated he was willing to negotiate on rules, including the touchy fireman-on-diesel issue. He agreed to a drastic revision of rules on the Reading and Jersey Central. He agreed to a massive crew reduction on the Penn Central. The only thing he would not tolerate was unilateral action by the railroad.[17]

That was why the trustees' decision to promulgate new work rules unilaterally in February 1973 looked as though it, too, was contrived to accomplish something bigger than the removal of one brakeman on freight trains. The UTU struck. Like any railroad strike, this one could cost a lot people a lot of money if it went on for long. The big shippers got in touch with their favorite congressmen and the strike was aborted. But in stopping the strike, Congress made itself responsible for the PC's problems. It ordered the Department of Transportation to devise a comprehensive plan to restructure the northeastern railroads in 45 days. That wasn't much time.

3

Despite its troubles, the giant had an instinct for self-preservation and hovered like a vulture over the carcasses of its bankrupt rivals. It advocated the liquidation of the Jersey Central, with PC to inherit the choice, densely trafficked segments of that carrier's lines. In response to a suggestion from the ICC that it coordinate operations with the B&M across western Massachusets, its only reply was a demand for the B&M to abandon its line west of Ayer, Massachusetts, robbing that carrier of its greatest asset, its low-level crossing of the Berkshires through the Hoosac Tunnel. It advocated liquidation of the Lehigh Valley, noting that other railroads could easily meet any need for railroad transportation in the Lehigh's area. (Lehigh caustically noted the same could be said for Penn Central.)[18]

The little carriers, however, had an inner strength that PC had lost. They could merge, and perhaps make something out of the very device PC had blown so badly. The idea of a New England unification was reincarnated, this time with Fredrick Dumaine as the protagonist. Dumaine had been president of the New Haven in the 1950s until he had been ousted in a proxy fight. After that, he occupied himself with Amoskeag, a Boston-based investment firm, and with the Delaware & Hudson Company, the holding company that controlled the D&H railroad, of which he was the largest single stockholder. He loved railroads and did a stint at the helm of the D&H just on the eve of the inclusion crisis. He wanted D&H to stay out of Dereco and fought the Harriman interests who wanted it in. He thought D&H could build a better empire on its own by linking up with the independent lines of Maine, Maine Central, and Bangor & Aroostook. He was in touch with the owners of the B&A, the Bangor Punta Company, the corporate remnant of the Punta Alegre Sugar Company that had been restructured as a conglomerate after the nationalization of Cuban sugar.

After D&H entered Dereco, Dumaine's Amoskeag Company bought a large block of Maine Central stock and then bought the Bangor & Aroostook from Bangor Punta. Immediately, he got in touch with the trustees of the Boston & Maine, who were delighted that their company might be reorganized under Amoskeag's tutelage. The ICC administrative law judge, Victor von Rintelin, was impressed by Amoskeag's enthusiasm. In what came to be called the von Rintelin Report, he urged New England unification.[19]

But Amoskeag did not control Maine Central; in fact, those shares it owned had to be put in trust. At the helm of Maine Central was E. Spencer Miller, who wanted to be the kingpin of New England railroading himself, ever since he organized the New England conferences of the 1950s. He may even have seen himself as the William Wiggins of Edward Hungerford's *A Railroad for Tomorrow*, for he put forth a plan for an American Railroad Corporation that was remarkably similar to Hungerford's "United States Railroad."[20] He accused Amoskeag of being nothing but a stalking horse for the Canadian Pacific. (Amoskeag owned 25,000 shares of CPR, and Bangor & Aroostook was diverting 24,000 cars a year of westbound wood pulp from the Maine Central to the CPR.)

Meanwhile, Reading, Jersey Central, and Lehigh Valley were thinking about re-creating the old Reading anthracite empire of the 1890s. In those days, control of the three railroads meant a near monopoly of the distribution of anthracite coal, and Reading's attempt to control the others was broken up forcibly. Lehigh wound up in the PRR sphere, Reading and

Jersey Central in the B&O's. It suited PRR and B&O to keep their little orphans apart, but now bankruptcy had broken old ties.

It was not going to be easy to simultaneously reorganize three railroads whose affairs were in serious disarray. But studies were made, state authorities seemed responsive, and income-based reorganization into a Mid-Atlantic Railroad Corporation (MARC) seemed feasible. With merger in the offing, Jersey Central abandoned all operations in Pennsylvania, turning its traffic over to the Lehigh Valley as far as the New Jersey border, ending one of the most sadly duplicative operations in the country. A new run-through service between Potomac Yard in northern Virginia, over the B&O, Reading, Lehigh Valley, D&H, and B&M, to Portland, Maine, provided a new, fast, back-door route into northern New England and was a great success.[21] Revived Lehigh Valley run-throughs, the *Apollos* with the N&W, and later another with the C&O, were successful also.

Erie Lackawanna was sounded out about joining the new MARC. The long-haul to Chicago would enhance the viability of the otherwise short-haul railroad, and superior EL routes to Buffalo would permit the abandonment of most Lehigh trackage in western New York. The EL did not jump, but took the idea under consideration. So did the D&H, whose future was doomed if it were surrounded by a PC monopoly. The D&H was the link between the MARC-EL system and the Amoskeag System, and could wind up the keystone of a grand merger.

Regardless of the plans for MARC, Erie Lackawanna was looking forward to an income-based reorganization without all the drastic abandonments PC seemed to think were the salvation of railroading. It identified a few lines that could be dropped, but they added up to only 4 percent of mileage.[22] Traffic held up well, new locomotives and freight cars were bought, and Buffalo's Bison Yard was busy day and night with movements from many railroads. The N&W cut all ties with EL after bankruptcy, and John Fishwick, who returned to Roanoke as N&W's president, denounced anyone that might be interested in it. But EL was healthy enough to have some suitors. The C&O seemed impressed, and there were rumors that Santa Fe was taking a long, hard look. Imagine that. None of this was good news to Penn Central.

4

When annual losses of $100 million became the norm at Penn Central, and the railroad began to resemble a junkie living on regular fixes of money from the government, the old creditors began to dissociate themselves from the trustees' easy-step plan for revival. The new loans (trustees' certificates) were senior to the old securities. That was why the creditors began to talk ominously of the "rights of capital," which meant liquidating the railroad.

Whether or not capital had the right to liquidate was not clear. It had invested freely and taken risks freely. It knew that railroads were not ordinary enterprises, but special ones, "clothed in a public interest." In the days of canals, it was assumed the providing of transportation was a responsibility of the state. By the time the railroad came along, there were private investors willing to build them, and the state conferred a privilege on capital, in the railroad charters, to go ahead. Individual investors were free to sell their railroad securities, but capital in general was not free to shut the railroad down when it got tired of it. That was an implicit part of the original bargain. Had it been otherwise, the state would never have delegated the responsibility of building railroads in the first place. [23]

The coming of regulation had brought some changes to this, however. If the state was going to set the price of railroad service, if it wanted capital to continue to finance railroads, it implicitly had to guarantee a return. In *Brooks-Scanlon Company* v. *Railroad Commission of Louisiana*, the court ruled a railroad could not be required to remain in operation when all hope of profit was gone.[24]

There had been no governing precedent for the threatened abandonment of the New Haven Railroad, however, for no railroad in such straits before had been as vital to as many people. Even after NH entered the Penn Central, NH creditors continued to litigate for more money, and in 1968, convinced federal judges they deserved it.[25] Judge Robert Anderson in U.S. District Court in Connecticut added that the continued erosion of the creditors' estate by the forced continued operation of the railroad was unconstitutional. In its review, the Supreme Court did not exactly refute the judge, but reiterated the position it had taken in the *Penn Central Merger* case that the rights of bondholders command respect, but do not demand Procrustean measures.[26] But it also awarded the NH bondholders $28 million more, which they never received because of the PC's bankruptcy a week later. But now, PC's security holders were putting a great deal of stock in Judge Anderson's opinion, insisting that liquidation was constitutional, and imminent.

If capital was finding railroads a poor investment, it was obviously finding litigation a good one. Its lawyers were filling up thousands of pages of transcript in Judge Fullam's court, the index alone getting thicker than a Philadelphia phone book. The *New York Times* untactfully pointed out that if anything was eroding the PC's estate, it was legal fees. One day, before Judge Fullam's court, there were eighteen lawyers, each representing some vested interest, each reciting at length from mind-dulling statements. A reporter watching the show recalled a scene from Charles Dickens's *Bleak House,* when the law firm of Chizzle, Mizzle, Drizzle, Blowers and Tangle was sorting out the case of *Jarndyce v. Jarndyce.* "Eighteen of Mr. Tangle's friends, each armed with a little summary of 1800 sheets, bobbed up like 18 hammers in a pianoforte, made 18 bows, and dropped into their 18 places of obscurity.''[27] Lawyers were not amused.

If the Penn Central was liquidated, no one knew exactly what that was going to mean. It was assumed solvent railroads, the N&W or the Chessie, or maybe the Canadian National, would pick up important segments. But none of them were jumping at the chance. As for the rest of the PC, it might wind up as downtown parking lots or extra pasture in a farmer's field. It seemed incredible. To preserve the rights of big creditors, a national heritage in the form of irreplaceable rights-of-way might be allowed to slip away.

Nationalization was suddenly a very real alternative. The capitalists who precipitated the crisis deplored the idea on ideological grounds, but probably wanted it to bail them out, and hoped the threat of liquidation would trigger it. Nobody was talking about expropriation after all. In the event of nationalization, investors expected to get top dollar on their old securities from the government, something they could no longer expect from an income-based reorganization. But if capitalists were ready to make their peace with nationalization, was the American public?

It was still fashionable to denounce nationalization as socialism, which everyone knew was un-American. Some senators were beginning to come to grips with it, however. A staff study for Senator Hartke's Subcommittee on Surface Transportation recommended it. A forthright, even eloquent document, it said simply that existing private and public institutions had failed to provide a stable and adequate rail service and something radically different was needed. Nixon's Department of Transportation put out a staff paper which noted that long before the world even had socialist governments, nationalized railways had been the hallmark of conservative governments, as in Germany, Austria-Hungary, and Tsarist Russia before World War I. The more liberal the state, the less it had interfered with railroads. Canada, Great Britain, and France nationalized railroads, not for ideological reasons, but because those railroads collapsed under their own weight.[28] In fact, the circumstances leading to the creation of the Canadian National Railways seemed remarkably similar to what was happening in the northeastern United States.[29]

But the debate on whether to nationalize took place in that strange netherworld that was the Nixon administration. It wanted to appear as the great defender of rugged individualism in business, even as the chief executive grasped for more arbitrary power by government. It was sensitive to the interests of the South and West, where railroads were not in trouble and voters retained their macho fascination for big automobiles. It was an administration that had promised fiscal responsibility for moral, if not really economic, reasons, but was running up the biggest peacetime deficits in history, which a crash bailout of eastern railroads was not going to help.

Sometime in 1972, the trustees realized a traditional reorganization was impossible. The problem was how to convince a majority in Congress that the crisis was more real than all the other railroad crises of years gone by. The best way was to scare Congress with a super-crisis. The easy-step plan of salvation was recanted, and a requiem-like report was filed with Judge Fullam early in 1973. He responded with a dramatic order: a reasonable plan of reorganization must be filed with him by the end of June, or he would order liquidation on July 2.[30] That, together with the crisis over work rules that had prompted Congress to issue its forty-five-day order for a plan of reorganization, meant things were moving to a climax.

The Department of Transportation was the agent of the Nixon administration's paranoia about preserving the facade of private enterprise without the government appearing to put up the money. So it took up the trustees' easy-step plan. The railroad would revive by itself if all the branch lines were chopped off. It suggested the ICC be stripped of all power to stop this. Rivalry between the two government loci of transportation power was coming to a head. When DOT was created in 1966, it absorbed some thirty-one agencies, including the Coast Guard and the Panama Canal Company, but not the ICC. It was a burgeoning bureaucracy with an insatiable appetite for money and office space, made all the sadder because it had made so little visible progress in planning for, or coordinating, rival modes of transportation. When it first appeared before Congress in the northeastern rail crisis, it had done no thinking or investigating on its own, which had left Senator Hartke sputtering as a result.[31] Now, by echoing the trustees' contrived gimmicks, it was putting forth a disarmingly inexpensive plan for salvation that still reflected no thinking of its own.

The ICC had fumbled a lot of things during the merger movement, and had been inexcusably asleep for the onset of the Penn Central crisis. Everyone picked at it. It was called upon daily to make decisions which were always unpopular with somebody. Rare was the person in transportation who did not have some ICC horror story—which they would recite as their comprehensive analysis of the evils of regulation. If these same people had received many favorable rulings over the years, they never said so. The ICC knew a lot of people were gunning for it. Perhaps knowing judgment was at hand, the commission suddenly seemed self-conscious. If these were to be its last hours, they must be glorious.

Whereas DOT formulated its plans behind closed doors, with faceless staffers consulting unrevealed interested parties, the ICC at least tried to go about its planning in an open way. It solicited the opinions of all who cared to respond. It insisted that copies of everyone's statement be distributed to everyone else who responded. Duplicating costs and postage fees tended to close this procedure to individuals, but still, in the rising antidemocratic tide of Nixon's Washington, the old procedures that once seemed so cumbersome were now like a breath of democratic fresh air.

But the ICC's counterpart to the DOT studies, Ex Parte 293, *The Northeast Rail Investigation,* was doomed from the start. Some key parties, like Penn Central and N&W and Chessie, figured the real decisions were going to be made elsewhere, as if the transition of power had already taken place, and filed only cursory, even insulting, responses. Like any participatory procedure, this one invited disagreements which no plan could reconcile. Furthermore, time was running out on this time-consuming procedure. Quaker Oats, for example, complained that before the rebuttals were even due, the commission had gone ahead and drawn up a plan, so it wasn't going to waste any more of its time with this.

The ICC insisted it was not possible to dismantle vast sections of the eastern railroads without doing violence to the industrial fabric of the region. Some slimming down might be acceptable, but not mass abandonments all at once. Furthermore, it said, it was wishful thinking to suggest these railroads could be revitalized without massive financial aid. Funds for basic capital investment, it thought, could come from a 1 percent tax on all transportation. That brought howls from many quarters, but it was closer to reality than DOT's projections.

Congress had muffed everything it touched with regard to railroads so far. It had had fun exposing all the corporate rot in Penn Central; it had done some fine studies, most of them never acted upon; but when it came to doing something, it had shown no more imagination than to provide band-aid loan guarantees. Hartke, though sometimes described as Capitol Hill's expert in the railroad crisis, never demonstrated that his interest went beyond the fate of lines in his home state (Indiana).

The House Commerce Committee listened to all the plans in the spring of 1973. It heard the DOT plan and it heard the ICC plan.[32] Senator Saxbe of Ohio introduced legislation to study the feasibility of merging all railroads into one private corporation.[33] Senator Hartke was ready with a nationalization bill in the Senate. Labor testified, shippers testified, state utility commissions testified, but Congress couldn't seem to come to grips with any of it, and liquidation day grew nearer.

5

It was said the idea was Frank Barnett's. He was president of the Union Pacific. It was said the law was written by William McDonald.[34] He was the Union Pacific's general counsel. The UP didn't want to lose the 25 percent of its traffic that it sent to or received from the Northeast. It didn't want a free-for-all of southern and western roads grabbing for pieces of the northeastern net in case there should be a liquidation. Barnett was a director of the First National City Bank of New York, which was stuck with $120 million in PC securities, but that was probably not even relevant at a time like this. It was not easy to get a congressman to sponsor a bill that came directly from the legal department of the Union Pacific, but at last Congressman Dick Shoup of Montana said he would do it, and when it seemed like a workable bill, as good as any of the others around, Congressman Brock Adams of Washington and four others on the House Subcommittee on Transportation and Aeronautics joined him. It was call the Shoup-Adams bill.[35]

It would first establish a nonprofit, federally chartered corporation, eventually called the United States Railway Association, with a board of directors that included the secretaries of transportation and the treasury, the chairman of the ICC, and representatives of solvent railroads, creditors of the bankrupts, large shippers, small shippers, labor, and state and local government agencies.[36] It was to plan the configuration of a slimmed-down system and arrange the financing—which was crucial to the whole plan and the reason for creating this buffer agency in the first place. Like "Fannie Mae," the Federal National Mortgage Assistance Association, it would be able to issue loans and loan guarantees without being subject to the national debt ceiling and was thus beyond the veto power of the Office of the Management of the Budget. "Off-budget financing" it was called, and it was the only way to get around the Nixon administration's growing hysteria about its own inability to control spending. Up to $1.5 billion in loan guarantees were authorized, half to acquire the assets of the bankrupt companies and half for rehabilitation. Additional sums were earmarked for various forms of interim assistance. Loans could also go (1) to states or local communities that wished to buy and keep operating the lines designated for abandonment, (2) to Amtrak, and (3) to desperate railroads in other parts of the country, like the Katy or Rock Island.

When the planning was done, operation of the new system would go to Conrail, the Consolidated Rail Corporation, which, with this handsome start, would hopefully become a profitable enterprise. It was to be a private corporation, chartered in a state, headquartered in Philadelphia. Its stock would be parceled out to the security owners of the old railroads. They would choose Conrail's directors, except that so long as more than 50 percent of its outstanding debt was either owed to the government or guaranteed by it, a majority of the directors would be appointed by the president with the advice and consent of the Senate.

Negotiations with labor were no problem when the government paid the bills (up to $250 million of them through the Railroad Retirement Board). Employees could be transferred anywhere on any of the bankrupts that joined Conrail, as long as their moving expenses were paid and they were not required to cross craft lines. That was labor's main concession. In return, so long as a man had five years' seniority, he was protected with allowances that guaranteed his standard of living for life. In theory, a senior man who was laid off but remained available for work could get up to $2,500 a month to age sixty-five with full pension thereafter.[37] In practice, senior men were required to bump junior men wherever possible, and most of the junior men who would actually be vulnerable to layoff had less than five years' seniority. A man receiving a monthly allowance had to remain available for work and had to move if asked to do so. So in practice, more people were going to elect a lump-sum settlement, which was generous enough, but not like $2,500 a month.

Nevertheless, labor had been treated very well. When railroad men were out of a job, they were not going to have to scramble at the unemployment office like everyone else. Even some of labor's supporters winced at the extent to which the agreement insulated railroad workers from economic and technological change. But management had done the same thing for itself. It had built a welfare state with long-term contracts and fringe benefits and big pensions. Did those who begrudged a laid-off worker an allowance complain equally about the executives' stock options and expense accounts?

As major bills go, Congress did not put a lot of work into this one. Union Pacific supplied the bill. First National City Bank supplied the financial data. The United Transportation Union supplied the labor contracts. Committee work was minimal. So was floor debate. Support from the South and West was whipped into line with a tart reminder that x thousands of freight cars a day rolled into the Northeast with products from other regions. A largely disinterested House passed the bill in November 1973. There was some wrangling in the conference committee, but a largely disinterested Senate, already melting away for the Chrismas holiday, passed it in December. The administration put on a blustery show of defiance, claiming it was too costly a burden on the taxpayer (which it wasn't—banks were going to supply most of the capital), but Nixon signed it early in January. Such was the Regional Rail Reorganization Act of 1973.

6

Congress prescribed a rigid timetable for the studies necessary to put the law into effect. The U.S. Railway Association was to have an elaborate "Preliminary System Plan" for the complete restructuring of the railroads ready within 300 days after the act became law. In the meantime, within 45 days, DOT was to work up a pre-preliminary report to lay out the basic direction of future planning.

Admittedly, forty-five days was too short a time for meaningful research. But like the Ripley Report of 1921, this first blossom of the planners' minds would probably be the most powerful influence on the second. Later plans might correct the details, but the basic assumptions, good or bad, would remain intact. As such, this first report, *Rail Services in the Midwest and*

Northeast Region, was very important and profoundly disturbing.

It clung tenaciously to the idea that railroad mileage had to be ruthlessly slashed. This was the battle cry of the Penn Central trustees. The causes, if they were real, must have been coming on for years, but no private management had recognized them until just a few months before. The DOT made no attempt to analyze if this were the correct solution. Its only effort was to cite the declining percentage of traffic carried by rail. No mention was made of the fact that total tonnage carried by rail had increased dramatically in the 1960s and early 1970s. Instead, the statement was simply repeated, over and over, in the report, in hearings, and to the press that students of transportation agreed that slashing mileage was the proper solution.[38]

The DOT collected all of its data from the railroads, doing no research of its own. It took a 1 percent sample of waybills from the year 1969, and from this claimed to have analyzed the basic traffic flows. Then it took the number of cars originated and terminated at each station in the year 1972, and from that determined which stations were entitled to continued service. Stations that originated and terminated less than seventy-five cars a year were dropped immediately. For the rest, a formula, developed for DOT by R.L. Banks Associates, was used to determine the potential future profitability of continued operation. It balanced traffic density against cost of operation per mile. Only if a line met the "DOT Upper Criteria," which meant a 90 percent chance of earning a profit, or about ninety cars per year per mile, would the line be retained. (This contrasted with a long-standing rule-of-thumb used by the ICC in abandonment cases of 34 cars per mile.) The DOT cited the possible fallacies of the Banks formula and then proceeded to use it.

The report was an elaborate thing, with a two-color cover on each of its three volumes, with detailed maps of each of the 202 zones in the region, each with many lines ominously labeled "potentially excess." When it was issued, the ICC, through its newly created bureau, the Rail Services Planning Office, conducted hearings to find out what the public thought of DOT's handiwork. First, the ICC found the interested public had been virtually unable to get copies of it, even though Congress had supposedly provided for as wide a distribution as possible. Some people were quite upset about this because they knew the report contained recommendations that could ruin them. Next, the ICC found the public thought the report was sloppy, or worse.

1. Determinations for abandonment were based on carloads only. No account was taken of whether more tonnage actually passed over the line in fewer, but larger-capacity cars such as the Big John hoppers. No account was taken of the commodities in those cars or of the revenues they produced. One carload of pharmaceuticals, for example, might produce more revenue than thirty cars of gravel.

2. There was no account taken of what branchline traffic contributed to overall system revenue. Ten cars coming down a branch and moving 1,000 miles over the mainline could produce more revenue than 100 cars coming down a branch and moving only ten miles on the mainline.
3. Since Congress mandated that any private group or local government willing to operate lines designated for abandonment be allowed to do so, no account was made of the fact that shortline railroads normally took a substantial division (cut) of the through rate on each car. Hence, Conrail might be better off operating some marginal branches itself than having them operated as shortlines.
4. The DOT's basic data, the 1969 1 percent waybill sample and the 1972 origin-termination figures were narrow and misleading. There had been substantial changes in the volume of traffic on some lines since the mid-1960s, frequently dependent on the ups and downs of Penn Central service. The use of figures for any one year, rather than averages over many years, could be deceptive. The 1972 figures, for example, showed little or no traffic on certain lines in New York and Pennsylvania, not because there was no demand for their services, but because they were washed out by Hurricane Agnes and never replaced.
5. The DOT study was studded with errors, including the designation of lines as potentially excess when in fact they met the "DOT Upper Crieteria"; the designation of lines as required for service when in fact they had already been abandoned; and the recommendation of continuing service at certain stations, while at the same time suggesting that the tracks over which most of their traffic flowed be abandoned.[39]

Applying just a single test, whether a line could earn a profit all by itself, raised the deepest questions about the new panacea. If the concept were carried to its logical conclusion, there would be no excess capacity on the northeastern railroads. But excess capacity was essential. It allowed for business expansion and national emergencies (of which Hurricane Agnes should have been a visible reminder). A lack of it was cited as one of the great economic bottlenecks of the Soviet Union. It also permitted "down time" so maintenance crews could do their work; lack of provision for this had made a bottleneck of PC's River Division.

Was profit and loss all that mattered? Once abandoned, a right-of-way was likely to be gone forever. At least, some thought, a "rail-bank" ought to be created to insure preservation of the right-of-way, even if the lines were abandoned. But even if the government did have to subsidize certain lines, might it not get more money back from shippers and shippers' employees in tax revenues than would be lost if the line were abandoned?

In short, the DOT report was either a set of poor conclusions, based on incorrect data and assembled under bad assumptions, or else it was a deliberate blueprint for the destruction of the northeastern railroads, which some people thought was not surprising from the highway and oil and aerospace interests that financed and otherwise dominated the Nixon administration.

7

With the DOT report providing a dubious kind of guide, the U.S. Railway Association began work on the Preliminary System Plan. Perfect plans had eluded everyone for fifty years, and this was going to be no exception.

Congress wanted rail competition for the Conrail behemoth, and presumably the solvent roads in the East would provide it—N&W via the Dereco Roads and Chessie through the Reading-Jersey Central. The N&W and C&O were vague on what they would do, but were clear on what they would not do—which was to acquire any routes east of a line between Albany and Harrisburg (the firewall, as John Fishwick called it). East of the firewall lay some of the most complex terminal trackage in America and, said the solvents, no railroad could serve it profitably. If that were true, it kicked a prop from under the rosy predictions that Conrail would realize a net operating income by 1978.

If the solvents wouldn't participate, the preliminary plan suggested the Pennsylvania and New York Central might be un-merged into Conrail North and South. If that couldn't be done, perhaps the Mid-Atlantic (MARC) group of Reading, Jersey Central, and Lehigh Valley could be coupled with Erie Lackawanna (MARC-EL), perhaps with trackage rights into Cincinnati and St. Louis. This was confused by the announcement that EL, along with Boston & Maine, would reorganize separately and not participate in Conrail. So in regard to overall structure, the preliminary plan was not a plan, but a disconnected set of options.

As in the DOT report, the real controversy swirled about the "light density" lines. The preliminary plan remedied some of the DOT report's worst shortcomings—it took into account tonnage and revenue, for example, rather than just car loadings. But it still relied entirely on information supplied by the railroads, notably questionnaires filled out by local supervisory people on the cost and frequency of train operations. These were estimates or guesses, and the association did no field work of its own to check them. The ICC went out in the field, however, and concluded that branchline costs had been overstated—by as much as 34 percent—and revenues understated. In estimating the time it took a crew to do branchline work, for example, a five-minute error, when multiplied over an entire year, worked out to more than $1,000 in the final calculation. After getting its data from the railroads, the association turned the analysis over to consulting firms whose clients were normally the railroads. Over $16.25 million was paid in consulting fees.[40]

Branchlines were still required to show potential profit on their own, taking no account of the revenue they generated for the system as a whole. Take the Cairo branch, as it was known in Illinois, the old NYC line from Chicago to the Little Egypt coal fields. Whether this was a branch or mainline was a matter of subtle definition. It generated traffic only at its two

ends and hauled it better than three hundred miles in between. By dividing it
into segments, it was easy to justify the abandonment of the middle portions. If, on the other hand, account was taken of the traffic passing over
them, rather than just originating or terminating on them, they would have
met the test to remain in Conrail with ease—at least so said the State of
Illinois. "What they have done," said State Representative Garmisa of
Illinois, "is take the front of the line and the end of the line, and it would be
just like your water hose without the center in between."[41]

Even the method by which lines were selected for study was open to criticism. Lines labeled "potentially excess" in the DOT report were studied
automatically, even if that report had been almost universally condemned
as a misuse of statistical evidence. So were lines labeled by the railroads as
"out of service," whether that was due to lack of demand or Hurricane
Agnes. Once identified as a potential loser, the line had to meet a test of
profitability—roughly net revenues against salvage value—which the ICC
thought was an unreasonable burden to put on any railroad. Since no railroad earned what was normally considered a "reasonable return on investment," there was probably not a segment of track in the country that could
meet this test.

The ICC did not question the association's motives, but it questioned its
attitude. "From the beginning," said the ICC, "the Association asked itself
'how many of these lines can we get rid of,' rather than 'how much could
they contribute to Conrail?'" Even Penn Central, which insisted its
bankruptcy was caused by light-density lines and not by mismanagement or
miscalculation in the merger, admitted these lines lost only $38 million, or
17 percent of its total losses. The ICC calculated that they accounted for
only $17.5 million, or 7 percent of total losses.[42] So at best, eliminating
them could solve only a fraction of the overall problem.

That raised another serious problem—the potential profitability of Conrail. The association assumed the merger of the bankrupts would solve
operational inefficiencies. It never had before. It assumed rate increases
would compensate for inflation and wage increases. They never had before.
In fact, they often drove business away and resulted in a net loss. The association assumed tonnage on Conrail would grow by 1.4 percent a year,
largely through increases in coal shipments. In fact, coal tonnage on Conrail was declining. The association projected an operating ratio of 71.7
percent, as good as the most efficient railroads in the country, but offered
no indication of how this was going to be achieved. The association said
Conrail would use a concept known as "modified betterment accounting"
(which capitalized maintenance and rehabilitation expenses), a device that
inflated income and deflated expenses. Lehigh Valley said that if it had used
modified betterment accounting in 1974, it would have shown a profit of
$200,000 instead of a loss of $5.8 million.[43]

The plan, in other words, was totally pessimistic about branches and totally optimistic about everything else. It was a political document, meant to show there were easy solutions that were not going to cost a lot of money. It was the same panacea mentality on which the mergers had been based.

8

Despite its kick in the teeth from the N&W, it looked for a time as though Erie Lackawanna were going to make it on its own. Then the recession hit in the fall of 1974. For EL, it was the most rapid decline in its history, its fortunes falling from normal to rock bottom in a period of three weeks. It was said that over the Thanksgiving weekend, a blanket of snow lay undisturbed on the mainline between Scranton and Binghamton for a period of forty-eight hours, indicating that no trains had passed over the line. On January 5, 1975, EL notified the association that it would be unable to reorganize on its own and would enter Conrail. This meant the preliminary plan, its ink hardly dry, was out of date, its financial projections invalid.

Meanwhile, the Justice Department was preparing a case against a monopolistic Conrail, using roughly the same argument it presented in the merger cases that competition was desirable and required by law.[44] Once EL crashed and burned, it was more important than ever to breathe some kind of life into the MARC-EL scheme. Unhappily, no one was too optimistic, save perhaps the trustees of the Lehigh Valley, who were fighting tenaciously to save their hapless little company. John Fishwick said MARC-EL would preserve nothing but the facade of competition in the face of the Conrail juggernaut. The ICC thought MARC-EL offered too much competition, at least in the West, where its lines to Chicago, Cincinnati, and St. Louis would needlessly compete with N&W and Chessie. Both arguments were familiar from the merger days.

By the time Congress got around to holding hearings on the preliminary plan, something of even more gravity was in the wind, namely, that the administration, now the Ford administration, was out to undermine the whole idea. "A Ford aide," reported the *Wall Street Journal* one morning while the hearings were going on, recommended "controlled liquidation" of the northeastern railroads, which meant auctioning off the valuable lines to the solvent roads or Amtrak (if it could come up with the money) and junking the rest. Secretary of Transportation William Coleman was questioned relentlessly by congressmen. Was he that aide? Did he prefer controlled liquidation to Conrail? Was he personally working against the congressional plan? What was DOT's position? Did DOT speak for the administration? Did the administration know what it was doing? Answers were not altogether clear.[45]

Three days later, Coleman went to Philadelphia and said "the nation's profitable railroad companies appeared willing to buy substantially all of the Penn Central and other bankrupt rail lines." He said such a sale would save U.S. taxpayers "at least $10 billion." The article in the *Philadelphia Inquirer* by John Holland continued:

It was two days ago that Coleman first proposed the sale of the bankrupt lines, but until yesterday, no federal official had attempted to predict how much of the bankrupt system could be sold.

"Somebody got the message because they're coming in to see me," Coleman said, although he did not identify the prospective buyers. . . .

He added: "I think it's a hell of a way to run a railroad when a public official who has never had experience in the railroad business has to tell the railroads how to get out of the box.

"If it can be done, I think it will save the American people at least $10 billion."

Coleman also had some advice for the rail companies thinking about buying the insolvent lines: "The first two or three guys at the gate will get a good deal. Those who come in and do it will get the profits and the rest of them will lose out."

Coleman, suitably, was in town to receive the annual award of the Philadelphia Council for Economic Education, which yearly cites a Philadelphian who promotes "the precepts and objectives of the private enterprise system."[46]

"I must say," said Congressman Fred Rooney (D-Pennsylvania), "that Chessie and N&W, the two railroads who have been reported as interested by the Administration, are not interested according to my information." The N&W's John Fishwick and Chessie's Hays Watkins verified that when they testified. Penn Central trustees told the committee they had held a big meeting of all their friends on the solvent railroads, including the Canadian carriers, and held up a big map of the railroad and asked which lines the others might be interested in. The answer was very few of them, and none east of the firewall.[47]

So controlled liquidation looked like another administration pipe dream, which was gambling, desperately it appeared, that private enterprise might still fly in, like Captain Marvel, and save the day. Even if the solvents had a desire, said John Fishwick, they didn't have the resources. Yet by indicating it was not giving what had now become the congressional plan its full support, the administration could almost make failure a self-fulfilling prophecy. If Conrail was treated like Amtrak, with appropriations today, impoundments tomorrow, and budget cuts the day after, long-range planning would be impossible and the thing would be a gigantic turkey at Congress's doorstep.

9

As prescribed by the Conrail Act, the association proceeded now to draw up the final system plan, presumably to incorporate the criticisms of the preliminary plan. The final plan was presented to Congress in September 1975. The *Washington Star* had reported a titanic struggle between ICC Chairman George Stafford and Secretary Coleman, both on the association board, over the issue of light-density lines.[48] Coleman was in favor of wholesale abandonment, while Stafford insisted it was a self-defeating remedy. Stafford had lost, and the abandonment program was going to be pushed vigorously. Communities would be given a two-year notice of intent to discontinue service, during which time they might find ways to operate them as short lines if they wished. Total savings were estimated at $33 million a year. Coleman said flatly that moving freight over these lines at 10 mph was not economical and that highways could do it better.[49]

The nagging feeling that the project was underfinanced was not laid to rest. Discrepancy between the association's estimates (now $2 billion) and the ICC's ($8 billion) were great. The tenacity with which the association clung to the lower figure had political implications. It allowed the public to believe it was going to get a super railroad, even with high-speed passenger trains, but with a budget-minded administration keeping an eagle eye on costs. For immediate political gain, it was insinuated this money was going to come from the taxpayers' pockets, which it wasn't. Most of it would come from private sources, guaranteed by the government. Money would come out of the taxpayers' pockets only if the whole idea were a flop. Building faults into the plan that would cause it to flop, such as providing it a budget so skinny, in inflationary times, that it could not rehabilitate its facilities properly, was the cruelest thing that could be done to the taxpayers.

10

With the announcement of Erie Lackawanna's inability to reorganize, the MARC-EL idea was dropped, although it was not certain it was given a fighting chance. The MARC partners, Reading, Jersey Central, and Lehigh Valley, wanted hard evidence that it was not viable. They extracted a promise from the association to do a joint study using the association's data and computers to see which was preferable, a unified Conrail or a Conrail competing with a MARC-EL. The agreement, said Robert Haldeman, trustee of the Lehigh Valley, was that we would see all the final computer printouts. If the competitive structure were worse than the monopoly structure, we would drop the whole line of argument.

We got to see the MARC-EL projections, he said, and they "were very, very good." But we were never shown the Conrail projections. That was in mid-May (1975). On May 29, the association board met, with William Scranton, a MARC-EL defender, absent, and rejected MARC-EL either for

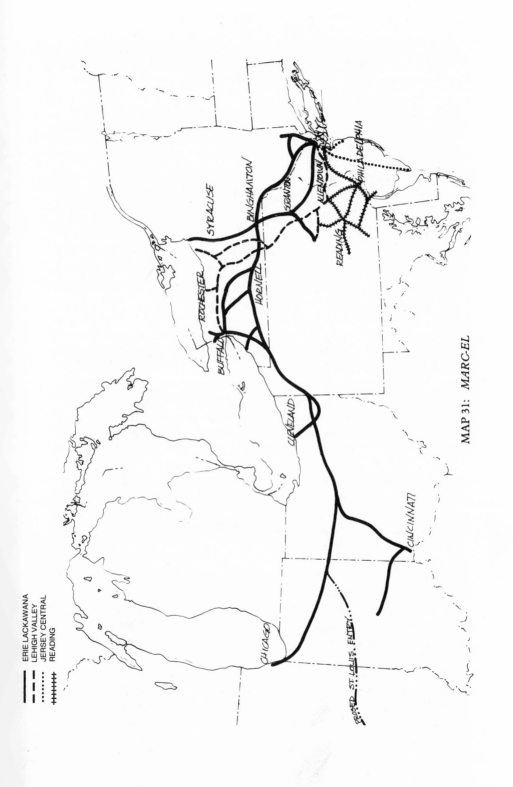

ERIE LACKAWANNA
LEHIGH VALLEY
JERSEY CENTRAL
READING

MAP 31: *MARC-EL*

primary recommendation or fallback. We assumed the Conrail projections, which they still refused to give us, in violation of their promise, must have been simply amazing. When the ICC finally obtained the figures for us, "we were shocked." The MARC-EL showed a much greater potential for profit than Conrail. "We asked the Association how their board had reached this decision based on the figures we had in hand. Their response, apart from shock and concern that we had somehow obtained material that they considered confidential, only vaguely alluded to 'other considerations' which would be published in the Final System Plan."[50]

Grand Trunk Western said they, too, had found it difficult to get information or explanations from the association. The New York Dock Railway called the association "secretive." Pittsburgh & Lake Erie said the association's closed-door decisions were inexplicable, like the one which gave P&LE trackage rights to Astabula, Ohio, but refused to allow it to interchange with the N&W, the only reason for such trackage rights. Here was a publicly created body, deliberating in secret over matters that had no legitimate reason to be secret. This was not the way government planning in a democracy was supposed to operate.

The decision to drop MARC-EL would either result in a monopoly for Conrail, or enrich a big private company, namely, Chessie, which had been induced to pick up Erie Lackawanna lines east of Akron (but not the commuter lines east of the firewall). The arrangement was sweetened with the Reading's choice freight lines in the Schuylkill Valley, and the New York Central's coal-hauling line to Charleston, West Virginia. Chessie would pay $22 million in cash and put up bonds with a face value of $82 million.[51]

Unfortunately, the Chessie deal rested on little more than ill feelings and mistrust. Chessie had not determined whether it could make money on such a deal. The EL had balked at providing the traffic and operating data it needed to make up its mind. Chessie demanded protection against deficiency judgments—the lawsuits for extra compensation that the creditors of the bankrupts were preparing to file against everyone who wound up in possession of their old railroads. The reason EL balked at supplying Chessie information was because Chessie refused to supply EL with the information it needed to prepare its deficiency judgment case.[52]

Nor was it clear that a Chessie invasion of the East was a good thing. It was a strong railroad, but it had recently taken an antagonistic attitude toward piggyback traffic (now generally called TOFC/COFC—trailers or containers on flat cars). It said it made no money at such traffic and that it diverted more from boxcars than from trucks. It precipitously closed its department of intermodal services. But, said Robert Haldeman of the Lehigh Valley, piggyback was the most profitable and expanding traffic his railroad had and the least affected by recession. It was inaugurating new services all the time, and the *Apollos,* the piggyback run-throughs with the

N&W, were winning national attention and bringing the Lehigh traffic it never had before. Whatever was behind the Chessie decision, he thought, it was a bad mentality to bring into the East.[53]

11

Such was the result of congressional handiwork in the Rail Reorganization Act of 1973. There was little choice but to see it through, or risk delaying a decision for three or four more years, in which time the Penn Central track would be beyond repair. The final system plan was approved.

Chessie, and the Southern Railway (which was going to take PC lines on the Delmarva Peninsula as far north as Wilmington) pulled out at the last minute, not for fear of deficiency judgment, but because they could not reach agreement with labor unions. Congress had been so generous, no private enterprise could match it. That left the final system plan a wreckage even before it was instituted.

On April 1, 1976, Conrail took over the operations of the bankrupts. The Washington-New York corridor eventually went to Amtrak, but only after a bitter hassle with Coleman over the release of impounded Amtrak funds. Boston & Maine stayed out, still hoping to reorganize on its own. Whether or not the light-density lines could be abandoned at all was in doubt, as a citizen, Lettie Gay Carson, had gone to court to test whether the idea was acceptable under the National Environmental Policy Act. From then on, environmental impact was a very serious consideration.[54]

The State of Michigan and Michigan's Hillsdale County prepared to operate large segments of the bankrupts' trackage independent of Conrail.[55] Delaware & Hudson, according to the fallback plan, prepared to double its size, with trackage rights over former EL to the Bison Yard at Buffalo, over former Lehigh Valley to Oak Island Yard in Newark, over former PRR to Potomac Yard at Alexandria, Virginia, and over former Reading to Philadelphia. Whether or not D&H was going to be able to digest this was yet to be seen. There was no precedent in railroading.[56]

There was a kind of celebration the day Conrail was inaugurated. Chairman Jordan quoted Shakespeare and spoke of resurrection. The plans of supposedly the best experts in government and business said it was going to work. Even the computer said it was going to work. Once again, the East was going to have fine railroads as in the days when the ground shook with the passage of the great expresses, and the companies had pride.

But somehow, it was a day of sadness. It was not really the memory of the great railroads whose banners were being furled forever that day. Only the rail buffs shed a tear over that. It was the gut feeling that the computers were wrong, the planning sloppy, the deals made in secret, and the public

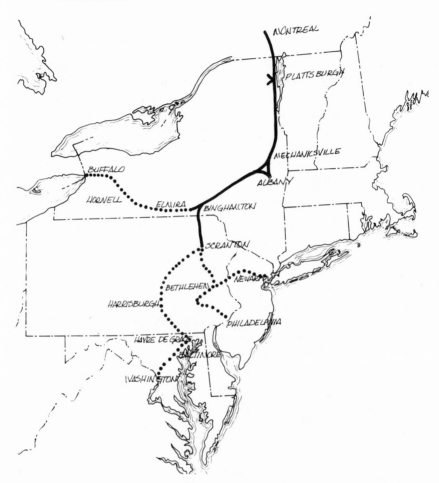

MAP 32:   *The Expansion of the Delaware & Hudson*

deceived about the cost, not because it wanted to be deceived, but because its government thought it ought to be deceived.

1. It was hard to be confident when Conrail immediately sent locomotives from the component roads all over the system, far from home shops, in much the same way Pennsylvania and New York Central threw two railroads together in order to get the "savings" quickly.
2. It was hard to be confident when congressmen from the South and West were already thumping the tom-toms about taxpayer bailouts to another region of the country.
3. It was hard to be confident when the computers that were simulating Conrail operations in preparation for actual operations called the Conrail Analysis Model, or CRAM, dispatched a train from New York to St. Louis, and it wound up at Pittsfield, Massachusetts, and then vanished. "It's the kind of thing that can happen," said a supervisor, who also confessed a key-puncher had programmed a train ten miles long.[57]
4. It was hard to be sympathetic about the creditors when the Canada Southern Railroad, a Penn Central subsidiary between Buffalo and Detroit that had remained solvent, declared a dividend of $60 a share in order to exhaust its $9 million reserve fund two days before Conrail took over. "Blatant" and "nervy" were the private comments of Conrail officials. A Canada Southern executive explained, "it just happened."[58]

In Hornell, New York, the little city prepared for the end. Its main industry had always been the Erie shops. If Chessie had taken over, it was going to keep them open. Conrail was not. Some of the Erie Lackawanna men who voted against the Chessie's offer said it made no difference what happened to Hornell; they had welfare-for-life. Others were sad. The life of the city—their city—was doomed.[59]

Other nations underwrote the cost of vital transportation so that industry and cities might prosper. The United States underwrote the cost of highway and air transportation because they were politically powerful. But the pathological need to preserve the facade of for-profit railroading, something every other nation had scrapped decades before, had it spooked. Other towns were going to become familiar with Hornell's plight. The branches were going to be killed; the factories would shut down; the young people would move; the towns would die. Somehow, for all the planning, the government rescue of northeastern railroading had come without an infusion of optimism. The panacea of retrenchment that had helped to wreck the private railroads was to be continued.

After a year and a half, it appeared the rail competition offered Conrail by the expanded Delaware & Hudson was an illusion. D&H believed its losses on Bison Yard-Oak Island piggyback traffic were so severe that it petitioned for a rate increase that would, in all probability, write *finis* to the *Apollo* service that had sustained the Lehigh Valley Railroad in its last days. In the first nine months of 1977, D&H's gross revenue was up 21 percent over the same period of 1976, but its operating ratio had climbed three percentage points (to 87.4) and the losses for this former profit-earner were better than $6 million.[60] The USRA, as D&H's largest creditor (since it put up the capital to finance the overnight expansion), forced out the company's old management headed by Bruce Sterzing and brought in one acceptable to it headed by Charles Bertrand, formerly of the B&O, Reading, and Amtrak. On a railroad that as late as 1975 had gone out of its way for the New York State Transportation Authority to field an Albany-Montreal passenger train with pride and care and distinction, everything began to smack of austerity.

At the end of one year of operation, Conrail boasted that it had not lost as much as originally projected. Track reconstruction went ahead, especially along the Water Level Route. At least part of the disappointing results of 1977 was caused by the severe winter, the worst in the century, that closed yards across the northern tier for weeks at a time. In the first six months of 1977, Conrail's operating deficit was $342 million, considerably more than anticipated, and its operating ratio climbed from 96 in 1976 to 99.6.[61]

It was then that Conrail management began to get shrill. In its second quarterly financial report for 1977, it said:

In recent months, in the press and in statements by public officials, there has been growing reference to Conrail as a quasi-governmental corporation similar in character to Comsat, the Postal Service, or Amtrak. This is not true. The law that established Conrail . . . states: "The Corporation [Conrail] shall be a for-profit corporation . . . shall not be an agency or instrumentality of the Federal Government." The U.S. Supreme Court, in upholding the constitutionality of the Act, said in part "Conrail is not a federal instrumentality. . . . Thus Conrail will be basically a private, not a government, enterprise." Continuing misconceptions of the true purpose and structure of Conrail could materially affect the achievement of the ultimate objective of the Conrail mandate—an economically viable solution to the Northeast rail crisis. If political and other constituencies incorrectly construe the Corporation as a government entity, then expectations about its operating policies will be greatly altered, with the result that economic viability for Conrail may never be achieved. That result could trigger a new rail crisis—which could eventually lead to the nationalization of Conrail, and parts, if not all, of the rest of the rail industry.[62]

Conrail had diagnosed its own flaw. With an operating ratio at nearly 100, it was not going to make a profit for a long, long time, and probably not ever. But of course it was going to have to meet socially useful goals—"serve many constituencies," in the words of its management. That was the justification for the expenditure of federal monies in the first place. Fiscal conservatives, by insisting that Conrail go through the empty motions of acting like a for-profit company, had insured—perhaps deliberately—that the Northeast would have the worst of both worlds, a perennial drain of cash without providing the distributive mechanism for a truly healthy economy. Congress and the nation had failed to come to grips with the fact that industrial capitalism was crossing a major watershed, where simple-minded profit-and-loss was no longer an adequate measure of success at every stage of production and distribution.

By the summer of 1977, the American steel industry seemed to be approaching a crisis very much like the railroads. It was an industry that was basic to an advanced economy. Just as railroad ton-miles had increased, so had the demand for steel. Neither were products that were no longer useful. Yet an unwillingness or an inability to reinvest capital in new technology had left American steel vulnerable to the competition of foreigners. They had used public monies freely to develop technology, specifically the basic oxygen furnace and the continuous casting process. Bethlehem Steel reported a third-quarter loss of more than $500 million in 1977, the worst of any American corporation ever, including Penn Central. It prepared to phase out many of its operations at Lackawanna, New York, and Johnstown, Pennsylvania, precipitating a potential economic disaster for thousands.[63] It appeared that another industry was about to join railroads in industrial maturity, where capital needs regularly outran the ability to raise that capital.

That was the state of American industrial capitalism with the coming of Conrail.

CHAPTER 15

The Railroad Mergers

Recall those jittery June days of 1970. The Penn Central crisis was deepening. The railroad, that magnificent national resource, lay in ruins. Emissaries of management and creditors were scurrying back and forth from Philadelphia to Washington. Closed conference doors would open and perspiring, exhausted faces would emerge, giving "no comment" to waiting reporters.

The economy was already over-hyped from the Vietnam War. Inflation and unemployment that were supposed to be mutually exclusive were taking hold simultaneously, and in an ominously virulent form. It was widely believed the announcement of the biggest business failure in history at this critical juncture, when both the old theory and the old institutions seemed unable to cope, would set off a panic as disastrous as October 1929. Perhaps those June days would, in retrospect, be remembered as a watershed of capitalism.

Merger was not the cause of what had happened on the railroad. It was not responsible for the decayed roadbed, where, in front of television cameras on CBS's *Sixty Minutes,* Senator Hartke could bend over and pull out by hand a spike from track over which passenger trains rolled. Merger had not produced the poor judgment by management, which could have infected any institution. But merger was supposed to have been the remedy for problems. A decade had been wasted on the wrong medicine, on a panacea that was a placebo. Warnings—like the disappointing performance of Erie Lackawanna, or the testimony of Kent Healy and John Meyer and James Nelson before the Kefauver hearings in 1962—had been ignored. Those days, like the bittersweet afternoons of Indian summer, had slipped away, one by one, when good minds from business and labor and government, fueled with imagination, might have sought an effective medicine. Now the patient lay dying, and whether life could be pumped back in was a matter of doubt. One thing was soon certain. Private enterprise was not capable of its own salvation. Capitalism's most sacred institution was beginning a transformation—first in railroads, as the railroads had always been first before—and probably into forms yet unknown.

Nor was the railroads' gangrene isolated in the Northeast. The infection had spread:

1. On the Milwaukee Road, where consolidation might have helped ease the problems of redundant granger railroading, but which had been excluded from all mergers, long stretches of the mainline between Chicago and St. Paul were under slow orders of 30 mph or less. It was along this line where, in the midst of depression, when the spirit of capitalism was at a low ebb, the orange-and-maroon Hiawatha streamliners helped revive it by speeding mile after mile at 110 mph.
2. The Illinois Central Gulf, the product of a merger, where as late as 1969 the University of Illinois student specials of orange-and-brown 1920-era cars flashed over the 126 miles between Champaign and Chicago in two hours flat, was ordered to restore track to 1971 standards in accordance with its obligation under the Amtrak law. On a typical day in 1975, there were two dozen slow orders on the first hundred miles out of Chicago.[1]
3. The Securities and Exchange Commission threatened suit against the Burlington Northern, another product of merger, unless it revealed to investors the extent to which their equity was being eroded by the deterioration of fixed plant, notably track.[2]

The implications were awesome. Frightened by the possibility of a general collapse, Congress produced the "4R Act," as it was called, the Railroad Revitalization and Regulatory Reform Act of 1976. It grew specifically out of the experience in the *Rock Island* case, but its applications were to be nationwide. It prescribed some familiar medicines—mergers and chopping off the branches.[3]

If merger was going to be pushed more strenuously than before, at least some of the shortcomings of past regulatory procedure were to be remedied. Proceedings were to be completed within a rigid timetable—twenty-four months to gather evidence in major cases plus 180 days for the ICC to reach a decision. Traffic diversion studies were to be based on probability sampling according to prescribed guidelines. The Rail Services Planning Office of the ICC, created by the Conrail Act, would provide the aggressive public-interest analysis previous mergers had lacked. The Office of Public Counsel, also under the ICC, would attempt to represent the interests of small businesses and individuals who otherwise could not afford to take part in the regulatory process. Whether the complexity these new players would add to proceedings could be neatly resolved in the prescribed time limits was a matter of some doubt. But if anyone feared that the new legislation would trigger a wave of unchecked consolidation, they were wrong. The ICC denied the Milwaukee Road's inclusion in the Burlington Northern, the Southern Pacific's bid to buy the Tucumcari-Kansas City line of the Rock Island, and the Denver & Rio Grande's bid to buy the Rock's Denver-Omaha and Denver-Kansas city lines.[4]

For the newer panacea, chopping the branches, the law ordered the Department of Transportation to survey the density of traffic on all lines in the United States. In case all of railroading should follow the Penn Central into the holocaust, there would be priorities on which lines to salvage. It was not clear what the multi-colored maps in the "Final Standards" Report meant when it was released on January 19, 1977.[5] It looked, in case the worst should happen, that service would remain on only the few lines that met the magic criterion of twenty million gross tons per mile per year. This would leave mainlines stripped of feeders. It would leave through lines stub-ended by abandonments in the middle. If such were to happen, the twenty million gross tons would quickly disappear from the lines slated for reha-bilitation. As in the Preliminary Plan for Conrail, the ICC's Rail Services Planning Office ripped into the dubious and dangerous implications of the study and left it in shreds.[6] The same question that had been raised in the planning for Conrail was raised again: Was this another panacea to replace the discredited mergers, or was it the deliberate blueprint for the destruction of railroads as a useful mechanism of transportation in the United States?

This was in a nation whose prosperity depended on the division of labor, which in turn demanded massive quantities of cheap transportation; a nation whose victory in two World Wars and whose status as a superpower depended largely on its ability to mass-produce (and the essential corollary of mass production, the ability to mass-distribute). How incredible that it should risk the destruction of its low-cost system of transport, a system that was already built. Once destroyed, it would be prohibitively expensive to rebuild. Once having placed its reliance on convenient and politically powerful, but cost- and fuel-inefficient modes of transportation, the nation would have willfully placed its status as a superpower at the mercy of oil-producing foreign powers, even risking the collapse of its very civilization if that fuel were not forthcoming. After the experience of the mergers, the challenge was too great to risk another panacea.

1

Not everyone was ready to admit the mergers had been a failure. Those who had staked their careers and their reputations on them were under-standably defensive.

Statistics can be slippery. Every company had its special circumstances, so no two can quite be compared. Every year had its special economic characteristics, so no two of them can be quite compared, either. But if one were to take six roads that were products of major consolidations and six that were not and compare them before the consolidations (1955) and after (1974) both years of general prosperity, some rough indications are evident.

1. Table 1: Roads that consolidated showed less ability to reduce mileage than roads which did not.
2. Table 2: Roads that consolidated didn't show a significantly greater ability to reduce employment than roads which did not.
3. Table 3: Roads that consolidated showed a somewhat better ability to concentrate traffic, although of all roads listed, the second and third best records were by roads which did not consolidate.
4. Table 4: Roads that consolidated showed no significantly better ability to bring fruits of productivity down to the bottom line.

After the cost of the mergers and all the dislocation they caused, roads that were strong stayed strong; roads that were marginal stayed marginal, whether they merged or not.

Table 1

Comparative Mileage of Representative Roads

	1955	1974	Percent Reduction
Six Merged Roads			
Seaboard Coast Line	9,375	9,040	3.6
Burlington Northern	24,969	22,722	9.0
Chicago & North Western	10,724	10,236	4.6
Illinois Central Gulf	9,757	9,568	1.9
Norfolk & Western	7,589	7,593	0.0
Chessie System	12,127	11,189	7.7
Six Unmerged Roads			
Delaware & Hudson	792	716	9.6
Union Pacific	9,811	9,464	3.5
Milwaukee Road	10,674	10,373*	2.8
Frisco Lines	5,096	4,776	6.3
Southern Pacific	12,439	11,602	6.7
Santa Fe	13,102	12,531	4.4

Average Percent Reduction

Six Merged Roads	4.5
Six Unmerged Roads	5.6

Source: *Moody's Transportation Manual.*
*Figures are for 1972.

Table 2

Comparative Number of Employees

	1955	1974	Percent Reduction
Six Merged Roads			
Seaboard Coast Line	33,922	22,390	34.0
Burlington Northern	80,791	44,417	45.0
Chicago & North Western	27,913	14,250	49.0
Illinois Central Gulf	42,545	18,610	56.3
Norfolk & Western	45,044	27,602	38.7
Chessie System	78,671	38,199	51.4
Six Unmerged Roads			
Delaware & Hudson	5,738	N.A.	—
Union Pacific	49,744	27,066	45.6
Milwaukee Road	27,936	14,143*	49.4
Frisco Lines	13,506	8,898	34.1
Southern Pacific	59,843	N.A.	—
Santa Fe	57,146	35,215	38.4

Average Percent Reduction

Six Merged Roads	45.7
Six Unmerged Roads	41.9

Source: *Moody's Transportation Manual.*
*Figures are for 1972.

Table 3

Comparative Efficiency: Net Tons per Train Mile

	1955	1974	Percent Increase
Six Merged Roads			
Seaboard Coast Line	1,170	1,974	68.7
Burlington Northern	1,303	1,804	38.5
Chicago & North Western	1,426	1,704	19.5
Illinois Central Gulf	1,628	2,262	38.9
Norfolk & Western	1,665	2,407	44.6
Chessie System	1,819	2,359	29.7

Six Unmerged Roads

Delaware & Hudson	1,844	1,936	5.0
Union Pacific	1,254	1,839	46.7
Milwaukee Road	1,323	1,574*	19.0
Frisco Lines	1,219	1,512	24.0
Southern Pacific	1,244	1,901	52.8
Santa Fe	1,167	1,398	19.8

Average Percent Increase

Six Merged Roads	40.0
Six Unmerged Roads	27.9

Source: *Moody's Transportation Manual.*
*Figures are for 1972.

Table 4

Comparative Operating Ratios

	1955	*1974*	*Net Change*
Six Merged Roads			
Seaboard Coast Line	77.67	76.99	− .68
Burlington Northern	76.00	79.53	+ 3.53
Chicago & North Western	79.82	81.44	+ 1.62
Illinois Central Gulf	72.73	77.74	+ 5.01
Norfolk & Western	69.19	70.78	+ 1.59
Chessie System	74.59	70.83	− 3.76
Six Unmerged Roads			
Delaware & Hudson	69.82	78.88	+ 9.06
Union Pacific	72.74	73.62	+ .88
Milwaukee Road	83.86	84.84*	+ .98
Frisco Lines	76.80	75.81	− .99
Southern Pacific	79.97	77.27	− 2.70
Santa Fe	71.86	80.63	+ 8.77

Average Net Change

Six Merged Roads	+ 1.22
Six Unmerged Roads	+ 2.66

Source: *Moody's Transportation Manual.*
*Figures are for 1972.

By 1977, even the railroad trade press seemed to discard merger as a source of "savings," that magical word of the sixties. Instead, merger was now touted as a way for strong companies to extend their marketing area. "Market penetration" was the fashionable new concept and was the apparent motive for the active studies between the Burlington Northern and the Frisco. Yet whether or not shippers had ever gotten the advantages they were promised by merger was not known, for no systematic study was made, except of the Penn Central, which was probably exceptional. There were new services both on roads that merged and those that did not. But in the dockets of even the successful mergers, the last entries in the correspondence files were usually complaints from shippers who felt service had deteriorated.[7]

Whether or not the "secret motives" of merger; like tax benefits (particularly tax loss carry-forwards), or the desire to reduce competition, or the sheer lust for personal power and glory were worth the price of merger, it did not seem to show on the bottom line. The mergers had simply not lived up to their advance billing.

2

The idea had been sound enough. There were some economies to be legitimately gained. It was called the "Lemly Thesis" in chapter 4, an idea that grew specifically out of a modest little merger in 1940 that produced a successful Gulf, Mobile & Ohio Railroad where two wheezing failures stood before. If it worked for them, why didn't it work for others?

One error was not recognizing at an early date that good consolidations which seemed to offer legitimate opportunities for increased efficiency were seldom being suggested, or when they were, were falling through—like a Lehigh Valley-Jersey Central combination, for example, or a Milwaukee Road-North Western one. Too many unseen obstacles and hidden interests lay in the path. A stronger motivation than voluntary initiative was necessary, whether it be provided by incentive or compulsion. There was nothing new about this. It was Albert Cummins's original argument in 1920; Joseph Eastman had taken it up later on, and John Leonard had been its protagonist throughout the merger movement.

More serious was a second error, which was implicit in the Lemly Thesis. It was the failure to recognize that the applicability of consolidation was very limited. The Erie, for example, was parallel to the Lackawanna east of Buffalo; west of Akron, it was parallel to the B&O and the Nickel Plate; in the Cleveland-Youngstown area, it was parallel to a number of roads. Merger with any one of them could realize only a fraction of the potential economies. Unless all roads were merged into a giant monopoly, an idea that was suggested from time to time, but which never had a significant following, consolidation could never reduce much mileage or concentrate much traffic. Hence, the tragedy of the merger movement was placing hope in a false remedy, when better tools to solve the problems of efficiency might have been found.

Furthermore, where real economies did exist, they were so scattered and diffuse that only a master manager, an Ike Tigrett on the GM&O, for example, or a William White on the Erie Lackawanna, had a fighting chance to bring them down to net. It is implicit in the thesis of Albro Martin (in *Enterprise Denied,* which argued that Progressive Era regulation crippled the railroads before the onslaught of competitive forms of transportation) that regulation so frustrated the ideas of truly creative men that few of them stuck around in railroading after 1920. I suggested, in trying to explain the advent of the merger movement in the 1950s, that it was in part a camouflage for the lackluster performance of management. Since it was always implicit that megalomania was a driving force, at least behind the bigger mergers, it is understandable that management never took account of its own shortcomings in its calculations.

If consolidation had such limited applicability, would anything have worked? We can't know. The past is not an experiment to be returned to the test tube and tried again. However, at least one possibility seems to emerge from the evidence. Coordination was probably a better avenue to savings than consolidation. Each project might not have produced as much savings when two companies were involved rather than one, but the number of opportunities for many projects with many different roads should have more than compensated—all possible without the trauma of merger. Railroaders denied that coordination was possible, or even desirable, for having decided on merger, they could never admit there was a less radical way to get more extensive savings. Though there were exceptions, railroads had usually been able to make coordination work when they wanted to. Even as the merger movement was in full bloom, run-through freights between independent roads were one of the truly innovative ideas of railroading.[8]

As the merger orthodoxy took hold, management and regulators seemed ominously immune to evidence that suggested the orthodoxy was wrong. No one looked back to learn by experience. In 1961, when the Nickel Plate was trying to merge with the Norfolk & Western, Outboard Marine Corporation, the makers of Johnson and Evinrude motors, wrote the commission. It had held its tongue up to now, it said, because it felt each carrier ought to be able to defend its best interests. But years before, when the Nickel Plate took over the Wheeling, and OMC had been promised better service to its plant on the Wheeling, service had deteriorated remarkably. Now that everyone had clambered aboard a counterproductive bandwagon, it feared for private enterprise itself.[9] All the rigidities of socialism—the inability to respond pragmatically, the inability to learn by past mistakes—seemed to reflect from the calcified heart of the free market system as well.

Similar comments were scattered in the other merger dockets. Was no one prompted to investigate? There had been the disappointing experience of Erie Lackawanna, for example, and the breakdown of the Penn Central was the scandal of railroading, even reported in the *New York Times* long before the ICC began an investigation.[10] The commission's adversary procedure, suitable to civil or criminal cases, was inexcusably inadequate for investigatory ones, and evidence of that came at least as early as the hearings on the Ripley Report in 1921.

The ICC did show a capacity to grow in wisdom. By the time of the "3R Act," its Rail Services Planning Office became the focus of participatory analysis, and it promised to be more active in planning under the "4R Act". An initial survey said bluntly, "Although Congress has adopted mergers and restructuring as one way to correct some of the current industry problems, the Office is not convinced that this approach is the panacea for the industry."[11] But by that time, the Department of Transportation had usurped much of the ICC's prestige in transportation matters and appeared ready to make all of the ICC's mistakes over again.

3

But scapegoating the ICC, or any other single party, was not quite fair, for it was the totality of the breakdown of all institutions that was so ominous. The ICC, after all, was caught between the inadequacy of the law under which it had to operate, and the tenacity and high-powered budgets of the railroads who wanted to get their mergers through.

Of the other parties, labor probably deserved the least of the blame. The standard protective conditions imposed by the ICC were a small percentage of anticipated savings and should have been a small price to pay for human decency if the merger savings had been real. Even the attrition agreements of the later mergers should only have delayed savings a little longer. The fact, as revealed in the Penn Central postmortem, that management could not make productive use of labor even as many jobs were going undone, was not labor's fault. Perhaps in the Conrail settlement, labor grasped too hard, a settlement that privately funded railroads would be hard pressed to match. But that, after all, was in response to what labor saw as two decades of merger graspingness by the other side.

Management can be criticized for its rigidity, its lack of imagination, and its reliance on studies that were almost certainly window dressing for previous decisions. If business came regularly to respond dogmatically rather than pragmatically, its future was not likely to measure up to its past performance. Also, management can be criticized for its faith in litigation. Early in the merger movement, in the Erie Lackawanna merger, for example, testimony ran about 1,500 pages and briefs were 75 to 100 pages each. As time went on, testimony regularly came to run from 10,000 to 25,000 pages, and briefs, with multicolored maps, went upwards of 1,000 pages. Points were more obfuscated than ever. Might the money have better been spent on air-slide grain cars? It may be that this consuming plague of litigation will become the most serious threat to efficient capitalism.

Capital—the investors—meaning primarily insurance companies, banks, and pension plans—deserves a great deal of the blame for the merger fiasco. Capital retained its ultimate veto over the structure of railroading but took little of the responsibility. It was the reluctance of capital to invest in railroads that prompted the merger movement in the first place. Capital could turn thumbs down on proposals that didn't please it, and was free to withdraw funds anyway if the going got rough. It had no permanent commitment to the industry. Of course, it had responsibilities on the other side to its depositors and policyholders. It may be a lesson of the merger story that some change in the strictly voluntary allocation of the nation's capital is needed.

But finally, it was Congress that deserved most, if not all, the blame. By its open subsidy of other forms of transportation, it had largely created the railroads' impasse that triggered the merger movement. It had left the law on mergers vague, with action dependent on management, subject to capital's veto, for reasons that applied to 1920 and 1940. It had been made aware that things were not turning out well in the Kefauver hearings of 1962, but had done nothing about it. How was it that a prominent senator of the majority party could conduct extensive hearings and then have his bill vanish without a trace? There had to be some powerful lobbying somewhere, behind the scenes, to get that bill suppressed. Congressional leadership obviously chose not to push it. Even after the fall, Congress seemed unable to cope until the Union Pacific wrote it a bill, and said, in effect, "Ok, here is a way out of the wilderness."

The way chosen—Conrail—was a plan remarkably similar to the Plumb Plan or to Edward Hungerford's blueprint in *A Railroad For Tomorrow*. In the past, such creative thinking had met with snarls, or guffaws, or both. Congress had been too unimaginative, or too scared, to tamper with the structure of capitalist institutions. Finally, capitalist enterprise itself had to do the prodding. Other Western democracies had not quailed at the challenge. Ultimately, they opted for state railways, which lost money by the shopworn definition of profit-and-loss but which provided the distributive mechanism for economies that were in some cases—the German, the French, and the Japanese, to name the most prominent—showing greater signs of vitality than the American. Perhaps it was lamentable that so many problems, like railroad mergers, required a "Washington" solution; but that being the case, it was more lamentable that Congress could not provide the needed direction.

However, since the blame for the disappointment of consolidation can be parceled out among so many institutions and individuals, therein lay the clue to the real problem. It was the diffusion of power. No one, ultimately, was responsible, or at least, everyone had others on whom to blame failure. Management could blame the regulators or labor, and they could blame Congress; individual congressmen could always blame other congressmen without ever revealing the interested parties that had influenced them behind closed doors. As for the president, even in the 1960s, when presidential power was supposedly reaching a new zenith, he was an ineffectual appendage to the chain of shrugged responsibility. Creditors, who controlled the life-giving capital, hovered above the scene, amoral, waiting to put their money where the return was. And so, as it was back in the days when the Plumb Plan had helped to whip the nation into an anti-innovative hysteria, the problem boiled down to a lack of leadership, of commitment, and of goodwill.

4

In the mid-1960s, Louis Armand, then director-general of the French National Railroads, came to the United States and was entertained by American railroad presidents. "I told them," he said, "that sooner or later they would have face the question of nationalizing American railroads. They all roared with laughter."[12] Nationalization was the old bugaboo. Americans had been told over and over by those whom it suited to keep a weak railroad system in private hands, that anything must be done to avoid it, even liquidate key railroads if necessary. Despite the essentially socialist underpinning of highways and waterways and airways, nationalized railroads were somehow the unmistakable sign that the old notions of big enterprise, as they had developed in the United States in the twentieth century, were no longer adequate. Yet in the summer of 1977, the Canadian National Railways was laying second track along its routes in British Columbia to accomodate the upsurge in traffic.[13] Its former president, Donald Gordon, had warned years before that demand for CN service was so strong that the line would soon have bottlenecks if it did not begin immediately to expand facilities. Also that summer, when the credit of the Milwaukee Road and other American carriers was exhausted the French National Railroads were borrowing freely on the New York money markets at the prime rate for capital improvements to a system that was already the distributive underpinning of one of the world's vibrant economies.[14]

Along Lake Ontario, below the Niagara Escarpment, that geological formation which created the falls, there was a Penn Central line called the Hojack. In the desperate days after the bankruptcy, when the trustees were hacking and chopping at anything that looked marginal, they tore out one thousand feet from the middle of this line, under dubious authority, so that it became two long sidings, one stretching down from Niagara Falls, the other from Rochester. What traffic there was declined precipitously. The vines took over, and a picture of a train that had made it as far as the village of Ransomville in 1975 was titled "Jungle Patrol" in *Trains*.[15] There were shippers on the line who demanded, even pleaded, that through service be restored. Jobs were hanging in the balance. But in the meantime, in the suburbs of Niagara Falls, some new arrivals had bought property that abutted the tracks, and now that service was all but gone, they insisted that restoring it would ruin their property values. One had to feel sympathy for Congressman John La Falce, who took the heat on both sides. The argument was still unresolved when Conrail took over, by which time the Hojack was lost in so many bigger problems. It was probable that the three-county area below the escarpment would never have rail service again. Its future would live or die with the highway.[16]

In 1974, in the former Wabash yards in Decatur, Illinois, a cut of tank cars carrying volatile chemicals, moving at a "higher than acceptable switching speed," slammed into a boxcar and ruptured. Sheets of flame engulfed the heart of this major downstate city. The pictures, published in *Trains,* were awesome; like the aftermath of a fire-bomb run, the haggard faces of the firefighters looked as though they had seen the very gates of hell. Broken wheels or broken rails caused similar accidents on the Southern Railway at Laurel, Mississippi, on the Illinois Central at New Athens, Illinois, on the Toledo, Peoria & Western at Crescent City, Illinois, and on the Penn Central near Indianapolis. "It's like a time bomb every time a train passes over these tracks," a Pensacola resident told ABC reporters after a series of explosive wrecks on the Louisville & Nashville forced local authorities to shut the line down. *Labor,* the old organ of the Plumb Plan League, which ran front-page pictures of these holocausts in almost every issue, sensed the seriousness of it all.

It was the heritage of a decade wasted on the false panacea of consolidation. On the one hand it was a whimpering death; on the other, an apocalypse.

Notes

Chapter 1

1. William Leonard, *Railroad Consolidation Under the Transportation Act of 1920.*

2. *Fixed charges* are total payments for the use of capital (interest and guaranteed dividends), not to be confused with *fixed costs,* an operating expense.

3. The fight was technically for control of the Northern Pacific. Hill had the Burlington, but controlled the NP only through a minority interest. Harriman's chance to get the Burlington, which would bring his Union Pacific rails to Chicago, was to secretly buy NP and force Hill's hand.

4. U.S. Senate, Committee on Interstate Commerce, *Railroad Combination in the Eastern Region* (1940), pp. 16–24.

5. *Consolidations and Combinations of Carriers,* 12 ICC 277 (1907).

6. U.S. House of Representatives, *Pere Marquette Railroad Co. and Cincinnati, Hamilton & Dayton Ry. Co.,* doc. 137 (1917), p. 217.

7. Henry Lee Staples and Alpheus T. Mason, *The Fall of a Railroad Empire;* Richard M. Abrams, "Brandeis and the New Haven-Boston & Maine Merger Battle Revisited," *Business History Review,* Winter 1962; and U.S. Senate, NYNH&H RR Co., *Evidence Taken Before the ICC,* doc. 542 (1914).

8. *Northern Securities Co.* v. *United States,* 193 US 197, 230 (1904).

9. Albro Martin, *Enterprise Denied;* Gabriel Kolko, *Railroads and Regulation, 1877–1916;* and I. Leon Sharfman, *The American Railroad Problem.*

10. U.S. Senate, Committee on Interstate Commerce, *Government Control and Operation of Railroads* (1918), p. 89.

11. *Government Control and Operation,* pp. 124, 349.

12. *Government Control and Operation,* p. 123.

13. Such as Louis Brandeis's famous, but largely unsupported claim that scientific management could save the roads $1 million a day. U.S. Senate, *Five Per Cent Case* (1915) vol. 14, pt. 6, p. 5248.

14. The *Royal Blue* line was named for the principal passenger train that once traveled the route; it consists of the B&O between Washington and Park Junction in Philadelphia, the Reading from there to Bound Brook, New Jersey, and the Jersey Central from there to Jersey City, with ferry and lighter connection to New York. It was the B&O's entrance to New York Harbor, sometimes called the Park Junction route. The B&O owns the Staten Island Rapid Transit Line and extensive terminal and harbor facilities.

15. U.S. Senate, Committee on Interstate Commerce, *Extension of Government Control of Railroads* (1919), pp. 12, 15.

16. Ralph M. Sayre, *Albert Baird Cummins and the Progressive Movement in Iowa,* pp. 228, 263–65.

17. Of 118 class I railroads in 1919, only 18 earned a return of 6 percent.

18. *Congressional Record,* vol. 56, pt. 1, pp. 131–32 (Dec. 4, 1919).

19. In the summer of 1919, Cummins told the Iowa legislature: "I look upon transportation by rail as a government function. I believe it is as much the duty of government to provide people with adequate transportation at low cost as it is to provide them with adequate highways, water supplies and courts of justice." U.S. Senate, doc. #19, vol. 14, 66th Cong., 1st sess. (1919).

20. *Blair* v. *City of Chicago,* 201 US 400 (1906) and *Washington Evening Star,* Aug. 2, 1922.

21. Glenn Plumb, "The Plan of Organized Employees for Railroad Reorganization" *Commerce and Finance,* July 23, 1919.

22. Undocumented clippings in the ICC Library, and U.S. House of Representatives, *Return of Railroads to Private Enterprise,* (1919).

23. W.E. Simnett, *Railway Amalgamation in Great Britain;* K.A. Doukas, *The French Railroads and the State;* G.R. Stevens, *The History of the Canadian National Railways.* The French railroads were nationalized in 1937 and the British in 1945.

24. Senator Lenroot offered a bill that provided for national consolidation into a single system, hence the questions on its practicality. *Congressional Record,* vol. 56, pt. 1, p. 132, Dec. 4, 1919.

25. K. Austin Kerr, *American Railroad Politics, 1914–1920.*

26. Samuel Rea, *Our Railroad Problem;* Howard Elliott, *An Efficient Transportation Machine* (pamphlets of limited distribution).

Chapter 2

1. *Consolidation of Railroads,* 63 ICC 455 (1921) contains the Ripley Report and the Tentative Plan. Mimeographed excerpts of the hearings are at the ICC Library.

2. *Congressional Record,* vol. 67, pt. 7, p. 7331.

3. S. 1175, 70th Cong., 1st sess. (1928).

4. U.S. Senate, *Railroad Combination in the Eastern Region* (1940), pp. 618–20.

5. U.S. Senate Committee on Interstate Commerce, *The Van Sweringen Corporate System* (1941).

6. *Operation of Lines and Issue of Capital Stock by NYC&StL RR Co.,* 79 ICC 581 (1923).

7. The Wabash Railroad was never considered suitable because it had to ferry traffic across the Detroit River and because the line from Detroit to Buffalo passed through Canada over a single-track line owned by the Canadian government.

8. *Railroad Combination in the Eastern Region,* ex. C-979, C-1015.

9. A.J. County, *Consolidation of Railroads into Systems; A Review of Some Financial Considerations That Consolidation Under the Transportation Act Imposes* (Washington, D.C., Dec. 28, 1923).

10. *Railroad Combination in the Eastern Region,* pp. 2027-38.

11. *Railroad Combination in the Eastern Region,* p. 1981 and *Proposed Construction and Extension by the P&WV Ry. Co.,* 138 ICC 755 (1928).

12. *Railroad Combination in the Eastern Region,* pp. 1228-30.

13. *Proposed Acquistion and Control of Virginian Ry. by N&W Ry.,* 117 ICC 67 (1926).

14. *Virginian Ry., Extension,* 162 ICC 552 (1930).

15. *Railroad Combination in the Eastern Region,* p. 2143.

16. *ICC* v. *B&O RR Co.,* 152 ICC 721 (1929) and *ICC* v. *B&O RR. Co.,* 160 ICC 785 (1930).

17. *ICC* v. *PRR Co.,* 169 ICC 618 (1930) and *ICC* v. *PRR Co.,* 291 US 651 (1934).

18. The B&O eventually took the Buffalo, Rochester & Pittsburgh (1930) and the Buffalo & Susquehanna (1932).

19. *Railroad Combination in the Eastern Region,* pp. 2075-122.

20. *In the Matter of Consolidation of Railway Properties in the U.S. into a Limited Number of Systems,* 159 ICC 522 (1929) and *Railroad Combination in the Eastern Region,* ex. C-2821.

21. *In the Matter of Consolidation of the Railway Properties in the U.S. into a Limited Number of Systems,* 185 ICC 402 (1932).

22. See Stuart Daggett, *Railroad Consolidation West of the Mississippi.*

23. Frederick H. Prince, *A Plan for Consolidating the Operation of the Railroads of the United States* (mimeo, no place, Mar. 15, 1933).

24. Earl Latham, *The Politics of Railroad Coordination, 1933-1936,* p. 38.

25. *Ibid.,* p. 57.

26. It also took over functions such as car reporting from predecessor organizations.

27. U.S. Senate, *First Report of the Federal Coordinator of Transportation,* Doc. # 119, 74th Cong., 2d sess. (1934).

28. U.S. House of Representatives, *Report of the Federal Coordinator of Transportation,* Doc. 89, 74th Cong., 1st sess. (1935).

29. William Leonard, *Railroad Consolidation Under the Transportation Act of 1920,* cites these as single copies at the Bureau of Railway Economics Library of the Association of American Railroads.

30. U.S. House of Representatives, *Omnibus Transportation Bill,* 76th Cong., 1st sess., hearings (Jan. 24-Mar. 3, 1939).

31. *Congressional Record,* vol. 86, pt. 11, p. 11766.

Chapter 3

1. U.S. Senate, *Railroad Combination in the Eastern Region* (1940), p. 2110.

2. *New York Times,* Mar. 29, 1940, p. 31.

3. *Overfield v. Pennroad,* 113 F. 2d. 6 (1941), rev. 39 F. Supp. 482 (1942) and 42 F. Supp. 586 (1941), 48 F. Supp. 1008 (1943), 146 F. 2d. 889 (1944). *Perrine v. Pennroad,* 28 Del. ch. 342 (1945), 29 Del. ch. 423 (1947). *Swacker* v. *Pennroad,* 30 Del. ch. 495 (1947), 333 US 862 (1948).

4. ICC Finance Docket (FD) 14530, *Pennsylvania Co., Notes,* Shipstead to Patterson (May 26, 1944).

5. *Wabash Ry. Co., Receivership,* 247 ICC 581, 584 (1941).

6. *NYNH&H RR Co., Reorganization,* 247 ICC 365 (1941), and FD 13235, *Wabash Ry. Co., Control,* tr. 192–204.

7. FD 13235, tr. 40.

8. FD 13235, tr. 154–59.

9. FD 13235, tr. 6.

10. FD 13235, tr. 156–64.

11. Joseph Borkin, *Robert R. Young, the Populist of Wall Street,* ch. 3, and Matthew Josephson, "The Darling Young Man of Wall Street," *Saturday Evening Post,* Aug. 18, 1945.

12. ICC Docket 29085, In Re *Alleghany,* examiner's report, as recounted in Borkin and Josephson.

13. Quoted in Joseph Borkin, *Robert R. Young,* p. 47.

14. *W&LE, Control,* 249 ICC 490 (1941).

15. See John A. Rehor, *The Nickel Plate Story,* an excellent company history.

16. The PM served GM plants in Detroit, Flint, Saginaw, and Lansing.

17. FD 15228, *Pere Marquette Ry. Co., Merger,* tr. 206–39, 361.

18. FD 15228, tr. 469.

19. The PM wanted the new C&O preferred stock that was to be issued in exchange for PM's own preferred stock, to be non-callable, since it was expected to be a prime dividend-paying issue. The C&O agreed to make it non-callable until Nov. 1, 1950. FD 15228, tr. 480.

20. FD 15228, tr. 37.

21. FD 15228, tr. 1082.

22. FD 15228, tr. 39, 179, 337–8, 379.

23. *PM Ry., Merger,* 267 ICC 207, 237–8 (1947).

24. *Schwabacher* v. *ICC,* 72 F. Supp. 560 (1948), and *Schwabacher* v. *United States,* 334 US 182 (1948).

25. *W&LE Ry. Co., Control,* 257 ICC 713 (1944) and 267 ICC 163 (1946).

26. FD 15685, *Wheeling & Lake Erie Ry. Co., Control,* tr. 40, and FD 16308, *Wheeling & Lake Erie R. Co., Control,* tr. 31, 38, 65, 164.

27. FD 15685, tr. 74.

28. ICC Docket 12964, In Re *Consolidation of Railroads* (1925), digest of testimony and exhibits of eastern carriers.

29. FD 17803, *NYC&StL RR Co., Control,* tr. 259.

30. FD 17803, tr. 144.

31. *NYC&StL RR Co., Control,* 295 ICC 131, 152 (1955).

32. FD 14692, *Chesapeake & Ohio Ry., Purchase,* tr. 1019.

33. *New York Times,* Dec. 4, 1946, p. 49.

34. FD 14692, corres., vol. 1-C.

35. *New York Times,* Mar. 4, 1946, p. 15.

36. FD 14692, tr. 1027.

37. Reproduced in Borkin, p. 2.

38. *New York Times,* July 9, 1948, p. 23, and FD 14692, Geo. Estin corres., vol. 1-C.

39. *New Automobiles in Interstate Commerce,* 259 ICC 475 (1945) and FD 14692, tr. 538, 1089.

40. FD 14692, brief of Virginian Ry, vol. 3, and tr. 538.

41. FD 14692, tr. 852, 909. The commission had always been reluctant to approve interlocking directorates: In Re *Boatner,* 257 ICC 369 (1944), based on In Re *Coverdale,* 252 ICC 672 (1942), In Re *Astor,* 193 ICC 528 (1933), and In Re *Rand,* 175 ICC 587 (1931).

42. FD 14692, tr. 1023–86.

43. FD 14692, tr. 1149--268.

44. *C&O Ry., Purchase,* 271 ICC 5 (1948).

45. *New York Times,* Dec. 11, 1947, p. 55.

46. Advertisement in *Time,* Jan. 19, 1948, p. 67; Feb. 2, 1948, p. 41; and Feb. 23, 1948, p. 41.

47. *Trains,* May 1948, p. 3.

48. *New York Times,* Feb. 5, 1947, p. 32; May 21, 1948, p. 35; and Nov. 28, 1951, p. 45.

49. John Brooks in the *New Yorker,* July 3, 1954, p. 44.

50. For more details, see Borkin, ch. 6.

51. *New York Times,* July 12, 1954, p. 1.

Chapter 4

1. The publisher (Kalmbach, Milwaukee) still had first edition copies for sale as late as 1960.

2. Edward Hungerford, *A Railroad for Tomorrow* (Milwaukee, 1945), pp. 77-79. Each was a consolidated system based on one of the principal railroads of old. A favorite game of rail fans during the merger discussion was to sketch on a map a favorite line and add to it choice lines of detested rivals. Hungerford partook of this liberally.

3. James H. Lemly, *The Gulf, Mobile & Ohio,* and *GM&O, RR. Co., Purchase Securities,* 267 ICC 265 (1947).

4. The famous New York Central tests of 1946 pitted steam against diesel to determine precisely the total operating costs of each. Diesels won, but by a surprisingly small margin. See Bill Withuhn, "Did We Scrap Steam Too Soon?" *Trains,* June 1974, p. 38.

5. *Noerr Motor Freight* v. *Eastern Railroad Presidents' Conference,* 155 F. Supp. 768 (1957).

6. *McLean Trucking Co.* v. *United States,* 321 US 67 (1944).

7. *CB&Q RR. Co., Control,* 271 ICC 63 (1948).

8. William Leonard, "Decline of Railroad Consolidation," *Journal of Economic History,* May 1949.

9. *New York Central Securities Co.* v. *United States,* 287 US 12 (1932).

10. *DT&I RR Co., Control,* 275 ICC 455 (1950).

11. *TP&W RR Co., Control,* 295 ICC 523 (1957), affirmed *M&StL Ry, Co.* v. *United States,* 361 US 173 (1959).

12. *St. Joe Paper Co.* v. *ACL RR Co.,* 347 US 298 (1954).

13. Railway Labor Executives' Association, untitled collection of documents relating to labor protective conditions in consolidation cases (Washington, D.C., reprinted 1968).

14. *United States* v. *Lowden,* 308 US 225 (1939).

15. *Congressional Record,* vol. 84, pt. 9, p. 9882.

16. *Congressional Record,* vol. 86, pt. 6, p. 5869.

17. *Fort Worth & Denver City Ry. Co., Lease,* 247 ICC 119 (1941); *Texas & Pacific Ry. Co., Operation,* 247 ICC 285 (1942); *CMS&P&P RR Co., Trustees' Construction,* 252 ICC 49 (1942); *C&NW Ry., Trustees' Abandonment,* 254 ICC 820 (1944); and *Oklahoma Ry., Trustees' Abandonment,* 257 ICC 177 (1944).

18. *New Orleans Union Passenger Terminal Case,* 267 ICC 763 (1948); *Railway Labor Association* v. *United States,* 339 US 142 (1950); and *New Orleans Union Passenger Terminal Case,* 282 ICC 271 (1952).

19. *L&N RR Co., Merger,* 295 ICC 457 (1957).

20. U.S. Senate, Subcommittee on Surface Transportation, *Problems of the Railroads,* hearings (1958), testimony of John M. Budd, pp. 437-40.

21. *Trains,* April 1956, p. 6.

22. *New York Times,* Nov. 3, 1958, p. 43, and *Nation,* Nov. 30, 1957, p. 406.

23. *New York Times,* Nov. 20, 1958, p. 49.

24. *New York Times,* Nov. 14, 1958, p. 1.

25. FD 21160, *C&O R. Co.—Control—B&O R. Co.,* tr. 2145.

26. *N&W R. Co.—Merger—Vgn. Ry.,* 307 ICC 401 (1959).

27. Evidence was the reduced coal rates requested in *Coal from Kentucky and West Virginia to Virginia,* 308 ICC 99 (1959), *Coal to New York Harbor Area,* 311 ICC 355 (1960), and *Coal from Southern Mines to Tampa and Sutton,* 318 ICC 371 (1962).

28. FD 20599, *N&W R. Co.—Merger—Vgn. Ry.,* agreement of June 18, 1959, signed by Stuart Saunders, Frank Beale, and George Leighty, after which the RLEA withdrew from the proceedings.

29. *Duluth, South Shore & Atlantic RR. Co., Merger, Minneapolis, St. Paul & Sault Ste. Marie RR Co. and Wisconsin Central R. Co.* 312 ICC 341 (1960), and U.S. Senate, Subcommittee on Antitrust and Monopoly, *Rail Merger Legislation* (1962).

30. *C&NW Purchase, etc., Minneapolis & St. Louis,* 312 ICC 285 (1960), and *Brotherhood of Locomotive Engineers* v. *C&NW R. Co.,* 314 F. 2d 424 (8th circuit, 1963).

31. *Rail Merger Legislation,* pp. 1000-10, and *Enforcement of Conditions on Merger Proceedings,* 313 ICC 191 (1961).

32. *Central of Georgia Ry. Co., Control,* 295 ICC 523 (1957) and 307 ICC 39 (1958).

33. John W. Barriger, "Why Consolidation? Remarks Before the Transportation Management Institute." (Stanford Univ., June 17, 1959; mimeo copy, Northwestern Univ. Transportation Library); *Super Railroads for a Dynamic American Economy* (New York, 1956).

34. *New York Times,* Oct. 26, 1958, III, p. 1.

35. U.S. Senate, Committee on Commerce, *National Transportation Policy* (1961). Specifically, the Doyle Report recommended that:

   (a) general consolidation be approached on a national or regional basis;
   (b) effective intramodal competition be preserved between a minimal number of systems where traffic is justified;

(c) rail monopoly should result only in restricted areas where traffic flow is inadequate for competition;

(d) no obstacle should be placed in the way of joint use of facilities by competing systems where economy and service advantages justify;

(e) no system involved in a program of general consolidation should be required to absorb a carrier or portion of carrier which it did not consider desirable or useful; and

(f) the overall public interest should supersede that of participants or of opposing interests in consolidation.

There was no satisfactory discussion of how (f) was to be reconciled to (e). In areas other than consolidation, the Doyle Report made some useful suggestions. Congress never did anything about it.

Chapter 5

1. *Trains,* September 1959, p. 6.

2. The most elaborate was a printed affair by Charles C. Henkel, an Erie stockholder, titled *The Proposed Erie-Lackawanna and D&H Consolidation; Let's Stop, Look and Listen* (in FD 20707, *Erie R. Co.—Merger—DL&W R. Co.*) Some highlights:

It is bewildering how the Erie is bailing out the Lackawanna. . . . It is difficult to understand why the Erie management has retained the firm of Wyer, Dick & Co. to make a study . . . when its own operating, engineering and traffic departments should be able to tell there would be little or no benefit from consolidation. . . . Left to its own devices, the Lackawanna, which has the heaviest grades of any eastern trunk . . . is a dying industry and will probably follow the Ontario & Western to the junk heap.

3. The Clark's Summitt Cutoff (forty miles) and the Hopatcong-Slateford Cutoff (twenty-eight miles). See Robert J. Casey and W.A.S. Douglas, *The Lackawanna Story.*

4. *Erie R. Co., Reorganization,* 239 ICC 653 (1940).

5. Henry S. Sturgis, *A New Chapter of Erie, The Story of the Erie's Reorganization, 1938-1941* (New York, 1948).

6. *N.Y., Lackawanna & Wn. R. Co., Merger,* 257 ICC 91 (1944).

7. The following account is gleaned from exhibits in FD 20707 and personal diaries of the author.

8. *New York Times,* Aug. 20, 1955, p. 8.

9. *Mohawk Air Lines, Mail Rates,* 29 CAB 198 (1959).

10. *Railway Age,* Apr. 13, 1960, p. 27.

11. *Railway Age,* May 5, 1958, p. 7.

12. Sponsored by the National Railway Historical Society, Buffalo Chapter. Neither the railroad nor the society was responsible for the gin.

13. FD 19182, *Erie R. Co.,* et al., *Trackage Rights,* reported 295 ICC 303 (1956).

14. *Erie R. Co., Ferry Abandonment,* 295 ICC 549 (1957), and *Erie R. Co.* v. *Board of Public Utility Commissioners,* 359 US 957 (1959).

15. FD 19989, *Erie R. Co.,* et al., *Trackage Rights,* et al., *Binghamton-Gibson, N. Y.,* reported 295 ICC 743 (1958).

16. FD 20707, tr. 853.

17. FD 20707, tr. 857, 969.

18. FD 20707, tr. 664.

19. FD 20707, tr. 189, 787.

20. FD 20707, tr. 47-49.

21. FD 20707, ex. H-48, Aug. 6, 1959 (the Wyer Report).

22. Telephone interview, Charles Meyers, executive vice president, Wyer, Dick & Co., Mar. 26, 1969.

23. *Erie R. Co., Abandonment,* 252 ICC 697 (1944).

24. FD 20707, corres., vol. 1-C.

25. Buffalo would be the hardest hit with 136 operating and 121 nonoperating jobs eliminated. Total job loss in northern New Jersey would be 160. Projecting the employment records of 1954 to 1956 into the future, it was figured 60 percent of those displaced would be taken care of by attrition. In metropolitan areas, it was estimated 35 percent of those would have to move their homes; in nonmetropolitan areas, 60 percent would have to move—a total of 259 homes sold across the system at an average loss of $2,500 each. It was estimated that displaced employees in metropolitan areas would earn up to 80 percent of their former salary in other occupations; in nonmetropolitan areas, no more than 20 percent. The average length of service for displaced employees would be three years; therefore, average protection allowances would last eighteen months. FD 20707, ex. H-48.

26. *United States* v. *Lowden,* 308 US 225 (1939), *ICC* v. *Railway Labor Association,* 315 US 373 (1942), and *Railway Labor Association* v. *United States,* 339 US 142 (1950).

27. *Brotherhood of Maintenance of Way Employees* v. *United States,* 366 US 169 (1961). The House had approved the Harrington Amendment, the Senate rejected it. When Congressman Lea presented the House with the final conference committee report, he said:

The substitute we bring in here provides two additional things. First, there is a limitation on the operation of the Harrington Amendment for four years. . . . In other words, employees have protection against unemployment for four years.

But moments after that was spoken, the following colloquy took place:

Cong. O'Connor: As I want to see those who lose their jobs as a result of consolidation protected, I should like to have the gentleman's interpretation of the phrase that the employee will not be placed in a worse position with respect to his employment. Does "worse position" as used mean that his compensation will be just the same for four years . . . as it would if no consolidation were effected?

Cong. Lea: I take that to be the correct interpretation. Our conference followed the instructions of the House in that respect. It gives railway labor generous protection against sudden and long unemployment.

That was from the *Congressional Record,* vol. 86, pt. 9, p. 10167. The Court thought that since it was spoken moments before the final vote, it would have been the last impression on the matter left with the House.

28. Examples: a car of fresh meat from Omaha to Brooklyn, routed Rock Island-Chicago-Nickel Plate-Buffalo—DL&W, lost to Erie Lackawanna because believed to have been solicited by Nickel Plate; a car of woodenware, Depew, New York, to Bessemer, Alabama, originated on DL&W, routed Nickel Plate-C&O-Cincinnati, L&N to destination. The DL&W revenue was $38. New route via Erie Lackawanna to Cincinnati produced revenue of $384. FD 20707, tr. 381-95.

29. FD 20707, tr. 1138-41.

30. FD 20707, tr. 1672-73.

31. *Railway Age,* Nov. 16, 1959, p. 34.

32. FD 20707, corres., vol. 1-C.

33. FD 20707, tr. 821-22 and *Trains,* December 1959, p. 5.

34. FD 20707, exhibits.

35. *Fried* v. *United States,* 212 F. Supp. 887 (S.D.N.Y., 1963).

36. FD 20707, corres., vol. 1-C.

37. FD 20707, tr. 1067-73.

38. *New York Times,* May 4, 1963, p. 28.

39. This and following stories from the *Wall Street Journal,* Feb. 12, 1962, p. 1, and Nardreen A. Burnie, *Transportation Mergers and Acquisitions,* pp. 49-56.

40. FD 20707, corres., mostly in vol. 1-C.

41. *New York Times,* Feb. 28, 1962, p. 41.

42. FD 23422, *Erie Lackawanna* v. *Lehigh Valley,* reported 330 ICC 306 (1966), tr. 131-39.

43. FD 21494, *In the Matter of EL RR Co., and the First National City Bank of New York as Trustee.*

44. EL Annual Report, 1963, interim report.

45. *Wall Street Journal,* June 14, 1963, p. 14.

46. EL Annual Report, 1963, interim report, p. 13.

47. *Trains,* January 1965, p. 9.

48. FD 20707, tr. 1099-100.

49. EL RR Co. and the New Jersey Division of Railroad Transportation, *The Erie Lackawanna Railroad Co., and Suburban Passenger Service in New Jersey,* report to Gov. Hughes, March, 1965.

50. *New York Times,* Feb. 12, 1969, p. 28.

51. EL Annual Report, 1965, p. 3.

52. *Wall Street Journal,* Feb. 12, 1962, p. 1.

53. *Hearings before a Special Committee of the New Jersey State Senate to Study Passenger and Freight Operations,* Nov. 30, 1965, p. 50.

Chapter 6

1. FD 21160, *Chesapeake & Ohio R. Co.—Control—Baltimore & Ohio R. Co.,* reported 317 ICC 261 (1962), tr. 62.

2. FD 21160, tr. 332.

3. FD 21160, tr. 24.

4. FD 21510, *Norfolk & Wn. Ry. Co., and New York, Chicago & St. Louis R. Co., Merger,* etc., reported 324 ICC 1 (1964), tr. 53-78, 497. The N&W's principal route was to Columbus. The Cincinnati line was single-track and not high speed; therefore, it was not considered a suitable connection to the Nickel Plate.

5. FD 21160, tr. 60.

6. *New York Times,* July 17, 1960, III, p. 3.

7. *New York Times,* Dec. 15, 1960, p. 69.

8. FD 21160, tr. 138.

9. FD 21160, tr. 140, 1924.

10. FD 21160, tr. 28-30.

11. FD 21160, tr. 1928.

12. *New York Times,* articles appearing May 27, June 4, June 14 (1960).

13. *New York Times,* articles appearing July 17, June 25, June 29 (1960).

14. *New York Times,* articles appearing July 30, Aug. 13, 26, 27, 31 (1960).

15. *Trains,* October 1960, p. 5.

16. *New York Times,* June 26, 1960, III, p. 3.

17. FD 21160, minutes of meeting Nov. 21, 1960, vol. 4.

18. Among Young's former bankrollers, Murchison was trying to wrest control from Kirby.

19. *New York Times,* articles appearing Sept. 18, Oct. 5, Dec. 15 (1960).

20. FD 21160, tr. 38-39.

21. FD 21160, tr. 2525.

22. *New York Times,* Jan. 20, 1961, p. 1.

23. From statements filed with the SEC. *New York Times,* Feb. 21, 1961, p. 48.

24. C&O Annual Report, 1962.

25. FD 23422, *Erie Lackawanna* v. *Lehigh Valley,* reported 330 ICC 306 (1966), tr. 30.

26. *New York Times,* Feb. 13, 1959, p. 12. Other judgments on LV management made largely on their testimony in FD 20707.

27. J.A. Pinkepank, "A Tale of Two Railroads," *Trains,* February 1965.

28. FD 21459, *Pennsylvania R. Co.—Control—Lehigh Valley R. Co.,* reported 317 ICC 139 (1962), tr. 38-42.

29. FD 21459, tr. 68-125.

30. FD 21459, tr. 167.

31. FD 21459, tr. 291, 396.

32. FD 21459, tr. 218.

33. FD 21459, tr. 427.

34. *New York Times,* Dec. 22, 1960, p. 33.

35. FD 21459, tr. 469-535.

36. FD 21459, tr. 199-207.

37. FD 21459, tr. 591-92.

38. FD 21160, tr. 3903.

39. FD 21160, tr. 520-21, 5696-98.

40. FD 21160, tr. 1261-62.

41. FD 21160, tr. 1568.

42. FD 21160, ex. H-9, H-121 and tr. 2364.

43. FD 21160, ex. H-98. Estimated savings for C&O-B&O were:

Common points	$6,976,724
Duplicate lines	37,346
Duplicate passenger trains	566,875
Administration	3,033,560
Equipment pool	3,725,402

44. FD 21160, tr. 576-77.

45. FD 21160, tr. 5750. Cars bearing C&O markings were preferable to B&O cars because they were protected by the C-411 car order. In the 1920s, when coal from the southern fields first became significant in northern markets, the C&O, N&W, and L&N were reluctant to buy a fleet of hopper cars because there was no commodity to bring them back to home rails. The C-411 ordered their immediate return, without exception, unless the coal had been delivered to a Lake Erie port, in which case it could make a single roundtrip to the steel district before return home.

46. FD 21160, tr. 1875.

47. FD 21160, tr. 93.

48. FD 21160, tr. 847.

49. FD 21160, tr. 2879.

50. FD 21160, tr. 847, 866, 1507.

51. FD 21160, tr. 135.

52. FD 21160, 578.

53. FD 21160, tr. 2169-956. A boomer in railroad lore is a man who worked at many places on many railroads, leading a happy-go-lucky life but never building up seniority.

54. FD 21510, ex. H-30.

55. 324 ICC 1, 18 (1964).

56. FD 21510, tr. 780-811.

57. The N&W coal was delivered as follows: 21 percent to tidewater; 38.2 percent all-rail eastbound; 22.3 percent westbound to the steel district, and 18.3 percent general westbound. FD 21150, prepared testimony of W.L. Bailes, vol. 3.

58. FD 21510, tr. 821 (Kansas City Board of Trade), 835 (Hercules Powder), 912 (Missouri Farmers' Association).

59. FD 21510, tr. 912 (Missouri Farmers' Association).

60. FD 21510, tr. 810 (Cargill).

61. FD 21510, tr 810 (Cargill), 898 (Ralston Purina), and 944 (Spencer Chemical).

62. FD 21510, tr. 760 (Detroit Steel Co.).

63. FD 21510, tr 792 (Continental Grain), 840 (Streitman Biscuit), 929 (Allied Chemical).

64. FD 21510, tr. 810 (Cargill).

65. FD 21160, tr. 2558-70.

66. FD 21510, tr. 737-38.

67. FD 21510, tr. 719.

68. FD 21510, tr. 715-25.

69. FD 21510, ex. H-138.

70. FD 21510, ex. H-120.
71. FD 21510, ex. H-137.
72. FD 21510, tr. 1231.
73. FD 21510, tr. 748-9.
74. FD 21510, tr. 1359-60.
75. FD 21510, tr 1073-76.
76. FD 21510, ex. H-177.
77. FD 21510, tr. 1023-62 and ex. H-140.
78. FD 21510, tr. 1724-25 and ex. H-121.
79. FD 21510, tr. 1514-21, 1599-602 and ex. H-41. This was particularly painful for the New York people who at long last had won favorable rulings to equalize rates for the North Atlantic ports. For years, the greater sea distance from Europe to southerly ports had been compensated by a shorter rail distance and lower rail rates to the interior. Conversely, the northerly ports, New York and Boston, took a higher rail rate and lower sea rates. But these "Atlantic port differentials" had become obsolete as the sea rates had tended to equalize, leaving the northerly ports at a disadvantage. Boston had brought suit to have the rail rates equalized (Civil Action 61-38-3, *B&M RR* et al. v *ICC and U.S.*). New York feared the arrangements among the railroads might freeze rates at the old differential level.
80. *Trains,* August 1960, p. 8.
81. *New York Times,* Nov. 7, 1961, p. 47.

Chapter 7

1. The builders of the Central Pacific, the so-called Pacific Associates of Huntington, Crocker, Stanford, and Hopkins, had gone on to build the SP, and had tended to divert traffic away from the Ogden gateway. So E.H. Harriman bought control of the SP, a move that was found to violate the antitrust laws. *United States* v. *Union Pacific,* 226 US 61 (1912). The SP was ordered to give up the Central Pacific when it was found that keeping it could ruin the UP. *United States* v. *Southern Pacific,* 259 US 214 (1922). But when it was found the Central Pacific could not survive alone, the ICC let SP have it under the condition that all traffic moving from Oregon and northern California to points west of an arc from Niagara Falls, New York, to Wheeling, West Virginia, be routed via Ogden. *Control of Central Pacific by Southern Pacific,* 76 ICC 508 (1923).
2. *Control of El Paso & Southwestern,* 90 ICC 732 (1924).
3. *Unification of Southwestern Lines,* 124 ICC 401 (1927).
4. *St. Louis Southwestern Ry. Co., Control,* 180 ICC 175 (1932).
5. Western Pacific originated 5.4 percent, terminated 3.8 percent; Santa Fe originated 20 percent, terminated 26 percent; Union Pacific and various shortlines handled the remainder. FD 21314, *Southern Pacific—Control—Western Pacific,* reported 327 ICC 387 (1965), brief of AT&SF, vol. 17.
6. *Great Northern Ry. Co., Construction,* 166 ICC 3 (1930).
7. FD 21314, tr. 85-87.
8. FD 21314, tr. 3928.
9. FD 21314, exceptions of the RLEA, vol. 1-L; tr. 3402-03.
10. FD 21314, vol. 1-B.

11. FD 21314, application of the SP, vol. 1.

12. FD 21314, tr. 91-92.

13. The Great Northern; Northern Pacific; Chicago, Burlington & Quincy, and the Spokane, Portland & Seattle. The NP and GN each owned 48 percent of the Burlington and 50 percent of the SP&S. Originally, the merged company was to be called the Great Northern Pacific, but Burlington, larger than either of its parents, induced them to change it to Great Northern Pacific & Burlington Lines. The name GNP&BL was so awkward, the eventual change to Burlington Northern was wise.

14. Max Lowenthal, *The Investor Pays.* In those days, the Milwaukee Road was popularly known as the "St. Paul."

15. FD 21478, *Great Northern—Merger—Northern Pacific,* reported 328 ICC 460 (1966), exceptions of Dep. of Justice, Jan. 15, 1965. Remaining traffic was handled by the Union Pacific. Other traffic percentages, based on ton miles:

	Montana	*North Dakota*	*Minnesota*
.GN	40.9	48.2	30.7
NP	39.4	33.0	13.3
Milw.	24.77	7.06	15.98

16. *Great Northern Pacific Ry. Co., Acquisition,* 162 ICC 37 (1930).

17. 328 ICC 460, 504

18. FD 21478, exceptions of Minn. R&W Comm., Jan. 15, 1965, p. 171. It was thought the low per diem rental charge for cars off home rails discouraged new car purchases.

19. FD 21478, exceptions of Minn. R&W Comm., p. 128. A copy of *Consolidation—Key to Transportation Progress* is in U.S. Senate, *Rail Merger Legislation* (1962) p. 801.

20. FD 21478, tr. 810-11, 1320.

21. *Pearsall* v. *GN Ry.,* 161 US 646, 677 (1896).

22. 328 ICC 460, 512. They also thought another study was deceptive that purported to show the impact of intermodal competition. It cited only the years 1947, at the peak of the postwar boom, and 1960, a recession year for railroads. If all the years in between had been listed, the picture would have been one of undulating peaks and valleys until the recession, and if the years 1961 to 1964 were added, it would have shown figures soaring above the 1950s highs.

23. FD 21478, exceptions of Dept. of Justice, p. 103.

24. FD 21478, petition of Baukol-Noonan, Inc., Feb. 5, 1968.

25. FD 21478, brief of Minn. R&W Comm., June 5, 1967. The C&NW wanted a gateway opened up to it at Oakes, North Dakota, in order to get its long haul.

26. *Rail Merger Legislation,* pp. 239-41. It should be added, however, that Rasmussen was sometimes given to intemperate remarks that he could not adequately substantiate. A particularly nasty illustration of this was an exchange of letters between him and Ben Heineman of the C&NW, reprinted in *Rail Merger Legislation,* pp. 1000-10, including the statement by him that hundreds of complaints had been received about C&NW's service on the newly acquired M&StL line. When pressed, he would not or could not produce the evidence, but suggested the inadequacy of

service was so well known that questioning the existence of these letters was "ridiculous" and "childish."

27. FD 21478, reply of 230 Pacific Northwest Shippers.

28. FD 21478, exceptions of Dept. of Justice, Jan. 15, 1965.

29. FD 21478, brief of Dept. of Justice, appendix X.

30. Notably Burdick (D-N. Dak.), Church (D-Idaho), Humphrey (D-Minn.), McCarthy (D-Minn.), Mansfield (D-Mont.), Metcalf (D-Mont.), Morse (I-Oreg.), Moss (D-Utah), and Schoepple (R-Kans.).

31. Minnesota, Montana, Oregon, and Washington were opposed. South Dakota, North Dakota, Michigan, Iowa, and Wisconsin sought substantial concessions by the applicants. In North Dakota, Gov. Guy and one of the state commissioners were opposed, but the other two commissioners were in favor with conditions.

Chapter 8

1. Derounian (R), Dooley (R), Dulski (D), Healy (D), King (R), and Ostertag (R). U.S. Senate, *Rail Merger Legislation* (1962), pp. 1216-18.

2. William H. Tucker and John H. O'Brien, "The Public Interest in Railroad Mergers" in *Rail Merger Legislation,* p. 911.

3. "Railroad Merger Mania: Its Causes and Cure," in *Rail Merger Legislation,* p. 1261.

4. Message from the President of the United States Relative to the Transportation System of the United States, in *Rail Merger Legislation,* p. 718.

5. *Report of the Interagency Committee on Transport Mergers* (ICC-CAB-FMC), Jan. 17, 1963.

6. James Symes (PRR), Leonard Murray (Soo Line), Jervis Langdon (B&O).

7. Harold Crotty (Maintenance of Way), George Harrison (Clerks), George Leighty (Telegraphers), William Kennedy (Trainmen), and Paul O'Dwyer (Transport Workers). Harrison served on FDR's "Committee of Six" in 1938.

8. Walter McDonald (Georgia PSC) and Paul Rasmussen (Minn. R&W Comm.).

9. George Baker (Harvard), Kent Healy (Yale), William Leonard (Hofstra), John Meyer (Harvard), James Nelson (Washington State), Merrill Roberts (Pittsburgh).

10. Some samples from Symes's chart at p. 339 of *Rail Merger Legislation:*

Industry	% Rate of Return	Industry	% Rate of Return
Drugs	19.7	Petroleum	10.4
Soap/cosmetics	17.2	Brewing	8.0
Soft drinks	15.8	Coal	7.5
Tobacco	14.8	Iron/steel	6.4
Automotive	14.2	Lumber	5.9
Finance	12.9	Meat packing	4.7
Chain food stores	12.3	*Class I RR*	2.2
Chemicals	11.5	Air transport	deficit
Construction	10.5		

11. Mainly, that railroads did not depreciate rights-of-way unless they were totally abandoned, which meant the investment base on which the rate of return was calculated was overstated.

12. U.S. House of Representatives, Committee on Armed Services, *Adequacy of Transportation Systems in Support of the National Defense Effort in Event of Mobilization* (1959).

13. *Rail Merger Legislation,* p. 371.

14. *Rail Merger Legislation,* pp. 235-36.

15. *Rail Merger Legislation,* p. 559.

16. *Rail Merger Legislation,* pp. 305, 313.

17. The Bureau of Inquiry and Compliance did not take a very active role. Its initial study, reprinted in *Rail Merger Legislation,* titled "Railroad Consolidations and the Public Interest—A Preliminary Study," supposedly the first of several installments, was all that ever came out. The author judged its sporadic presentations in the cases as poor. It has since been reorganized as the Bureau of Enforcement.

18. Max Malin, "A Realistic Appraisal of the Financial Condition of Railroads," published by the Brotherhood of Locomotive Engineers, reprinted in *Rail Merger Legislation,* is much too detailed to summarize here, but is an important antidote to the railroad crying-towel. Mr. Keyserling compiled a detailed chart of interlocking financial relationships, in *Rail Merger Legislation,* pp. 669-74. Derek Bok, "Section Seven of the Clayton Act and the Merging of Law and Economics," *Harvard Law Review,* December 1960, at p. 233 discounted this motive:

. . . Though it is generally conceded that the great combinations at the turn of the century were often the result of a desire to gain control of the market, the anticompetitive motive seems to have become increasingly rare in later years, having been replaced by a number of tax, managerial and commercial considerations of rather neutral value from an antitrust standpoint.

19. See J.A. Van Fleet, "Why the Railroads Never Stopped Running in Korea," *Trains,* July 1956, p. 16.

20. *Rail Merger Legislation,* P. 126.

21. *Rail Merger Legislation,* p. 26.

22. Healy's paper reprinted in *Rail Merger Legislation,* p. 735.

23. The commission even cited the "world crisis" as a reason for its approval. *C&O R. Co.—Control—B&O R. Co.* 317 ICC 261, 291 (1962).

24. 317 ICC 261, 298-99.

25. 317 ICC 261, 298.

26. 317 ICC 261, 331.

27. *Brotherhood of Maintenance of Way Employees,* et al., v. *United States,* 221 F. Supp. 19 (E.D. Mich., 1963) affirmed 375 US 216 (1963).

28. FD 21510, *N&W Ry. Co.—Merger—NYC&StL R. Co.,* tr. 136, 1150, 1738.

29. FD 21510, Dept. of Justice, motion for dismissal, vol, 1-D.

30. *Rochester Telephone Corp.* v. *United States,* 307 US 125 (1939).

31. U.S. Senate, Committee on Commerce, *The Penn Central and Other Railroads* (1972). Memo by David Bevan, Apr. 30, 1963, reprinted on p. 389.

32. *N&W Ry.—Merger—NYC&StL R. Co.,* 324 ICC 1 (1964), 148.

Chapter 9

1. *Boston & Maine Discontinuance of Passenger Service,* 324 ICC 418 (1965), and George W. Hilton, *The Transportation Act of 1958; A Decade of Experience,* ch. 4.

2. *NYNH&H RR Co., Trustees' Discontinuance of All Interstate Passenger Trains,* 327 ICC 151 (1966).

3. FD 21989, *Pennsylvania R. Co.—Merger—New York Central RR Co.,* reported 327 ICC 475 (1966), tr. 194, 1061.

4. In Re *Consolidation of Merger Proceedings,* Oct. 24, 1962, tr. 73.

5. FD 21989, tr. 1078.

6. FD 21989, tr. 1164.

7. James R. Nelson, *Railroad Mergers and the Economy of New England.* This is the most thoughtful analysis of New England railroad problems in the early 1960s, and the following analysis draws heavily upon it.

8. 62 ICC 513 (1921).

9. Nelson, *Railroad Mergers, p. 80.*

10. *Movement of Highway Trailers by Rail,* 293 ICC 93 (1954).

11. FD 21989, tr. 18, 469 and 6488.

12. FD 21989, tr. 1104.

13. FD 21989, tr. 11,574.

14. FD 21989, tr. 545.

15. FD 21989, tr. l032, 1460.

16. FD 21989, tr. 866-77.

17. An analysis is in U.S. Senate, Committee on Commerce, *The Penn Central and Other Railroads* (1972) at pp. 11-15 and 79-121.

18. Cole to Kattau, Aug. 30, 1965. *Penn Central and Other Railroads,* ex. 63. Some outside consultation was employed, but only for technical advice and with little discretionary power.

19. FD 21989, tr. 11,044.

20. FD 21989, tr. 5916.

21. FD 21989, tr. 6742-46.

22. Ibid.

23. Smucker to Saunders, Nov. 13, 1969. *Penn Central and Other Railroads,* ex. 65.

24. FD 21989, tr. 6245.

25. FD 21989, tr. 1104.

26. FD 21989, tr. 5893.

27. FD 21989, tr. 8563.

28. FD 21989, tr. 8949.

29. FD 21989, tr. 7082-95.

30. FD 21989, tr. 1598.

31. FD 21989, tr. 571-75.

32. FD 21989, tr. 1397-1508.

33. FD 21989, tr. 19,639-94 and ex. S-291 and H-349.

34. Katzenbach to Saunders, Sept. 4, 1964. *Penn Central and Other Railroads, ex. 67.*

35. *FD 21989, ex. NH-1 and tr. 24,* 549-52.

36. Saunders to Tate, July 13, 1965, in FD 21989, vol. 1-K.

37. Joseph Daughen and Peter Binzen, *The Wreck of the Penn Central,* p. 88.

38. FD 21989, petition of M.J. Shapp, Jan. 3, 1966, vol. 1-L.

39. See *Wall Street Journal,* July 20, 1964, p. 20.

40. 327 ICC 475, 532-34 and 561-63.

41. FD 21989, petition of N&W, June 13, 1966, vol. 1-M.

Chapter 10

1. Based on 1968 gross revenues, they ranked (in millions):

SCL Line (inc. L&N)	$733,905
Southern Ry.	493,390
MoPac System	465,654
Ill. Cent. Gulf	400,718

2. FD 21215, *Seaboard Air Line—Merger—Atlantic Coast Line,* reported 320 ICC 122 (1963), ex. 232 (not accepted in evidence), vol. 1-G.

3. FD 21215, ex. 232.

4. 320 ICC 122, 150-53.

5. 320 ICC 122, 239.

6. FD 21215, brief of RLEA, vol. 18. Coverdale & Colpitts also made some of the studies.

7. FD 21215, brief of FEC, vol. 18.

8. FD 21215, corres., vol. 1-A. The Georgia PSC, however, was an opponent.

9. FD 21215, petition of Southern, Aug. 23, 1960, vol. 1.

10. *United States* v. *Philadelphia National Bank,* 374 US 321, 372 (1963).

11. 320 ICC 122, 239.

12. *Florida East Coast Ry. v. United States,* 242 F. Supp. 14 (M.D. Fla., 1965) reversed in *Seaboard Air Line R. Co.* v. *United States,* 382 US 154 (1965).

13. FD 21215, ex. 232.

14. *Sou. Ry.—Control—Central of Ga. Ry.,* 317 ICC 557 (1967) and *Sou. Ry.—Control—Ga. & Fla. Ry.,* 317 ICC 745 (1963).

15. *Brotherhood of Maintenance of Way Employees* v. *United States,* 366 US 169 (1961).

16. *Arnold* v. *L&N R. Co.,* 180 F. Supp. 429 (M.D. Tenn., 1960); *Batts* v. *L&N* and *L&N* v. *Cantrell,* 316 F. 2d. 22 (6th cir., 1963). A subsequent decision on this issue was *Clemens* v. *CRR of NJ,* 264 F. Supp. 551 (E.D. Pa., 1967).

17. *Brotherhood of Locomotive Engineers,* v. *C&NW R. Co.,* 314 F. 2d, 424 (8th cir., 1963).

18. *Nemitz* v. *N&W R. Co.,* 404 US 37 (1971).

19. 317 ICC 557, 588-91.

20. *Railway Labor Executives' Assn.* v. *United States,* 226 F. Supp. 521 (E.D. Va., 1964) reversed and remanded, 379 US 199 (1964).

21. *Sou. Ry.—Control—Central of Ga. Ry.,* 320 ICC 377 (1964).

22. *Sou. Ry.—Control—Central of Ga. Ry.,* 331 ICC 151 (1967).

23. FD 21755, *Missouri R. Co.—Control—Chicago & Eastern Illinois R. Co.,* reported 327 ICC 279 (1965), affidavit of intervening security holders, May 5, 1965, vol. 1-D.

24. FD 21755, ex. H-1, H-78, H-79, and exception of Bureau of Inquiry and Compliance, vol. 1-B.

25. 327 ICC 279, 316-21, 336-38, and *Illinois Central R. Co.* v. *United States,* 263 F. Supp. 421 (N.D. Ill., 1967).

26. FD 21755, tr. 2596.

27. FD 21755, statement of D.O. Mathews, vol. 1-A.

28. FD 21755, ex. H-188, H-198.

29. 263 F. Supp. 421, affirmed 385 US 457 (1967).

30. FD 25103, *Ill. Cent. Gulf. R. Co., Acquisition, GM&O R. Co., Ill. Cent. R. Co.,* et al, reported 338 ICC 805 (1971) tr. 2062-63, 2210, 2261, and brief of Missouri Pacific RR.

31. FD 25103, Williams to ICC, Oct. 10, 1968, vol. 1-B.

32. *Trains,* August 1977, p. 7.

33. *Trains,* October 1972, pp. 3-4.

34. *Tennessee Central Ry. Co., Abandonment,* 334 ICC 235 (1969).

35. *L&N R. Co.—Merger—Monon RR.,* 338 ICC 134 (1970).

36. FD 28417, *FEC Ry.* v. *SCL RR.,* cited in *Trains,* June 1977, p. 7.

37. Bill Anderson, "The Merger Movement," *Passenger Train Journal,* March 1977, p. 23.

Chapter 11

1. Account of the proxy fight gleaned from FD 2268, *Chicago & North Western R. Co.—Control—Chi., Rock Island & Pac. R. Co.,* joint brief of UP, SP, and RI, brief of C&NW, and from *New York Times,* June 23, 26, 28, Nov. 15 (1963), Jan. 17, June 19, Nov. 12 (1964), and Jan. 11, 1965.

2. Based on 1969 market prices, it was $30.66 versus $21.37 market price of RI stock.

3. FD 22688, Klitenic Report, pt. 1.

4. The pamphlet was prepared by Hayden, Stone & Co.

5. *Chicago Daily News,* April 30, 1968, p. 16.

6. *C&NW Ry. Co.—Merger—CGW R. Co.,* 330 ICC 13 (1967).

7. *Soo Line RR* v. *United States,* 280 F. supp. 907 (1968) and *C&NW Ry. Co.—Merger—CGW R. Co.,* 333 ICC 235 (1968).

8. *United States* v. *ICC,* civil action 1132-68, Nov. 20, 1968, p. 40.

9. FD 24182, *Chicago, Milwaukee, St. Paul & Pacific R. Co.—Merger—Chicago & North Western R. Co.,* (not reported) exceptions of applicants.

10. Dudley Pegrum, "The Chicago & North Western-Chicago, Milwaukee St. Paul & Pacific Merger: A Case Study in Transportation Economics," *Transportation Journal,* Winter 1969, pp. 43-50.

11. FD 24182, corres., vols. 1-L and 1-M.

12. *Chicago Daily News,* Feb. 27, 1970.

13. *Chicago Daily News,* April 14, 1970, and March 19, 1971.

14. *Great Northern Pacific & Burlington Lines—Merger—Great Northern Ry.,* et al., 331 ICC 869 (1968).

15. *United States* v. *ICC (Northern Lines Merger Cases)* 396 US 491 (1970).

16. FD 21503, *Illinois Central Gulf-Merger,* C&NW motion for discovery, Jan. 24, 1969, with supporting memorandum; and 338 ICC 805, 866-73 (1971).

17. FD 22688, vol. 1—U.

18. Even John Barriger had been unable to bring it back. It had come under a holding company that used it, at first, for tax loss purposes. Its funded debt was very high, and Santa Fe was given mild compensation by the requirement that Katy's owners negotiate a sale based on earning power or scrap value, not on the debt that was largely in the hands of speculators.

19. *New York Times,* Sept. 19 and Sept. 24, 1975.

20. *New York Times,* Sept. 3, 1971.

21. Rush Loving, Jr., "A Railroad Merger That Worked," *Fortune,* August 1972.

22. *New York Times,* Dec. 23, 1970, p. 35.

23. *Trains,* December 1977, p. 3, June 1977, p. 8; and November 1977, p. 9.

Chapter 12

1. *New York Times,* Jan. 8, 1967, III, p. 3.

2. FD 21510, *N&W Ry. Co—Merger—NYC&StL R. Co.,* supplemental report, 330 ICC 780 (1967), statement NW-1, vol. 13.

3. FD 21510, tr. 1386.

4. FD 23422, *Erie Lackawanna* v. *Lehigh Valley,* reported 330 ICC 306 (1966) tr. 30-50, 131-39.

5. FD 23422, tr. 122-23.

6. FD 23422, tr. 89.

7. FD 21510, statement EL-3, vol. 9.

8. FD 21510, statement EL-1, vol. 9.

9. FD 21510, statement EL-4, vol. 9.

10. FD 21510, ex. NW-4, pp. 31-33, vol. 14.

11. FD 23178, *Western Maryland Ry. Co., Control by Chesapeake & Ohio R. Co.,* reported 328 ICC 684 (1967).

12. FD 23832, *Norfolk & Western Ry.—Merger—Chesapeake & Ohio R. Co.,* not reported, tr. 253.

13. FD 23832, tr. 262.

14. FD 23832, tr. 630.

15. FD 23832, tr. 249.

16. FD 23832, tr. 419-29.

17. FD 21510, statement EL-1, vol. 9.

18. FD 21510, tr. 1289, 1295, 1347.

19. *New York Times,* Mar. 17, 1968.

20. FD 21510, statements DH-1 to DH-5, vol. 11.

21. FD 21510, ex. NW-4, pp. 53-54.

22. FD 21510, ex. NW-4, pp. 53-54.

23. FD 21510, proxy statement at annual meeting of stockholders, April 13, 1966, attached to ex. NW-4 and NW-45, vol. 15. See *Galcy* v. *United States,* Docs. 6652-66, U.S. Cir. Ct. Appeals, May 25, 1966, and *United States* v. *Boston & Maine,* 380 US 57 (1965).

24. FD 23832, ex. A-11, vol. 8 and FD 21510, ex. NW-9, vol. 15.

25. FD 23832, tr. 631-32.

26. FD 23832, tr. 251-52.

27. FD 23832, tr. 249 and ex. 146, rebuttal of John Fishwick, Dec. 14, 1967, vol. 16.

28. FD 23832, tr. 630.

29. FD 23832, tr. 228.

30. *Erie Lackawanna RR Co.,* v. *United States,* 259 F. Supp. 964 (S.D.N.Y., 1966).

31. *Baltimore & Ohio R. Co.* v. *United States,* 386 US 372 (1967), 392.

32. 386 US 372, 442.

33. *Erie Lackawanna RR Co.,* v. *United States,* 279 F. Supp. 303 (S.D.N.Y., 1967).

34. *Oscar Gruss and Son* v. *United States,* 261 F. Supp. 386 (S.D.N.Y., 1966).

35. *Pennsylvania RR. Co.—Merger—New York Central,* 331 ICC 643 (1967).

36. *Penn Central Merger and N&W Inclusion Cases,* 389 US 486 (1968), 510-11.

37. *New York Times,* Mar. 17, 1968 and FD 23832, tr. 9826.

38. See Ken Kraemer and Devan Lawton, "Buffalo Terminal," *Trains,* February 1976.

39. FD 23832, address to Security Analysts of San Francisco, Nov. 9, 1967, vol. 16.

Chapter 13

1. U.S. Senate, Committee on Commerce, *Penn Central and Other Railroads,* Bevan to Saunders, Nov. 8, 1967, p. 559.

2. FD 35291, *Investigation into the Management of the Business of the Penn Central Transportation Company and Affiliated Companies.* Accused of being asleep at the switch, the ICC undertook this investigation in 1970 to 1971. It is a series of reports by field staff from points all over the PC system. Most of the material in this chapter up to part 5 is drawn from these reports. Further citation will refer only to documents cited internally within that docket.

3. Rush Loving, Jr., "The Penn Central Bankruptcy Express," *Fortune,* August 1970. This was the first real analysis of the PC disaster in the press, and most of Loving's conclusions stood up well in later investigation. There were inaccuracies with regard to accounting techniques, and *Fortune* had to make a partial retraction. See *Wall Street Journal,* Aug. 1, 1970, p. 4.

4. FD 35291, statement 16.

5. FD 35291, Large to Saunders, Nov. 14, 1969.

6. FD 35291, Large to Saunders, May 1, 1967.

7. FD 35291, Bossler to Ring, Dec. 3, 1968.

8. FD 35291, Lamprecht to Smucker, Sept. 4, 1968; Hasselman to Taylor, Sept. 10, 1968; Taylor to Hasselman, Sept. 10, 1968.

9. FD 35291, Flannery to Harrison, Aug. 26, 1969.

10. FD 35291, statement 35, Langdon to Perlman, Apr. 21, 1969.

11. FD 35291, statements 16 and 26.

12. FD 35291, statement 16.

13. FD 35291, statement 30.

14. FD 35291, report of J.F. Aigeltinger of the ICC Bureau of Enforcement after a visit to the Altoona Shops, Apr. 8, 1971.

15. FD 35291, statement 33.

16. FD 35291, statement 32.

17. A discussion of the different rate policy, with documentation, is in *Penn Central and Other Railroads,* pp. 87-92.

18. Preparations for the Tarrytown meeting are discussed in FD 35291, Smucker to Perlman, Oct. 1, 1969. The journalistic accounts referred to are in the Loving article, cited above, and in Joseph Daughen and Peter Binzen, *The Wreck of the Penn Central,* p. 121.

19. The memo is reproduced in *Penn Central and Other Railroads,* pp. 704-05.

20. *The Magazine of Sigma Chi,* Winter 1963, p. 34.

21. U.S. Senate, Committee on Commerce, *Failing Railroads, (1970), p. 324.*

22. *Failing Railroads, p. 324.*

23. *Failing Railroads,* p. 396.

24. *Failing Railroads,* p. 388.

25. U.S. House of Representatives, Committee on Banking Staff Report, *The Penn Central Failure and the Role of Financial Institutions* (1972), p. 156.

26. *Penn Central and Other Railroads,* p. 343. The whole section titled "Corporate Character" is filled with insight.

27. *The Penn Central Failure* discusses this with supporting evidence at pp. 280-84.

28. *The Penn Central Failure* discusses this with supporting evidence at pp. 189-271.

29. Daughen and Binzen, p. 85.

30. Most of the acquisitions were made by the Pennsylvania Company, not the railroad. The Pennsylvania Company was wholly owned by the railroad, but to imply the railroad made the purchases is technically in error. For a description of the financing of diversification, see *Penn Central and Other Railroads,* pp. 387-430.

31. *Failing Railroads,* pp. 329-31.

32. For a discussion with supporting documentation, see U.S. House of Representatives, Committee on Commerce, staff study, *Inadequacies of Protections for Investors in Penn Central and Other ICC-Regulated Companies (1971).*

33. The guest list is reproduced in *Penn Central and Other Railroads,* p. 527, and a discussion of the Hodge-Bevan relationship is at pp. 404-06.

34. A lengthy discussion of Penphil, with supporting documentation, is in *The Penn Central Failure,* pp. 189-254.

35. A lengthy discussion of Executive Jet, with supporting documentation, including a verbatim transcript of the Ricciardi deposition, is in *The Penn Central Failure,* pp. 55-148.

36. *The Penn Central Failure,* pp. 112-114.

37. *The Penn Central Failure,* pp. 129-42.

38. *Penn Central and Other Railroads,* Cook to Bevan, Oct. 5, 1967, p. 732.

39. Bevan to Saunders, Nov. 21, 1966, in *Penn Central and Other Railroads,* p. 616.

40. FD 35291, Weitzner to Saunders, Dec. 10, 1968.

41. Bevan to Saunders, Nov. 21, 1966, in *Penn Central and Other Railroads,* p. 616.

42. FD 35291, Saunders to Day, Dec. 8, 1969.

43. *The Penn Central Failure,* correspondence and memos, pp. 163-7.

44. *The Penn Central Failure,* minutes, Nov. 26, 1969, p. 150.

45. *The Penn Central Failure* gives a chronology of both the publicly known events leading to bankruptcy and those not publicly known, at pp. 318-20, and then continues with a discussion with supporting documentation of possible illegal trading by banks.

46. Perlman refused to resign until his employment contract was up.

47. *New York Times,* Jan. 7, 1972, p. 41, and July 30, 1974, p. 43.

Chapter 14

1. Equitable Life, Metropolitan Life, Connecticut Life, and Northwestern Mutual.

2. ICC Ex Parte 293, *Northeastern Railroad Investigation,* statement of the Reading Co., Mar. 12, 1973.

3. Cleveland *Plain Dealer,* June 27, 1972, p. 1.

4. Ex Parte 293, statement of the D&H, Mar. 12, 1973.

5. FD 35291, *Investigation into the Management of the Business of the Penn Central Transportation Company and Affiliated Companies,* handwritten note on a memo from Forrester to Hasselman, Mar. 18, 1969.

6. *Erie Lackawanna Ry Co.* v. *Penn Central Co.,* 338 ICC 513 (1969).

7. See Bob Mahowski, "The Poughkeepsie Bridge is Burning," *Railfan,* Winter 1974, p. 18.

8. *Congressional Record,* vol. 119, p. 36,349.

9. Marshall Smith, "'We're Going Broke,' He Told the Workers," *Life,* Sept. 24, 1969, p. 69; and *New York Times,* Jan. 26, 1974, p. 1.

10. *Penn Central Transportation Co., Discontinuance of 34 Passenger Trains,* 338 ICC 380 (1970).

11. U.S. House of Representatives, Committee on Commerce, *Northeast Rail Transportation (1973) beginning p. 288.*

12. A list of the segments and the status of their case before the ICC is in U.S. Senate, Committee on Commerce, hearings, *Review of the Penn Central's Condition—1971,* pp. 6-9.

13. *New York Times,* Jan. 13, 1972, p. 41. Erie Lackawanna and Boston & Maine paid the increases, but all other eastern bankrupts reneged on at least some of them. *Northeast Rail Transportation,* p. 475.

14. Figures cited in *Northeastern Railroad Problem,* report to Congress, Department of Transportation, Mar. 26, 1973 at p. 30:

Carrier	Net Ton Miles per Employee, 1970 (in thousands)
Southern	2,000
Missouri Pacific	1,800
Southern Pacific	1,700
Union Pacific	1,600
Norfolk & Western	1,600
Illinois Central	1,500
Seaboard Coast Line	1,400
Burlington Northern	1,400
Chessie System	1,300
Erie Lackawanna	1,100
Penn Central	900

15. Those bodies, cited in *Review of the Penn Central's Condition* at p. 133, were Emergency Board 109 (1955), the Presidential Railroad Commission (1962), Arbitration Board 282 (1963), Emergency Board 154 (1963), Emergency Board 172 (1968), Emergency Board 177 (1970), and Emergency Board 178 (1970).

16. *Northeast Rail Transportation*, prepared statement of L.E. Dennis, pp. 471-85.

17. Ex Parte 293, statement of the Lehigh Valley; *New York Times,* July 16, 1972, p. 1; and *Trains,* May 1967, p. 3.

18. Ex Parte 293, statements of Reading, Penn Central, Boston & Maine, and Lehigh Valley, Mar. 12, 1973.

19. FD 26115, *Boston & Maine Reorganization,* report and order, cited in Ex Parte 293, statement of Amoskeag Co.

20. Ex Parte 293, statement of Maine Central, with attached annual reports of MEC and Amoskeag, and the *Maine Central Messenger,* June-July 1972, pp. 2-3.

21. Ex Parte 293, statements of LV and D&H.

22. U.S. District Court, N.D. Ohio, doc. B-72-2838, *Erie Lackawanna Ry. Co., Reorganization,* doc. 158.

23. *Reconstruction Finance Corp.* v. *Denver & Rio Grande Wn. RR,* 328 US 535,536 (1946).

24. 251 US 396, 399 (1920), upheld in *Bullock* v. *Railroad Commission of Florida,* 254 US 513 (1921) and *Railroad Commission of Texas* v. *East Texas Railroad,* 264 US 79 (1927).

25. *NYNH&H RR Co. First Mortgage 4% Bondholder Committee* v. *United States,* 289 F. Supp. 418 (S.D.N.Y., 1968) and In Re *NYNH&H RR Co.,* 289 F. Supp. 451 (D. Conn., 1968).

26. *New Haven Inclusion Cases,* 399 US 392 (1970).

27. *New York Times,* Jan. 22, 1973, pp. 1, 39 and Mar. 6, 1973, p. 40.

28. *Review of the Penn Central's Condition—1971,* pp. 46-58.

29. In *Northeast Rail Transportation,* p. 175:

Class I RR in U.S. Outperform All Major Government-Controlled Roads

	Profit (loss) in millions	Shipper cost/ ton mile (cents)	Employees/ mile	Labor as % op. rev.
U.S. Class I RR	$569	1.31	2.8	53.7
Canadian Pacific	21	1.28	3.6	53.1
Canadian National	(116)	1.32	3.5	65.1
British Rys.	(354)	3.34	25.5	79.6
French National Rys.	(901)	2.83	13.5	86.4
German Federal Rys.	(704)	2.88	21.6	85.9
Italian State Rys.	(578)	2.40	18.7	111.0
Netherland Rys.	(41)	2.07	13.3	62.8
Japanese National Rys.	(376)	1.66	36.0	47.2

The figures, however, have no validity, as they attempt to compare dissimilar things. Foreign railroads carry more passengers, and are a more labor-intensive kind of railroading. Their freight tends to have a high proportion of manufactured items, often in containers, hence higher cost/mile to shippers. Notice that in terms of cost efficiency, Japanese Railways deploys labor as efficiently as the best U.S. railroads, almost 40 percent more effectively than Penn Central.

30. The Interim Reports of Jan. 1 and Feb. 1, 1973, are reprinted in *Northeast Rail Transportation,* beginning p. 255.

31. *Review of the Penn Central's Condition—1971,* testimony of James M. Beggs, beginning p. 3.

32. *Northeast Rail Transportation.* The ICC's plan was H.R. 6591. A modified version of DOT's plan was H.R. 5485. H.R. 4897 proposed to have the government acquire and rehabilitate rights-of-way, with reorganized private railroads operating on them.

33. S. 2526, cited in William Bush, "Western Railroad Mergers—Then and Now," ICC Practitioners' Journal.

34. See Joseph Albright, "The Penn Central, A Hell of a Way to Run a Government," *New York Times Magazine,* Nov. 3, 1974.

35. H.R. 9142 became Public Law 92-236, The Regional Rail Reorganization Act of 1973, reprinted in USRA *Preliminary System Plan,* vol. 1.

36. Named to the board: for solvent railroads, Gale Aydelott, D&RGW RR; for local governments, Frank Blatz, past president of New Jersey Conference of Mayors; for labor, James Burke of the UTU; for banks, Samuel B. Payne of Morgan, Stanley & Co.; for states, William Scranton, former governor of Pennsylvania; for large shippers, William K. Smith of General Mills; for small shippers, Charles Schuman, former president of the American Farm Bureau Federation. Arthur D. Lewis, selected as chairman, was formerly chief operating officer for Eastern Airlines.

37. See *Congressional Record,* vol. 119, pp. 36,346-49.

38. See, for example, the bravura remarks of Arthur Lewis, chairman, USRA, in U.S. House of Representatives, Committee on Commerce, *United States Railway*

Association Preliminary System Plan (1975), p. 6. (Hereafter cited as *Hearings on the Preliminary Plan.)*

39. *Evaluation of the Secretary of Transportation's Rail Services Report,* a report of the Rail Services Planning Office of the ICC, May 1974, pp. 18-27.

40. *Hearings on the Preliminary Plan,* pp. 16-17.

41. U.S. House of Representatives, Committee on Commerce, *USRA Final System Plan* (1975) p. 766. (Hereafter cited as *Hearings on the Final Plan.)*

42. *Evaluation of the Preliminary Plan,* p. 50, and *Hearings on the Final Plan,* p. 115.

43. *Evaluation of the Preliminarry Plan,* pp. 13, 37-47.

44. *Hearings on the Preliminary Plan,* pp. 183-93.

45. *Hearings on the Preliminary Plan,* pp. 159-62.

46. *Philadelphia Inquirer,* May 9, 1975, reproduced in *Hearings on the Preliminary Plan,* p. 349.

47. *Hearings on the Preliminary Plan,* p. 420.

48. *Hearings on the Final Plan,* p. 105.

49. *Hearings on the Final Plan,* p. 16.

50. Haldeman to Rooney, Oct. 6, 1975, in *Hearings on the Final Plan,* p. 99.

51. ICC RSPO, *Evaluation of the USRA's Final System Plan,* Aug. 25, 1975, pp. 6-9.

52. *Hearings on the Final Plan,* p. 466.

53. *Hearings on the Final Plan,* p. 83.

54. *Time,* July 9, 1973, p. 53.

55. Kevin Keefe, "How Michigan Got Into the Railroad Business." *Trains,* October 1976, p. 46.

56. *New York Times,* Apr. 1, 1976, p. 47.

57. *New York Times,* Dec. 1, 1975, p. 49.

58. *New York Times,* Mar. 4, 1976, p. 1.

59. *New York Times,* Mar. 20, 1976, p. 37.

60. *Moody's Transportation News Reports,* May 20, 1977.

61. *Moody's Transportation News Reports,* August 19, 1977.

62. Conrail Second Quarterly Financial Report, quoted in *Trains,* Nov. 1977, p. 16.

63. *Business Week,* Sept. 19, 1977, pp. 66-88.

Chapter 15

1. National Arbitration Panel, Case 11, In Re *Level of Rail Utility,* Nov. 20, 1973, Mar. 5, 1974 and Dec. 31, 1974; *Passenger Train Journal,* February/March, 1976, p. 18.

2. Burlington Northern Quarterly Report to Stockholders, May 4, 1977.

3. U.S. House of Representatives, Committee on Interstate Commerce, *Railroad Revitalization,* hearings, 94th Cong., 1st sess., June 1975.

4. T.P. Ellsworth, Jr., "The Merger Merry-Go-Round: Rail Consolidations Under the 4-R Act," *ICC Practitioners' Journal,* May/June, 1977.

5. U.S. Department of Transportation, *Final Standards, Classification and*

Designation of Lines of Class I Railroads in the United States, Jan. 19, 1977.

6. ICC Rail Services Planning Office, *Evaluation Report of the Secretary of Transportation's Preliminary Classification and Designation of Rail Lines,* Dec. 1, 1976.

7. Even an upbeat article on the Burlington Northern noted that, among numerous complaints, one shipper claimed that certain deliveries which took five days before merger took upward of thirty days after. Robert A. Wright, "The Way West Looks Bright for Merged Railway," *New York Times,* March 25, 1973, III, p. 1.

8. In an extensive study of consolidation in 1977, the ICC's Rail Services Planning Office devoted an entire volume to "Alternatives to Merger" and found there were many that railroads had barely explored. As part of that study, R.L. Banks Associates studied run-through trains and concluded they were a "harbinger of future railroad operations in which traffic decline is arrested and industry expansion is once again a forseeable near-term objective." RSPO, "Study of Merger Alternatives: Run-Through Trains," *Rail Merger Study,* September 21, 1977, p. 6.

9. FD 21510, *Norfolk & Wn. R. Co.-New York, Chi. & St. L. R. Co., Merger,* corres., vol. 1-B.

10. *New York Times,* March 9, 1969, III, p. 1.

11. RSPO, "Merger White Paper," *Rail Merger Study,* April 15, 1977.

12. *Time,* July 6, 1970, p. 59. See also syndicated column of Ernest B. Furgurson, "Nationalization or Death?" which appeared in *Greenville* (S.C.) *News,* March 3, 1975, p. 4.

13. *Trains,* December 1977, p. 18.

14. *Time,* December 5, 1977, p. 65.

15. *Trains,* April 1975, p. 4.

16. *Niagara Gazette,* Nov. 15, 1974; Dec. 19, 1975; Aug. 12, 1977; and Nov. 16, 1977.

17. National Rail Safety Board, report, and *Trains,* October, 1974, p. 13. See also Todd E. Fandell, "Our Railroads are No Longer Safe," *This Week,* Nov. 2, 1969.

Bibliography

The principal source for this book was the written record of the merger cases as found in the ICC's dockets. These consist of transcripts, exhibits, briefs, orders, and reports. They do not reveal everything about a merger, but only what was officially known. However, as cases became intertwined, each successive docket revealed new facets about previous ones. Unfortunately, they contain no record of the debates of commissioners, or what, if any, unofficial pressures were applied to them. Recent cases are available at the Dockets File Room of the ICC on Constitution Avenue in Washington, D.C. Older dockets are stored at the Federal Records Center at Suitland, Maryland, and the ICC will arrange to have them made available. Mergers, along with passenger train discontinuances and corporate reorganizations, all come under the commission's division of finance and are called finance dockets. Hence their citation in notes throughout this book by the abbreviation "FD."

The reports, which summarize the docket and explain the commission's decision, are also cited frequently in standard legal form, giving volume number, series, and page, in that order. (For example: 133 ICC 487.) These reports are available in major libraries, including all law libraries in the United States, and contain a great deal of information. They are not substitutes for the docket, however. They contain only what the commission thought was important to support its decision, which is not necessarily what the historian finds important in the raw materials of the docket.

Many of these cases eventually wound up in litigation before federal courts, with district court cases reported in the *Federal Supplement,* and Supreme Court cases in the *United States Reports.* These are available at law libraries.

After the bankruptcies of the eastern railroads, reorganizations were assigned to Federal District Courts—the New Haven in Connecticut, the Penn Central, Lehigh Valley, and Reading in Philadelphia, the Boston & Maine in Boston, the Jersey Central in Newark, and the Erie Lackawanna in Cleveland. These dockets contain an enormous amount of material, only a fraction of which is included in this research. An index and digest of the Penn Central docket is at the ICC library.

Another important source was congressional reports and hearings. Hearings contain the verbatim testimony of experts and interested witnesses, which usually runs the gamut of opinion. Reports often contain monumental quantities of research, sometimes made especially valuable because the investigators were able to subpoena key private documents into the public record. However, these written sources give no clues as to the lobbying that went on behind the scenes of political Washington.

Sometimes, journalists were able to fill in the gaps. Robert Bedingfield's coverage in the *New York Times* was most important. The *Wall Street Journal* did several in-depth stories, as did the *Buffalo Evening News,* the *Philadelphia Inquirer,* the *Cleveland Plain Dealer,* the *Washington Star,* and the *Niagara Gazette.* Drew Pearson's and later Jack Anderson's *Washington Merry-Go-Round* was valuable at times. Articles by Rush Loving, Jr., in *Fortune* and *The Wreck of the Penn Central* by Joseph Daughen and Peter Binzen, are really primary, rather than secondary sources, because they relied heavily on direct interviews. *Trains,* a magazine for mature rail fans, is read by many who are associated with railroading. Its news reporting is slow but excellent, and the editorial comments of its editor, David P. Morgan, have been outstanding since the magazine's founding in 1940. *Railway Age* sometimes had news items of interest, but generally its articles were too short and too bland to be of use.

I was able to fill in some of the gaps in the written record myself in conversations with some of the participants in the mergers. However, with one exception, these were not the principal figures in the cases. Some of these people asked that I not mention their names, as they were talking candidly about colleagues and bosses. I decided it was best not to mention any of them. None of my conclusions are based on anything that they told me that was not also confirmed by the written record. By and large, what they said simply reaffirmed my previous judgments or suspicions.

When Helen R. Richardson was librarian at the Library of the Bureau of Railway Economics of the Association of American Railroads, she compiled a magnificent bibliography of that library's material on mergers. There were several supplements to it, with entries dating up to 1965. These included many rare items, some printed, some mimeographed. Some of these may have been the only copy preserved in a regular depository. When the Association of American Railroads moved to its new headquarters in Washington, D.C., it discarded a great deal of that material. Some, I was told, went to the Library of Congress, which seemed unable to locate any of it. Some was supposed to have been returned to railroad companies. Only a fraction of the items in the card catalog are actually on the shelves. In addition, the shelves are closed to the public. I found the personnel indifferent to outsiders. As a result, the library has been largely destroyed as a place for historical research.

Happily, two other libraries have acquired very exciting collections and are worthwhile for research in transportation. These are the ICC Library in Washington and the Northwestern University Transportation Library in Evanston, Illinois.

Some of the following may be of use to the reader who wishes to pursue particular topics:

Books and Dissertations

Alberts, William W., and Joel E. Segall, eds. *The Corporate Merger.* Chicago, 1966.

Anderson, James, *The Emergence of the Modern Regulatory State.* Washington, D.C., 1962.

Barriger, John. *Super Railroads for a Dynamic American Economy.* New York, 1956.

Bernstein, Marver. *Regulating Business by Independent Commission.* Princeton, N.J., 1955.

Bishop, David. *Railroad Decisions of the Interstate Commerce Commission*. Washington, D.C., 1961.

Bogen, Jules. *The Anthracite Railroads: A Study in American Enterprise*. New York, 1927.

Borkin, Joseph. *Robert R. Young: The Populist of Wall Street*. New York, 1969.

Bryant, Keith. *History of the Atchison, Topeka and Santa Fe*. New York, 1975.

Burnie, Nardreen A., ed. *Transportation Mergers and Acquisitions*. Evanston, Ill., 1962.

Caine, Stanley. *The Myth of Progressive Reform*. Madison, Wisc., 1970.

Campbell, E.G. *The Reorganization of the American Railroad System, 1893-1900*. New York, 1938.

Carson, Clarence. *Throttling the Railroads*. Indianapolis, 1971.

Carson, Robert. *Main Line to Oblivion*. New York, 1971.

Casey, Robert J., and W.A.S. Douglas. *The Lackawanna Story*. New York, 1951.

Chandler, Alfred D., Jr., ed. *The Railroads: The Nation's First Big Business*. New York, 1965.

Cherington, Charles. *The Regulation of Railroad Abandonments*. Cambridge, Mass., 1948.

Cleveland, Frederick A., and Fred W. Powell. *Railroad Promotion and Capitalization in the United States*. New York, 1909.

Conant, Michael. *Railroad Mergers and Abandonments*. Berkeley, 1964.

Cunningham, William. *American Railroads: Government Control and Reconstruction Policies*. Chicago, 1922.

Cushman, Robert. *The Independent Regulatory Commissions*. New York, 1941.

Daggett, Stuart. *Principles of Inland Transportation*. New York, 1934.

Daggett, Stuart. *Railroad Consolidation West of the Mississippi River*. Berkeley, 1933.

Daggett, Stuart. *Railroad Reorganization*. New York, 1908.

Daughen, Joseph, and Peter Binzen. *The Wreck of the Penn Central*. New York, 1971.

Davies, Richard. *The Age of Asphalt*. Philadelphia, 1975.

Deakin, B.M., and T. Seward. *Productivity in Transport: A Study of Employment, Capital, Output, Productivity and Technical Change*. London, 1960.

Dearing, Charles, and Wilfred Owen. *National Transportation Policy*. Washington, D.C., 1949.

Dewing, Arthur S. *The Financial Policy of Corporations*. New York, 1953.

Dixon, Frank. *Railroads and Government, 1910-1921*. New York, 1922.

Doukas, K.A. *The French Railroads and the State*. New York, 1945.

Fellmeth, Robert C. (for the Ralph Nader Organization). *The Interstate Commerce Omission: The Public Interest and the ICC*. New York, 1970.

Feuss, Claude M. *Joseph B. Eastman; Servant of the People*. New York, 1952.

Fogel, Robert. *Railroads and American Economic Growth: Essays in Econometric History*. Baltimore, 1964.

Friedlaender, Ann F., et al. *The Dilemma of Freight Transport Regulation*. Washington, D.C., 1969.

Friendly, Henry J. *The Federal Administrative Agencies: The Need for a Better Definition of Standards*. Cambridge, Mass., 1962.

Gallamore, Robert E. *Railroad Mergers: Costs, Competition and the Future Organization of the American Railroad* (unpublished dissertation, Department of Economics, Harvard University, 1968).

Gartner, Michael. *Riding the Pennsy to Ruin; A Wall Street Journal Chronicle of the Penn Central Debacle.* Princeton, N.J., 1971.

Gooch, Tarrant Alan. *An Analysis of ICC Policy with respect to Traffic Factors Inherent in Problems of Railroad Consolidation* (unpublished dissertation, University of Tennessee, 1962).

Grodinsky, Julius. *Railroad Consolidation, Its Economics and Guiding Principles.* New York, 1930.

Hare, Jay. *History of the Reading.* Philadelphia, 1966.

Healy, Kent. *The Effects of Scale in the Railroad Industry.* New Haven, Conn., 1961.

Herring, J.M. *The Problem of Weak Railroads.* Philadelphia, 1929.

Hilton, George W. *The Transportation Act of 1958; A Decade of Experience.* Bloomington, Ind., 1969.

Hines, Walker. *War History of American Railroads.* New Haven, Conn., 1928.

Hoogenboom, Ari and Olive. *A History of the ICC: From Panacea to Palliative.* New York, 1976.

Horton, George R. *Railroad Unification* (unpublished dissertation, University of Virginia, 1962).

Hungerford, Edward. *Men of Erie.* New York, 1946.

Hungerford, Edward. *A Railroad for Tomorrow.* Milwaukee, 1945.

Kelly, Eamon M. *The Profitability of Growth Through Mergers.* University Park, Pa., 1967.

Kerr, K. Austin. *American Railroad Politics, 1914-1920: Rates, Wages and Efficiency.* Pittsburgh, 1968.

Kneafsey, James T. *An Economic Evaluation of Mergers in the Railroad Industry: The C&O-B&O Consolidation—A Case Study* (unpublished dissertation, Department of Economics, Ohio State University. 1971.

Kneafsey, James T. *The Economics of the Transportation Firm.* Lexington, Mass., 1974.

Kneafsey, James T. *Transportation Economic Analysis.* Lexington, Mass., 1975.

Kohlmeier, Louis. *The Regulators: Watchdog Agencies and the Public Interest.* New York, 1969.

Kolko, Gabriel. *Railroads and Regulation, 1877-1916.* Princeton, N.J. 1965.

Langsroth, Charles, and Wilson Stilz. *Railway Cooperation.* Philadelphia, 1899.

Latham, Earl. *The Politics of Railroad Coordination, 1933-1936.* Cambridge, Mass., 1959.

Lemly, James H. *The Gulf Mobile & Ohio, A Railroad That Had to Expand or Expire.* Homewood, Ill., 1953.

Leonard, William N. *Railroad Consolidation Under the Transportation Act of 1920.* New York, 1946.

Locklin, D. Philip. *Railroad Regulation Since 1920.* New York, 1928.

Lowenthal, Max. *The Investor Pays.* New York, 1933.

MacAvoy, Paul, ed. *The Crisis of the Regulatory Commissions.* New York, 1970.

MacAvoy, Paul. *The Economic Effects of Regulation; The Trunk Line Railroad*

Cartels and the Interstate Commerce Commission Before 1900. Cambridge Mass., 1970.

Martin, Albro. *Enterprise Denied: Origins of the Decline of American Railroads, 1897-1917.* New York, 1971.

Martin, David D. *Mergers and the Clayton Act.* Berkeley, 1959.

Meyer, John, Merton Peck, John Stenason, and Charles Zwick. *The Economics of Competition in the Transportation Industry.* Cambridge, Mass., 1959.

Miller, Clarence A. *The Lives of the Interstate Commerce Commissioners and the Commission's Secretaries.* Washington, D.C., 1946.

Moore, Thomas G. *Freight Transport Regulation; Surface Freight and the ICC.* Washington, D.C., 1972.

Mowbray, A.Q. *Road to Ruin.* Philadelphia, 1969.

Muhfeld, John. *The Railroad Problem and Its Solution.* New York, 1941.

Nelson, James. *Railroad Mergers and the Economy of New England.* New England Economic Research Council, 1966.

Nelson, James. *Railroad Transportation and Public Policy.* Washington, D.C., 1959.

Overton, Richard. *Burlington Route.* New York, 1965.

Parsons, Frank. *The Heart of the Railroad Problem.* Boston, 1906.

Pierce, Harry. *Railroads of New York: A Study of Government Aid, 1826-1875.* Cambridge, Mass., 1953.

Rehor, John A. *The Nickel Plate Story.* Milwaukee, 1965.

Ripley, William Z. *Railroads: Finance and Organization.* New York, 1915.

Ripley, William Z. *Railway Problems.* New York, 1907.

Sampson, Roy J. *Obstacles to Railroad Unification* (unpublished dissertation, Oregon State University, 1960).

Sayre, Robert M. *Alfred Baird Cummins and the Progressive Movement in Iowa* (unpublished dissertation, Columbia University, 1958).

Schubert, Glendon. *The Public Interest.* Glencoe, Ill., 1960.

Sharfman, I. Leo. *The American Railroad Problem.* New York, 1921.

Sharfman, I. Leo. *The Interstate Commerce Commission.* New York, 1931.

Shaughnessy, Jim. *Delaware & Hudson.* Berkeley, 1967.

Shott, John. *The Railroad Monopoly.* Washington, D.C., 1950.

Simnett, W.E. *Railway Amalgamation in Great Britain.* London, 1923.

Sobel, Robert. *The Entrepreneurs.* New York, 1975.

Sobel, Robert. *The Fallen Colossus* (Penn Central). New York, 1977.

Sorrell, Lewis. *Government Ownership and Operation of Railways for the United States.* New York, 1937.

Spearman, Frank. *The Strategy of the Great Railroads.* New York, 1904.

Staples, Henry Lee, and Mason, Alpheus T. *The Fall of a Railroad Empire.* Syracuse, N.Y., 1947.

Stevens, G.R. *History of the Canadian National Railways.* New York, 1973.

Stickney, A.B. *The Railway Problem.* St. Paul, Minn., 1891.

Stover, John. *The Life and Decline of the American Railroads.* New York, 1970.

Sussman, Joseph M., C.D. Marland, and A.S. Lang. *Reliability in Railroad Operations: Executive Summary.* Dept. of Civil Engineering, Massachusetts

Institute of Technology Research Report R73-4, Studies in Railroad Operations and Economics, vol. 9, 1973.

Taylor, George, and Neu, Irene. *The American Railroad Network,* 1866-1890. Cambridge, Mass., 1956.

Wycoff, D. Daryl. *Railroad Management.* Lexington, Mass., 1976.

Articles and Addresses

Abrams, Richard M. "Brandeis and the New Haven-Boston & Maine Merger Battle Revisited." *Business History Review,* Winter 1962.

Albright, Joseph. "The Penn Central: A Hell of a Way to Run a Government." *New York Times Magazine,* 3 November 1974.

Allen, W. Bruce. "Some Observations on Improving Railroad Productivity." *Proceedings of the Transportation Research Form,* 1976.

Altman, Edward I. "Predicting Railroad Bankruptcies in America." *The Bell Journal of Economics and Management Science,* Spring 1973.

Anderson, Bill, "The Merger Movement," *Passenger Train Journal,* March, April, and May 1977.

Beverly, Philip C. "The Consideration of Antitrust Policy in the Determination of Mergers and Consolidations Under Section 5 of the Interstate Commerce Act." *ICC Practitioners' Journal,* November 1961.

Blaze, James R. "Towards a National Policy of Super Railroads." *Proceedings of the Transportation Research Forum,* 1974.

Bok, Derek. "Section 7 of the Clayton Act and the Merging of Law and Economics." *Harvard Law Review,* December 1960.

Burck, Gilbert. "Merging Time for the Railroads." *Fortune,* January 1961.

Burck, Gilbert. "The Railroads Are Running Scared." *Fortune,* June 1969.

Bush, William L. "Western Railroad Mergers—Then and Now." *ICC Practitioners' Journal,* January/February 1975.

Claytor, W. Graham, Jr. "A Single Intermodal Transportation Company." *Transportation Journal,* Spring 1972.

Conant, Michael. "Merger Valuation of Net Loss Railroads." *ICC Practitioners' Journal,* March/April 1975.

Conant, Michael. "Two, Not Three Eastern Rail Systems Make Economic Sense." *Transportation Journal,* Fall 1963.

Cordtz, Dan. "The Fight for the Rock Island." *Fortune,* June 1966.

Creedy, John A. "The Built-In Bias Against Efficiency in Transportation." *ICC Practitioners' Journal,* January/February 1975.

Delaney, John J. "Rail Mergers vs. Antitrust Laws." *Distribution Age,* May 1967.

Due, John F. "Factors Affecting the Abandonment and Survival of Class II Railroads." *Transportation Journal,* Spring 1977.

Eads, George C. "Railroad Diversification: Where Lies the Public Interest?" *Bell Journal of Economics and Management Science,* Autumn 1974.

Ellsworth, T.P., Jr. "The Merger Merry-Go-Round: Rail Consolidation Under the 4-R Act." *ICC Practitioners' Journal,* May/June 1977.

Eno Foundation Board of Directors, "Report on Joint Conference: Restructuring the Railroads of the United States." *Traffic Quarterly,* April 1976.

Fair, Marvin L. "Railroad Mergers and the Public Interest." *Transportation Journal,* Winter 1966.

Faltermayer, Edmund K. "The Rail Route to a More Mobile America." *Fortune,* July 1966.

Farris, Martin T. "Rail Mergers: New Interest in an Old Approach." *Transportation Journal,* Summer 1962.

Fixler, L. Donald. "Less Than Arm's Length Relations: Interlocking Directorates and Railroad Mergers." *Quarterly Review of Economics and Business,* January 1965.

Graves, F.M., and W.A. Steger. "Management Systems Analyses and Administrative Law: A Railroad Merger Example." *Transportation Journal,* Winter 1964.

Griliches, Zvi. "Cost Allocation in Railroad Regulation." *Bell Journal of Economics and Management Science,* Spring 1972.

Hale, G.E. "Mergers in Regulated Industries." *Northwestern University Law Review,* April 1964.

Harbeson, Robert W. "New Patterns in Railway Consolidation." *Quarterly Review of Economics and Business,* February 1962.

Harbeson, Robert W. "Railroad Regulation, 1877-1916: Conspiracy or Public Interest?" *Journal of Economic History,* June 1967.

Harbeson, Robert W. "Some Policy Implications of Northeastern Railroad Problems." *Transportation Journal,* Fall 1974.

Harbridge House, Inc. "A Review of National Railroad Issues." Prepared for U.S. Congress, Office of Technology Assessment, Boston, 1975.

Hasenkamp, G. "A Study of Multiple-Output Production Functions: Klein's Railroad Study Results." *Journal of Econometrics,* August 1976.

Hilton, George W. "Basic Behavior of Regulatory Commissions." *Papers and Proceedings of the American Economic Association,* May 1972.

Hilton, George W. "The Consistency of the Interstate Commerce Act." *Journal of Law and Economics,* February 1966.

Horton, George A., and L.A. Drewry, Jr. "Railway Mergers; Recent ICC Policy." *Traffic Quarterly,* January 1967.

Huntington, Samuel P. "The Marasmus of the ICC: The Commission, the Railroads and the Public Interest." *Yale Law Journal,* Fall, 1952.

Ingles, J. David, and David P. Morgan. "Fallen Flags: Memories of the Merged." *Trains,* April, May, and June 1974.

"Is it Endsville for the Railroads?" *Forbes,* 15 October 1969.

"Jervis Langdon, Jr. Contemplates Conrail." *Trains,* June 1976;

Johnson, James C., and Donald V. Harper. "The Shipper Views Proposed Solutions to the Northeast Railroad Problem." *Transportation Journal,* Summer 1974.

Johnson, James C., and Terry C. Whiteside. "Professor Ripley Revisited: A Current Analysis of Railroad Mergers." *ICC Practitioners' Journal,* March/April 1975.

Josephson, Matthew. "The Daring Young Man of Wall Street." *Saturday Evening*

Post, 18 August 1945.

Kahn, Fritz R. "The Reformation of Railroad Regulation." *ICC Practitioners' Journal,* May/June 1976.

Keefe, Kevin P. "How Michigan Got into the Railroad Business." *Trains,* October 1976, p. 46.

Keeler, Theodore E. "Railroad Costs, Returns to Scale and Excess Capacity." *Review of Economics and Statistics,* May 1974.

Kefauver, Estes. "Why I Prefer a Moratorium on Railroad Mergers." *Progressive Railroading.* September/October 1962.

Kidder, Tracy. "Trains in Trouble." *Atlantic,* August 1976.

Kneiling, John G. "How to Run a Railroad in the Northeast." *Trains,* August 1974.

Kneiling, John G. "Kneiling vs. USRA." *Trains,* September 1975, p. 52.

Korbel, Herbert J. "The ICC and Monopoly—A Study of the Commission's Powers and Duties in the Antitrust Field: The Commission and Railroad Unifications." *ICC Practitioners' Journal,* December 1961.

Lackman, Conway L. "Implication of Conglomerates for Transportation in the 1970s." *Transportation Journal,* Fall 1974.

"Learning the Alphabet." *Trains,* July 1974.

Leonard, William N. "The Decline of Railroad Consolidation." *Journal of Economic History,* May 1949.

Leonard, William N. "Issue of Competition and Monopoly in Railroad Mergers." *Transportation Journal,* Summer 1964.

Leonard, William N. "Rail Mergers: A Common Sense Approach." *Challenge,* November 1962.

Lev, Baruch, and Gershon Mandelker. "The Microeconomic Consequences of Corporate Mergers." *Journal of Business,* January 1972.

Levin, Richard C., and Merton J. Peck. "Allocation in Surface Freight Transportation: Does Rate Regulation Matter?" Working Paper 31, Department of Economics, Yale University, August 1976.

Locklin, David P. "Do We or Do We Not Want Railroad Mergers." *Traffic Topics,* September 1963.

Loving, Rush, Jr. "Getting the Eastern Railroads Back on the Track." *Fortune,* December 1972.

Loving, Rush, Jr. "The Penn Central Bankruptcy Express." *Fortune,* August 1970.

Loving, Rush, Jr. "A Railroad Merger that Worked." *Fortune,* August 1972.

Mahowski, Bob. "The Poughkeepsie Bridge Is Burning," *Railfan,* Winter 1974.

Malin, Max. "A Realistic Appraisal of the Financial Condition of Railroads." Brotherhood of Locomotive Engineers, pamphlet, 1961.

Martin, Albro. "Railroads and the Equity Receivership; An Essay on Institutional Change." *Journal of Economic History,* September 1974.

Martin, Albro. "The Troubled Subject of Railroad Regulation in the Gilded Age; A Reappraisal." *Journal of American History,* September 1974.

Mauer, Herrymon. "Central Rolls Again." *Fortune,* May 1954.

McFarland, Walter R. "Unification of Carriers Under the Interstate Commerce Act." *ICC Practitioners' Journal,* January 1942.

Miller, E. Spencer. "A Prescription for Railroad Recovery." *New York Times,* 10 September 1972, p. 17.

Monroe, J. Elmer. "Comment on 'The Effects of Scale in the Railroad Industry.'"
Yale University pamphlet, 26 October 1961.
Montgomery, Alan J. "The Role of Intermodal Service in Improving Railroad
Productivity." *Proceedings of the Transportation Research Forum,* 1974.
Morgan, David P. "The Ironies of Penn Central." *Trains,* November 1972, p. 25.
Morton, Alexander L. "Balkanization in the Railroad Industry." *Proceedings of the
Transportation Research Forum, 1974.*
Payne, Jr. Stanley. "History of the Consolidation Provisions of the Interstate Com-
merce Act." *ICC Practitioners' Journal,* February 1962.
Pearce, C. Jack, and Keith I. Clearwaters. "Rate Bureaus and the Railroad Revital-
ization and Regulatory Reform Act of 1976—Truman Revisited." *ICC Prac-
titioners' Journal,* May/June 1976.
Pegrum, Dudley F. "The Chicago & North Western-Chicago, Milwaukee, St. Paul
& Pacific Merger: A Case Study in Transport Economics." *Transportation
Journal,* Winter 1969.
"Pennsy's Predicament." *Fortune,* March 1948.
Phillips, Charles F., Jr. "Railroad Mergers: Competition, Monopoly and Anti-
trust." *Washington and Lee Review,* Spring 1962.
Phillips, Don. "The Feds Look at Trains vs. Trucks." *Trains,* October 1976, p. 14.
Pinkepank, Jerry. "A Tale of Two Railroads." *Trains,* February 1965.
Purcell, Edward A., Jr. "Ideas and Interests: Businessmen and the Interstate Com-
merce Act." *Journal of American History,* December 1967.
"Railroad-Trucker Brawl." *Fortune,* June 1953.
Seneca, Rosalind S. "Inherent Advantage, Costs and Resource Allocation in the
Transportation Industry." *American Economic Review,* December 1973.
Shaw, Robert. "A Case Study of Railway Mania." *Trains,* May 1977.
Shoemaker, Perry M. "Should Railroads Diversify for Growth and Profits." *Trans-
portation Journal,* Fall 1969.
Smith, Marshall. "'Were Going Broke,' He Told the Workers." *Life,* 24 September
1971.
Tucker, William H., and John H. O'Brien. "The Public Interest in Railroad Merg-
ers." Boston University Law Review, Spring 1962.
Tuggle, Kenneth. "The Outlook for Railroad Consolidation and Mergers." Speech
before the National Association of Railroad and Utilities Commissioners, Las
Vegas, 30 November 1960.
Van Fleet, James A. "Why We Never Stopped the Red Railroads in Korea." *Trains,*
July 1956.
"Western Railroads: Merge or Go Broke." *Business Week,* 24 May 1976.

Government Documents (other than ICC reports, dockets, or court cases)

U.S. Congress: House of Representatives

*Adequacy of Transportation Systems in Support of the National Defense Effort in
Event of Mobilization,* Committee on Armed Forces, 86th Cong., 1st sess.,
1959.
Inadequacies of Protection for Investors in Penn Central and Other ICC-Regulated

Companies, Committee on Interstate and Foreign Commerce, staff study, 92d Cong., 1st sess., 1971.

Northeast Rail Transportation, Committee on Interstate and Foreign Commerce, hearings, 93d Cong., 1st sess., 1973.

Omnibus Transportation Bill, Committee on Interstate and Foreign Commerce, hearings, 76th Cong., 1st sess., 1939.

The Penn Central Failure and the Role of Financial Institutions, Committee on Banking and Currency, staff report, 92d Cong., 1st sess., 1972.

Pere Marquette Railroad Co., and Cincinnati, Hamilton & Dayton Railroad Co., doc. 137, 65th Cong., 1st sess., 1917.

Railroad Revitalization, Committee on Interstate and Foreign Commerce, hearings, 94th Cong., 1st sess., 1975.

Railroad Revitalization and Regulatory Reform Act, Committee on Interstate and Foreign Commerce, report, 94th Cong., 1st sess., 1975, and report of conference committee, 19 December 1975.

Reports of the Federal Coordinator of Transportation, doc. 119, 73d Cong., 2d sess., 1935.

Return of the Railroads to Private Enterprise, hearings, 66th Cong., 2d sess., 1919.

United States Railway Association Final System Plan, Committee on Interstate and Foreign Commerce, hearings, 94th Cong. 1st sess., 1975.

United States Railway Association, Preliminary System Plan, Committee on Interstate and Foreign Commerce, hearings, 94th Cong., 1st sess., 1975.

U.S. Congress: Senate

The American Railroad: Posture, Problems and Prospects, Committee on Commerce, staff report, 28 August 1972.

Extension of Control, Government Control of Railroads, Committee on Interstate Commerce, hearings, 65th Cong., 3d sess., 1919.

Failing Railroads, Committee on Commerce, hearings, 91st Cong., 2d sess., 1970.

Five Per Cent Case, doc. 466, 63d Cong., 2d sess., 1915.

Government Control and Operation of Railroads, Committee on Interstate Commerce, hearings, 66th Cong., 2d sess., 1918.

National Transportation Policy, Committee on Commerce, report, 86th Cong., 1st sess., 1961.

New York, New Haven & Hartford RR Co., Evidence Taken Before the ICC, doc. 542, 63d Cong., 2d sess., 1914.

Northeastern Railroad Transportation Crisis, Committee on Commerce, hearings, 93d Cong., 1st sess., 1973.

Penn Central and Other Railroads, Committee on Commerce, report, 92d Cong., 2d sess., 1972.

Rail Merger Legislation, Committee on the Judiciary, hearings, 87th Cong, 2d sess., 1962.

Railroad Consolidation in the Eastern Region, Committee on Interstate Commerce, report, 73d Cong., 3d sess., 1940.

Railroads—1975, Committee on Commerce, hearings, 94th Cong., 1st sess., 1975.

Review of the Penn Central's Condition, Committee on Commerce, hearings, 92d

Cong., 1st sess., 1971.

Surface Transport Legislation, Committee on Commerce, hearings, 92d Cong., 1st sess., 1972.

The Van Sweringen Corporate System; A Study in Holding Company Financing, Committee on Interstate Commerce, report, 77th Cong., 1st sess., 1941.

U.S. Council of Economic Advisors

Improving Railroad Productivity, Task Force on Railroad Productivity, National Commission on Productivity, November 1963.

U.S. Department of Transportation

Decade of Decision: Terminals, and Track and Roadway, Report of the Task Force to the Labor and Management Committee, 23 April 1971.

Final Standards, Classification and Designation of Lines of Class I Railroads in the United States, vol. 1, 19 January 1977 and vol. 2, 30 June 1977.

National Transportation Report: Current Performance and Future Prospects, July 1975.

National Transportation Report: Present Status, Future Alternatives, July 1972.

National Transportation Trends and Choices to the Year 2000, 12 January 1977.

Northeastern Railroad Problem, report to Congress, 26 March 1973.

Railroad Abandonments, and Alternatives: A Report on Effects Outside the Northeastern Region, submitted in accordance with section 904 of the 4R Act, May 1976.

Rail Service in the Midwest and Northeast Region, 3 vols., 1 February 1974.

United States Railway Association, *Annual Report,* 3 June 1974.

United States Raillway Association, *News,* 26 February 1975.

United States Railway Association, *Preliminary System Plan,* 26 February 1975.

U.S. Interstate Commerce Commission

Evaluation of the Secretary of Transportation's Rail Services Report, Rail Services Planning Office, 2 May 1974.

Evaluation of the United States Railway Association's Final System Plan, Rail Services Planning Office, 25 August 1975.

Evaluation of the United States Railway Association's Preliminary System Plan, Rail Services Planning Office, 28 April 1975.

Evaluation Report of the Secretary of Transportation's Preliminary Classification of Rail Lines, Rail Services Planning Office, 1 December 1976.

Rail Merger Study, Rail Services Planning Office. *Initial White Paper,* 15 August 1977; vol. 1, *Service,* 1 August 1977; vol. 2, *Impacts on Other Carriers,* 12 August 1977; vol. 3, *Labor Impact,* vol. 4, *Environmental and Community Impact,* and vol. 5, *Role of Government,* 1 August 1977; vol. 6, *National Defense,* 12 August 1977; vol. 7, *Alternatives to Merger,* 1 September 1977.

Railroad Conglomerates and Other Corporate Structures, 1977.

Railroad Consolidation and the Public Interest, A Preliminary Examination, Bureau of Transport Economics and Statistics, 1962.

Index

Pittsburgh & West Virginia Ry., 49-52, 59, 147
Plumb Plan, 40-42, 54, 334-35
Pocahontas Railroads described, 14
Point of no return (on railroads) defined, 6, 215-16
Poland Report, 56
Portland, Oregon, 244
Preliminary System Plan, 309-11
Presspritch, R.W., Co., 253
Prince, Frederick (Prince Plan), 55-56
Progressive movement and railroads, 38-43
Prudential Insurance Co., 256
Public interest (legal definition), 82

Quaker Oats Co., 307
Quinn, William, 162-63

Railroad for Tomorrow, A, 76-78, 302
Railroad Revitalization and Regulatory Reform Act of 1976, 325, 332
Railroad Unification Act of 1931, 54-55
Railroad War Board, 36
Railroads: capital needs and finances, 31, 35, 50, 174-75, 203; competition among, 7, 29, 31-32, 77-78 (*see also* Railroads and consolidation); competition with other modes, 5, 349n; coordination, 103-05, 108, 161, 245, 331; diversification, 219, 232-33, 283-88; economic problems, 6, 12 (in New England, 181-85; in Northeast, 9-14, 169; in South, 201-02; in West, 150); efficiency and technology, 6, 34, 80, 335; and foreign railroads, compared, 41-42, 360n; and individualism, 30; and industrialization, 30-31; and labor, 6, 39-42, 77-78, 83-85, 308-09, 319, 359n (*see also* Railroads and consolidation, and labor); leadership, 102-03, 123, 139, 172, 175, 209 (Penn Central, 279-83; 331-33); ownership, 194,

205-06 (Erie Lackawanna, 205-07, 249, 256, 259, 304-05, 333); and war, 35, 169, 172
Railroads and consolidation: and capital investment, 123, 160-61, 168-69, 215-16; and competition, 112, 145-47, 152-56, 162-63, 167-68, 170, 182, 204-05, 219-20, 227-30, 232-34, 238, 270, 312; compulsory, 39-41, 83; fallacies of, 118-19, 123, 172-74, 263-64, 326-32; history of (early), 5-8, 31-32, 78-81; illegal, 93-94; interlocking directorate, 70-72, 341n; justification of, 5-8, 108, 136, 157, 159-60, 168-69, 172-74, 187-88, 203, 219, 227-29; and labor, 83-85, 111, 118-19, 166, 171-72, 174-75, 178, 195-96, 211-14, 267, 271, 273-79, 300-01, 328, 332; planned, 39-57, 148, 170, 177, 198, 267; public reaction, 7-8, 104, 108-11, 142, 166, 176-77, 183-85, 207-08; and shippers, 142, 153-55, 160-61, 268-75; and states, 66-67, 82, 207, 210-21; stock control, 60-62, 127-29, 138-40, 151, 179, 217; and stockholders, 66-67, 105, 106, 115-16, 186, 227; studies for, 86, 105-08, 119, 131-32, 138, 176-77, 141-42, 145, 187-91, 205, 219, 227
Rail Services Planning Office. *See* ICC and Rail Services Planning Office
Railway Age, 94
Railway Labor Executives' Association, 92, 165, 174, 193, 212-14
Raskob, Jacob, 62
Rasmussen, Paul, 163, 168, 170, 349n
Rea, Samuel, 43
Reading Railroad, 14, 32, 45-46, 53, 138; and Western Maryland Ry., 251-52, 257, 270; bankrupt, 295, 298; and Penn Central, 296, 301; and MARC-EL, 302-03, 312

Wyer, William, 97, 105, 113, 134
Wyer, Dick & Co.: merger studies for
  Erie Lackawanna, 106-08; for
  C&O-B&O, 130, 133; for New
  Haven RR, 196; for Seaboard

Coast Line, 203, 205; for Missouri Pacific, 217; for *Rock
Island* case, 227

Young, Robert, 4, 62-67, 69-75, 89-90

ABOUT THE AUTHOR

Richard Saunders, Associate Professor of History at Clemson University, Clemson, South Carolina, specializes in post-World War II American history, and the history of business in the United States.